Building
Sustainable Worlds

LATINOS IN CHICAGO AND THE MIDWEST

Series Editors
Omar Valerio-Jiménez, *University of Texas at San Antonio*
Sujey Vega, *Arizona State University*

Founding Editor
Frances R. Aparicio

*A list of books in the series appears
at the end of this book.*

Building Sustainable Worlds

Latinx Placemaking in the Midwest

Edited by
THERESA DELGADILLO,
RAMÓN H. RIVERA-SERVERA,
GERALDO L. CADAVA,
AND CLAIRE F. FOX

UNIVERSITY OF
ILLINOIS PRESS
Urbana, Chicago, and Springfield

Library of Congress Cataloging-in-Publication Data
Names: Delgadillo, Theresa, 1959– editor. | Rivera-Servera,
    Ramón H., 1973– editor. | Cadava, Geraldo L., 1977–
    editor. | Fox, Claire F., editor.
Title: Building sustainable worlds : Latinx placemaking in
    the Midwest / edited by Theresa Delgadillo, Ramón H.
    Rivera-Servera, Geraldo L. Cadava, and Claire F. Fox.
Other titles: Latinx placemaking in the Midwest
Description: Urbana : University of Illinois Press, [2022] |
    Series: Latinos in Chicago and the Midwest | Collection
    of essays by Theresa Delgadillo and others. | Includes
    bibliographical references and index.
Identifiers: LCCN 2021055879 (print) | LCCN 2021055880
    (ebook) | ISBN 9780252044540 (hardback) | ISBN
    9780252086618 (paperback) | ISBN 9780252053542
    (ebook)
Subjects: LCSH: Hispanic Americans—Middle West—
    Social life and customs. | Hispanic Americans—Middle
    West—Ethnic identity. | Hispanic Americans—Middle
    West—Social conditions. | Middle West—Ethnic
    relations.
Classification: LCC F358.2.S75 B85 2022 (print) | LCC
    F358.2.S75 (ebook) | DDC 305.89/68073—dc23/
    eng/20220126
LC record available at https://lccn.loc.gov/2021055879
LC ebook record available at https://lccn.loc.gov/2021055880

Contents

Acknowledgments

We owe an enormous debt of gratitude to the many scholars who have studied and written about Latinxs in the Midwest. Some are individuals in whose footsteps we walk, while others are our colleagues and peers in this ongoing work. Our chapter endnotes and the volume's bibliography include numerous references to many of these sources, but here we acknowledge how deeply we admire and draw from this important body of work.

We thank the many individuals, leaders, event participants, artists, and activists who agreed to share their perspectives, materials, words, and time with us in the course of this research. We have learned much from you and much about Latinx communities in this region. Lourdes Torres, Ana Aparicio, Amalia Pallares, and Teresa Magnum graciously shared their expertise and guidance with us at the first gathering of this research collaborative at Northwestern University in August 2017, helping us to launch our shared work. We are also grateful to the National Museum of Mexican Art in Chicago and especially Cesario Moreno, chief curator and visual arts director of the museum, for hosting our gathering with a group of leaders from community cultural centers in the region in 2017. Thank you to Roberto Torres, Carmen Hernandez, Gibran Villalobos, and Cesario Moreno for talking with us about the work of cultural and community organizing in varied Latinx communities in the Midwest. Louis Mendoza, Gina Pérez, and George Sanchez provided invaluable feedback on our work in progress at our second gathering in the spring of 2018 at the Ohio State University, nudging us to consider unexplored questions or alternative explanations or to consider our evidence in new ways. We are also grateful to colleagues at OSU who joined in parts of our discussions there and helped us to think through what we were finding in our research. We could not have asked for a more supportive and relaxing environment for further thought, discussion, and editing than the summer of 2018 at the Obermann Center for Advanced Studies in Iowa City, Iowa. Thank you, Teresa Magnum, director of the Obermann Center, for hosting us, and many thanks to Obermann staff Erin Hackathorn and Jenna Hammerich for assisting with arrangements. We are also grateful to Gerardo Sandoval for partnering with our project for the week to create three different local public-access TV programs to share our research with Iowans and communities beyond the university.

We thank our collaborators in this volume not only for their keen insight, generosity in feedback and ideas, openness to collaboration, and extremely hard work on this volume but also for much shared joy, laughter, and pleasure in our gatherings, including walks along the lakeshore in Chicago and hikes in Iowa state parks. We recall evenings of shared conviviality at long dining tables in Chicago, Columbus, and Iowa City with much fondness. We valued the opportunity to learn more about each other and to better understand how this research mattered in each of our lives professionally and personally.

We are grateful for the funding that allowed us to launch a multiyear collaboration among scholars across the Midwest that culminates in this volume. Our discussions began in 2014 as we worked to craft a proposal that addressed Latinx cultural and social life in the region as a question about "climate." We are grateful to the Ohio State University Humanities Institute, especially Rick Livingston, the associate director, for encouraging this project with a $5,000 seed grant. This allowed us to land a 2017–19 grant from Humanities Without Walls based at the University of Illinois Urbana-Champaign's Humanities Research Institute and funded by a grant from the Andrew W. Mellon Foundation. Thank you to Antoinette Burton, director of the Humanities Research Institute, and to Jason Mierek, director of operations for Humanities Without Walls, who answered many questions along the way.

The support we received from the Humanities Without Walls consortium was supplemented by additional administrative and facilities support from the Ohio State University, the University of Iowa, and Northwestern University, including the absolutely outstanding work of several individuals at our respective universities who helped us to navigate the demands of grant records, reports, and reimbursements. Our hats off in particular to Nick Spitulski, administrative coordinator for the Latina/o Studies Program and the Center for Ethnic Studies at Ohio State University, who provided amazing, outstanding, and excellent support at every step, ensuring that bills were paid, travel went smoothly, and facilities functioned as we needed them. Thank you, Nick! We also thank Corey Campbell of the University of Iowa Department of English, who graciously dedicated her exceptional organizational skills and attention to detail to make our Iowa City gatherings and public events a success.

The publication of this book also received support from our academic institutions, including Northwestern University, the Office of the Vice Chancellor for Research and Graduate Education at the University of Wisconsin–Madison with funding from the Wisconsin Alumni Research Foundation, and the University of Iowa College of Liberal Arts and Sciences and Office of the Vice President for Research.

This volume was much improved by the comments and suggestions of two peer reviewers for the University of Illinois Press, Jason Ruiz and an anonymous reviewer. We are grateful to the Latinos in Chicago and the Midwest series editors, Sujey Vega and Omar Valerio-Jiménez, as well as Frances R. Aparicio before them, who encouraged this project early on, and to the University of Illinois Press editors Dominique Moore and Alison Syring for their support of our project. Our thanks to the wonderful editorial and marketing staff of the University of Illinois Press, including Ellie Hinton, Jennifer Argo, Roberta Sparenberg, Dustin Hubbart, and Kevin Cunningham. Of course, any errors or shortcomings in this publication remain ours.

Building
Sustainable Worlds

Introduction

THERESA DELGADILLO, RAMÓN H. RIVERA-SERVERA,
GERALDO L. CADAVA, AND CLAIRE F. FOX

This volume examines the ways that expressive culture constitutes and sustains diverse Latinx communities in the midwestern United States, enacting a desire to live and thrive in a region where Latinxs have resided for over one hundred years. Over and over again, Latinxs, interacting with others, have established, cultivated, and maintained worlds for themselves in the Midwest amid often harsh social, cultural, and political climates, as well as in environmentally challenging workplaces. They have done so in large and midsize urban and small-town rural locations in ways that seek not only to bridge their distance from others like them or their difference from others in the Midwest but also to cultivate a knowledge of place that can construct a more just Midwest. We are urgently invested in understanding how Latinx dynamics of placemaking and the worlds Latinxs imagine and enact constitute both practices of sustenance and knowledge of sustainability for communities in the region. Our essays are dedicated to highlighting these efforts, while at the same time, they represent our own gesture—in collaborating together over four years to create not only this volume but also a network of Latinx studies scholars in the Midwest—toward building, repeating, and sustaining the practice of Latinx placemaking.

This volume examines environmental concerns that surface in Latinx cultural expressions, yet equally important is our focus on the intimate connection between place and culture, on the one hand, and sustenance and sustainability, on the other hand—a focus that Priscilla Solis Ybarra advocates in her analysis of the desire for sustainable environment alongside communal survival in Chicanx literatures.[1] As Julie Sze observes, the question of "place" is key to thinking about sustainability in the concrete and therefore requires that scholars both "contextualize and situate" sustainability in relation to specific locations, peoples, natures, cultures, and periods in order to achieve a just sustainability.[2] Through this approach, we suggest that the study of Latinx placemaking in the Midwest and its engagement with varied temporal, spatial, and scalar concerns can inform the creation of more sustainable cultural and material environments in the region. In seeking out explicitly environmental knowledge in Latinx cultural expression, we find ourselves in agreement with Barbara Deutsch Lynch, who suggests that "where power in society is unequally distributed, not all environmental discourses will be heard equally."[3] Like the studies by Ybarra and Lynch, our work unearths some of those previously unheard Latinx perspectives on the environment, understood not only as climate and nature but also as the spaces and communities across many different times and scales that Latinxs in the Midwest have built for themselves. In this volume, therefore, we propose that building sustainable worlds requires us to attend to difference, and the essays collected here explore the extent to which Latinx discourses of environmental sustainability are deeply connected to questions of social, cultural, political, and economic sustainability.[4]

While significant scholarship on Latinx labor and activism for social justice in the Midwest exists, we have more limited knowledge of how Latinxs in this region have transformed the region and created homes for themselves by building cultural, social, and artistic communities. We understand expressive culture broadly in this volume as the creative communicative practices that have assembled Latinx communities as publics in the region. By this we mean that Latinx communities become tangible collectives not only through the historical political-economic conditions that have compelled them to migrate to the region or the shared experiences of marginalization that shape the material infrastructure of the environments they inhabit but also through the exchanges facilitated by cultural practices as platforms for imagining and actively enacting a Latinx world in the Midwest. The present volume thus develops unique perspectives from anthropology, history, literature, media, and performance studies to consider how Latinx populations in the Midwest create community through cultural forms including zines, film, videos, literature, festivals, and activist events. These media help us illuminate the wide variety of Latinx placemaking practices that bring questions of sustenance and sustainability to the fore.

Many of the chapters in this volume explore cultural practices that are not unique to Latinxs, yet what is unique is how Latinxs create cultural forms with new meanings in specific eras. In this way, our essays engage with Elizabeth A. Povinelli's call to unpack "the ways that alternative social projects aggregate life diagonal to hegemonic ways of life" in order to examine how "new forms of social life" emerge amid persistence.[5] Povinelli's "alternative social projects" interrupt or puncture the force of combined human, discursive, and material figurations that impose harm with impunity.[6] Her insistence on the examination of "alternative forms of social belonging, abandonment and endurance" becomes another strategy for us to think through the ways that both sustenance and sustainability are obstructed for Latinxs through abandonment, such as exclusion, dispossession, marginalization, colonialism, or, as Lisa Marie Cacho outlines, social death.[7] We also tend to the ways Latinxs counter such abandonment through persistence, which may involve multiple "tenses" or temporalities and scales (as in transnational) of placemaking and perhaps gaining recognition or forming as a counterpublic. The essays in this volume wrestle with these ideas by exploring Latinx placemaking as an "alternative social project" that activates varied temporalities in seeking to sustain Latinx communities and operates at multiple scales in creating place for diverse communities.

We recognize, too, that this volume continues to build on important work that both precedes and accompanies us. *Building Sustainable Worlds* extends and deepens the focus of *The Latina/o Midwest Reader* (2017), an edited volume in which several editors of this book had a hand, and of the more recent innovative studies of Latinx populations in the Midwest in what is now a long line of scholarship centered on this region.[8] We are indebted to numerous scholars whose invaluable work has documented and examined the routes and modes of Latinx migration, work, and existence in the region; made known the pathbreaking cultural projects created by Latinx in the region, including journals, presses, museums, literature, arts, music, performance, and theater; recorded and analyzed Latinx involvement in civil rights, *movimiento*, and immigration politics and activism; sought to understand the transnational civic, cultural, and economic networks that connect the Midwest with Latin American countries; and examined the relationships among differing Latinx groups and between Latinxs and other minorities rather than exclusively Latinx-white relations.[9] This previous work marks the historical presence and contributions of Latinx communities, as well as the sustenance of the Midwest as an important economic and cultural region of the United States, a critical global hub of exchange, and a significant resource for the creation of new modalities of being in light of our ever-changing societies.

Political and Cultural Transformations in Our Time

The urgency of our project has been continuously impelled by inescapable dilemmas of communal survival during the years in which we produced this volume, including a deep well of hateful rhetoric about Latinxs, as well as Black, Indigenous, and Asian Americans, women, and LGBTQ people. It also accounts for a global political economy accruing through the long timeline of colonialism and its variant forms of capitalist modification and the resulting environmental and social degradation these have brought forth. Latinxs are, by now, deeply rooted in almost every civic, political, social, economic, and cultural activity in the Midwest.[10] But during the past five years, the world has changed dramatically and along with it our understanding—as scholars, as citizens—of the region that is our home.

To begin with the obvious, for most of the period in which we worked on this volume, a white supremacist, misogynist xenophobe occupied the White House. We did not imagine we would ever see a president who described Mexicans as rapists, murderers, and thieves; regularly engaged in immigrant-bashing; and boasted about assaulting women. Even more disturbing for us in the Midwest is how much his message seems to have resonated here. He won every midwestern state except for Minnesota and Illinois—often narrowly, shifting regional and national discourses about whether Latinx communities and Latin American migrants truly belong into a more intensely xenophobic, even genocidal period if we consider the separation of children from their parents at the border. We cannot ignore the depth of white patriarchal griev-ance and resentment in the Midwest in addition to all of the other things the region might be. In 2020, Joseph Biden flipped many of the states Trump won in 2016 to take the presidency, though his sometimes narrow margins of victory demonstrate that much of what Trump (re)activated remains alive and well.

The Midwest was not a bulwark for pro-Latinx and proimmigrant or pro-Black or prowoman sentiment before Trump's election, and activism by and on behalf of these communities has not subsided since November 2016. Yet much has changed. The hate-filled rhetoric, exacerbation of economic inequal-ity, public health disaster, and environmental calamities of the past four years have taken a significant toll on Latinx communities, the focus of our work. The disproportionate rates of infection and death among Latinxs during the Covid-19 pandemic undermine the very claims to belonging we have insisted upon for decades as much as they have confirmed Latinxs' critical role in sustaining the region as frontline workers. In light of this, our volume's focus on sustenance and sustainability offers readers an opportunity to understand the present moment in light of the historic and contemporary placemaking projects we make known in this volume.

Another world-shattering event that emerged from our region during this collaboration is the massive and powerful expansion of Black Lives Matter mobilizations in Minneapolis and across the Midwest, the nation, and, in-deed, the globe in response to the brutal murder of George Floyd by police in Minneapolis. This resounding cry for social justice brought Native Ameri-can and Latinx activists to stand with Black midwestern communities, but it also sparked frank conversations about anti-Blackness and the positionality of Black Latinxs within the field of Latinx studies. This massive antiracist movement also inspired us to transform our region in solidarity with Black, Native American, and Asian American scholars and activists. We see the potential for coalitions to emerge from these conversations that are committed to building more equitable communities and institutions across our region. Black Lives Matter's opposition to state-sanctioned violence, for example, also lends itself to analysis of the terror perpetrated on Latinxs by ICE and the status of child detainees at the US-Mexico border. For those of us who work in predominantly white midwestern academic institutions, this is not only a challenging but also a thrilling moment, as our students are often taking the lead in organizing for curricular and institutional change. The strategies that they are using to bring visibility to BIPOC midwesterners resonate with many of the placemaking efforts examined in this volume.

We trace the recent escalations in hateful rhetoric and punitive policies toward Latinx communities back through the past three decades, making public assertions of Latinx existence and belonging through cultural events that are significant for both Latinxs and broader communities, from the Illegal Immigration Reform and Immigrant Responsibility Act (IIRIRA) of 1996 (also known as the Mexican Exclusionary Act) to the massive 2006 immigration rights marches following the passage of the Border Protection, Anti-terrorism, and Illegal Immigration Control Act of 2005 in the House of Representatives.[11] Furthermore, in the wake of those 2006 marches, the 2008 implementation of the Secure Communities, or S-Comm, program by US Immigration and Customs Enforcement (ICE) effectively drove millions into the shadows by seeking to pressure local law enforcement into participating in immigrant detention and deportation. The effort to exclude, demonize, and scapegoat Latinx migrants has been unrelenting. As the battles in Arizona over Mexican American studies and the racial profiling of residents authorized by the "anti–illegal immigrant law" (Support Our Law Enforcement and Safe Neighborhoods Act, known as Arizona SB 1070) make clear, this decades-long discourse has impacted everyone who is Latinx. This is why we believe that Latinx claims on public spaces in the Midwest in the variety of ways that these unfold in the chapters of this volume carry significant weight as evidence of endurance.

In their moments, each of the actions, events, and performances have built and sustained Latinx spaces in the Midwest and represent an assertion of the right to be and the right to create place. They also offer an alternative understanding of the spaces in which they coexist with others. These efforts involve cultural, social, and artistic forms of expression, as well as organizing in both rural and urban locations, by diverse Latinx communities that include individuals from multiple national backgrounds and diverse racial, sexual, and gender subjectivities. We note that this volume addresses activities of people descended from Central American, Caribbean, and South American populations in the region, though our collective expertise leads to a heavier emphasis on Chicanx, Mexican, and Puerto Rican activities. In considering how the cultural expressions of Latinxs bring places of nurture, support, and sustenance into being and cultivate interethnic awareness and relationships, it became ever more clear to us that these efforts also evince a profound appreciation for the varied scales at which Latinxs live and for the unique desires to maintain transnational communities.

The Temporal Dimensions of Culture in Placemaking

To know place, we ought to consider the dynamics of time. If collective place is constituted through processes of extended interaction, including creative and intentional expressive gestures, then our conceptualization of place shifts from a noun that names a site or location to verbs that describe the procedures through which place is constituted as such. Thus, what we understand as the Latinx Midwest is not just a collection of sites or enclaves that mark Latinx presence but a map of actions accumulating into a felt sense of belonging and not belonging to the region.

The concept of performance as embodied communicative practice offers a capacious framework for understanding the range of expressive cultures discussed in this collection, as well as the temporal logics so crucial to understanding Latinx placemaking. At its very core, performance is understood as an intentional communicative enactment directed at an audience, be it human or nonhuman, such as a deity or nature. Repetition has been the central theoretical paradigm for understanding performance, assuming, as Richard Schechner has advanced, that performance is always "twice behaved behavior."[12] This paradigm of repetition is also at the core of understandings of performativity as the practiced ways social categories take form. Understanding social categories as doings has served to destabilize long-established truisms about the essential coherence of the subject. It has also introduced more process-oriented frameworks for narrating the emergence of categories such as gender, not from predetermined biological truths but from the habituated norms we have enacted so often that we have rendered them as if they were natural.[13] The focus on repetition or iteration in formal performance, as well as in understandings of performativity, directs us toward the required ongoingness of an action to sustain what we might otherwise assume as simply structural fixities of the social realm. In the case of placemaking, it is then through the actions that we sustain collectively in relation to our environment that we come to institute something of a known sense of place.

Pursuing Latinx placemaking in the Midwest as a performative achievement or as the processual sustenance of a collective identity resulting from action across time allows us to account for what Frances Aparicio has so aptly described as the "convergences and divergences" that *latinidad* invokes: the dynamic amalgamation of a vast range of experiences from Latin American–descent communities with a range of race, ethnicity, and class backgrounds, as well as a range of histories of migration, settlement, and legal status in the United States.[14] In her milestone study of Latinx queer performativity, Juana María Rodríguez pursued precisely the ways in which the discursive performativities of *latinidad* across a range of platforms enabled the transformation of queer Latinx discursive spaces into social realities.[15]

The interdisciplinary collective of scholars and cultural workers assembled here thinks about Latinx places as tangible physical phenomena—the places where our lives unfold—with infrastructural, economic, and environmental variables to consider. We also think of places as created through performative, activist, aesthetic, and representational practices that render the Latinx Midwest through writing, photography, film, theater, dance, and everyday acts of invention. In sum, we understand culture as action and experiences of place as resulting from such doings. Many of the contributions to this volume and much scholarship on placemaking successfully argue that culture itself—the arts, spirituality, food, and other forms of expression—ought to be considered as a principal factor concentrating and animating economic and social participation within Latinx enclaves and routes.

While we draw from the work of colleagues in architecture and urban planning who have studied how Latinx immigrants breathe new life into neighborhoods in decline by buying homes and starting new businesses in urban areas, we do not often see cultural phenomena addressed within the developmental economics approaches that predominate in theories of placemaking.[16] To be sure, some urban studies placemaking work acknowledges the importance of culture, and this allows us to move from an infrastructural conception of place onto a performative one. Andrew Sandoval-Strausz, for example, underscores the important idea, articulated across the late twentieth century, that the "built environment"—our homes, our neighborhoods, our places of work and leisure—are important reflections of who we are, while Jesus Lara stresses the significance of a "third space" outside of home and work in the creation of community.[17] Also relevant here is Mike Davis's work examining how the "social reproduction of *latinidad*" is already well under way and touches on multiple aspects of life in the United States.[18] Taking as our point of departure the daily practices that connect Latinxs to a place, we observe that over the past thirty to forty years, the stories that emerge from the Midwest describe neither decline nor renaissance but rather continual struggle to survive and to extend to new generations the claims to belonging in place that previous generations fought so hard to achieve.

This volume, therefore, considers ways that the durée and force of quotidian and performative cultural practices as iterative doings over time create place rather than singular events or movements or alterations to built environments. It invites us all to examine different routes, itineraries, and strategies for orienting toward, inhabiting, and creating place in the Midwest.[19] Understanding that no choice is neutral in a territorial expanse riddled with power struggles over resources and legacies, regarding placemaking as performance allows for itinerant, visitor, refugee, and other less static positionalities to assume their due role in the accruing formation of anything we might come to call the Latinization of the region. As each of the chapters in this volume demonstrates through its respective forms of evidence, it is through the sharing occasioned by our everyday and formal collective rituals that we build up our sense of place through what sociologists Milagros Ricourt and Ruby Danta have conceptualized as "*convivencia diaria*," or daily conviviality.[20] Through the creation of cultural forms that facilitate ongoing interaction among Latinxs and between Latinxs and others, as Sujey Vega suggests, Latinx communities in the Midwest advance their belonging with difference.[21]

The range of chapter topics in this volume demonstrates that the impulse to excavate a history of Latinx placemaking cannot yield a unitary narrative of arrival and settlement nor a singular account of the strategies or characteristics of what might make the Midwest a Latinx place. These variegated efforts cohere precisely through their dynamism. Our collection attends to large migratory patterns of Latinx arrivals, but it also examines fleeting or even temporarily curated emergences of Latinx presence. We find that making place is a process that may unfold at the scale of the micro, the local, the regional, or the transnational by individuals and groups who choose to explore their difference together, however imperfect or incomplete the effort.[22] This is the work done by events that bring together individuals from distinct cultures and ethnic/racial backgrounds in the region. It is what Marisol de la Cadena meant by the term "composition," which she uses to signify a place that "has never been singular or plural, never one world and therefore never many either, but a composition (perhaps a constant translation) in which the languages and practices of its worlds constantly overlap and exceed each other."[23]

We take up this idea of the "composition" of Latinx places in the region in reference to the layered and overlapping histories and knowledges, and therefore temporalities, they embody as we also recognize that Latinx places become through the performative dynamism of culture and identity and engagement with the aesthetics of time as both representational paradigm and social theory. These kinds of temporalities are implied in our thinking about sustainability because it is our hope that the places Latinx communities have made not only will endure but also will thrive, even as they change and manifest in different ways. We pursue a focus on persistence and resilience—efforts to sustain in the now—without defaulting into fantasies of a predictable futurity we remain critically uncertain about. As the history of struggles our volume illustrates, *latinidad* in the Midwest is neither a historically neutral category (we are a settler-colonial presence in Indigenous lands) nor a universally welcomed or rejected identity (our chapters document ways in which Latinxs have been variably embraced, marginalized, and persecuted in the region).

If placemaking results from action across time, then our attention to the cultural phenomena contributing to the imagination and enactment of a Latinx Midwest requires that we tend to both the historical contexts that undergird them as much as the emergences or futurities recorded and proposed in those cultural practices. That is, we ought to understand that *latinidad* stands in relation to other significant historical and ongoing dynamics that position the Latinx Midwest as always after and in the midst of a settler-colonial history. It also invites us to see the history and present of our presence in the region in relation to the longer histories of economic, political, social, and environmental changes that continue to change and shape it. Most importantly, it demands that we do not see the Latinx Midwest as a static object attached to a single narrative of arrival and settlement shaped by the historical milestone established by what sociologists of migration have, problematically from the vantage point of Indigenous critique, termed "pioneer migrants."[24] Instead, Latinx settlement continuously gets refreshed and transformed by new patterns of migration (transnational, intranational, regional, and local) that continue to reshape how Latinx place is imagined, practiced, and represented.

Multiple Scales in Placemaking Projects

These observations regarding the cultural, temporal, and performative aspects of placemaking remind us also that the spatial categories defining our project, especially the Midwest, are not static; instead, they are constantly evolving and affirmed through iterative gestures. Regions, in addition to geographical designations such as nations, cities, towns, rural areas, and wilderness areas, are both produced and historic. Our invocation of the Midwest in the volume's subtitle intentionally embraces a flexible set of identifications that have accrued to the Midwest historically while also striving to capture the utopian possibilities inherent in that very flexibility for the sustainability of Latinx communities. Conceptualizing the Midwest as a territory, historian Doug Kiel argues that the region's boundaries are elusive. He describes the Midwest as a "nonplace" that is eclipsed in historiography by US westward expansion and defined in everyday discourse by what it is not: "[The Midwest] is at once the anti-East, not primarily urban or industrial or powerful; the anti-South, not chiefly typified by black-white racial discord and its legacies; and the anti-West, neither wild nor rugged nor tainted by a history of protracted Indian wars. . . . It is a floating signifier of progress, closure, whiteness, and the absence of violence—an idea that closes space for a wide range of multiethnic experiences, not just American Indian histories."[25] Following Kiel's appeal to contemporary scholars that they reopen study of the Midwest to a "wide range of multiethnic experiences," our volume foregrounds placemaking practices of the Latinx Midwest that challenge the prevailing stereotypes of whiteness, tranquility, homogeneity, and normative Americanness that accrue to the heartland. In an effort to illuminate a multiethnic Midwest, we stress the ways in which Latinx midwesterners interact with European-descended, African American, and Native American people historically and into the present. Our work in this volume, therefore, joins with parallel projects such as the Humanities Without Walls research group, dedicated to "Indigenous Art and Activism in Changing Climates: The Mississippi River Valley, Colonialism, and Environmental Change," and the Black Midwest Initiative, based at the University of Minnesota, in exploring a diverse Midwest.

Each of our chapters in some way registers what Kiel describes as the Midwest's "transition from frontier to modern industrial region," a profile that encompasses historic settler colonialism and dispossession of Native peoples, migration, and immigration, which subtend and inform contemporary regional patterns of urbanization, labor recruitment, and demographic shifts, including emergent Latinx Midwest communities in the post-NAFTA era.[26] In addition to recalling the Midwest as a former frontier in the manner that Kiel advocates, we also invoke the Latinx Midwest as a regional designation, drawing on insights from geography and political economy. For geographer Neil Smith, the boundaries of a region are not foreordained but rather emerge through uneven development within the global economic framework of capitalism.[27] Through his long career, Smith posited that capital moves from areas characterized by high wages, unionization, and employment to areas where low levels of wages, worker organization, and employment predominate. Regions emerge through patterns of capital movement as "peripheries become cores and cores peripheries, and the see-saw process repeats itself."[28]

When viewed through the lens of Latinx studies, it is not just the historic movement of capital from "militant" unionized shops in Chicago or on the East Coast to more "docile" small-town locations that produces the Midwest as a region.[29] It is also the transnational and transregional processes that connect this part of the United States to other regional and global locations. Midwestern normativity has in fact been exported and exploited insidiously, both globally, as in the sweeping neoliberal restructuration associated with the Chicago school of economics, and nationally, as in Wisconsin's campaign against welfare mothers and Iowa's dubious distinction, until recently, as the location of the largest workplace immigration raid in US history. José E. Limón and Marc Rodriguez have charted the long-standing transregional migratory circuits linking Tejano and Mexicano agricultural workers to the upper Midwest since the nineteenth century.[30] To these patterns, recent decades of neoliberal economic policies have heightened the "push" factors that compel Latinxs to make homes in the Midwest, even as "the bonds of loyalty and mutual obligation" that characterize "traditional midwestern capitalism" have eroded at an accelerated pace since the 1980s.[31]

The chapters in this volume describe Latinx placemaking in a range of locations and also often track events across scales. Latinx becoming occurs everywhere, from the midwestern metropolis of Chicago to large cities such as Cleveland, Ohio, and Milwaukee, Wisconsin, to midsized cities with established Latinx populations such as East Chicago, Indiana, and Grand Rapids, Michigan, and to rural and small-town locations that have experienced long-standing patterns of agricultural labor migration such as Hampton, Iowa, and Campbell, Ohio. We even describe placemaking efforts in college towns such as Urbana-Champaign, Illinois, and Madison, Wisconsin. Several chapters also track events across scales or reflect on cultural forms that show Latinx, Black, and Native American people's movement across a range of places or engaging in shared struggles or leisure in ways that bring the local, regional, national, and transnational into dialogue. The heterogeneous places that comprise the Latinx Midwest in this volume attest to nineteenth-century and early twentieth-century processes of urban industrialization; deunionization and deindustrialization; the postwar growth of metropolitan service sectors and cultural industries; the farm crisis of the 1980s and 1990s; and, in recent decades, the reindustrialization of rural and small-town communities through the establishment of meatpacking and agricultural processing industries in these locations.

As Jefferson Cowie notes in his study of long-twentieth-century capital flight, "The pull of place and community has been a powerful force in labor relations, but the limitations of local identity also create constraints on a more expansive notion of working-class politics in an era in which capital transcends boundaries with complete ease."[32] His argument applies to the Latinx midwesterners profiled in this volume, who are bearers of transnational histories, including ones shaped by US policy toward the countries of

Latin America and US immigration policy. They are witnesses, survivors, and descendants of the Mexican Revolution, Operation Bootstrap, Operation Peter Pan, the Trujillato, Central American civil wars, border blockades, and NAFTA, to name but a few major events. The transnational histories borne by Latinx midwesterners discussed in these essays as they create literature, zines, videos, and dance, organize parades, social events, festivals, and exhibitions, and advocate for labor rights and social justice offer valuable perspectives as to how twenty-first-century residents of the Midwest actively challenge the limits of narrowly defined location-based and territorially bound concepts of community. Through creative placemaking, Latinx communities theorize relationships across what Cowie terms the material world of "life space" and the "abstract and discontinuous" realm of the global economy.[33]

The plenitude of cultural expression and activist movements that define our project, as we have discussed above, often exceeds the boundaries of neighborhood, town, city, and region both culturally and affectively. Our chapters thus put regional, urban, and small-town scalar metrics of the Latinx Midwest into dialogue with practices of Latinx placemaking. According to literary and cultural studies scholar Mary Pat Brady, scale is associated with "imposed regimes of spatial domination, with abstract space that is universal," and this top-down hierarchy pertains to both the material environment and disciplinary studies: "As a vertical metric, scale reinforces hierarchies, assigns glamour and power to larger scales, and denigrates and dismisses the quotidian, gendered female, and parochial local practices by scaffolding meaning within relations of value."[34] The chapters in this volume seek out those occluded registers of experience described by Brady through attending to the horizontality of movement from one place to another, interpersonal interactions, and affective and remembered placemaking.

Our collective discussions leading up to this volume resulted in some place-oriented neologisms of our own, especially in regard to activist movements. For example, we observed sanctuary, labor, and immigrant rights activists invoking "hyperlocality," that is, intimate, specialized, and seemingly non-transferable place knowledges, as they maneuvered through legal systems and material environments. At the same time, however, those activists developed extensive regional networks and interregional mobility animated by activist commitment to broader social movements, faith, and ideology. In light of challenges and threats to Latinx sustainability outlined in our chapters, we also noted that "bubbles" aptly referred not just to enclaves of white privilege and bigotry but also to the relative sense of security associated with particular neighborhoods, streets, and places in rural, small-town, and other Latinx majority locations. "All brown all around, we are safe," a phrase related by Sandra Cisneros's narrator, Esperanza, as she recalls her Near West Side Chicago neighborhood in *The House on Mango Street*, identifies this security in what Lara refers to as a "third space," or place of community formation that is neither work nor home.[35]

Organization of This Volume

Building Sustainable Worlds is divided into three parts that detail the interrelated themes of sustainability, temporality, and scale in cultural practices of placemaking outlined in this introduction. The essays collected in this volume take a variety of methodological, analytical, and interpretive approaches, and, taken together, they reflect the innovative interdisciplinarity of Latinx studies. Several scholars engaged in embodied research write in the first person or adopt an intimate *testimonio* voice, while others make their positionality as scholars from the region evident. Yet others pursue more traditional lines of academic analysis and with significant citation of important Latinx studies research. This volume also intentionally includes the voices of community builders, advocates, and activists speaking directly of their experience of placemaking. The contributions gathered here often attend to the ways that Latinx have interacted with African Americans, Native Americans, and other immigrants from Europe, Asia, and Africa in the region, because Latinx Midwest experiences involve not only adaptation or assimilation but also creative transculturation.

Part I explores practices in the interstitial and dynamic sense described by Brady, in which Latinx midwesterners devise creative temporalities and geographies that elude or maneuver through scalar categories and exclusive temporalities. Theresa Delgadillo advances the idea that the invocation of alternative place-times in fiction reveals struggles with midwestern environments that prompt us to revalue the alternative knowledge produced by Chicanx and Latinx memory, cultural inheritance, labor, and creativity. Claire F. Fox offers an intimate exploration of the Latinx history of Hampton, Iowa, a small town linked to agribusiness that can be plotted within unequal processes of national and international capital movement, documenting pockets of vibrant small-town compassion. Lawrence La Fountain-Stokes breaks new ground in documenting the prolific work of Latinx queer performer Fausto Fernós, revealing wide audiences for Latinx performers, the depth of Latinx engagement with digital media, and intraethnic collaborations among Latinxs. Delia Fernández-Jones analyzes the mid-twentieth-century social networks and cultural celebrations of Mexicans and Puerto Ricans in western Michigan, revealing long-standing intraethnic socialities and cultural exchange. Ariana Ruiz unsettles the whiteness of zine studies by examining zine festivals that invest in a performance of *latinidad* as an alternative or underground cultural space to contest gentrification and construct such space as a transnational one that links concerns in Chicago to those in Mexico. These various iterations of *latinidad*, which collectively accrue into what we understand as a Latinx Midwest, not only record a difference in the repertoires and the directionalities of placemaking but also mark historically different moments in the formation of *latinidad* in the Midwest, from early labor migration and settlement at the height of the postwar industrial boom, to ascendancy dreams in the "Decade of the Hispanic," to the rise of Latinx underground millennial cultural practices. In each of these cases, the contingencies and the strategies for performing *latinidad* are driven by significantly different contexts and by changing articulations of what specific communities need.

Part II is comprised of three testimonial narratives and features activists describing how they have made Latinx places within, across, and in opposition to existing institutions. Sandra Ruiz both documents the collaborative process of creating a unique gallery space for Latinx art on the campus of the University of Illinois Urbana-Champaign and analyzes the sensory and environmental dimensions of its first exhibition by Erica Gressman. The next chapter offers us the first-person *testimonio* of Carmen Hernandez, PBVM, the founder of La Luz Hispana in Hampton, Iowa, on her commitment and that of her religious community in welcoming migrants. J. Gibran Villalobos describes the progress and challenges of building a Latinx arts network of artists and professionals in Chicago.

Part III includes essays that feature an exploration of placemaking through culture at varied scales of significance and often across scales. Karen Mary Davalos focuses on a Day of the Dead celebration in Minnesota, illustrating the tension of sustaining transmigrated Mexican indigeneity in a territory from which Indigenous communities were violently displaced. She also conveys the minute somatic experience of her own participation in the ceremony as a recently relocated Chicana scholar into the Latinx Midwest. Sergio González's essay reveals the emergence of multiracial religious coalitions to offer sanctuary in Wisconsin to Central Americans fleeing US-supported wars in what became the 1980s sanctuary movement. We then turn to East Chicago, Indiana, in the 1970s, and here Emiliano Aguilar Jr. documents the spirited forms and legal avenues, sometimes in collaboration with regional and national organizations, that East Chicago Latinxs pursued in their quest for equal opportunity. Aguilar and González show how Latinx activists enact "scale-jumping" as a strategy by bringing local struggles and intimate place knowledge to bear in national arenas and, in some cases, bypassing the presumed hierarchy of nesting scales.[36] In a collaboratively written chapter, Theresa Delgadillo, Laura Fernández, Marie Lerma, and Leila Vieira consider the sensory, spatial, affective, and sociopolitical dimensions of cultural expression at a series of Ohio Latinx festivals in 2017, illuminating the force of repetition in seemingly ephemeral events. Geraldo L. Cadava explores the work that the Chicago Latino Film Festival does in effecting Latinx inclusion in the city through the transnational and hemispheric framing of *latinidad*. Lastly, Ramón H. Rivera-Servera offers both a narrative of relocation to the Midwest and a meditation on the choreographic remembrance of urban and rural places of labor and leisure for Black and Latinx midwesterners in the work of Joel Valentín-Martínez and Anita González.

How Latinx communities enact their placemaking strategies is thus contingent on conditions that are constantly changing and shaped as much by global shifts as they are by local exchanges. What is critical to our approach in this volume is that we understand the productive potential of this dynamism, that we commit to tend to it with careful contextualization, and that we dare to ride the utopian possibilities of what each of these actions proposes as a possibility for sustaining an effort to make the Midwest livable for Latinx communities into the future.

Nonetheless, part III's scalar designations "plumb decolonial depths," to use Brady's phrase, and as an ensemble, the essays of all parts affirm our desire to invoke scale in two directions at once: in relation to a regional identification that acquires weight for Latinx midwesterners who take up existing discourses about the Midwest at the same time that their placemaking strategies actively seek to reshape the very concepts of home and community that subtend this region. In their exploration of the cultural expressions that come to life in advocacy, community-building, and leisure, these essays affirm our understanding of the Midwest as an industrialized, deindustrialized, and reindustrializing region, to echo Doug Kiel, "the outcome of many contested frontiers."[37]

Our Own Placemaking Efforts

As part of our effort to move the field forward, the essays in the present volume address intersections of class, gender, race, and ethnicity among Latinxs and between Latinxs and others in the region. In the four years that our collective has met to discuss our individual and shared enterprise, we have proceeded with the understanding that the Latinx Midwest has been built on several earlier Midwests: the Indigenous Midwest, the Midwest created by a European settler colony, the African American Midwest, the Midwest that various white ethnic immigrants and their descendants have called and continue to call home, and the Asian American Midwest.

In this collaborative project, we were eager to learn from those engaged in building Latinx communities in the Midwest. Over the course of our four-year collaboration, the authors included here traversed the region together, traveling to Chicago, Columbus, and Iowa City to participate in extensive dialogue about our individual research projects and our shared lines of inquiry. Our efforts to gather the group of scholars assembled in the volume before you constituted our practice of Latinx placemaking in the Midwest. Each time we coordinated our time together, identified potential cultural agents to engage, prepared writing and responses, and invested in aligning our thinking with one another we imagined and enacted in the collectivity of our effort a Latinx Midwest. At our editing meeting held in Iowa City, for example, the chapter authors organized several public-facing events that drew participation from the broader university and surrounding communities, including a talk by Lawrence La Fountain-Stokes at a local LGBTQIA+ club, a public-access television show, and an open mic at a local café, bookstore, and community center.[38]

As we prepared the final version of this manuscript, we, the coeditors, gathered in Chicago for our final editorial retreat. This time our gathering coincided with the third Chicago International Latino Theater Festival, organized by the Chicago Latino Theater Alliance to showcase the work of local and national Latinx and Latin American theater talent. So of course we ventured into the theater together to witness productions of Evelina Fernández's *Hope*, the second part of her Mexican trilogy, and Nilo Cruz's *Exquisita Agonía*. These were just two of twelve plays offered at the festival, and in our different experiences of those two plays we encountered many of the questions and the premises that animate this volume.

Hope is a drama about history, about 1960s working-class Mexican American history, to be exact. It tells the story of a family unit struggling with change, with the dissatisfaction of gender inequality, and with the promise of doing things otherwise in the solidarity that may emerge among women and friends as alternative to heteropatriarchal obedience. *Exquisita Agonía* is a melodramatic flirtation with loss and love as an opera singer struggles to find her dead husband in the young man who received the husband's heart as a transplant. Presented in Spanish with nonidentified Latinx specificity, the piece continues Cruz's exploration of European high-cultural classicism as backdrop and metaphor. Here we were, coeditors from wide-ranging backgrounds—a white European-descended midwesterner, a Chicana midwesterner, and a Puerto Rican queer transplant to the Midwest, one accompanied by family members from the region—in the collective ritual of assembling at the theater to experience *latinidad* staged before us in an effort not unlike many of the cultural projects discussed in this volume. And here we were in an attempt to make sense of all this difference before us, on the stage and in our seats, and with a commitment to understanding how gatherings such as these performances and cultural objects such as these plays make the Midwest Latinx.

With this collection we are invested in marking the historical strategies through which Latinx communities have carved out spaces for themselves in the region. However, our agenda is not the neutral development of an archive of Latinx placemaking. We are invested in these histories and in the ethnographic accounts of contemporary efforts as a way to amass a methodological toolbox to ensure the sustainability of a Latinx Midwest. Understanding that new forms of placemaking are still happening and that academic understanding of the Latinx Midwest is in and of itself a form of academic placemaking, we mine the past to better understand and model our actions in the present to ensure that our efforts endure and carry on into a future in the Midwest that recognizes, honors, respects, includes, and enables *latinidad*.

Notes

1. Priscilla Solis Ybarra, *Writing the Goodlife: Mexican American Literature and the Environment* (Tucson: University of Arizona Press, 2016).

2. Julie Sze, introduction to *Sustainability: Approaches to Environmental Justice and Social Power*, ed. Julie Sze (New York: NYU Press Scholarship Online, 2018), 1–18, DOI: 10.18574/nyu/9781479894567.001.0001.

3. Barbara Deutsch Lynch, "The Garden and the Sea: U.S. Latino Environmental Discourses and Mainstream Environmentalism," *Social Problems* 40, no. 1 (February 1993): 108–24, 110.

4. Lynch observes that "environmental problems are inseparable from the social and political systems in which they are embedded" (ibid., 116).

5. Elizabeth A. Povinelli, *Economies of Abandonment: Social Belonging and Endurance in Late Liberalism* (Durham, NC: Duke University Press, 2011), 30.

6. Ibid.

7. See the introduction in ibid., 1–30; and see Lisa Marie Cacho, *Social Death: Racialized Rightlessness and the Criminalization of the Unprotected* (New York: New York University Press, 2012).

8. Omar Valerio-Jiménez, Santiago Vaquera-Vásquez, and Claire F. Fox, eds., *The Latina/o Midwest Reader* (Urbana: University of Illinois Press, 2017).

9. Individual chapter endnotes include references to numerous works, and the bibliography provides a comprehensive list of scholarship on Latinxs in the Midwest.

10. Accounts of racist beatings and police harassment against Latinx in Chicago, for example, figure in Jennifer Domino Rudolph's analysis of Latinx narratives by former gang members in *Embodying Latino Masculinities: Producing Masculatinidad* (New York: Palgrave Macmillan, 2012), 47–51.

11. Illegal Immigration Reform and Immigrant Responsibility Act of 1996, Pub. L. No. 104-208, September 20, 1996; H.R. 4437, Border Protection, Antiterrorism, and

Illegal Immigration Control Act of 2005, H. Rept. 109-345, introduced December 6, 2005.

12. Richard Schechner, *Performance Theory* (New York: Routledge, 1988).

13. Judith Butler, *Gender Trouble: Feminism and the Subversion of Identity* (New York: Routledge, 1991).

14. Frances R. Aparicio, *Negotiating Latinidad: Intralatina/o Lives in Chicago* (Urbana: University of Illinois Press, 2019), 52.

15. Juana María Rodríguez, *Queer Latinidad: Identity Practices, Discursive Places* (New York: NYU Press, 2003).

16. In addition to the work of Sandoval-Strausz and Lara, see also Richard Florida, *The Rise of the Creative Class and How It's Transforming Work, Leisure, Community and Everyday Life* (New York: Basic Books, 2002).

17. Andrew Sandoval-Strausz, *Barrio America: How Latino Immigrants Saved the American City* (New York: Basic Books, 2019); Jesus J. Lara, *Latino Placemaking and Planning: Cultural Resilience and Strategies for Reurbanization* (Tucson: University of Arizona Press, 2018).

18. Mike Davis, *Magical Urbanism: Latinos Reinvent the U.S. City* (London: Verso, 2007), 65.

19. Social geographers, for example, have generated important studies of placemaking as changes to physical environments inhabited by Latinx communities. See Christopher A. Airriess and Ines M. Miyares, eds., *Contemporary Ethnic Geographies in America* (Lanham, MD: Rowman & Littlefield, 2016); Daniel D. Arreola, ed., *Hispanic Spaces, Latino Places: Community and Cultural Diversity in Contemporary America* (Austin: University of Texas Press, 2004).

20. Milagros Ricourt and Ruby Danta, *Hispanas de Queens: Latino Panethnicity in a NYC Neighborhood* (Ithaca, NY: Cornell University Press, 2002).

21. Sujey Vega, *Latino Heartland: Of Borders and Belonging in the Midwest* (New York: NYU Press, 2015).

22. We are borrowing and modifying a phrase from Marisol de la Cadena's work *Earth Beings: Ecologies of Practice across Andean Worlds* (Durham, NC: Duke University Press, 2015). Cadena states that she and her ethnographic partners "knew that our being together joined worlds that were distinct and also the same. And rather than maintaining the separation that the difference caused, we chose to explore the difference together" (4).

23. Ibid., 5.

24. David P. Lindstrom and Adriana López Ramírez, "Pioneers and Followers: Migrant Selectivity and the Development of U.S. Migration Streams in Latin America," *Annals of the American Academy of Political and Social Science* 63, no. 1 (2010): 53–77.

25. Doug Kiel, "Untaming the Mild Frontier: In Search of New Midwestern Histories," *Middle West Review* 1, no. 1 (Fall 2014): 20.

26. Ibid., 27.

27. John Paul Jones III et al., "Neil Smith's Scale," *Antipode* 49, no. S1 (2017): 139.

28. Ibid., 141.

29. See, e.g., Chad Broughton, *Boom, Bust, Exodus: The Rust Belt, the Maquilas, and a Tale of Two Cities* (Oxford: Oxford University Press, 2015).

30. José E. Limón, "*Al Norte* toward Home: Texas, the Midwest, and Mexican American Critical Regionalism," in Valerio-Jiménez, Vaquera-Vásquez, and Fox, *The Latina/o Midwest Reader*, 40–56; Marc Simon Rodriguez, *The Tejano Diaspora: Mexican Americanism and Ethnic Politics in Texas and Wisconsin* (Chapel Hill: University of North Carolina Press, 2014).

31. Broughton, *Boom, Bust, Exodus*, 86.

32. Jefferson Cowie, *Capital Moves: RCA's Seventy-Year Quest for Cheap Labor* (New York: New Press, 2001).

33. Ibid., 198.

34. Mary Pat Brady, "Territoriality," in *Keywords for Latina/o Studies,* ed. Deborah R. Vargas, Lawrence La Fountain-Stokes, and Nancy Raquel Mirabal (New York: New York University Press, 2017), http://proxy.lib.uiowa.edu/login?url=https://search.credoreference.com/content/entry/nyupresskls/territoriality/0?institutionId=1049.

35. Sandra Cisneros, *The House on Mango Street* (Houston: Arte Público Press, 1985), 29.

36. Jones et al., "Neil Smith's Scale," 145.

37. Kiel, "Untaming the Mild Frontier," 11.

38. See https://www.youtube.com/watch?v=5Po7mJaCnXA.

PART I

Emergent Futures

CHAPTER 1

Unsustainable Environments and Place in Latinx Literature

THERESA DELGADILLO

In the short memoir "Hurricane," by Aurora Levins Morales, collected in the volume *Cosecha and Other Stories* (2014), the narrator recounts her experience as a young Puerto Rican woman integrating into life at a majority white school in an exclusive neighborhood on Chicago's South Side. She contrasts the rhythm of life, the aural environment, and the landscape of the Puerto Rican farming community of Candelarias, where she grew up, with those of her new school: "The days were minced into tiny bits. . . . Cabs, buses, people, dogs, garbage cans rattling in the wind, but no rustle of leaves, no hawks' cries, no coquís, no rain pounding on a tin roof. And no distances to look into even when it was day."[1] These observations contain the seed of a critique of the space of the modern city and the logics that inform it. The hollow "rattle" of the city driven by the ticking time clock of Fordist industrial production is devoid of subtlety ("rustling"), affect ("cries"), and passion ("pounding"), as well as the vistas or vision that she associates with Candelarias. Hemmed in and constrained by cityscapes that do not allow for a view of the horizon, the narrator recalls the expansiveness and lushness of Candelarias, which her new classmates mistakenly view as "more primitive." The reversal of values ascribed to city and rural landscapes in this excerpt does not merely propose a romantic view of the natural world in contrast to the city—a literary trope with a long history.[2] Instead, it forms part of a narrative that examines the relationship between human society and physical environment with a critical eye on the specific histories of power embodied in distinct local spaces. The story's speaker must also learn to adjust to the way that she is perceived by others in this new location: "They let me know that my voice was too expressive, my gestures too flamboyant, my friendliness undignified."[3] As a result, she quickly learns that "being from another country was odd and uncouth, but that *knowing* someone from another country made you sophisticated and cosmopolitan."[4] For the narrator's classmates, sophistication in knowing people from other countries is a symbol of their place in the empire/center, a place that affords them travel to the periphery, those lesser spaces—to them—where the exploitation of natural and human resources fuels the development of the modern world and city.[5] "Hurricane" thereby conveys the migrant's acute sense of surroundings—both former and new, cultural and material—when placed in a new environment.

In both this story and the larger volume in which it appears, the authors refuse a romantic view of Candelarias, explicitly narrating its many drawbacks and limitations while also advancing a sustained consideration of political economy, nationalism, gender, and colonialism in the history of Puerto Rico's inhabitants. "Hurricane," therefore, is also a consideration of power, one that the light-skinned Puerto Rican narrator considers in another episode. When assigned to tutor a young Black girl from the "dangerous" neighborhood near hers, she doesn't do what she is supposed to do (tutor her in homework); instead, she does what the girl wants her to do (listen to her many stories of surviving tornados back in Arkansas).[6] Something in her current environment prompts the girl to dwell on these stories of surviving disasters, which leads our narrator to recall Ramona, a Black schoolmate back in Puerto Rico who was without fail constantly singled out for ridicule by teachers, leading the narrator to conclude, "I knew now that where you stood, and in whose shoes, changed everything about what was visible. You learn what you need to know. In Candelarias, nothing had forced me to recognize the daily, deadly grind of racism. In Chicago, everything did."[7] In narrating her newfound understanding of racism, Levins Morales joins in "a moment of newly concerted will to face down the pestilential afterlife of slavery" in order to undo what Christina Sharpe identifies as the deadly force of prevailing "conventions of antiblackness."[8] In "Hurricane" the struggle to make place in the Midwest can generate new critical insight about both places of origin and spaces of arrival, potentially bringing Latinxs into coalition with others in the region. The memoir, therefore, touches on the twin themes of this essay: environmental sustainability and cultural sustainability in Midwest Latinx literature precisely because it lays bare the racialized colonial logics that make, for example, "possession" of Puerto Rico possible while it also critiques the consequences of such possessiveness both in the modern city and as they manifest in Puerto Rico. The story, therefore, offers us a decolonial commentary on environment and place.

This chapter proposes that in literature produced by Latinxs in the Midwest about making home in the region we can identify an environmental critique that recognizes the interplay between cultural and physical environments and unfolds through the invocation of alternative place-times in literature to join in the project of what Priscilla Ybarra terms "goodlife writing."[9] This chapter examines how the focus on social relationship in Latinx literature about making place in the Midwest involves a negotiation of urban industrial and agroindustrial spaces whose social construction did not involve Latinxs as equal participants. Making place in Latinx literature, therefore, is sometimes a reckoning with these environments and other times a contestation of these environments with a different kind of place-time that derives from social relations outside of capitalist, colonialist, and neocolonialist logics. These alternative place-times are not merely nostalgia for the precapitalist or a return to idyllic "natural" environments, nor are they portrayals of the kind of environmental writing that has been most widely recognized and studied (individuals alone with nature). Instead, they are an invocation of knowledge from the Americas about living with the natural world in contemporary literature, suggesting that Latinx literature is also engaged in imagining futures alternative to the present.[10]

How does Latinx literature about the Midwest disrupt capitalist and industrial-era values about space, place, and environment?[11] What does Latinx literature about the Midwest tell us about alternative sustainable modes of living? This chapter will examine several Latinx literary works in addition to *Cosecha* for the reckoning with industrial and urban space that they represent: Hugo Martinez-Serros's *The Last Laugh and Other Stories* (1988), an interrelated set of fictional narratives focusing on the lives of a Mexican American steelworker family in Chicago in the mid-twentieth century; Rubén Martinez's nonfiction journalistic chronicle of Mexican migration to rural areas and small towns in the Midwest in the late twentieth century in *Crossing Over: A Mexican Family on the Migrant Trail* (2002); Sandra Cisneros's novel *Caramelo* (2002), about a transnational Mexican American family who creates home in the large urban centers of Chicago, Mexico City, and San Antonio; and Fred Arroyo's *Western Avenue and Other Stories* (2012), which focuses on Puerto Rican migrants in Indiana, Pennsylvania, and Chicago. This chapter suggests that Midwest Latinx literature's representation of alternative place-times becomes a lens for communicating a complex and interrelated set of concerns: an intimate examination of landscapes, built environments, and ecologies that bespeaks Latinx belonging in the region; an ambivalence about patterns of consumption that the industrial and agroindustrial economies of the region afford; and an expression of Latinx alienation and marginalization in the region that is driven not only by hostile social and cultural climates but also by a deep dissatisfaction with the environmental degradation that Latinx characters encounter as workers in the region.

From Nature Writing to Goodlife Writing:
New Paradigms for Reading

In this study, I want to underline the distinction between "space" and "place." The first is devoid of attachments, and the second is a site of belonging, of affective attachments and memories and interrelationship—what Lawrence Buell describes as "associatively thick."[12] What is "space" to one group may well be "place" to another, and vice versa. Buell furthermore suggests that "the concept of place gestures in at least three directions at once—toward environmental materiality, toward social perception or construction, and toward individual affect or bond—makes it an additionally rich and tangled arena for environmental criticism."[13] As this passage suggests, thinking about the representation of space and place in Latinx fiction is also thinking about environment. In considering how Latinx literature imagines place for Latinxs in the Midwest, I recall Edward Soja's insight that "spatiality is a substantiated and recognizable social product" that "socializes and transforms both physical and psychological spaces." It is both a "medium and outcome" of "social action and relationship," that is, "an arena for struggles over social production and reproduction."[14] Particular spaces, such as cities, neighborhoods, and zones, don't just pop up "naturally" but are, as Soja argues, produced through social relations that are themselves often a contest, and these spaces have a profound physical and psychological impact on those who inhabit them. Environmentalists concur when they note that what we consider "environmental" is a cultural construction, and they ask us, "How is bounded and managed wilderness area designated a national park more 'natural' than a city?" As I will discuss shortly, this has led to greater incorporation of ecocritical assessments of all kinds of built environments, including "natural preserves," within the field.[15] As I have already noted above, the fact that Latinxs did not participate equally in the construction of the spaces they enter into in the Midwest matters in their ability to make place.

Ecocriticism, or literary environmental studies, has shifted away from a strict focus on "nature writing" and into more sustained considerations of the interrelationship between the realms of the cultural and social, on the one hand, and the material and natural environment, on the other hand.[16] In the United States, an ecocritical movement attentive to questions of social justice has been working to decenter an earlier exclusive focus on wilderness experience or living (usually of white male subjects) or nature writing (usually of white male and female subjects) in order to also examine urban landscapes, questions of environmental justice, and the experiences of ethnic and racialized minorities in relation to environment.[17] For these reasons, until recently, little critical attention has been devoted to the treatment of ecology and environment in Latinx literature, a gap that Ybarra addresses with her conception of "goodlife writing" as descriptive of a unique Mexican American literary consciousness about the environment that is driven not by an individual narrator's experience of nature but instead by advancing ideas of humans living in healthy relationship with each other and the natural environment. Several aspects of goodlife writing emerge in Midwest Latinx literature, including tension around issues of possession and control of land.[18] The latter may be relevant to considering how Latinxs see themselves in relation to others in the Midwest, given that this literature is produced by descendants of migrants and migrants to the region with no ancestral claim to the lands or region they now inhabit and where indigenous peoples continue to reside as federally recognized tribes.

Latinx Literature's Environmental Critique of Industrial and Agricultural Economies

The histories and experiences of Latinxs in the Midwest since the early twentieth century have been dominated by migration to the region for industrial, agricultural, and agroindustrial labor, including rail, steel, and auto industries; leather production; harvesting of beets, berries, cucumbers, potatoes, and canning crops; meat and poultry processing; and dairy production.[19] Manufacturers, growers, and local governments in the region were known to manipulate labor economies and state resources in ways that contributed to challenging social climates for Latinxs in the region as well.[20] In early twentieth-century Detroit, Mexican auto workers, according to one social worker, were reported to "have more money but less air and fresh vegetables."[21] There, "unhealthy living conditions and improper nutrition coupled with cold weather produced a high incidence of tuberculosis, measles, and rickets," while workplace conditions were no better, as they were "polluted with dust, smoke, and coal gases."[22] The pollution and degraded environments that Mexican steel workers in Chicago faced were often blamed on the workers themselves when "acceptable levels of pollution were sometimes couched in racialized terms."[23] And Latinx industrial workers often lived in close proximity to the industries where they worked, heightening their exposure to polluted environments. While later generations of Latinxs may no longer work in these industries, and some of these industries have left the region, the industrial and agricultural labor experience and corollary exposure to dangerous and degraded environments, as well as challenging social climates, remain at the core of the historical experience of Latinx placemaking in the Midwest, recalled and analyzed in histories and reimagined, remembered, and critiqued in literature.

While we might today imagine that the industrial experience is far behind us and that Latinxs have seamlessly blended into middle-class professional employment throughout the region, the slaughterhouses and industrial meat-packing plants that first brought Mexican migrants to Kansas City in the early twentieth century, for example, have become, with further mechanization, industries on steroids that still continue to rely on Mexican immigrant labor.[24] Rubén Martinez's work of nonfiction, *Crossing Over*, offers us an extended chronicle of the lives of a family of migrants from Cherán, Michoacán, who have relocated to Norwalk, Wisconsin, to work in the Valley Pride Meat Plant. Martinez's narrative reveals how industrialization that "creates jobs" operates in a context of colonial paradigms underpinning modernity that prompts us to consider whether Latinxs, specifically Mexicans, in the Midwest have become a permanently disenfranchised citizenry by virtue of their race, ethnicity, and legal status. In the chapter "Princes of Norwalk," Tom Powell, the owner of the Valley Pride Meat Plant, referring to the Enríquez family he employs, says, "I don't think they're a typical Spanish family. They're pretty clean people," repeating an old eugenicist claim deployed against Mexicans and others wherein Mexican/Other = natural = primitive = dirty.[25] Martinez's chronicle of the Enríquezes' journeys between Mexico and the United States, when considered in this context, conveys a strong sense of enduring racist logics while it also captures the complexity of the lives of contemporary immigrants, who are both strivers and neighbors, Mexicans and midwesterners in a labor economy no longer dominated by organized labor. The 1980s industry attacks on meatpackers disabled labor's control over working conditions, wages, and benefits in ways that continue to resonate today in favor of companies such as the Valley Pride Meat Plant, and have contributed to the growth of immigrant labor in the United States.[26] One Norwalk resident, Frank Ettinger, a former worker at Valley Pride who was fired for complaining about unsafe conditions, comments on this changed labor market in the chronicle, though there may be gender bias in how easily he assigns blame to the woman owner and not the male owner of Valley Pride: "You can't blame the Mexicans for all this, Frank says, but that's what people in town talk about: Mexicans bring down wages, making it more dangerous, Mexicans this, Mexicans that. Bullshit. It's Rhonda who lowers the wages. It's Rhonda who makes it more dangerous. The Mexicans, after all, don't own anything. Rhonda's the one with a stake in the plant."[27] In Ettinger's perspective, he is more like the Enríquezes than he is like the plant owners, Rhonda and Tom Powell, and his words highlight his sense of class solidarity versus the antiworker sentiments expressed by the plant owners. Martinez's description of the plant makes readers aware of both the toll this work environment takes on its workers and its toll on the environment: the massive scale of equipment and energy use, the extreme hot and cold temperatures of the plant, the slippery and bloody surfaces throughout, the loudness, the intense pace, and the monotony and exhaustion of the work for everyone on the plant floor.[28] His chronicle bears witness to Frank Ettinger's observations about how all workers suffer under antilabor conditions.

A sense of affiliation and connection between white midwesterners and Mexican immigrants emerges again, with a twist, when the narrative describes the Enríquez family practicing a "traditional Purépecha dance called los viejitos (the elders)," which they will perform for a meeting of the town's Latino Task Force: "It is a pre-Columbian ritual and, as such, older by centuries than the Euro-American presence in Norwalk."[29] With this simple observation, the chronicle upends a sense of place based on modern nation-states and instead voices an older indigenous claim to belonging in the Americas that the Enríquezes enact in their performance. But in revealing the Enríquezes to be friendly indigenous neighbors, the chronicle troubles us by leaving unspoken a dark undercurrent in the trope of friendly Indians who share their ways with the dominant culture, and we must wonder about the price the Enríquezes will pay, or are paying, for their generosity. Martinez's chronicle offers several such scenes of stark juxtaposition that create an undercurrent of uncertainty hovering at the edges about the ability to overcome deeply embedded social structures of capitalism and ethnonationalism, contributing to a sense of the in-betweenness and peril in which migrants reside. In the rare free moments they enjoy, the migrants from Cherán to the Midwest underscore this in-between state when they also imagine a future for themselves and their children far from the difficult labor in the agricultural industry that brought them there.[30] "Princes of Norwalk" thereby joins in "goodlife writing" by prompting readers to consider the relationship between labor abuse, compromised environment, and "larger oppressions of colonization, imperialism, modernity, and neoliberal globalization."[31]

Consumption, Craft, and Sociality in *Caramelo*

A fictional representation of transnational life for Mexican immigrants unfolds in Sandra Cisneros's rich and expansive 2002 novel, *Caramelo*, which takes readers from Chicago to Mexico City and back again as it tracks the Reyes family on their annual summer visit to Mexico City, home of Inocencio Reyes, the father in the story, and then to San Antonio, where the family moves.[32] This reading proposes that *Caramelo* offers us a critique of capitalist commodity production and the material and environmental waste it produces by juxtaposing it to artisanal and craft production and by contrasting the then still artisanal place of Mexico with the industrial space of Chicago.

The *caramelo*-colored *rebozo*, or shawl, at the center of the novel embodies the novel's invocation of another place-time. The *rebozo* in *Caramelo* has been inherited by Soledad Reyes, grandmother of Celaya Reyes, who narrates the novel, from its makers, her father, Ambrosio, and mother, Guillermina, widely known for their dyeing, weaving, and *empuntadora* (a technique of taking up threads to create a design akin to embossing) skills, even among their fellow *rebozo* makers in the town of Santa María del Río, in the state of San Luis Potosí, a town famous for the artisanal production of this garment in another era.[33] The unmistakable black color of Ambrosio's shawls derived from soaking the fabric in water filled with old iron objects, discarded items reused in dyeing, while the intricate knotting of the fringe in Guillermina's "signature design" was said to take "one hundred and forty-six hours to complete."[34] Unfinished at the time of Guillermina's death, the child Soledad claims the *caramelo rebozo*—"a beautiful blend of toffee, licorice, and vanilla stripes flecked with black and white"—and carries it with her throughout her life, proud of the exquisite artistry it represents and treasured as a piece of her long-gone mother.[35] Soledad eventually stores the delicate silk *rebozo*, wrapped in paper, in the armoire of her Mexico City bedroom, where the object piques the interest of the young Celaya Reyes, her granddaughter, years later.

When Inocencio Reyes tells his mother, Soledad, that he wants to buy his daughter Celaya a silk *rebozo* from Santa María, the grandmother scoffs that such shawls are "disappearing," since all that is sold nowadays is made in a factory, and those shawls that do exist "cost a fortune."[36] I suggest that Inocencio's and Celaya's desire for a silk *rebozo* like the grandmother's represents and conveys a complex amalgamation of nostalgia that is also knowledge, acquisitiveness for a scarce/rare object, and memory of place. The nostalgia for this object from the past suggests a still-present desire for materials traceable to their local sources and handcrafted in excellence by people in a specific place that is emotionally significant for the Reyes family as a place of belonging. Because it conveys these meanings, the *rebozo* itself takes on talismanic qualities in the narrative, becoming the title for a narrative that not only remembers events but also reknits the relationship of a family to its past and to each other. The *rebozo* comes to stand for place, belonging, interrelationship, and, I suggest, a sustainable environment. As an object of use, it contrasts sharply with the carloads of gadgets and merchandise gathered at the Maxwell Street flea market in Chicago by Celaya's Uncle Fat-Face and Aunty Licha to sell in Mexico: "Topo Gigio key rings. Eyelash curlers. Wind Song perfume sets. Plastic rain bonnets. . . . [G]low-in-the-dark yo-yos."[37] While the sale of the latter funds the annual summer visit to Mexico, the items are not valued or valuable. They are trinkets that lose their attraction after initial fascination with them fades, not items packed away and saved for decades, not like the *rebozo*. In this way, *Caramelo* also engages in goodlife writing by offering readers a critique of the "consumer desire that creates the outsized U.S. ecological footprint," and in this case, the novel shows us how that consumer desire is reproduced abroad.[38] The alternative place-time that the treasured *rebozo* embodies, however, continues to circulate as knowledge in the narrator's consciousness, and it colors her apprehension of desired socialities.

Caramelo's environmental critique extends to the space of the city as it contrasts the experience of living in Chicago to that of living in Mexico City— both large urban centers but with differing approaches to public and private space. The novel's description of the "original Maxwell Street" in Chicago as a vibrant neighborhood contrasts with its description of the landscape that replaced it: expressways.[39] From the windows of her Aunty Licha's home, Celaya observes, "Outside, roaring like the ocean, Chicago traffic from the Northwest and Congress Expressways. Inside, another roar; in Spanish from the kitchen radio, in English from TV cartoons."[40] Celaya and her siblings experience Aunty Ninfa's home, full of beautiful gold-and-white furniture that is covered in plastic and that is too big for the apartment, as one that inhibits their movement, and they consequently avoid visits there: "Whenever some- one wants to pass, someone else has to sit down."[41] Celaya's home does not feature glamorous furniture; instead, it is filled with mismatched furniture on loan from her father's upholstery business and "too many things" purchased by him at Maxwell Street and by her mother at secondhand stores. The space of Chicago, for the Reyes family, is cramped, constrained, and filled with too many things whose immediate usefulness is in question, an echo of the "con- fining, violently punctuated barrio apartments" that John Alba Cutler notes in *The House on Mango Street*.[42] The expressway just outside the window is a sign of a cityscape reshaped by the demands of automobiles and the ideas of urban planners who do not value difference or social interaction in the city.[43]

However, when Celaya arrives with her family in Mexico City, she describes a public place of interaction and commerce and work and relationship, of fresh food and the smells, tastes, and sights of sensory interaction with others: "above doorways, faded wreaths from an anniversary or a death till the wind and rain erase them," "a workman carrying a long metal pipe on his shoulder, whistling ffftt-fffttt to warn people," "the smell of hot corn tortillas along with the pat-pat of the women's hands making them."[44] Unlike the description of Mexico City streets, which conveys vibrant interaction, the description of the Chicago apartments conveys stultification and out-of-placeness, where the proliferation of objects is experienced as a burden. In this way, *Caramelo* prompts us to consider the social relations that create and are created by built environment designed for cars and not people.

Even the *Milpa* Is Corrupted

Hugo Martínez-Serros's 1988 collection of short stories portrays the experience of growing up on Chicago's working-class South Side during the mid-twentieth century from the perspective of Lázaro and Jaime Rivera, who at ages eight and eleven are the oldest sons of José María, who is a steelworker. Like the narrator of "Hurricane," Lázaro and Jaime experience the disdain of classmates and teachers, though here, far from the cutting politeness of elite South Side spaces described in "Hurricane," hostility is openly expressed by white adults who call the boys "Panchos" and inflict violence on them or classmates who call them "Fuckin' Messkin" and dismiss them.[45] As "outsiders," the boys are as perceptive and observant of their surroundings as the narrator of "Hurricane," aware that what they do and how they do it are dependent on the spaces they move through: "They were quick to spot a hostile eye, to see bodies stiffen at their entry, to detect disapproving silences."[46] Their perceptiveness leads them to conclude that what their father encounters at the steel plant is similar to what they encounter, though they are never privy to the character of those exchanges. In "Killdeer," the narrator describes some of the taunting the father experiences in the steel plant: "José María paused to observe his sons. They would grow up one day and the thought of their working in the steel mill tormented him. He slashed the earth but could not still his foreman's voice—'Your sons will work for me too, Hoezay, you'll see.' He slashed harder, faster, angry with his foreman, and himself for having brought his sons to a life of possible entrapment in the mill."[47] At another point, the narrator describes José María arriving at the family's plot, where the boys are working, barely a half hour after his shift at the mill has ended, full of pent-up rage and looking to discharge it in some way. After he finds fault with the boys' work and beats them, he feels his anger released. The boys, trying to understand his rage, say, "Maybe somebody said somethin' to him at work. You know how he gets when they ask him if we're gonna work in the mill."[48] Although they also discuss the possibility that their father remained angry with them over an earlier transgression, the boys intuit but can't fully know that there is a link between their father's work experience and his anger, that the space of the steel mill has invaded his psyche. In the present day, where we hear much longing for the good old days of well-paying industrial jobs in the region, what are we to make of this story, which openly rejects the steel mill as a future and reveals the frustration and anger of individuals bound by it?

The fierceness of José María's desire for something different, something better for his children, is palpable, particularly in "Distillation," in which the father bears the brunt of a hailstorm to protect his children from danger in a way that metaphorically evokes his daily sacrifice for what he hopes will be a future for them.[49] In these short stories we learn that work in the steel mill was not always reliable or adequately compensated: José María sometimes works "short weeks," and the family makes ends meet by scavenging the city dump for food on Saturdays. We also learn from both the boys' experience and that of their father that racism and xenophobia are useful in creating hierarchies of opportunity in the workforce. The stories recognize a generation's skill and hard work in negotiating both a degraded urban environment and a demanding, though limiting, job, but they betray no love for that built environment, and they do not offer readers the comforts of nostalgia about an industrial past.

Instead, in *The Last Laugh*, the family's shared and collective attempt to live an alternative place-time in the cultivation of a *milpa* at the edge of the city forces a reckoning with how much they have been negatively transformed by the urban industrial space. In the short story "Victor and David," readers meet two brothers who are friends of Lázaro and Jaime and whose father, Damian, a railroad worker, maintains a vegetable garden in their backyard.[50] In "Jitomates," told retrospectively from Jaime's perspective, the narrator lovingly recalls how his mother canned the tomatoes that he, Lázaro, and their father, José María, grew in the *milpa*.[51] In the course of the story, we learn how the family kept dried corn in the attic to use in spring planting and how Jaime and Lázaro collected, in the spring, horse manure around the neighborhood—to the amusement of all who passed by and who were unaware of its use—to fertilize their *milpa*.[52] These stories portray Mexican workers and their families making place in the space of South Chicago through their friendships and shared efforts in cultivating food in the ways and with the knowledge they carried with them from Mexico to Chicago. These practices of cultivation, particularly that of the *milpa*, which is a form of permaculture that involves the planting of complementary regional crops in the same plot (such as corn, beans, and squash) and the rotation of fields, have a long history in Mesoamerica.[53]

The depiction of creating a *milpa* in both "Jitomates" and "Killdeer" presents an alternative place-time to that of the urban industrial economy, one that appears essential to the family's survival, requires skills and knowledge of natural and built environments, provides a green summer respite from the city for the family, and represents the continuation of inherited indigenous traditions and knowledges.[54] The *milpa* is also an attempt to counter the degraded urban environment of South Chicago. "Killdeer" portrays, in detail, the entire process of creating the *milpa*, from clearing the land in the very early spring to planting and the summer growing season, which Jaime and Lázaro largely carry out under the direction of their father, José María.[55]

In describing the location of their *milpa* in South Chicago, the story reveals a Mexican approach to sustainability practiced by many in that northern urban site:

> Acres of land with few trees reached south as far as the 103rd Street bridge and west to the highway—railroad land fallen into disuse. It hid old wells and scant remains of structures razed long ago. Their *milpa* was off Torrence Avenue, just west of where the long curve ended. José María, like other Mexican immigrants, had found his way there some years earlier, had cleared several acres, turned them over with a hoe and worked the simple magic that gave him corn, tomatoes, potatoes, squash, coriander and much more. It was more land and richer than any his father cultivated in Mexico. He took it, worked it and felt like a landowner.[56]

While the Riveras, like other Mexican immigrants, are making use of fallow and discarded land to create a place out of "no place"—echoing, in a parallel realm, the work of Los Angeles Chicanx performance art group Asco in the 1970s and 1980s to create Chicanx art out of the "no place for art" of Chicanx experiences and neighborhoods—the last line of the above passage signals a dangerous shift into possessiveness that encroaches on the family's *milpa* efforts.[57]

This story conveys how this alternative place-time, which has provided food, respite, togetherness, and knowledge of the landscape around them to the Riveras (Jaime, for example, had previously enjoyed the song of the meadowlarks there), eventually becomes a site corrupted by the logics of the industrial urban environment in which it exists.[58] Jaime's remembrance of happier times there in his youth contrasts with the growing sense of oppressiveness both he and Lázaro feel under the thumb of a father whose eagerness to outshine and beat all the other *milpa* growers and whose pent-up rage over his place in the steel mill finds an outlet in his harsh judgments and treatment of Lázaro and Jaime for their efforts in managing the *milpa*. Unwittingly, José María, whose knowledgeable and careful instruction of his sons in making *milpa* echoes his similarly knowledgeable and careful instruction of the boys in tending a furnace in the first story of the collection, has begun to treat his sons as workers and to be motivated by competition and not community in relation to other *milpa* growers. When the boys, unconsciously seeking to vent their own anger about their new situation, buy into the competitiveness of their father and brazenly destroy the *casita* of another *milpa* grower as they alternate between joy and terror over their actions, we know that the corruption of industrial space has now made itself manifest in their lives, though the story's end suggests a sliver of hope that perhaps the boys will not entirely lose their knowledge of living in connection with plants, animals, and others.

If "Jitomates" offers us a tender view of the fruits of cultivation and human interaction, then "Killdeer"—the name of the migratory plover whose territory includes Canada, the United States, and Mexico and that Jaime hears in the *milpa*—reminds us of the wildness and ecological competition also at play throughout these stories, as well as the omnipresent economic structure influencing human behavior. In the story, the Killdeer bird itself symbolizes the environmental interconnections in North America, while its song may convey knowledge that most no longer hear. In the end, one isolated nuclear family of Mexican migrants cannot sustain a challenge to an overwhelming industrial environment, and the only hope that remains, for both Jaime and readers, is in listening to the Killdeer's song.

Cultivating Another Place-Time for Survival

Fred Arroyo's *Western Avenue and Other Fictions* (2012) is a series of interconnected stories that largely revolve around events in the lives of Manuel Perez, a.k.a. Boogaloo, his friends Tino, Arturo, and Changó, and their wives and children—a small network of Puerto Rican friends and workmates who accompany each other through shifting employment opportunities that carry them from Puerto Rico to New York and Connecticut to Michigan and Indiana and finally Chicago, where the story "A Case of Consolation" takes place. Short stories alternate with vignettes of experiences in Puerto Rico throughout the narrative in a way that conveys the transnational dimensions of migrant lives as it weaves together interconnected narrative threads. Like *The Last Laugh and Other Stories*, Arroyo's work offers us a novel-like text but not quite a novel, as each story also stands alone as a piece of short fiction. In form, it is, therefore, reminiscent of other important works of American literature from the Midwest such as *The House on Mango Street* (1984) by Sandra Cisneros, *Blacks* (1945) by Gwendolyn Brooks, and *Winesburg, Ohio* (1919) by Sherwood Anderson.

In "A Case of Consolation," we meet Manuel Perez when he has already experienced multiple displacements and hardship in the United States through his industrial and agricultural labors and has slowly lost touch with his friends and family due to death, distance, and drink over the years of moving from Connecticut to Michigan and then Chicago, where he is in this story, living like a hermit, unconnected to those around him. He exists in the sparest of surroundings, with unadorned walls and few possessions—a folding chair, a table, seven books, butcher paper, index cards, and pencils—but with a keen sense of the sights, sounds, and flavors around him, particularly the sight of green trees, sun, and sky. Manuel, who we are told is now ten years sober, is described in this way: "Without ever understanding the gradual changes to his emotional life, Boogaloo was slowly transformed into a man without likes or dislikes, without a strong sense of desire or remorse, a shell alone on an empty beach without the inner, passionate song of the sea found in that place where shell, ear, and sea meet in the radiance of music. Continually in motion—adrift in work—he seemed to simply stand still."[59] In casting Manuel as "continually in motion" yet standing still, the narrative suggests that migration for work might be a false promise or trick, as it also reveals Manuel to be the one sanded down by motion, stripped of strong desire or dislike, and shaped into a quiet and willing cog in the machine. But the text, in suggesting that "he *seemed* to simply stand still," opens the possibility that Manuel may not be standing still at all, or possibly that standing still might mean something other than immobility—might mean an interruption or disruption of the ever-forward motion and logic of modernity.[60]

The only pleasure in Manuel's life is the time and energy he invests in creating new recipes for the restaurant Cassava, where he is employed, a task described as a mesmerizing immersion in flavors, and smells, and memories as he improvises on an established recipe by adding his own personal touches, recording the provisional recipe on the butcher paper, practicing it in the restaurant, and testing it on coworkers, carefully noting their reactions as they eat in case adjustments are necessary before finally recording the final recipe, in English, on a recipe card for his boss, who distributes it to his other restaurant locations.[61] Two of the books in Manuel's small library are *Comida Criollas* and "the late eighteenth century" volume on "new Hispanio vegetation and foodstuffs, *Fruiticas Paradisio*," both titles that suggest the unfamiliarity of Latin America to other regions of the world.[62] Yet Manuel's reliance on memories of watching his mother cook in her own kitchen—how she flavored a simmering *sancocho* with mango, for example—rather than on cookbooks is the key resource that transports him and his recipes into another realm, if his coworkers' reactions are any gauge. In this story, those memories suggest what María DeGuzmán terms "LatinX botanical epistemology," or a knowledge of plants and plant-derived materials that inform the labor of cooking.[63] In this portrayal, Manuel's cooking is not merely a job; instead, it is an art and an act of making place, where the selection and combination of flavors and textures are infused with his memories of his mother's and *abuela*'s cooking and of his time with them in their kitchens and where the recipes he creates become, in turn, an experience shared with his two coworkers and incorporated into the place of the restaurant.

This new vocation fills him with a sensation of rich stillness and a sense of wonder, being so completely different from all other jobs he's held. Manuel's life, generally, is a new experience to him as a recovering alcoholic with ten years of sobriety under his belt. On the outside, he might seem to be still, but the text frequently describes how aware Manuel is of the sight, texture, sound, and smell of his surroundings, especially the natural elements and plants, when he watched "for the tops of the trees suddenly to bud green" or "listened to the robins chirping outside his window" or noticed the "air smelling clean and tinted with the lilacs [he] had stopped to savor."[64] These moments of attentiveness to his surroundings, of appreciation for the natural world around him, appear to be an achievement of his recovery and healing from alcoholism, but they are also linked to his development of a culinary repertoire. I suggest that Manuel is engaged in actively cultivating another place-time—that of his life in Puerto Rico, of his family in Puerto Rico—in order to survive life in the northern urban environment where he finds himself, and in this cultivation, Manuel experiences a gradual reawakening, but not before one last, painful loss.

The owner of Cassava, an East Asian man, takes Manuel's recipes and shares them with his other restaurants, and this raises questions about exchange versus appropriation. The narrative conveys the delivery of recipes in a neutral way, suggesting that creative menu creation is part of Manuel's job, what he is paid for, rather than the act of one person profiting from the labor of another. Manuel expects additional compensation in the form of an annual raise for this work, but he decides that he will decline the raise in favor of awarding greater pay to his coworkers, Tomás, who is Peruvian, and Rosita, who is Nicaraguan. Manuel thereby acts in solidarity with his coworkers and fellow Latinxs, whose need he recognizes as greater than his. Perhaps Manuel's awareness that he is cultivating alternative knowledge of his environment keeps him from seeing his boss's action as appropriation. More important is Manuel's eschewal of possession over the recipes and his decision to act in solidarity with his coworkers, acts that suggest both community and sociality, as well as the refusal to put a price on memory, on family recipes. These are not things that can be owned, and even in his isolated, alienated life, he still recognizes what supersedes economies of commodity production.[65]

In the midst of Miguel's process of awakening consciousness from the stillness that enveloped him at the beginning of the story, he coincidentally runs into Rosita at a café outside of work, and they fall into an easy and growing friendship. At the moment when their friendship begins to yield to an intimate relationship, when Rosita invites him to accompany her home, the space-time of manufacture, of "continually in motion," prevents Manuel from seizing the moment: "He closed his eyes for a moment. In the distance, train wheels ground against steel, a horn honked, and a roar of wind filled him with the smell of cooking chocolate from the candy factory on the river. He pressed his hands against his chest, felt for a moment the purple rising in his fingers. Before words arose in his throat, as the wind seemed to die, he heard Rosita say, No worries, Manuel, we'll ride together another day."[66] We intuit here how Manuel's emotional life has been gradually malformed and stunted by the space-time of industrial life—the exacting rhythms and clocks and enclosures and the forced, continual movement "forward" that leads to lost friends, lost ties, isolation. This scene reinforces that understanding of Manuel, were it not for what comes afterward. Feeling remorse for letting Rosita down and for depriving himself of her company, he seeks her out when she doesn't show up to work, fearing that she may have been taken in an ICE raid. The story signals Manuel's awakened desire for relationship and interconnection in his new observations of families and children on the city streets, and soon Manuel is remembering and wondering about his grown daughter and nodding a greeting to two Latinos who pass him. Suddenly, "the sidewalk seemed like a slice of the world he would learn to accept." He took a turn onto a tree-covered avenue, and "he saw within the trees arching over the avenue infinite doorways, opening and closing, some with and some without promise. He took each threshold encountered with surprise and wonder, crossing over without any sense of right or wrong. Tomorrow, Rosita, tomorrow if it's warm like today I will slice fruit, wherever you are, wherever we won't meet, Rosita, tomorrow, please don't be alone."[67] Although Manuel has missed out on the opportunity for a life shared with Rosita because his own journey to overcoming the damage and isolation wrought by his experience as an itinerant laborer remains incomplete, his cultivation of homegrown knowledge and alternative place-time has fueled his rebirth into a life where loneliness and isolation will be less acceptable.

Conclusion

If we fully embrace Latinx difference in the region as it intersects with prevailing paradigms and populations, we can see how Latinx literature might be speaking to all of us in our current contemporary moment of environmental crisis. It is not surprising that Latinx literature about the Midwest, born of people drawn to the region for work, would address working-class experience and social justice issues, yet as this chapter has explored, this experience is also the ground for an environmental consciousness that recognizes the interplay between cultural and physical environments that we see in this literature. This recognition is at play in Ariana Ruiz's essay in this volume examining changing urban spaces and the mobilities of Chicago Latinx zine production. In this chapter Latinx texts reveal Latinxs working to make place amid urban industrial and agroindustrial spaces whose social construction did not involve them as equal participants, drawing from knowledge and experience of alternative place-times that point us to decolonial modes for renewal, even if the characters themselves continue to reside in that in-between space of both loss and hope. In this way, these stories echo the call for a synthesis of philosophies that could lead to a new environmental ethics, one that "would take from primitivism the idea of *diversity*, from peasant cultures the ideal of *sustainability*, and from modern society in general, rather than from scientific conservation in particular, the value of *equity*" while also making plain just how challenging the path toward that goal is.[68]

Notes

1. Aurora Levins Morales and Rosario Morales, "Hurricane," in *Cosecha and Other Stories* (Cambridge, MA: Palabrera Press, 2014), 57–64, 58.

2. Timothy Clark, *The Cambridge Introduction to Literature and the Environment* (Cambridge: Cambridge University Press, 2011), 13–18; Lawrence Buell, *The Future of Environmental Criticism: Environmental Crisis and Literary Imagination* (Malden, MA: Blackwell Publishing, 2005), 23.

3. Levins Morales and Morales, "Hurricane," 59.

4. Ibid., 60. The irony of this observation is that it also applies to higher education, the location from which I write, where the unwillingness to invest in critical ethnic studies contrasts with the insistence that we develop so-called global citizens who know the languages and literatures of the world.

5. Anibal Quijano and Immanuel Wallerstein, "Americanity as a Concept, or the Americas in the Modern World-System," *International Social Science Journal* 44, no. 4 (1992): 549–57.

6. Levins Morales and Morales, "Hurricane," 61–62.

7. Ibid., 63–64.

8. Peter Schjeldahl, "The Song of a Nation: Walt Whitman at Two Hundred," *New Yorker Magazine*, 24 June 2019, Art World, 74–75, 75; Christina Sharpe, *In the Wake: On Blackness and Being* (Durham, NC: Duke University Press, 2016), 21.

9. Ybarra, *Writing the Goodlife*.

10. As I have noted elsewhere, "neither the colonial nor the postcolonial, neither the settler nor the nation-state, succeeds in erasing native worldviews or cultures from memory or practice" (Theresa Delgadillo, *Spiritual Mestizaje: Religion, Gender, Race, and Nation in Contemporary Chicana Narrative* [Durham, NC: Duke University Press, 2011], 181). In this way, these texts also echo José David Saldívar's observation about the complexity of the "conjunctural present—where multiple times exist simultaneously within and across the same planetary location or co-exist as uneven subaltern temporalities" (*Trans-Americanity: Subaltern Modernities, Global Coloniality, and the Cultures of Greater Mexico* [Durham, NC: Duke University Press, 2011], xxviii). As Priscilla Ybarra notes in her discussion of environmentalism in Mexican American literature, this literature offers "an approach [that] is at once nonmodern and decolonial" and presents "an alternative set of traditions and insights with which to approach today's challenges" (*Writing the Goodlife*, 6). This reading has some affinities with the

Latin Americanist view that in certain hands an embrace of primitivism might be a kind of "returning gaze of the colonized," but it principally draws from Chicanx and Latinx decolonial studies. For primitivism as challenge to capitalist modernity in Latin America, see Erik Camayd-Freixas and José Eduardo González, eds., *Primitivism and Identity in Latin America: Essays on Art, Literature, and Culture* (Tucson: University of Arizona Press, 2000).

11. For more on the "spatial matrix" of industrial capitalism, see Edward Soja, *Postmodern Geographies: The Reassertion of Space in Critical Social Theory* (London: Verso, 2011), 128.

12. Buell, *The Future of Environmental Criticism*, 63. See also Tuan Yi-Fu, "Place: An Experiential Perspective," *Geographical Review* 65, no. 2 (1975): 151–65; Lynda H. Schneekloth and Robert G. Shibley, *Placemaking: The Art and Practice of Building Communities* (New York: John Wiley & Sons, 1995); Katia Balassiano and Marta Maria Maldonado, "Placemaking in Rural New Gateway Communities," *Community Development Journal* 50, no. 4 (2015): 644–60; Raymond W. Rast, "Cultivating a Shared Sense of Place: Ethnic Mexicans and the Environment in Twentieth-Century Kansas City," *Diálogo* 21, no. 1 (2018): 35–49.

13. Buell, *The Future of Environmental Criticism*, 63.

14. Soja, *Postmodern Geographies*, 120–30.

15. Clark, *The Cambridge Introduction*, calls this the "antinomy of environmental criticism" (94).

16. For an overview of the field, see ibid.

17. Buell writes: "Literature-and-environment studies must develop a 'social ecocriticism' that takes urban and degraded landscapes just as seriously as 'natural' landscapes (Bennett 2001: 32). Its traditional commitment to the nature protection ethic must be revised to accommodate the claims of environmental justice (Adamson, Evans, and Stein 2002)" (*The Future of Environmental Criticism*, 22). Ybarra notes that "in the United States, it is the middle- and upper-class Anglo-American population that has always seen itself as taking the lead on environmental reforms and innovations, such as the establishment of national parks and the management of natural resources such as forests. Partly understanding this disconnect between environment and the marginalized, some scholars (myself included) have tried to make connections to the environmental movement with the idea of environmental justice. Environmental justice, with its central concern for human access to nontoxic living and working spaces, as well as to clean water and healthy food, has made some progress toward connecting the marginalized with environmental concerns" (*Writing the Goodlife*, 15).

18. Ybarra, *Writing the Goodlife*, 17.

19. Dennis Nodin Valdes, *Barrios Norteños: St. Paul and Midwestern Mexican Communities in the Twentieth Century* (Austin: University of Texas Press, 2000); Rodriguez, *The Tejano Diaspora*, 62, 75.

20. Zaragosa Vargas, *Labor Rights Are Civil Rights: Mexican American Workers in 20th Century America* (Princeton, NJ: Princeton University Press, 2007), 54, 79, 149.

21. Quoted in Zaragosa Vargas, *Proletarians of the North: Mexican Industrial Workers in Detroit and the Midwest, 1917–1933* (Berkeley: University of California Press, 1999), 125.

22. Ibid., 125.

23. Michael Innis-Jimenez, *Steel Barrio: The Great Mexican Migration to South Chicago, 1915–1940* (New York: New York University Press, 2013), 14.

24. Rast, "Cultivating"; Michael Grabell, "Sold for Parts: Case Farms Took Advantage of Immigrant Workers Then Used U.S. Immigration Law Against Them When They Got Hurt or Fought Back," *ProPublica*, May 1, 2017; Rubén Martinez, *Crossing Over: A Mexican Family on the Migrant Trail* (New York: Picador, 2002), 247, 255, 257–58, 265.

25. Martinez, *Crossing Over*, 245. Throughout the 1920s eugenicists circulated claims about so-called Mexican primitiveness, filth, and disease and subjected Mexican migrants to stringent and sometimes dangerous sanitation measures at the border. Meanwhile, migrants from Canada were exempted from such measures. See Alexandra Minna Stern, *Eugenic Nation: Faults and Frontiers of Better Breeding in Modern America* (Berkeley: University of California Press, 2005), 68–69, 67.

26. Elizabeth Baier, "25 Years Ago, Hormel Strike Changed Austin, Industry," *MPR News*, August 17, 2010, https://www.mprnews.org/story/2010/08/17/austin-hormel -strike; Barbara Kopple, *American Dream*, 1990.

27. Martinez, *Crossing Over*, 258.

28. Ibid., 246–48.

29. Ibid., 259.

30. Ibid., 65.

31. Ybarra, *Writing the Goodlife*, 18.

32. Sandra Cisneros, *Caramelo* (New York: Vintage / Random House, 2002).

33. Ibid., 92.

34. Ibid., 92, 93.

35. Ibid., 94.

36. Ibid., 38.

37. Ibid., 7.

38. Ybarra, *Writing the Goodlife*, 18.

39. Cisneros, *Caramelo*, 9.

40. Ibid., 6.

41. Ibid., 12–13.

42. John Alba Cutler, "Lyric Subjects, Cultures of Poverty, and Sandra Cisneros's Wicked Wicked Ways," in *The Ends of Assimilation: The Formation of Chicano Literature* (Oxford: Oxford University Press, 2015), 131.

43. For further reading on expressways in literature and culture, see Raúl Homero Villa, *Barrio Logos: Space and Place in Urban Chicano Literature and Culture* (Austin: University of Texas Press, 2000); Eric Avila, *Popular Culture in the Age of White Flight: Fear and Fantasy in Suburban Los Angeles* (Berkeley: University of California Press, 2006).

44. Cisneros, *Caramelo*, 18.

45. Hugo Martínez-Serros, "The Last Laugh" and "Her," in *The Last Laugh and Other Stories* (Houston: Arte Público Press, 1988), 7, 36.

46. Martínez-Serros, "The Last Laugh," 10.

47. Martínez-Serros, "Killdeer," in *The Last Laugh*, 59.

48. Ibid., 78, 82.

49. Martínez-Serros, "Distillation," in *The Last Laugh*, 21–32.

50. Martínez-Serros, "Victor and David," in *The Last Laugh*, 129–73.

51. Martínez-Serros, "Jitomates," in *The Last Laugh*, 123–28.

52. Ibid., 124, 128. Although horses were still used for milk deliveries into the 1950s in Chicago, the stories, with their descriptions of coal-fired furnaces and horses used for hauling yet in an era of steel mills and railroads, appear to be set earlier in the twentieth century, possibly the 1930s or 1940s. By 1966 only sixteen working horses were licensed in Chicago. See "City's Vehicle License Sales Rise in 1966," *Chicago Tribune*, January 3, 1967, B13, ProQuest Historical Newspapers: *Chicago Tribune*; Donald Yabush, "Milk Drivers Still Like the Old Gray Mare," *Chicago Daily Tribune*, May 5, 1957, SW12, ProQuest Historical Newspapers: *Chicago Tribune*; Henry Greene Jr., "Modern Times Bring Bad Luck to Horseshoer: Cars, Trucks Put Hex on Blacksmith," *Chicago Daily Tribune*, February 17, 1955, W4, ProQuest Historical Newspapers: *Chicago Tribune*. Thank you to the Chicago Public Library staff for this information.

53. A group of ecologically minded students and faculty in the School of Environment and Natural Resources held a two-day workshop on making *milpa* at the Ohio State University farm in May 2018. Participants were able to learn about the ecological benefits of this indigenous method of planting complementary crops in the same plots and were instructed and led in traditional ways of planting by a visiting Mayan farmer from Belize, Central America. This workshop was supported by the Initiative for Food and AgriCultural Transformation at OSU, which aims to develop conceptual models and practical examples of climate-resilient, secure, and equitable agricultural and food systems. See also http://www.marc.ucsb.edu/research/maya-forest-is-a-garden/ maya-forest-gardens/milpa-cycle.

54. Barbara Deutsch Lynch suggests that the "environmental significance of the pre-Columbian past" continues to signify in Latinx communities and that we can learn from these communities how "differently imagined ideal landscapes offer differing definitions of environmental good and evil" ("The Garden and the Sea," 111, 112).

55. Martínez-Serros, "Killdeer," 55–84.

56. Ibid., 57.

57. C. Ondine Chavoya and Rita Gonzalez, eds., *Asco: Elite of the Obscure; A Retrospective, 1972–1987* (Ostfildern, Germany: Hatje Cantz; Williamstown, Mass: Williams College Museum of Art; Los Angeles: Los Angeles County Museum of Art, 2011). For Ybarra, land figures centrally in good life writing, but she identifies a rejection of land "possession" and the colonialist logics that undergird that approach as key to good life writing in Mexican American letters.

58. Martínez-Serros, "Killdeer," 72.

59. Fred Arroyo, "A Case of Consolation," in *Western Avenue and Other Fictions* (Tucson: University of Arizona Press, 2012), 3–15, 4.

60. André Lepecki, *Exhausting Dance: Performance and the Politics of Movement* (New York: Routledge, 2006).

61. Arroyo, "A Case of Consolation," 5.

62. Ibid., 3.

63. María DeGúzman, "LatinX Botanical Epistemologies," *Cultural Dynamics* 31, no. 1–2 (2019): 108–24, 115.

64. Arroyo, "A Case of Consolation," 3, 4, 6.

65. Ybarra, *Writing the Goodlife*, 17. Although the possession discussed here is not of land, which constitutes a characteristic of goodlife writing, but instead of recipes, there is a consonance here with the ethos of goodlife writing as Ybarra defines it.

66. Ibid., 9.

67. Ibid., 15.

68. Ramachandra Guha and J. Martinez-Alier, *Varieties of Environmentalism: Essays North and South* (London: Earthscan Publications, 1997), 91.

CHAPTER 2

Radical Hospitality in a Small Iowa Town

CLAIRE F. FOX

Zoo Island

In "Zoo Island," a story by Tomás Rivera, the fifteen-year-old protagonist, José, wakes up "with a great desire of taking a census count, of making a town and making everybody in it do what he said."[1] Due to rain that pre-empts another long day of agricultural labor with his family, what begins as a sleepy-eyed fantasy of adolescent power becomes a more ambitious project to survey his neighbors, Mexican and Tejana/o migrant laborers who dwell in repurposed chicken coops on an Iowa farm. Dressed in their Sunday best and armed with a notebook, questionnaire, and wristwatch, José and his friends set to work conducting an official head count. Their efforts culminate in a community self-portrait as residents gather for a photograph before a sign that says "Zoo Island, Pop. 88 ½," the fraction indicating a baby on the way.[2]

By appropriating the techniques of US census-takers, José and his companions make the farm field visible to themselves and others as something more than a worksite—it is a residential community, a place of birth and death, leisure and homemaking. The Zoo Islanders take pleasure in the realization that "the farm settlement was really a town and bigger than the one where they bought their groceries every Saturday," the implication being that it is their labor that sustains the nearby community.[3] And for José, this act of placemaking awakens his sense of belonging in the world: "He was a part of that number, he was in Zoo Island, in Iowa, and like Don Simon said, in the world."[4] When Sunday drivers cruise by the farm to gawk and laugh at the migrants, José perceives the satiric force of naming his town after the monkey habitat at the San Antonio zoo so as to reflect the tourists' dehumanizing gaze back at them. Through simple acts—visiting neighbors, making a list, placing a sign, taking a photo—a transregional migrant collective claims its place in the Midwest just days before breaking camp, and in doing so, it wryly manipulates the operative tropes of liberal citizenship and sovereignty in a settler-colonial state: visibility, voice, representation, and incorporation.

Much scholarship on placemaking in the Latinx Midwest focuses on legacy neighborhoods in urban areas that date from nineteenth- and twentieth-century waves of industrialization, places where collective memory accrues to the built environment through residents' interactions in and with particular dwellings, commercial and industrial districts, parks, schools, and churches. In such neighborhoods, community organizing often avails itself of pride in barriology, that is, the residents' deep knowledge of place stories and ways of being in the neighborhood, in order to combat pathologizing or remediating discourses wielded by external authorities.[5] But what are the techniques of placemaking in the Midwest's small-town and rural communities, where Latinx presence has also been crucial to the development of agriculture and industry since the late nineteenth century, but without a demarcated territory or roster of heritage places that attests to this long history? How do the legacies of racial and spatial segregation described by Rivera bear on small towns where Latinxs are increasingly making homes in the twenty-first century? In addressing these questions, I take a cue from the Zoo Islanders' placemaking strategies under the voyeuristic gaze of their neighbors by looking to storytelling, visual culture, and performance as important means through which Latinxs and non-Latinxs alike assert, foster, and transmit collective memory about Latinx presence in rural and small-town communities.

Two decades ago, I arrived in Iowa from California, the daughter of small-town midwesterners of European descent, and with academic training in US-Mexico border studies. As I adjusted to my new university position, I turned to midwestern locations as a way to make my interest in NAFTA-era policy relevant for my students. The borderlands and the Rust Belt have long-standing connections, I learned, and many small midwestern towns are becoming destinations for immigrants who have been obliged to leave family farms in Mexico due to the economic stress that the North American trade agreement placed on their livelihood.[6] The writings of Tomás Rivera, who spent his youth as a migrant worker in South Texas and the Upper Midwest, also helped me to perceive the established migratory circuits that link the borderlands to the Midwest.[7] As Theresa Delgadillo has observed, midwestern settings figure prominently in Rivera's poetry and fiction, yet most readers associate the author with South Texas, in part because four of Rivera's midwestern stories were ultimately excluded from his best-known work, . . . *y no se lo tragó la tierra* (. . . *And the Earth Did Not Devour Him*, 1971). Had "Zoo Island" been included in this novel as Rivera initially intended, Delgadillo argues, this story about becoming Chicanx in Iowa "would significantly alter the [novel's] emphasis on the powerlessness and confusion of migrant workers, endowing them with greater agency—which in the current published version emerges only among a few characters and only in the Southwest."[8]

My interest in Rivera led me to retrace the author's journeys in north-central Iowa and to one small town in particular, Hampton (pop. 4,337), which today has a significant and growing Latinx population.[9] I became interested in how contemporary Hamptonians understand the history of Latinx presence in their community and how Latinxs make places for themselves there, especially in light of the intensified anti-immigrant movements that have gripped the United States in recent years. With Rivera's Iowa-based stories as my guide, in this chapter I examine the ways in which Hamptonians enact the dyadic roles of guest and host, traveler and stayer, which are integral to hospitality scenarios, through their storytelling and public events.[10]

Hospitality is a great mythos of the Midwest, one that is seemingly inexhaustible in regional development initiatives and cultural heritage tourism designed to lure visitors to friendly, small-town destinations. As such, the ethics of hospitality in both ideal and lived manifestations provide a rich point of entry to the examination of small-town intercultural relations in a moment of danger, when hospitality's mandate to "welcome the stranger" is at odds with the national climate in which Latinxs routinely risk arrest, deportation, social exclusion, and interpersonal and institutional violence. In the absence of Latinx neighborhoods, small-town hospitality lends itself to forms of placemaking that can be ephemeral, contingent, and strategic yet are nevertheless profoundly impactful on how people perceive their belonging in a community. As Julia Reinhard Lupton observes, hospitality "crafts scenes for appearing" in the theater of everyday life, insofar as its rituals feature "the tremulous and risky appearing of persons to each other in moments of quasi-public encounter and acknowledgment."[11] In Hampton, such moments of "risky appearing" sometimes depend on bonds of trust to adhere among strangers who are also neighbors. Such encounters also have the potential to "clear a stage for actors unaccustomed to or excluded from political speech" and thus, in this small-town setting, to foster the inclusion of undocumented people, racial and ethnic minorities, and Spanish speakers in the broader community.[12]

In Rivera's "Zoo Island," the host community's failure to extend hospitality to migrants results in two adjacent yet incommensurate societies. However, José's consciousness is transformed when he and his neighbors temporarily reject the roles of guest and traveler, which are often used to marginalize Latinxs as perpetual newcomers or transients in rural midwestern settings, and instead begin to act as though they were residents of a town like any other in the region. In order for Latinx placemaking to be successful in a small town such as Hampton, I argue, it is important not only for established European-descended communities to welcome new Latinx residents but also for both groups to imagine hospitality as a reciprocal process in which the roles of guest and host can be fluidly embodied and exchanged.

My thinking on this topic is informed by Mireille Rosello, whose study *Postcolonial Hospitality: The Immigrant as Guest* identifies ways in which hospitality has served as a driving metaphor for immigration policy and international relations at the same time that it is embedded in unwritten, culturally relative, and age-old practices of everyday human interaction. In the former arenas, Rosello notes, the "vision of the immigrant as a guest is a metaphor that has forgotten it is a metaphor."[13] One need only recall phrases common to contemporary discussions about immigration policy, such as "host nation," "donor country," "guest worker," "sanctuary city," and "refugee," to grasp the ubiquity of hospitality as an operative scenario in political and policymaking arenas. Ideals of equality and reciprocity underlie most cultural practices of hospitality, according to Rosello. By saying "Make yourself at home" or "Está en su casa," the host grants the guest the same privileges that the host enjoys, and the guest potentially can reciprocate this gesture at some point in the future by extending similar privileges within his or her own home.[14] Rosello goes on to observe, however, that the hospitality metaphor as it circulates politically with respect to immigration tends to mask inequalities and sometimes even serves as a platform for virulent anti-immigrant sentiment: rather than being welcomed as guests, immigrants are actively recruited as laborers, refused entry, or obliged to abandon their homes due to violence or poverty. And rather than receiving the unconditional gift of welcome, rest, and safety, immigrant guests are instead expected to pay a debt to the host nation through expressions of assimilation, gratitude, and loyalty.[15]

The creditor/debtor framework of conditional hospitality, familiar from contemporary political debates in the United States, sometimes manifests on a deeply confrontational level in small-town midwestern settings. A letter to the editor of the *Hampton Chronicle*, for example, refers explicitly to the "security deposit" that the author feels immigrants owe prior to receiving hospitality: "I owe you NOTHING. Hampton will never be a strong, vibrant, beautiful community unless they assimilate, learn English, obey the laws and take personal responsibility [what a concept]. You will be welcome then."[16] Even as this writer extends a conditional invitation to a presumed Latinx interlocutor, she inserts an aside to fellow Hamptonians about the infractions that "they" commit, effectively conscribing all Latinx community members, historic and contemporary, migrant and immigrant, to the status of outsiders or uninvited newcomers. Arriving "in debt" and thoroughly bound to the role of guest, immigrants are frequently unable to act as hosts because they lack a stable residence or the necessary security that serves as a precondition for extending an invitation.[17] It is clear, then, that whether in reference to nations or individuals, the ability to extend hospitality hinges implicitly on the host's claim to safety and agency within a particular place, a claim that is often foreclosed to Latinxs in parts of the Midwest who lack a "home," though they might have a functional place of residence.

In my visits to Hampton over the past five years, I have encountered myriad hospitalities, conditional and unconditional, vulnerable and exuberant. As the county seat of Franklin County, Iowa, Hampton went from being located in a sanctuary county for undocumented people to having its sanctuary status repealed in the early months of the Trump presidency.[18] Even as these developments were occurring, La Luz Hispana, the newly established Latinx community center in Hampton, was acting boldly to challenge them. The center extended a form of unconditional hospitality, welcoming to all without question, while at the same time orchestrating the "risky appearing" of Latinx Hamptonians in events ranging from town meetings with the county sheriff to a large annual Latinx festival. I have personally enjoyed the hospitality of Hamptonians, who have welcomed me into their public institutions, parks, churches, festivals, and homes. In this chapter, I revisit a few of those memorable places and encounters: Band Shell Park, the Hampton Public Library, La Luz Hispana community center, a private home, and the vehicle moving between sites of risk. By asserting their agency and presence as hosts in midwestern hospitality scenarios, Latinx Hamptonians, like the Zoo Islanders of Rivera's story, are creating communities and making places even under inhospitable circumstances.

La Luz Hispana

Located in central Iowa near the Minnesota border, Hampton is surrounded by beautiful farms and woodlands. From almost any vantage, one can see the join between the vast Iowa sky and land that appears to extend forever in all directions. Hampton's walkable downtown clusters small businesses, including several Latinx-owned restaurants and two Latinx grocery stores, around a prominent group of public institutions: the county courthouse, a library constructed with funds from Andrew Carnegie, and Band Shell Park, which hosts musical performances in temperate months. During World War II, Italian POWs worked in sugar beet and hemp production in this area; so did Tomás Rivera's family, along with many other Tejanas/os and Mexicanas/os, inspiring the setting for several of Rivera's stories.[19] According to the 2010 census, 21 percent of Hampton's residents were Hispanic, though recent estimates place that percentage higher, while the town's European-descended majority population is declining.[20] Some Latinx families in this part of the state trace their ancestry to people who settled out during Rivera's time and even earlier, but today, adult Latinx Hamptonians hail from Texas, Mexico, Guatemala, Honduras, El Salvador, Puerto Rico, and the Dominican Republic, and they are raising families and buying homes here.[21] Like other Latinx, Southeast Asian, eastern European, and African Iowans, they arrived in the wake of the deunionization of meatpacking and agricultural industries that began in the mid-1980s, and they were recruited to work in this area's nearby egg-processing plants, hog confinements, and construction industry. Their presence has invigorated Hampton's economy while also dramatically changing the town's demographics and public culture.

Across the street from the courthouse in downtown Hampton, La Luz Hispana occupies a former law office; the center's interior space features a large meeting room, two classrooms, a computer lab, an office, and a kitchen.[22] The center was founded in 2013 by Sister Carmen Hernández and Sister Maura McCarthy of the Dubuque Sisters of the Presentation as a nonprofit organization dedicated to "education, service, and hospitality" for Hampton's Latinx community. La Luz Hispana benefits from its soft connections to other institutions and agencies, religious, academic, and governmental. It has a precarious funding structure, with operating costs covered mostly by grants and donations, and it functions through the paid and volunteer labor of professionals and community-based leaders.[23] A recent impact study conducted by the center among area residents and business owners led Sister Carmen to conclude that one of the center's greatest accomplishments in its first five years of existence has been to shift the needle appreciably from the "sentiment of negativity" that Hampton's majority white, European-descended population previously held toward Latinx residents. For La Luz Hispana's assistant director, Aimee Lenth, who arrived at the center after working for a refugee support center in Minneapolis, La Luz Hispana is instrumental in "bridging the cultural divide between Latinos and non-Latinos" in Hampton. Meanwhile, Sister Carmen aspires for the center to achieve a similar impact within Hampton's Latinx community by encouraging greater interaction among Latinx groups that remain somewhat isolated from one another, such as Guatemalans and Mexicans.

After working for a mobile women's health clinic that served this area, Sister Carmen saw the need for a Latinx-serving community center in Hampton. She founded La Luz Hispana with the intention of eventually turning over the center leadership and management to community members.[24] Like José and friends in "Zoo Island," Sisters Carmen and Maura began by conducting a survey among the town's Latinx residents, asking them "what do you need?"

and "how can we get there?" What they heard most often was that people "wanted a place they could call home and feel safe" and "a safe place to gather." At the center's inauguration, Sister Maura was gratified to hear one visitor say, "Me siento muy en casa aquí" (I feel very much at home here). Though La Luz Hispana is nondenominational, with both secular and religious allies, Sister Maura and Sister Carmen inevitably draw on their order's emphasis on hospitality in their daily work. Offering food and shelter to travelers is a long-standing practice of many Catholic orders, for which every encounter with a stranger is an opportunity to follow Jesus's example. Founded in eighteenth-century Ireland, the Presentations practiced hospitality by operating free schools for poor children in defiance of the English Penal Laws; the order followed the nineteenth-century Irish diaspora to establish convents and ministries in the Upper Midwest and throughout the world. Today, the congregation's commitment to live "radical hospitality in kinship with Earth and all people" and "in all relationships, especially with people made poor" is incorporated into its mission statement.[25]

In addition to the recent work on hospitality from immigration scholars, some Christian theologians are returning to hospitality as a model for how Christians should interact with non-Christians "in a context of deep diversity" and often in violent or conflictive societies.[26] In a manner similar to the ethical perspective advanced by Rosello, they maintain that the church should act as both a guest and a host to its neighbors, with the objective that Christians and non-Christians live well together.[27] This approach to hospitality lends itself to alliances with other social movements, including immigrant and refugee rights, as Sergio González illustrates in his chapter about the sanctuary movement in the Midwest, which was reanimated under the Obama and Trump administrations. The philosopher Ilsup Ahn further proposes that ethical and religious perspectives on hospitality should inform US immigration policy. For Ahn, "radical hospitality" can supplant the dominant political understanding of immigration's guest/host roles as a creditor/debtor relationship by extending amnesty to undocumented immigrants, that is, unconditional "forgiveness" of the "invisible debt" incurred by the immigrant as guest.[28] The crossing between the ethical-religious and political realms of hospitality seems relatively easy to ford in a town of Hampton's size, where everyday acts of hospitality in public settings and institutions have the potential to make visible the multidimensional life worlds of Latinx midwesterners and defamiliarize the well-worn metaphor of the immigrant as guest.

A key player in such efforts, La Luz Hispana does not function as a home for Latinx Hamptonians per se but rather as a facilitator of placemaking in which Latinxs may act as hosts. At the center, new and established Latinx community members meet one another, exchange phone numbers, and develop relationships and social networks. The center also serves as an advocate on behalf of the town's Spanish-speaking Latinx residents and the primarily English-speaking staff of public institutions and businesses. "We have the opportunity to model kindness, nonracist . . . hospitality, . . . treating the newcomer with patience and with kindness," says Sister Maura.[29] In practical terms, this means doing a bit of everything: the center offers translation services; advice about nutrition, health, childcare, and job applications; and assistance with navigating the immigration system, law enforcement, building permits, medical appointments, public schools, insurance agencies, the post office, and social services. La Luz Hispana offers citizenship and English classes, as well as lessons in driving, cooking, yoga, and banking. People come there to use the computers, sewing machines, and kitchen; send faxes; get documents notarized; and make phone calls. At a moment when community policing and US immigration policy are increasingly enmeshed, the two well-attended meetings that the center organized between local law enforcement and community members in 2017, shortly after the repeal of the county's sanctuary jurisdiction, were no small accomplishment. As the sponsor of a Grupo de Danza Folklórica, directed by an instructor from Veracruz, Mexico, and organizer of El Gran Festival North Iowa, held annually in Band Shell Park, the center also promotes cultural events that give Hampton's Latinx community visibility and status in Spanish- and English-language media in the region.

Iowa City

While traveling back and forth between Hampton and Iowa City in the years that Trump was president, I had several disconcerting conversations about travel with Latina and Black colleagues at the university. One who had just joined the faculty told me that while driving from Iowa City to Urbana-Champaign, Illinois, shortly after the election, she did not know where it would be safe for her to make a rest stop. "What happens when I leave the college-town bubble?" she wanted to know. How could I explain to her that there are lots of bubbles in Iowa, and some of the brownest communities are also located in the reddest parts of the state?

Hampton is located in Iowa's fourth congressional district, traditionally conservative and represented until 2020 by Steve King, known for his anti-immigrant and white nationalist views. King's birthplace, Storm Lake, is frequently described as Iowa's most diverse city, where eighteen languages are spoken in the community's public schools.[30] My hometown of Iowa City, on the other hand, prides itself on being a UNESCO City of Literature, with a highly educated population and progressive public culture. Many of my neighbors display yard signs that welcome the stranger in Spanish, English, and Arabic as an expression of solidarity with the immigrant rights and sanctuary movements. Yet my community is also grappling with systemic inequities in its public schools, poverty, food insecurity, and a shortage of affordable housing. Shortly after the conversation with my colleague, national news media reported that Iowa City also has the highest rate of mortgage denials to prospective Hispanic homeowners of any city in the United States.[31] Meanwhile, twenty minutes away from campus, the meatpacking town of West Liberty is Iowa's first Latinx-majority town, with vital cultural institutions, dual-language immersion public schools, and integrated sports teams.

While there are different kinds of bubbles, my colleagues certainly had reason to be concerned about traveling from one to another. Rather than think of midwestern places in terms of red and blue or welcoming and xenophobic, I am coming to see the rural areas of the region as a web of hyperlocal dynamics, a patchwork of travel deserts and oases. The labor recruitment that brought Latinxs and other ethnic groups to the Upper Midwest in recent decades means that two towns of similar size, appearance, and history might be only a few miles apart but also worlds apart in terms of who lives there. In his travels through small midwestern towns earlier this decade, Louis Mendoza found that high school sports teams fostered racial and ethnic inclusion among young people. In contrast, several recent small-town athletic events in Iowa have erupted in displays of racist and anti-immigrant sentiment when the "home" and "visitor" roles common both to hospitality and team sports became mapped onto the contrasting racial and ethnic demographics of neighboring communities.[32]

With ease of mobility circumscribed for Latinx Iowans, driving is a significant part of La Luz Hispana's community activism. In my visits to Hampton, I have observed the sisters' keen awareness about county lines, local law enforcement jurisdictions, and when and where it was safe for members of the Latinx community to travel. Getting to and from work does not seem to pose a problem for Latinx Hamptonians, but buying groceries, banking, attending medical and legal appointments, and visiting friends and family in nearby communities do. Without access to a public transportation system, La Luz Hispana staff use their personal vehicles to make long hauls with community members to Omaha, Chicago, and Des Moines. They make short hauls to the nearest pediatric dentist and to the hospital in Mason City and even shorter ones to Hampton's supermarket and the Walmart located twelve miles away. Some of these trips serve town residents who are isolated and do not own cars, but many simply assist people who are at risk of being profiled when driving outside the local area. The tension between creative placemaking and being confined to a place, eloquently dramatized in Rivera's

"Zoo Island," is heightened in a landscape of travel deserts and oases. While Latinx Hamptonians are increasingly assuming host roles in public settings within the town, their ability to exchange guest and host roles is frequently limited by the risk of being perceived as "out of place" when traveling beyond circumscribed environs.

The Hampton Public Library

The fact that one of its former residents went on to become an acclaimed scholar and writer and the first Chicano university president gives Hampton a unique point of entry in transmitting collective memory about Latinx historical presence. References to Hampton and other Iowa places, including Des Moines, Mason City, and Clear Lake, are scattered throughout Tomás Rivera's writings. School-age children in Hampton especially are aware of Rivera's historic presence in their town, though not necessarily through Rivera's stories themselves. Instead, the children access the stories through the children's book about Rivera, *Tomás and the Library Lady*, by Chicana poet and fiction writer Pat Mora. Mora's illustrated story celebrates Rivera's relationship to the town librarian, from whom Rivera learned to read in English. In addition to its success as a publication, *Tomás* has also been adapted and widely produced as a play, which embarked on its third national tour in 2018–19 and even had a streaming production at Northwestern University in the spring of 2021, during the pandemic.[33]

Pat Mora met Tomás Rivera on several occasions over the course of her career as an administrator at the University of Texas at El Paso, and the two of them developed a friendship and mutual admiration for one another's writing. Mora imaginatively filled in details about Rivera's relationship to the Iowan librarian on the basis of an anecdote from his biography.[34] Though Mora's story does not name the setting or the librarian, the Hampton Public Library has fleshed out those details in its own institutional historiography, which proudly highlights the library's role in Rivera's formation. Today, the children's reading room in the library prominently displays Spanish- and English-language versions of Mora's book, and at the circulation desk one can obtain a brochure featuring archival newspaper clippings about Bertha Gaulke, the librarian who befriended Rivera.[35]

In contrast to the failure of hospitality and imposed segregation that Rivera portrays in "Zoo Island," Mora's story presents a successful scenario in which a Tejano guest is welcomed by a European-descended host, resulting in a friendship that is cemented through the exchange of food, stories, and language lessons and the guest obtaining access to a public institution. The story begins with Tomás's journey from South Texas to Iowa, where his elders will spend the summer working in cornfields. Papá Grande, the family patriarch and storyteller, encourages Tomás to visit the town library so that he can begin to add to the family's oral storytelling repertoire. On his first visit, the librarian greets the shy young man and offers him water, a chair, and books about tigers and dinosaurs, cowboys and Indians. While reading, Tomás forgets about Iowa and Texas as he enters a world of fantasy, which he later describes to his family in bilingual storytelling sessions.[36] Over the course of the summer, Tomás learns to read English and teaches the librarian some Spanish words. The story concludes with Tomás bidding farewell to the librarian and offering her a gift of *pan dulce* from his mother. Tomás returns to Texas as the family's "new storyteller" with an expanded archive of stories enriched by all that he encountered in Iowa and at the library.[37]

Tomás and the Library Lady appeared during the US culture wars of the 1990s, shortly after Bill Clinton's election to a second term as president. The book was included in initiatives aimed at making K–12 curricula diverse and inclusive, and following its publication, it received numerous commendations, including the Tomás Rivera Mexican Children's Book Award.[38] Beyond this apogee of multiculturalism, *Tomás* has had a long afterlife and been endorsed by a range of public figures, including former First Lady Laura Bush, who lists it as a "family favorite"; it is also designated a Common Core Exemplar Text.[39] The book is an enduring emblem of Pat Mora's campaign in support of Latinx library patronage and literacy through an annual celebration that she founded, El día de los niños, el día de los libros. While a somewhat familiar story of educational uplift and assimilation via English-language literacy and the library, *Tomás* holds additional significance for Hamptonians in that it affirms the Midwest as a location of Latinx community formation rather than a mere ellipsis within Rivera's South Texas–based biography. The book offers Hampton a means to envision itself as a Latinx Midwest town and, broadly speaking, to build a bridge between new and established residents of the community.

I am welcomed at the Hampton Public Library by a warm, bilingual librarian who actively seeks to draw more Latinx patrons to the library. On this visit, I notice that the library's adult Spanish-language book section has shrunk to only a few titles since my first visit to this institution in 2014. With limited shelf space, she explains, the library must continually deaccession books that are underutilized in order to make room for new ones. The children's Spanish-language selection, on the other hand, has grown in size, and the librarian is pleased with the increase she sees in the number of women who are bringing their children to her bilingual story hour. She tells me that she used to teach computer classes at La Luz Hispana and wonders aloud whether offering a children's storytelling session there might prove popular.

As she and I converse, we are interrupted briefly by two Latinx elementary school boys who want to use the computers, and I observe a brief aside between the librarian and a volunteer in which I catch the phrases "the wrong crowd" and "well-behaved."

When we resume, our conversation turns to the local reception of *Tomás and the Library Lady*. The library staged the play based on the story several years ago, and field trips to area productions are a staple for Hampton elementary school children. Pat Mora's website in fact features a video about a production of the play at a public school in Des Moines, where groups of children enacted multiple, nontraditional casting versions of *Tomás* in which the race and gender of the guest and host characters are mutable.[40] The polite and respectful Tomás of Mora's book contrasts sharply with Rivera's own child protagonists who continually wrestle with anger, despair, racism, poverty, and the brutality of the migrant labor system.[41] Instead, Mora's story largely shields readers from scenes of labor and hardship through its focus on the library and imaginary worlds. The gap its narrative closes between Rivera's childhood in the 1940s and the book's publication in the 1990s elides the transformative decades of La Causa in Iowa. Yet as the *Tomás* story circulates locally in Hampton, I apprehend the present-day urgency in Mora's interpretation of Rivera's personal history: each dramatization and recitation of Mora's tale becomes a potential act of embodied placemaking that renews Rivera's demands for Latinx access to homes, leisure, and public culture.

Band Shell Park

"Are you here for the Franklin County Bluegrass Festival?" the clerk asks me when I check into the local hotel. "No, El Gran Festival," I respond. "You mean the *Mexican* festival?" Her voice drops to a whisper on that word, and I think, How often have I heard that shift when speaking with other white midwesterners? This is not the "fragility" I know well from my life in academia, where many white people who consider themselves to be progressive recoil at confronting their own racism; rather, it is something I learned from my extended rural midwestern family: a hesitancy about whether it is appropriate to name nonwhite racial and ethnic identifications and a fear of misspeaking before a white person who might not prove an ally.[42] But that thought is quickly interrupted by another: Should I be concerned about the festival?

On May 9, 2018, one month before El Gran Festival North Iowa, ICE arrested thirty-two workers at a cement plant in Mt. Pleasant, Iowa. The date seemed deliberately chosen to coincide with the ten-year anniversary of the massive raid at the Agriprocessors plant in Postville, Iowa, which resulted in the arrest of nearly four hundred people.[43] After persistent rumors about ICE sightings that had been spiking in Latinx communities since Trump's election, Iowa activists and communities were on high alert. El Gran Festival North Iowa has a reputation for being one of the best Latinx festivals in the state, attracting many visitors from nearby towns. At La Luz Hispana, Aimee had been working for months to confirm vendors, volunteers, and entertainment for the center's third and most ambitious festival yet. Sister Carmen and Sister Maura, who had recently relocated to Dubuque, were returning for it.

Band Shell Park occupies a shady square block of downtown Hampton. The park's most prominent structure is the bandstand, constructed in the late 1950s, opposite which benches are positioned to accommodate concertgoers. When my family and I arrive at the festival, we encounter attractions typical of small-town midwestern fairs: games of chance and skill, inflatable play structures, a petting zoo sponsored by Future Farmers of America, food trucks, and artisans' stalls. And, interspersed throughout, the sensorium of *latinidad*: the tastes, smells, sounds, and visual iconography that Theresa Delgadillo, Laura Fernández, Marie Lerma, and Leila Vieira vividly unfold in their chapter on Ohio ethnic festivals. In the afternoon heat, the Puerto Rican food vendor from Iowa Falls is making out well selling virgin *piña coladas*; others offer *pambazos veracruzanos, pupusas, aguas frescas*, ice cream cones, funnel cakes, and *pan de plátano al estilo Amish*.

The crowd is about half Latinx, half Anglo, with families clustered around the children's areas, elders seated on the benches, and pods of teenagers roaming around, while others congregate at the dunk tank. La Luz Hispana volunteers staff a table, and Sister Carmen and Sister Maura circulate throughout the crowd, seemingly knowing every individual among the hundreds in attendance and greeting each with big hugs. My teenage son, in possession of a freshly minted driving permit, cruises around a used Hyundai Elantra that has been donated by a local car dealer for a raffle drawing later tonight, a fantasy of mobility that seems to resonate broadly with this crowd, based on the brisk ticket sales. At the band shell, a bilingual DJ plays a range of Latinx pop music in between emceeing demonstrations by young pupils from the local martial arts club and dance academy. When La Luz Hispana's Grupo de Danza Folklórica takes the stage in midafternoon, they are the first in a series of headliners that will culminate with *veracruzano* and *norteño* musical acts later that night. As evening arrives, the crowd becomes a bit older and predominantly Latinx. And then, unexpected guests show up—Los Súper Caracoles, legendary rock stars from Xalapa, Veracruz, known for their repertoire combining glam, hair metal, and *cumbia*. The band must be touring the United States; they take the stage to perform "La traigo bien parada," one of their biggest hits.

Who are the guests and who are the hosts at this event? Is the town of Hampton hosting neighboring communities? Are European-descended Hamptonians ceding place to Latinx Hamptonians or vice versa? Are Latinx Hamptonians hosting everyone? Once the festival gets under way, the guest and host roles manifest and dissolve thousands of times, recalling Rosello's concept of hospitality as the potential for infinite reciprocity. In the face of the festival's relaxed conviviality—its successful uneventfulness, as it were—it is difficult to recall that in the current political climate, many participants are making themselves vulnerable simply by enjoying the company of their neighbors in a public place. Rosello cautions that risk, too, is an inherent aspect of hospitality, because in extending one's place to another, both guest and host can incur violence and loss. Some practices of hospitality, furthermore, are haunted by the image of a seigneurial property owner: when a powerful host extends his place on behalf of those who are subordinate to him, home itself can be a place of entrapment and subjugation rather than safety.[44] As important as having a home is to ethical hospitality, then, so too is having the freedom to leave it at will.

Despite its outward appearance of a laid-back small-town fair, the Gran Festival's atmosphere of unconditional welcome is one way in which it can be described as "radical." With its emphasis on being together in place, radical hospitality seeks to create events that will lead to mutual recognition and coexistence: it is a performance of equality through acts of ritual exchange and fluidity of roles. For me, accustomed to the oppositional stances that I associate with campus-based activism, "radical" means something entirely different from the social dynamics I witness at El Gran Festival. The aspect I find most challenging about the sisters' practice of hospitality is their willingness to dwell in an ever-expanding present; in Hampton, radical hospitality defers the friction that accompanies ethnic succession by ritualizing the transfer of privilege associated with the dominant group.[45] In towns like Hampton, where literally the entire population can stand together in Band Shell Park, embodied acts of hospitality effectively challenge the entrenched metaphor of the immigrant as guest. And in a moment of danger, such events guide the community into the future, welcoming a different configuration of populace and inviting it to stay.

Birthday Party

While visiting Hampton over the Feast Day of Guadalupe, I am invited to the home of Sister Carmen's goddaughter, who is celebrating her tenth birthday. We are well over twenty people gathered in a two-bedroom apartment.

The adult men are seated in a large circle in the kitchen drinking and talking, the women are in small groups in the living room doing the same, and kids are running around everywhere. Sister Carmen's *comadre* is offering me huge helpings of *barbacoa de res roja* and cake. And the awkward moment comes when she makes her shy daughter, the birthday girl, march over and say hello to me, "the professor"—a complete stranger, considerably older than most of the guests, and the only white woman present besides Sister Maura. The kids shout to the birthday girl, "Show her your present!" "What is it?" I ask. "It's a Hawkeye sweatshirt!" (I cannot underscore enough how shocking this is, given that I am in rival Cyclone territory.) Smiles. What a relief to meet someone from the same team, and so far from home.

Tomás Rivera's and Pat Mora's stories about hospitality have taught me to appreciate my complex roles at the birthday party as both a library lady and a guest of my ten-year-old host. Though these writers depict contrasting interethnic encounters set in Hampton, each constructs a powerful narrative of placemaking around child protagonists. José and the baby on the way in "Zoo Island," and young Tomás in *Tomás and the Library Lady* are more than children. They are emblems of futurity, repositories of the authors' own utopian longings, as well as those of their communities. In a Riveraesque fantasy that is coming true, Latinxs are making homes in Hampton, and the town's future, as well as the future of my university, rests with this ten-year-old's generation. Radical hospitality, or unconditional welcome, such as that practiced by La Luz Hispana, offers a way for midwestern small towns to recognize their Latinx histories and imagine collective futures. As for my young host, I hope that she will one day make uneventful trips back and forth between home and college, enlarging the bubbles that surround us.

Notes

1. Tomás Rivera, "Zoo Island," in *The Complete Works*, ed. Julián Olivares (Houston: Arte Público, 1991), 241.

2. Ibid., 245.

3. Ibid., 244.

4. Ibid., 245.

5. For an elaboration of barriology, see Villa, *Barrio Logos*, 1–19.

6. Meanwhile, the impact of capital flight on midwestern workers has been chronicled vividly in Cowie, *Capital Moves*; and Broughton, *Boom, Bust, Exodus*. Thank you to Geraldo Cadava for referring me to these sources.

7. For more on the transregional migrant circuits connecting Texas and the Midwest, see Limón, "*Al Norte* toward Home"; and Rodriguez, *The Tejano Diaspora*.

8. Theresa Delgadillo, "Exiles, Migrants, Settlers, and Natives: Literary Representa-

tions of Chicano/as and Mexicans in the Midwest," Occasional Paper No. 64, August 1999, 1–11, 6, Michigan State University, Julian Samora Research Institute.

9. The 2020 census reports Hampton's population at 4,337 and the town's Hispanic population at 28.8 percent. US Census Bureau, http://data.census.gov, accessed September 18, 2021.

10. Performance studies scholar Diana Taylor describes a scenario as a setup that provides a broadly recognizable interpretative framework for understanding events and social interactions that can be enacted with myriad outcomes and permutations. Diana Taylor, *The Archive and the Repertoire: Performing Cultural Memory in the Americas* (Durham, NC: Duke University Press, 2003), 1–52.

11. Julia Reinhard Lupton, "Hospitality," in *Early Modern Theatricality*, ed. Henry S. Turner, Oxford Twenty-First Century Approaches to Literature (Oxford: Oxford University Press, 2013), 424. Thank you to Lori Branch and Sergio González for recommending helpful sources on hospitality.

12. Ibid., 428.

13. Mireille Rosello, *Postcolonial Hospitality: The Immigrant as Guest* (Stanford, CA: Stanford University Press, 2001), 3.

14. This ethical approach to hospitality has been elaborated by Jacques Derrida, whose writings inform Rosello's study. While Derrida's important work tends to explore the dissolution of the guest/host roles synchronically and the problematic status of the "gift," Rosello, on the other hand, explores the guest/host roles' potential to shift diachronically through reciprocity.

15. Ilsup Ahn, "Economy of 'Invisible Debt' and Ethics of 'Radical Hospitality': Toward a Paradigm Change of Hospitality from 'Gift' to 'Forgiveness,'" *Journal of Religious Ethics* 38, no. 2 (June 2010): 243–67.

16. Karen Suter, letter to the editor, *Hampton Chronicle,* May 7, 2014, http://hampton chronicle.com/content/letter-editor-25. Brackets in the original.

17. Rosello, *Postcolonial Hospitality*, 17–18.

18. Franklin County sheriff Linn Larson revoked the sanctuary policy of Franklin County on January 23, 2017, three weeks after taking office and two days before President Trump signed an executive order to defund sanctuary jurisdictions. Mary Pieper, "County Debates Sanctuary Policy," *Globe Gazette*, February 15, 2017, A1–A2.

19. "War Prisoners to Shock Hemp," *Hampton Chronicle*, December 2, 1949, World War II Press Clippings, Iowa Digital Library, University of Iowa Libraries, http://digital.lib.uiowa.edu/cdm/singleitem/collection/wwii/id/519/rec/2. For details about Rivera's biography, see Rivera, *Complete Works*, 13–48.

20. According to the 2010 US Census, the population of Hampton was 21.5 percent Hispanic and 78.5 percent non-Hispanic, reflecting a 10 percent increase in the Hispanic population from the 2000 census. The 2020 census reports Hampton's Hispanic population at 28.8 percent. Many studies affirm that international migration is revitalizing rural and small-town areas that have shrunk due to outmigration. See, for example, Jed Kolko, "How Much Slower Would the U.S. Grow without Immigration? In Many Places, a Lot," *New York Times*, April 14, 2019, https://www .nytimes.com/2019/04/18/upshot/how-much-slower-would-the-us-grow-without

-immigration-in-many-places-a-lot.html; and Art Cullen, "The View from Iowa: Where Immigrants Are at the Heart of America's Culture War," *The Guardian*, September 17, 2018, https://www.theguardian.com/society/2018/sep/17/the-view-from-iowa-where-immigrants-are-at-the-heart-of-americas-culture-war?CMP=share_btn_fb. Thank you to Theresa Delgadillo for referring me to these articles.

21. La Luz Hispana, "Totals by Country, 2017–18," client data prepared by Aimee Lenth, obtained by the author, March 16, 2018.

22. Sister Carmen Hernández, Sister Maura McCarthy, and Aimee Lenth, interview with the author, March 16, 2018. The quotes from individuals that appear in this section are taken from this interview. The center, now called La Luz Centro Cultural, has since relocated to a larger building near its original location.

23. In addition to its original full-time staff, Sisters Carmen and Maura, the center hired program director Aimee Lenth in 2017.

24. In May 2018 Sister Carmen was named to the leadership team of the Sisters of the Presentation in Dubuque, obliging her to relocate to that city, and Sister Maura also returned to Dubuque, where she entered retirement. Aimee Lenth is now associate director and Claudia Rivera is executive director of La Luz Centro Cultural.

25. For more information about the order and its mission, see Dubuque Sisters of the Presentation, https://www.dbqpbvms.org/2020_communitygathering and https://www.dbqpbvms.org/who-we-are/; and M. Raphael Consedine, *One Pace Beyond: The Life of Nano Nagel* (Victoria, Australia: Presentation Congregation of Victoria, 1977). Additionally, Sister Maura bases her activism on her long-term experience in a Guarani Christian base community in Bolivia that supported Indigenous people's leadership in struggles against inequality based on race, language, and land tenure. Maura McCarthy, interview in Denis Lynn Daly Heyck, *Surviving Globalization in Three Latin American Communities*, Part Two: Bolivia (Peterborough, Ontario: Broadview, 2002), 182–93.

26. Luke Bretherton, *Hospitality as Holiness: Christian Witness amid Moral Diversity* (Hampshire, UK: Ashgate, 2006), 5.

27. Ibid., 197–98.

28. Ahn, "Economy."

29. Sister Carmen Hernández, Sister Maura McCarthy, and Aimee Lenth interview.

30. Art Cullen, "Melting Pot Never Boils," *Storm Lake Times*, April 26, 2016, http://www.stormlake.com/articles/melting-pot-never-boils; the population of Storm Lake is estimated to be 11,269, according to 2020 census data.

31. The loan denial rate for Latinxs was calculated in comparison with non-Hispanic whites. Ryan J. Foley, "In Iowa City, Latinos Faced the Nation's Worst Bias in Home Loans," *Iowa City Press-Citizen*, February 15, 2018, www.press-citizen.com.

32. Louis Mendoza, "Conversations across 'Our America': Latinoization and the New Geographies of Latinas/os," in Valerio-Jiménez, Vaquera-Vásquez, and Fox, *The Latina/o Midwest Reader*, 25–41; Linh Ta, "Racist Chant Targets Iowa High School Basketball Players," *Des Moines Register*, January 25, 2018, https://www.desmoinesregister.com/; Ryan Smith, "Students Meet to Discuss Trump Chants Made during Game," *KCCI Des Moines*, February 25, 2016, www.kcci.com.

33. Pat Mora, author's website: Pat Mora, author, presenter, literacy advocate, www .patmora.com; for the Northwestern University production, see https://wirtz.north western.edu/tomas-and-the-library-lady/, accessed February 17, 2021.

34. Pat Mora, "Meet the Author, Pat Mora," interview conducted by Toni Buzzeo. *LibrarySparks* web resources, November 2008, http://www.librarysparks.com/wp -content/uploads/2016/07/lsp_nov08_meet_pat_mora.pdf.

35. Gaulke was the librarian at the Hampton Public Library from 1923 to 1964. Brochures on the history of the Hampton Public Library and Bertha Gaulke obtained by the author, 2014, 2018.

36. Pat Mora, *Tomás and the Library Lady*, illustrated by Raúl Colón (New York: Knopf, 1997), 13.

37. Ibid., 25.

38. Mora, author's website.

39. Laura Bush, "Laura Bush's Family Favorites," George W. Bush White House Archives, https://georgewbush-whitehouse.archives.gov/firstlady/initiatives/family favorites.html, accessed February 17, 2021. See also Mora, author's website.

40. For a video about this workshop, see "*Tomás and the Library Lady* Experience," https://www.youtube.com/watch?time_continue=17&v=ME4RKb1TISA, accessed February 17, 2021.

41. Rivera's "The Salamanders" ("Las Salamandras"), set in the town of Clear Lake near Hampton, is another story of hospitality denied related from the perspective of a young man.

42. Robin DiAngelo, *White Fragility: Why It's So Hard for White People to Talk about Racism* (Boston: Beacon, 2018).

43. MacKenzie Elmer, "Dozens Rally in Mount Pleasant Day after ICE Arrested 32," *Des Moines Register,* May 10, 2018, www.desmoinesregister.com.

44. Rosello, *Postcolonial Hospitality*, 12–14.

45. For more on ceding privilege, see Ahn, "Economy," 264.

CHAPTER 3

Chicago Tropical

Fausto Fernós's *Transloca* Drag Performances

LAWRENCE LA FOUNTAIN-STOKES

Latinx drag performance has the power to transform, build awareness of social issues, and entertain. It can serve as a bridge to create networks of solidarity based on shared identities and common experiences, but it can also perpetuate stereotypes, offend, and create divisions. Complex, undomesticated, and at times transgressive, Latinx drag performance takes multiple forms in Chicago and in the broader Midwest. These performances are not always easily legible, and as queer (disruptive, alternative) interventions they do not necessarily serve the interests of traditional Latinx placemaking; in a sense, we can say that they push the envelope, question borders, and invite us to rethink what we know.[1]

Take the case of Fausto Fernós. In his more-than-thirty-year career as a performance artist, podcaster/journalist, multimedia content producer, and drag performer, the Chicago-based Puerto Rican *transloca* (Latinx queer translocal) artist has created, disseminated, and archived the experiences of a collective LGBTQ Texas-Chicago-Rican transnational community, one that frequently has been marginalized or simply ignored.[2] Fernós's intervention is a very particular kind of placemaking, one that negotiates the mediations of broadcast technology but resists the corporate-oriented impetus of "creative placemaking," which seeks a seamless integration of capital, communities, and urban design.[3]

This essay is an archival recovery and analysis of some of Fernós's mostly understudied drag performances. It is also a personal story of how I learned about him in Michigan (where I live and work), became a fan, met his family and his partner in Puerto Rico (where we are from), and eventually became a friend and collaborator in his podcasts and YouTube videos in Chicago, including dressing up in drag and performing as Lola von Miramar at his request. As a translocal, queer tale, it is a story with Caribbean and Texan roots that reflects colonial diasporic wanderings in the Midwest and that serves to bring into focus the rich queer Latinx culture of this region.

A close analysis of Fernós's Latinx drag performances in Chicago and elsewhere, particularly focusing on his cabaret shows, public-access cable television program, and YouTube videos, reveals how he challenges dominant heterosexist, colonialist, and masculinist narratives of self and nation, frequently by creating over-the-top feminine characters and highlighting humor, community building, and collaboration but also displeasing some audience/community members and media consumers.[4] Constantly "performing queer Latinidad" (to borrow Ramón H. Rivera-Servera's phrase) and "tropicalizing" culture (to cite Frances R. Aparicio and Susana Chávez-Silverman), Fernós is what I refer to as a *transloca*, that is to say, a diasporic Puerto Rican queer performer who negotiates the stigmatized Spanish-language vernacular category of *loca* (madwoman, sissy, fairy, or effeminate homosexual) in relation to linguistic, cultural, and geographical displacement, embracing multiple *latinidad/es*, particularly queer *latinidad*, while negotiating the perils of American and Latinx homophobia and transphobia.[5]

Inspired by the radical Mexican muralist David Alfaro Siqueiros's whitewashed and now partially restored Los Angeles mural *América Tropical* (1932), I propose we engage the work of Fernós in the context of "Chicago Tropical" as a reenvisioning of hemispheric relations and of the role of art, as well as a manifestation of what the queer Brazilian artist Hélio Oiticica called "tropicamp" in relation to the Puerto Rican drag performer Mario Montez's Caribbean-inflected (tropical, Latin American) camp performance.[6] For Oiticica, "tropicamp" is a culturally specific, decidedly not Anglo-American queer sensibility and practice that invokes a different universe of significations marked by glamour, humor, and Latin American referents. As an embodiment of "Chicago Tropical" and of "tropicamp," Fernós is a controversial, disruptive, and invaluable example of queer Latinx minoritarian placemaking in the Midwest.

With his collaborators, Fernós has transformed Puerto Rican and Latinx queer culture, first in Austin, Texas, where he went to college; then in Chicago; and now globally through cyberspace, taking advantage of public-access television, live cabaret performances, podcasts, YouTube video production, and online digital archive sharing. His drag has developed through character-based performances such as "Claraluz," "Faustina," "Fausto Fernós, the Fire-Eating Drag Princess," and "Saltina Obama Bouvier." Currently, his performance entails identifying as a bodybuilder and performing in drag using his given name.

Born in San Juan in 1972, Fernós has been performing in drag since 1990, when he studied with the Irish Italian American performance artist Linda Montano at the University of Texas at Austin and began collaborating with a fellow student, the Chicano artist Christopher Rincón.[7] Fernós moved to Chicago in 1995 to pursue graduate studies at the School of the Art Institute of Chicago (SAIC), where he obtained an MFA in 1997, and has lived in the city ever since. Food, comedy, humor, bilingualism, drag performance, and references to Puerto Rican and Latinx culture have always been at the heart of the artist's work, as have the mediations of technology. In spite of his copious artistic production, there are remarkably few scholarly analyses of his oeuvre.

Fernós is best known for his Chicago-based *Feast of Fools* cabaret show (1997–2004) and for the award-winning, ongoing daily podcast *Feast of Fun* (http://www.feastoffun.com/), which he created with his partner (now husband), Marc Felion, in 2005; as of November 21, 2021, the couple has recorded 2,995 hour-long episodes and has nearly 8,000 photos on the image-hosting service Flickr (https://www.flickr.com/photos/feastoffools/).[8] Numerous leading American drag and trans stars such as Holly Woodlawn, Lady Bunny, Latrice Royale, Hedda Lettuce, Coco Peru, RuPaul, Kate Bornstein, Sherry Vine, Bob the Drag Queen, Varla Jean Merman, Jackie Beat, Alaska Thunderfuck, Vivacious, Peaches Christ, and Barbra Herr have appeared on the show, as well as many of the Latinx contestants on *RuPaul's Drag Race* such as Jade Sotomayor, Monica Beverly Hillz, Bianca Del Rio, Adore Delano, Naysha Lopez, and Jaymes Mansfield. Since 2010, Fernós and Felion have also produced and starred in over thirty-five *Cooking with Drag Queens* videos, all currently available on YouTube, which have included Puerto Rican drag performers such as April Carrión making *quesitos*, which are a type of cheese-filled pastry (May 2014); Cynthia Lee Fontaine making *pastelón*, or "Puerto Rican lasagna" (September 2017); and Lola von Miramar (my drag persona) making *tostones*, or fried green plantains (November 2010).[9] These videos are key examples of Fernós's queer tropicalization of Chicago and of the broader Midwest, in which the artist celebrates, mocks, and transforms Puerto Ricanness and *latinidad* as a way to provoke, educate, and entertain.

In *Tropicalizations: Transcultural Representations of Latinidad*, Frances R. Aparicio and Susana Chávez-Silverman describe tropicalization "as a tool that foregrounds the transformative cultural agency of the subaltern subject."[10] This complex process can have a negative or positive valence, for, as they indicate, "to tropicalize, as we define it, means to trope, to imbue a particular space, geography, group, or nation with a set of traits, images, and values," which is potentially a hegemonic move that can reify stereotypes.[11] At the same time, "a different, more radical sort of tropicalization emerges from the cultural productions, political struggles, and oppositional strategies deployed by some

U.S. Latinos/as. The margins that bell hooks evokes as 'sites of radical possibilities' are the locations from which these retropicalizing tendencies are surfacing."[12] As Fernós's queer tropicalization is ambivalent (a recuperation but also a parody of the culture of origin), it works through hegemonic and antihegemonic postures.

Fernós's work occupies the complex and contradictory space of the middle: at times caricaturizing, oversimplifying, and relying on stereotypes; at others conveying very important cultural, linguistic, and political knowledge that is crucial for coalitional and panethnic progressive social agendas. Here Latinx queer tropicalization becomes a tool for social critique, as in the work of the Cuban American Carmelita Tropicana (Alina Troyano) and in that of the Colombian American John Leguizamo (when performing in drag or as a gay character), a type of "self-tropicalization" that uses comedy, camp, and Caribbean *choteo* or *relajo* for strategic ends, embracing the political potential of humor.[13]

In Fernós's solo and collective work, racialized, minoritarian, queer, gay, and transgender identities and practices intersect with transnational and translocal politics of cabaret, with critical independent media production, and with a valuable reconceptualization of Puerto Ricanness and *latinidad* in Chicago and elsewhere.[14] In this context, the translocality of *transloca performance* refers to the interlinked experiences of persons in diverse geographic locations, whether in the country of origin (such as Puerto Rico) or in the diaspora (e.g., in the Midwest), who nevertheless are in complex and constant daily, weekly, monthly, or yearly contact, be it through travel, migration, communications, or other forms of exchange; who live in the intimacy of these interactions and of the knowledge they generate; who might not even be living in different sovereign nations but instead in different locations marked by profound linguistic and cultural differences in the same nation-state, for example, as metropolitan subjects vis-à-vis colonial, insular ones or spread across the United States.[15]

As a Midwest-based, queer Latinx alternative media content creator, Fernós transforms social knowledge and builds bridges of information through comedy and entertainment.[16] His work creates "alternative spaces" for "unaccounted voices and images" of queer Puerto Ricans, Latinxs, and LGBTQ persons like myself that are similar to the alternative spaces for individuals who use social networking sites (SNS) (i.e., MySpace and Facebook) and user-generated content (UGC) platforms (i.e., YouTube). Manuel Avilés-Santiago has analyzed these in his book *Puerto Rican Soldiers and Second-Class Citizenship: Representations in Media*.[17] An important distinction is that unlike other largely heteronormative Latinx channels such as Pero Like and mitú and comedians such as Jenny Lorenzo, Joanna Hausmann, and LeJuan James,

Fernós centers queerness in the Midwest. The queer Puerto Rican performer also participates in the creation of the "virtual islands" of "translocal Caribeñidad" that Dara E. Goldman sees in the "Puerto Rican web."[18] He does this emphasizing a collaborative, tropicamp, *transloca* viewpoint that challenges prevailing norms.

While Fernós has lived in Chicago since 1995, it is important to note that his work does not come out of the traditional working-class Puerto Rican neighborhoods that scholars such as Mérida M. Rúa and Gina M. Pérez have studied and that have been portrayed in Henrique Cirne-Lima and Josué Pellot's documentary *I Am the Queen* (2010) and in its sequel, *The Other Side of the Queen* (2012), which focus on drag and transgender contestants participating in the Vida/Sida Paseo Boricua Cacica Queen Pageant, held in Humboldt Park.[19] It is also different from the classical lip-synch and comedy-oriented drag performance style of Ecuadorian Puerto Rican star Miss Ketty Teanga, a Chicago drag legend whom Rivera-Servera has carefully analyzed, and from the high femme, glamorous stage-performance drag that is celebrated at the renowned Miss Continental pageant, held yearly in Chicago since 1980, where many Latinxs have gone home with top prizes.[20]

Instead, Fernós's life experiences correspond more to the middle-class Puerto Rican lives documented by Ana Y. Ramos-Zayas in her book *National Performances: The Politics of Class, Race, and Space in Puerto Rican Chicago* and to the lives of queer Chicago Puerto Rican artists such as the filmmaker Rose Troche and the poet and playwright Rane Arroyo.[21] Fernós navigates these different spaces in complex ways, for example, by living in Andersonville, a middle-class neighborhood with an important queer presence, and by collaborating with other queer Chicago Puerto Rican artists such as Jade Sotomayor, Monica Beverly Hillz, and Naysha Lopez, who predominantly come from working-class backgrounds. It is important to acknowledge that Chicago and the Midwest are the site of different, competing, and at times clashing *latinidades* that bring together persons from diverse socioeconomic and geographical backgrounds and that are not easily homogenized in simplistic depictions.

Food, Drag, and Performative/Televisual Origins

In order to understand Fernos's Chicago performances and media and cultural production, it is crucial to contextualize his early years in Puerto Rico and Texas. The artist's celebrity began when he was young. At the age of eleven, Fernós appeared in a feature-length article in the leading Puerto Rican newspaper *El Nuevo Día*, where he was celebrated for his cake-baking skills and for being home-schooled in San Juan along with his sister, Talía, by their mother, Patricia Fernós, a La Leche League activist and educator who was born and raised in Monterrey, Mexico, of American parents and who met her husband at the University of Puerto Rico in Río Piedras.[22] A focus on food (particularly cooking) and family will continue to be central to the artist's aesthetic and cultural projects in his adult life.

As a teenager, Fernós dropped out of high school, received a distance-learning diploma from the Clonlara School, won a science fair award at his old high school (even though he was no longer enrolled there), and moved to Texas (where his mom had attended high school) in 1989 to attend a summer program at the University of Texas (UT) at Austin.[23] Fernós started his undergraduate degree that fall at the age of seventeen as an aspiring English honors and science student but quickly switched to drama. Frustrated with the rigidity of the theater program and with the need for extensive memorization, he changed his major again, this time to studio art, graduating from UT with a BFA in 1993.[24]

Encouraged by his friend Chris Rincón, Fernós enrolled as an undergraduate in a class with the performance artist Linda Montano in 1990.[25] In an interview that I conducted in 2011, Fernós emphasized his mentor's importance, particularly her exhortation that students should explore their own lives through their art.[26] As an assignment for her class, Rincón and Fernós created the drag performance duo of Montserrat and Claraluz, who would go on to star in a year-long live weekly performance soap opera titled *SoftMen* in 1991.[27] Rincón's character was inspired by the great Catalan soprano Montserrat Caballé, particularly by the diva's 1988 performance of the song "Barcelona" with the British queer rock singer Freddie Mercury. For the character of Claraluz, Fernós visually emulated the Mexican American singer Linda Ronstadt, an artist who "after becoming a rock and roll megastar in the 1970s and '80s . . . released *Canciones de mi Padre* in 1987, a double-platinum album that pays tribute to her family's Mexican heritage," but he named his character after an eccentric Puerto Rican paternal aunt, Clara Luz Fernós Echandi.[28] The character's full name, Claraluz Gómez Gutiérrez Guzmán Del Carmen Arroyo Rodríguez Alegría Fernós López Maldonado Morales, parodied perceptions of long Latino names; according to Fernós, "People in Texas nicknamed me 'Looze.'"[29] Soon after, Fernós parted ways with Rincón, who moved back to Houston to live with his family. The Puerto Rican artist continued to develop his drag performance in Austin in shows such as the *Big Wig Revue* in 1992 and in *Pe.A.Ch. (Performance Art Church)* in 1993.

Inspired by the New York City drag queens who were doing public-access cable TV programs, Fernós decided to start *El Chow de Faustina* in 1994, when he was twenty-two years old. The show consisted of eight thirty-minute episodes that aired at 11:00 p.m. on Channel 10 in Austin.[30] Public-access TV provided an ideal venue at the time.[31] According to Pamela Doty, "The idea behind public-access television is, in essence, a simple one: that you or I, the man or woman down the street, even the kid next door—in short, anyone who wishes—should have the opportunity to produce, direct, hold forth on our own television program."[32] Public-access TV, which is highly local programming, conjures a different form of placemaking from cabaret performance: community is created through the shared experience of collective viewership (whether with friends and neighbors or with strangers who live in the same city or region) thanks to the mediation of communications technology. Fernós based his drag character of Faustina on the Cuban American television host Cristina Saralegui, who was nationally and internationally renowned at the time for her very popular Miami-based Spanish-language program *El Show de Cristina* on Univision, which "sometimes covered controversial topics such as homosexuality and child abuse which had been taboo to broadcast in most Latin American countries," as media scholar Kenton T. Wilkinson has observed.[33] The parodic nonstandard spelling of "chow" in Fernós's title, meant to be pronounced in Spanish, accentuates the program's over-the-top nature and also hints at the English-language meaning of "chow" as food or victuals.

Two episodes of *El Chow de Faustina* stand out: the pilot episode ("How to Put on Makeup"), which originally aired on July 28, 1994, and the episode with Linda Montano, which led Fernós to win the *Austin Chronicle* Best Cable Access TV Show award in 1995.[34] The two episodes are very different: the first is hosted solo, although there is direct voice interaction with the production crew; the second focuses on a guest. Both demonstrate a certain lack of experience of the performer, who laughs inappropriately, jumps from topic to topic, occasionally says offensive things, and mixes the name of the guest (Linda Montano) with the name of the character she is portraying (Lenny Golden, Esq.). At the same time, the episodes are marked by the performer's charisma, beauty, and wit; by the transmission of relevant information (e.g., how to do drag makeup and how to make Caesar salad dressing, which is inaccurately described as vegan); by the entertaining and politically valuable linguistic practice of code-switching between English and Spanish by a queer Puerto Rican; by occasionally hilarious one-liners such as "You should make a baboon jealous!" uttered as an exhortation to apply colorful makeup, particularly around the eyes; and by an absolutely extraordinary and disquieting performance by Fernós's mentor, Linda Montano.

In a five-minute remix or mashup of the original thirty-minute pilot episode prepared for the *Feast of Fun* website by Matt Johnston in 2011, the blond-haired, pearl-bedecked, creamy-satin-dressed, blue-eye-shadowed, self-tropicalizing Faustina speaks with a noticeable accent, identifying herself as a Puerto Rican, that is, as a person from a very small country stuck between the Atlantic Ocean and the Caribbean Sea.[35] This spatial duality repeats itself linguistically through intersentential codeswitching in which Faustina alternates from English to Spanish (e.g., while speaking English, she proclaims, "Soy una puertorriqueña"), and biologically, as the host claims to be intersex ("Soy un hombre y una mujer. Tengo un penis, ¿tú sabes lo que es un penis, verdad? Y tengo una vagina").[36] Faustina's bilingual explanation of intersexuality in Spanglish with male genital terms in English ("penis" for the linguistically standard *pene*) leads to the (politically incorrect) existential question: "What does it mean to be a hermaphrodite in these days and times?," using a term that has currently fallen out of favor.[37] Faustina then misidentifies other supposedly famous intersexuals such as the performer Michael Jackson and a former First Lady of the United States, referred to as Barbara *Brush*. This sequence is disturbing in its casual lack of awareness of or perhaps campy engagement with the complex reality of intersexuality. At the same time, it is marked by tropicamp absurdity, mediatized narcissism, queer language politics, and the way it captures the schizophrenia of colonialism, perhaps in the vein of Charles Ludlam and the Theatre of the Ridiculous. The malapropisms also seem to be a humor inherent in live performance, suggesting a degree of improvisation and filming in one take, without much rehearsal.[38]

The episode of *El Chow de Faustina* with Linda Montano is also of great note, extending Fernós's performance of ethnic Latinx camp (what I have referred to as tropicamp) to the realm of Italian American embodiment (Montano's drag king character) and showcasing extreme physical discomfort as a performative act. In this video, Faustina appears wearing glasses and a red satin blouse and looks younger and less confident than in the premier episode as she struggles to introduce Lenny Golden, Esquire and Voice Teacher, and to read Lenny's handwriting. Always the consummate hostess, she serves Lenny some tea and lights Chanel No. 27 incense, a parody of the better-known Chanel No. 5 perfume. Orientalizing décor and music are reminiscent of those employed by Walter Mercado, a leading *transloca* Puerto Rican astrologer whose work has been discussed by performance studies scholar Diana Taylor, among others.[39] Lenny's butch outfit consists of dark glasses, a false moustache, a blue cap, blue jacket, and denim pants. Lenny proceeds to lubricate and insert a clear surgical tube into his nose until it comes out through his mouth; he then sings, so to speak, or rather gags, gasps, screams, and chokes while vocalizing the Italian American classic "That's Amore."[40] Looking concerned, Faustina pleads, "¡Ten cuidado, Linda!" (Be careful!), but then calmly sips her tea, later proclaiming: "That was wonderful! Give an applause for Lenny. His technique is very useful in clearing out the nasal passages." In fact, Faustina indicates that the exercise reminded her of an article she read in *Cristina* magazine about the Spanish tenor Plácido Domingo, supposedly a student of Lenny Golden, to whom she asks: "Los tenores tienen fama de ser vanidosos, ¿tú eres vanidoso?" (Tenors are famous for being vain. Are you vain?). Lenny then comes back onstage to continue his song, leaving many spectators in a state of bewilderment and shock.

Chicago Performance Art and Cabaret

Fernós moved to Chicago in 1995 to pursue graduate studies at SAIC. The next year, he presented his one-man show *Homosexual Personae* at the well-known Cleveland Performance Art Festival in Ohio, where he performed as Faustina with the assistance of his collaborators Kerthy Fix and Victoria Reis, who served as his "handmaiden" assistants.[41] A festival archival website describes the show as follows: "With his aluminum-foil costumes, letters from Eartha Kitt, and a melodious atonal tribute to Karen Carpenter, queer Latino art-diva Fausto Fernos [*sic*] of Chicago explodes under the pressures of sexual anonymity."

After receiving his MFA in 1997, Fernós cocreated the *Feast of Fools* stage show in collaboration with the Chicago Radical Faeries, initially at the then-struggling, important, artist-led Randolph Street Gallery, which was about to close, and later at different Chicago bars and performance venues such as Big Chicks, the HotHouse, and Schubas Tavern.[42] The Radical Faeries, a predominantly white alternative gay organization created by early homophile leader Harry Hay and others in 1979, borrowed from pagan religions, Native American culture, and new age, hippy, and anticapitalist sentiments; in their aesthetic and performance style, we also can see similarities with the San Francisco–based drag performance troupe the Cockettes, with the Brazilian show Dzi Croquettes, and with the French radical liberationist group Les Gazolines, which Jean-Yves Le Talec has analyzed.[43]

The *Feast of Fools* cabaret followed in the tradition of Austin, Texas, shows such as *Big Wig Revue* and *Pe.A.Ch.* but incorporated an important drag shift: Fernós no longer emulated famous Latinas such as Linda Ronstadt and Cristina Saralegui but rather self-identified with his Spanish-language birth name and with the title of "Fire-Eating Drag Princess." This shift might have been meant to overcome the psychological distancing effect (or internal alien-ation) that some drag performers experience as a result of the success of their stage characters, when it becomes difficult (or overwhelming or confusing) to maintain or negotiate between two distinct identities: that of the public persona (Faustina) and of the actual individual (Fausto); it might also simply have been a desire to consolidate a more-identifiable artist's name.[44]

The Fire-Eating Drag Princess's makeup, in Radical Faeries style, is exor-bitantly colorful (the face is made up in blue and orange), includes black ink

FIGURE 3.1. Fausto Fernós, the Fire-Eating Drag Princess, with his mother, Patricia Fernós, at a *Feast of Fools* show in Chicago, 2001. Photo by St. Sukie de la Croix.

swirls and rhinestones, and no longer emulates dominant notions of female beauty; the color patches, polka dots, lines, blue and red wigs, butterfly clips, and antennas are closer to carnival, clown/circus, or non-Western theatrical makeup, as we can see in a 2001 photo of Fernós and his mother, Patricia (whose face is all made up in green, black, and white), by the influential gay photographer and writer St. Sukie de la Croix (see figure 3.1).[45] Here, cabaret skills such as storytelling and singing are combined with circus skills such as fire eating, visible in a YouTube video of an April 1, 2000, performance at the HotHouse in Chicago ("Fire-Eating Drag Princess"), in which Fernós welcomes the audience, has them collectively recite an oath of affirmation, eats fire, and goes on to tell an origins story of Taina warrior Amazons in the rainforest before singing "La Era Acuario" ("Aquarius" from the musical *Hair*) in Spanish.[46] Fernós interrupts his musical rendition to offer horoscope predictions, or rather, "premiere Puerto Rican psychological psychic readings," clearly a reference to Walter Mercado, as an elaboration of a vernacular Puerto Rican *transloca* or tropicamp queerness.

In her March 31, 2000, *Chicago Tribune* profile of Fernós, the Cuban American lesbian writer and journalist Achy Obejas (for decades a mainstay of Chicago's queer Latinx community) quotes the artist's "myth of origins" as follows from what she describes as "a little comic book called 'The Radical Faeries of Chicago'":

> Not long ago, in the darkest parts of the Puerto Rican rainforest, two Nobel prize-winning scientists, along with their 6-month-old son, were seeking the Tainas, a secret tribe of Puerto Rican Amazons. Late at night the whole family was eaten alive by a giant snake. None would have heard of this had it not been for Gran Abuelita Pingan'chixlu Tautemoc, who with her mighty sword cut the snake's head off. The couple had been crushed, but miraculously the young boy was still alive. Thus Fausto, the fire-eating drag princess, was twice born.

Fernós continues this origins story in the performance and then bursts into song with live piano accompaniment. He later recites horoscopes to the rapt audience members, who sip cocktails while a waitress at times walks in front of the performer, partially blocking our view.

Appropriations of Indigenous origin myths by non-Native performers in the United States are long-standing, as Scott Lauria Morgensen highlights in *Spaces between Us: Queer Settler Colonialism and Indigenous Decolonization* (2011), where the scholar critically discusses the Radical Faeries.[47] When asked about this issue at a May 2013 event at Northwestern University in Evanston, Illinois, Fernós responded that in his case it had to do with his nation-specific, paradoxical situation as a Puerto Rican raised in a country where there is an insistence on narratives of extermination according to which there are no living Tainos; as such, Fernós's fantasy scenario, which presents him as the Tarzan-like rescued child of wildly successful professionals ("two Nobel prize–winning scientists" of unnamed ancestry) can be seen as an ambivalent queer validation of Indigenous heritage, as a nonnative reborn ("twice-born") due to a miraculous Indigenous intervention. This appeal to Taino heritage coincides with the more earnest, perhaps decolonial Humboldt Park Vida/Sida Paseo Boricua Cacica Queen Pageant organizers' gesture of crowning their winner as "Cacica Queen," using the Taino word *cacica* (Indigenous female chieftain) to identify their winner.

Fernós's parodic Taino reclamation is different from efforts by specific groups in Puerto Rico and the diaspora to disseminate, reenvision, and revive Taino language and culture, which have generated mixed responses from scholars such as Arlene Dávila, Jorge Duany, and Miriam Jiménez Román, who have argued that claims to indigeneity are a foil for minimizing African ancestry.[48] Other scholars, such as Sherina Feliciano-Santos, have highlighted current interest and identification with Taino culture as a valid, politically informed, and meaningful practice, but not one particularly marked by receptiveness to queerness.[49] For Fernós, the mention of Amazons is also important as a mythological woman-centered warrior society associated with lesbianism; while intrinsically a reference to Greek mythology, their placement in the tropics builds on their links to the South American rainforest.[50] Fernós's "playing Indian" (to cite Philip J. Deloria) is not about denying Blackness or asserting Latinx indigeneity as a primary identity (as discussed by Maylei Blackwell); it is more about queerness in a context of white (or light-skinned) privilege and about envisioning links to his home country.[51]

Fernós presents a hybrid (syncretic), invented (perhaps nonsensical) fantasy of Puerto Rican indigeneity in the Midwest, mixing Tainas and Amazons with Mesoamerican naming practices, as in the parodic (yet empowered and heroic) "Pingan'chixlu Tautemoc," which invokes Nahuatl naming practices ("Tautemoc" sounds like a variant of Cuauhtemoc, the last Aztec emperor) while incorporating the word *pinga* (Puerto Rican slang for penis) in Spanish. This potentially offensive tropicamp mixing of Caribbean and Mesoamerican referents can be seen as the result of Fernós's contact and collaborations in Texas and Chicago with Mexican/Chicanx/Texano populations and the processes of hybridization that occur in sites with multiple Latinx communities; in this case, it is marked by humor and not by nationalist affirmation.

The fact that Fernós sings a lengthy Broadway tune in Spanish also serves to transculturate and transform key American popular culture, highlighting how in fact Latinxs have always been at the heart of American musical theater, as scholars Brian Eugenio Herrera, Frances Negrón-Muntaner, David Román, and Alberto Sandoval-Sánchez have demonstrated.[52] In a sense, Fernós is queering and tropicalizing the Chicago cabaret scene, making the well-known unfamiliar through a Puerto Rican *transloca* and tropicamp lens. Here, Fernós is bringing Puerto Rican cultural referents and the Spanish language to alternative English-dominant audiences in a famously segregated city where Spanish-language speakers are often isolated in specific neighborhoods.[53]

The media scholar Ragan Fox has seen Fernós's and Marc Felion's invocation of the Puerto Rican tropical rainforest of El Yunque, or, more concretely, the experience of recording an early podcast there in 2006 that was later broadcast to an international audience (FOF #226: "Puerto Rican Rainforest Soundscape"), as a gesture of queer community making that intersects with environmental awareness and "cultural transference," referring to "cross-pollinations of cultures that occur in an increasingly globalized world."[54] This invocation of Puerto Rican Indigenous heritage and of the natural landscape has been a defining feature of many diasporic Puerto Rican artists, particularly of the Nuyorican poets, as Juan Flores insightfully noted in his pioneering essays in *Divided Borders* (1993); in his book *Defending Their Own in the Cold: The Cultural Turns of U.S. Puerto Ricans*, Marc Zimmerman identifies a similar phenomenon among Chicago Rican poets such as David Hernández and especially Salima Rivera.[55] Fernós's (and Felion's) return to the island and reappraisal of nature from a queer ecological standpoint coincides with Flores's interest in *The Diaspora Strikes Back* (2009), where the scholar prioritizes the positive impacts of return migrants in Puerto Rico and the diaspora's investment in placemaking back in the Caribbean.[56] Fernós's gesture can be seen (following Flores) as a "cultural remittance" that recuperates and highlights environmental awareness from a diasporic Puerto Rican perspective.

Recovering the Technological Twist

After fifteen years of ephemeral, mostly self-financed, and financially draining drag performance, Fernós decided to try a new medium in 2005 at the suggestion of his friend, the queer, Jewish, technologically savvy, Chicago-based drag queen and performance artist Richard Bluestein, who performs as "Madge Weinstein."[57] This new medium was podcasting, called oral blogging at the time, which has been described by Richard Berry as "liberating the listeners from time and place, and allowing them to talk back to the programme-makers."[58] Podcasting creates new possibilities for placemaking: while the content can be profoundly linked to the site of creation (e.g., Fernós and Felion invite multiple queer Chicago Latinx individuals to participate in the show and frequently discuss local issues and events), the inexpensive global distribution mechanism leads to the creation of a new transgeographic community of listeners who can participate and chime in in multiple ways by traditional mail, phone, Internet, and other means. And, as Ragan Fox notes, podcasting has enabled the creation of complex queer bridges.

In 2005 Fernós also abandoned drag, which he did not retake until 2009, when a conflict with some of the guests on the podcast led him to create the character of Saltina Obama Bouvier, an ornery, antinice queen who benefits from search engine optimization terms in her name as a strategy to increase Google hits.[59] The character was created for a video titled "Feast of Fun Forced Feminization," a parody of popular fetishistic male cisgender heterosexual fantasies of being forced to adopt a feminine appearance, seen as a form of humiliation but also of sexual pleasure.[60] Uploaded onto YouTube on June 3, 2009, the forced feminization video also featured the Chicago-based white trans performer Victoria Lamarr (V-Marr), who is now deceased, and Fernos's partner, Marc Felion, who performed as Daphne Dumount.[61]

According to the *Feast of Fun* website, "Saltina Obama Bouvier hails from Caricola, Texas, the 'Fruitcake Capitol [*sic*] of the World' and did in fact work at the famous fruitcake factory after her puppy farm, not a puppy mill as was printed in the newspaper, went out of business. She really loved each and every one of those puppies!"[62] Curiously, this biographical narrative does not point to more evident referents for the character's name: the ways in which "Saltina" (a variation of Faustina) refers to saltine crackers, which are extremely popular among Puerto Ricans (e.g., Galletas Sultana, manufactured in Mayagüez), but also refers to "salty" as a character trait; "Obama" as a reference to US president Barack Obama and to the then First Lady of the United States, Michelle Obama, who are former residents of Chicago; and "Bouvier," the French-origin maiden name of former First Lady of the United States Jacqueline Kennedy Onassis. As such, the name "Saltina Obama Bouvier" parodically invokes a wide range of referents linked to diverse cultures and geographies, including Chicago, but marked by political power and celebrity; the character, which sometimes features a rather masculine beard and a menacing grimace, as we can see in a photo by Marc Felion (see figure 3.2), is presented as Texan but created by a Puerto Rican who now lives in the Midwest, manifesting an intrinsically *transloca* tropicamp sensibility.

My own drag involvement with Fernós and his partner, Marc Felion, began in 2010 with the filming of the premier episode of the series *Cooking with Drag Queens*, titled "How to Make Tostones," which was uploaded onto YouTube on November 16, 2010. *Cooking with Drag Queens* follows the format of two very popular YouTube genres: the cooking show and the drag queen video.[63] In this episode, the production is marked by the Puerto Rican specificity of the creative talent (Fernós and myself) and of the plot line, which consists of making a very distinctive Puerto Rican (and, more broadly, Latin American and Caribbean) food item, *tostones,* or savory, twice-fried, crispy green plantains, but in Chicago. As in Fernós's early episodes of *El Chow de Faustina*, the video aims to be informative as much as entertaining; it is marked by extravagant, campy, and at times bawdy humor, following in the tradition of drag provocateurs such as Divine (Harris Glenn Milstead), particularly as portrayed in the films of John Waters, and of the intersexual artist Vaginal Davis.[64] Our drag performance does not quite achieve the radical disjuncture or political intervention and social critique of Davis's "terrorist drag" as discussed by José Esteban Muñoz in *Disidentifications: Queers of Color and the Performance of Politics* (1999), where the Cuban American critic describes how the Afro-Latina performer challenges white supremacy through the embodiment of a nationalist, white supremacist character called Clarence. At our most radical, Fernós (as Saltina), Felion (as Daphne), and I (as Lola) disrupt and confuse, for example, in the improvised crushing plantains scene, when we flatten the fried plantains with "cha cha heels" (silver and clear plastic high heel shoes, a reference to John Waters's 1974 film *Female Trouble*, in which Divine portrays

FIGURE 3.2. Fausto Fernós as Saltina Obama Bouvier, 2016. Photo by Marc Felion.

the character of Dawn Davenport), an act that is accompanied by a distorted soundtrack of the words "The crushing!"

Here, instead of making Caesar salad (as in episode 1 of *El Chow de Faustina*), the three drag queens present Puerto Rican cuisine as interesting and delicious in a bilingual format, albeit with a grotesque touch, picking shoes off the floor and using them as a cooking utensil to replace a *tostonera,* or *tostones* press. The combination of comedy, linguistic alternation, and cultural specificity envisions an audience of hip (queer) bilingual Puerto Ricans and other Latinxs as much as of lovers of camp (or tropicamp) but might also upset persons who feel it is too over the top, offensive, or simply gross. Clearly, the video flirts with stereotypes of Puerto Ricans and of gays but ultimately proposes the goal of eating good, tasty, delicious but perhaps dirty, contaminated, or *sucio* food and of understanding Puerto Rico as a site distinct from the Mexican imaginary that dominates mainstream American conceptualizations of *latinidad*, perhaps playing with or anticipating what scholar Deborah R. Vargas, drawing on the queer of color critique and on Muñoz's theorization of *chusmería* (Latinx low-brow humor), later identified as the "Latino queer analytic" of *lo sucio*, an optic that mixes sexuality, transgression, culturally specific humor, erotic attraction, and embodied knowledge.[65] Fernós's play with *tostones sucios* (dirty, potentially soiled, sexualized *tostones*) can also be seen as a push against the fad of "clean diets" that are often associated with white middle- and upper-class lifestyles.

At the same time, the *Cooking with Drag Queens* "How to Make Tostones" video engages a much longer and broader reimagining of Puerto Rican identity through food and agricultural products, specifically the green plantain and *la mancha de plátano* (the dark stain that remains on the hands after peeling green plantains), seen as transnational cultural signifiers involving the body, whether through the ingestion or preparation of food, as Cruz Miguel Ortiz Cuadra highlights in *Eating Puerto Rico: A History of Food, Culture, and Identity*.[66] There is widespread acknowledgment of *plátanos* as a cultural marker for Puerto Ricanness and, more broadly, Hispanic Caribbeanness; as the cultural journalist Ana Teresa Toro has noted, the 2015–18 exhibit of the permanent collection of the Museo de Arte de Puerto Rico (MAPR) in San Juan titled *Interconexiones: Lecturas curatoriales de la colección MAPR*, curated by Juan Carlos López Quintero, included a room dedicated to artistic portrayals of the *plátano* in Puerto Rican art, such as *El pan nuestro de cada día* by Víctor Vázquez and *Plátano Pride* by Miguel Luciano.[67]

Green plantains are not part of the vision that David Alfaro Siqueiros highlighted in his mural *América Tropical: Oprimida y Destrozada por los Imperialismos*, although they might have been part of the vision of the people who commissioned it. As Shifra M. Goldman describes, "[Siqueiro's] vision of tropical America differed sharply from prevailing folkloric ideas: instead of painting 'a continent of happy men, surrounded by palms and parrots where the fruit voluntarily detached itself to fall into the mouths of the happy mortals,' he said, 'I painted a man . . . crucified on a double cross, which had, proudly perched on the top, the eagle of North American coins'" (324). Fernós's Chicago Tropical maintains important differences with Siqueiros's (explicitly antitropicalizing) vision but shares the desire to use art to transform, educate, and create a space of home (i.e., to participate in Latinx placemaking); it moves in the direction of Chicago Tropicamp.

Conclusion

In this chapter I have mapped out three moments of Fernós's *transloca* drag performances, focusing on different types of placemaking, mainly those that occur in the intimate interactions in the space of the cabaret and the mediated ones enabled through broadcast technology. I have analyzed representations inflected by diasporic Puerto Ricanness and Latinx identity and by defining traits of mediatized femininity, including that of effeminate *transloca* figures such as Walter Mercado. Gay camp humor, a standard of drag performance in the United States, as Esther Newton noted in her pioneering 1972 ethnography *Mother Camp*, is another constant, but here refracted through the lens of tropicamp and of what Rosamond S. King has called the Caribglobal.[68] One of the particularities of Fernós's work is the way he has used different techniques of representation (whether live shows, public-access television, YouTube videos, or podcasts) to develop his work and to give other LGBT/queer individuals a space for expression. Another is his appeal to iconic Latina women, whether to the Mexican American Linda Ronstadt, the Cuban American Cristina Saralegui, or his Puerto Rican aunt Clara Luz Fernós Echandi.

Throughout the years, the *Feast of Fools* stage show and *Feast of Fun* podcast have also served as a platform for other drag queens and trans women, as well as a historical, documentary, archival, and community-building project, participating in Latinx and LGBTQ placemaking in Chicago and around the world: creating a virtual place of encounter, disagreement, and potential joy. Fernós's more than thirty-year career moving successfully back and forth from live performance to mediatized forms suggests a flexible engagement with dominant hegemonic forms of media representation. In his influential book *Liveness: Performance in a Mediatized Culture*, the performance studies scholar Philip Auslander theorizes the challenges presented to live performance in a day and age dominated by television and the Internet, and talks precisely about the interrelation of both.[69] Auslander argues against the notion that live is necessarily better than or different from mediatized. Fernós's work is exemplary in this respect.

In this essay I have not said much about the political economy of drag or what it means to not be able to survive off your work, a constant concern of Fernós. I have also not discussed Fernós's frustration at not being able to break into the mainstream; his mid-2010s turn to bodybuilding; and the role and centrality of collaboration, most consistently with his husband, Marc

Felion (who is not Latino), but also with a large cast of people throughout his entire performance career. The constraints of funding, market, and lifestyle and the question of what kind of an artist one wants to be and of how one makes one's art and one's living are also key, as well as what it means to be a middle-class, light-skinned, highly educated Puerto Rican artist in Chicago in a context where many people don't grasp the most basic facts about Puerto Rico and its colonial relationship with the United States. Fernós, who has a following among queer Latinx Chicagoans, combines efforts as a journalist, talk show host, performer, film/videomaker, and community builder, with its attendant inclusions and exclusions. His work is a fundamental contribution to translocal, transnational, queer Puerto Rican and Latinx performance in Chicago and elsewhere, given his important national and international following. Alas, his engagement with stereotypes and his occasional cultural appropriations (e.g., of indigeneity) also make him a slippery, uncomfortable subject that is bound to ruffle feathers and cause discomfort and censure and that challenges the utopian potential for placemaking in Chicago Tropical.

Notes

1. On Latinx placemaking, see Lara, *Latino Placemaking and Planning*.

2. On *translocas*, see Lawrence La Fountain-Stokes, "Translocas: Migration, Homosexuality, and Transvestism in Recent Puerto Rican Performance," *emisférica* 8, no. 1 (Summer 2011), https://hemisphericinstitute.org/en/emisferica-81/8-1-essays/translocas.html; La Fountain-Stokes, *Translocas: The Politics of Puerto Rican Drag and Trans Performance* (Ann Arbor: University of Michigan Press, 2021).

3. Ann Markusen and Anne Gadwa, *Creative Placemaking* (Washington, DC: National Endowment for the Arts, 2010).

4. Other Latinx performers who use comedy and negotiate stereotypes (at times falling into stereotype) are John Leguizamo, Culture Clash, and Carmelita Tropicana. On the complexities of race on the Internet, see Lisa Nakamura, *Digitizing Race: Visual Cultures of the Internet* (Minneapolis: University of Minnesota Press, 2007), particularly the chapter "Measuring Race on the Internet."

5. Ramón Rivera-Servera, *Performing Queer Latinidad: Dance, Sexuality, Politics* (Ann Arbor: University of Michigan Press, 2012); Frances R. Aparicio and Susana Chávez-Silverman, *Tropicalizations: Transcultural Representations of Latinidad* (Hanover, NH: University Press of New England, 1997); Frances R. Aparicio, "Latinidad/es," in *Keywords for Latina/o Studies*, ed. Deborah R. Vargas, Nancy Raquel Mirabal, and Lawrence La Fountain-Stokes (New York: New York University Press, 2017), 113–17; Rodríguez, *Queer Latinidad*. For a discussion of American and Latinx homophobia and transphobia, see Michael Hames-García and Ernesto Javier Martínez, *Gay Latino Studies: A Critical Reader* (Durham, NC: Duke University Press, 2011); José Esteban Muñoz, *Disidentifications: Queers of Color and the Performance of Politics* (Minneapolis: University of Minnesota Press, 1999).

6. On Siqueiros's mural, see Shifra M. Goldman, "Siqueiros and Three Early Murals in Los Angeles," *Art Journal* 33, no. 4 (Summer 1974): 321–27. On "tropicamp," see Arnaldo Cruz-Malavé, "Between Irony and Belief: The Queer Diasporic Underground Aesthetics of José Rodríguez-Soltero and Mario Montez," *GLQ* 21, no. 4 (October 2015): 585–615; Max Jorge Hinderer Cruz, "TROPICAMP: Some Notes on Hélio Oiticica's 1971 Text," *Afterall* 28 (Autumn/Winter), https://www.afterall.org/journal/issue.28/tropicamp-pre-and-post-tropic-lia-at-once-some-contextual-notes-onh-lio-oiticica-s-1971-te; Hélio Oiticica, "Mario Montez, Tropicamp," *Afterall* 28 (2011): 16–21, https://www.afterall.org/journal/issue.28/mario-montez-tropicamp; Hélio Oiticica and Mario Montez, "Héliotape with Mario Montez (1971)," *Criticism* 56, no. 2 (2014): 379–404; Juan A. Suárez, "Jack Smith, Hélio Oiticica, Tropicalism," *Criticism* 56, no. 2 (2014): 295–328.

7. Fausto Fernós is the son of the late Puerto Rican architect Gonzalo Fernós López and of the Mexican-born American educator Patricia Fernós. The Fernós family is well known in Puerto Rico, as his paternal relative Antonio Fernós-Isern was the island's resident commissioner in Washington, DC, from 1946 to 1965. See "Fausto Fernós" and "Feast of Fun" articles in Wikipedia; biography on "About Us" page on *Feast of Fun* website (http://feastoffun.com/about/); Fausto Fernós, unpublished interview with author, September 5, 2011; Lawrence La Fountain-Stokes, Lourdes Torres, and Ramón Rivera-Servera, "Towards an Archive of Latina/o Queer Chicago: Art, Politics, and Social Performance," in *Out in Chicago: LGBT History at the Crossroads*, ed. Jill Austin and Jennifer Brier (Chicago: Chicago History Museum, 2011), 127–53; Achy Obejas, "'Feast of Fools'—A Celebration of Diversity. Colorful Fausto Fernós—An Appropriate Host for Radical Faeries," *Chicago Tribune*, March 31, 2000, 28; Gregg Shapiro, "Feast of Fools Takes Gay Podcasting to New Heights," AfterElton.com, August 22, 2006, http://www.afterellen.com/archive/elton/people/2006/8/fausto.html; Albert Williams, "Faerie Frolic Arts Festival," *Chicago Reader*, March 12, 1998. A February 2018 article identifies Christopher Rincón as the executive director of the River Pierce Foundation in San Ygnacio, Texas; see Serena Solomon, "A Bold Artist, a Quiet Texas Town and the Heritage of the Borderland," *New York Times*, February 16, 2018, https://www.nytimes.com/2018/02/16/arts/design/michael-tracy-san-ygnacio-texas.html.

8. The podcast was known as *Feast of Fools* from 2005 until 2009. See Rex W. Huppke, "Gay Podcast Draws 70,000 a Week," *Chicago Tribune*, April 25, 2010, 14 (ProQuest); Jerry Nunn, "'Feast' Duo Still Having Fun after 13 Years," *Windy City Times*, December 27, 2017, 18 (ProQuest); Bradley Osborn, "The Feast of Fools: The Fiercest Gay Podcast in the Universe," BradleyOsborn.com, December 2006.

9. See, for example, Fausto Fernós, "Cooking with Drag Queens: How to Make Tostones," YouTube, November 16, 2010, http://youtu.be/TA05Vl3FoV0.

10. Aparicio and Chávez-Silverman, *Tropicalizations*, 2.

11. Ibid., 8.

12. Ibid., 12.

13. On "self-tropicalization," see Jillian M. Báez, *In Search of Belonging: Latinas, Media, and Citizenship* (Urbana: University of Illinois Press, 2018), 84, 109–11. On Leguizamo, see David Román, *Performance in America: Contemporary U.S. Culture*

and the Performing Arts (Durham, NC: Duke University Press, 2005), 109–36. On Tropicana and Cuban *choteo*, see Muñoz, *Disidentifications*, 119–41. On *relajo*, see Diana Taylor, *The Archive and the Repertoire* (Durham, NC: Duke University Press, 2003), 129–30.

14. On queer Latinx Chicago, see Lawrence La Fountain-Stokes, *Queer Ricans: Cultures and Sexualities in the Diaspora* (Minneapolis: University of Minnesota Press, 2009), 108–22; La Fountain-Stokes, Torres, and Rivera-Servera, "Towards an Archive"; Ramón Rivera-Servera, "History in Drag: Latina/o Queer Affective Circuits in Chicago," in Valerio-Jiménez, Vaquera-Vásquez, and Fox, *The Latina/o Midwest Reader*, 185–96. On the broader history of Puerto Ricans and other Latinxs in the Midwest, particularly in Chicago, see Frances R. Aparicio, *Negotiating Latinidad: Intralatina/o Lives in Chicago* (Urbana: University of Illinois Press, 2019); Nicholas De Genova and Ana Y. Ramos-Zayas, *Latino Crossings: Mexicans, Puerto Ricans, and the Politics of Race and Citizenship* (New York: Routledge, 2003); Lilia Fernández, *Brown in the Windy City: Mexicans and Puerto Ricans in Postwar Chicago* (Chicago: University of Chicago Press, 2012); Jesse Stewart Mumm, "When the White People Come: Gentrification and Race in Puerto Rican Chicago" (PhD diss., Northwestern University, 2014); Félix M. Padilla, *Latino Ethnic Consciousness: The Case of Mexican Americans and Puerto Ricans in Chicago* (Notre Dame, IN: University of Notre Dame Press, 1985); Padilla, *Puerto Rican Chicago* (Notre Dame, IN: University of Notre Dame Press, 1987); Gina M. Pérez, *The Near Northwest Side Story: Migration, Displacement, and Puerto Rican Families* (Berkeley: University of California Press, 2004); Ana Y. Ramos-Zayas, *National Performances: The Politics of Class, Race, and Space in Puerto Rican Chicago* (Chicago: University of Chicago Press, 2003); Mérida M. Rúa, *A Grounded Identidad: Making New Lives in Chicago's Puerto Rican Neighborhoods* (New York: Oxford University Press, 2012); Mérida M. Rúa, ed., *Latino Urban Ethnography and the Work of Elena Padilla* (Urbana: University of Illinois Press, 2010); Marc Zimmerman, *Defending Their Own in the Cold: The Cultural Turns of U.S. Puerto Ricans* (Urbana: University of Illinois Press, 2011).

15. On Puerto Rican translocality, see Jorge Duany, *Blurred Borders: Transnational Migration between the Hispanic Caribbean and the United States* (Chapel Hill: University of North Carolina Press, 2011); Duany, *The Puerto Rican Nation on the Move: Identities on the Island and in the Unites States* (Chapel Hill: University of North Carolina Press, 2002); Duany, *Puerto Rico: What Everyone Needs to Know®* (New York: Oxford University Press, 2017); Frances Negrón-Muntaner, *Boricua Pop: Puerto Ricans and the Latinization of American Culture* (New York: New York University Press, 2004); Frances Negrón-Muntaner, ed., *None of the Above: Puerto Ricans in the Global Era* (New York: Palgrave Macmillan, 2007).

16. On the centrality and challenges faced by Latinx alternative media content creators, see Ed Morales, "Latinos in Alternative Media: Latinos as an Alternative Media Paradigm," in *Contemporary Latina/o Media: Production, Circulation, Politics*, ed. Arlene Dávila and Yeidy M. Rivero (New York: New York University Press, 2014), 322–36; Frances Negrón-Muntaner, "The Gang's Not All Here: The State of Latinos in Contemporary US Media," in ibid., 103–24.

17. See Manuel G. Avilés-Santiago, *Puerto Rican Soldiers and Second-Class Citizenship: Representations in Media* (New York: Palgrave Macmillan, 2014), 3.

18. Dara E. Goldman, *Out of Bounds: Islands and the Demarcation of Identity in the Hispanic Caribbean* (Lewisburg, PA: Bucknell University Press, 2008), 196.

19. See Henrique Cirne-Lima and Josué Pellot, dir., *I Am the Queen* (Los Angeles: Cinema Libre Studio, [2010] 2015); *The Other Side of the Queen* (2012); Pérez, *The Near Northwest*; Ricki Reay, "I Am the Queen Latest Trailer Sashays In," Movie TV Tech Geeks, October 13, 2015, https://movietvtechgeeks.com/i-am-the-queen-latest-trailer-sashays-in/; Rúa, *A Grounded Identidad*.

20. On Miss Ketty Teanga, see Rivera-Servera, "History in Drag." On the Continental Pageantry System, see Tracy Baim and Owen Keehnen, *Jim Flint: The Boy from Peoria* (Chicago: Prairie Ave. Productions, 2011).

21. Hollywood filmmaker Rose Troche is a Puerto Rican lesbian artist raised in the suburbs of Chicago; her first film, *Go Fish*, profiled a group of multiracial young women in Wicker Park, a formerly working-class neighborhood in Chicago that was undergoing gentrification. See La Fountain-Stokes, *Queer Ricans*, 108–22. On queer poet Rane Arroyo, see La Fountain-Stokes, Torres, and Rivera-Servera, "Towards an Archive," 142–44.

22. The article ("Cocinerito en su casa") is from 1983 and appeared in a cooking dossier titled "Fausto Fernós Riddick, Calle Barbé 503, Santurce, Puerto Rico." See Fausto Fernós, "PHOTO: Time Traveling Bunny Cake Follows Gay Couple," Feast of Fun.com, December 1, 2010, https://feastoffun.com/topics/people/2010/12/01/photo-time-traveling-bunny-cake-follows-gay-couple/; Sanda Rentas Torres, "Cuando el hogar es la escuela," *El Nuevo Día*, April 13, 1983, 42–43. La Leche League is a global, nongovernmental, nonprofit organization that organizes advocacy, education, and training related to breastfeeding.

23. Fausto Fernós, unpublished interview with author, and Facebook communication and phone call, December 18, 2018.

24. See Belinda Acosta, "Fernos Tilts Gender Rules: Latino Artist Wants to Have Fun, Make a Statement," *Austin American Statesman*, August 13, 1994, 4 (ProQuest).

25. On Montano, see Linda M. Montano, *Letters from Linda M. Montano*, ed. Jennie Klein (London: Routledge, 2005).

26. Fernós, unpublished interview with author.

27. The African American artist A. (Andy) Rafael Johnson also performed in *SoftMen*. See http://www.arafaeljohnson.com/bio/.

28. See Sebastián Zubieta, "Interview with Linda Ronstadt," *Review: Literature and Arts of the Americas* 42, no. 1 (2009): 102–6, 102.

29. Fernós, personal communication with author, Facebook, June 16, 2013.

30. See "Best of Austin '95," *Austin Chronicle*, August 4, 1995; Fernós interview.

31. On public-access cable TV, see Pamela Doty, "Public-Access Cable TV: Who Cares?," *Journal of Communication* 25, no. 3 (September 1975): 33–41; Ralph Engelman, *The Origins of Public Access Cable Television 1966–1972* (Columbia, SC: Association for Education in Journalism and Mass Communication, 1990); Eric Freedman, "Public Access / Private Confession: Home Video as (Queer) Community Television," in *The*

Television Studies Reader, ed. Robert C. Allen and Annette Hill (London: Routledge, 2004), 343–53.

32. Doty, "Public-Access Cable TV," 33.

33. Kenton T. Wilkinson, "Spanish Language Media in the United States," in *The Handbook of Spanish Language Media*, ed. Alan B. Albarran (New York: Routledge, 2009), 3–16, 10. *El Show de Cristina* premiered nationally in 1989. Saralegui's show was also accompanied by *Cristina* magazine, years before Oprah Winfrey created her own magazine, *O*. Also see "Cristina Saralegui," *Encyclopædia Britannica*, January 25, 2020, https://www.britannica.com/biography/Cristina-Saralegui; Kenton T. Wilkinson, *Spanish-Language Television in the United States: Fifty Years of Development* (New York: Routledge, 2016).

34. Fausto Fernós, "Faustina—Mini Episode #1—How to Apply Makeup (1994)," *Feast of Fun*, November 11, 2011, http://feastoffun.com/videos/2011/11/11/video-faustina-mini-episode-1-how-to-apply-makeup/ and *El Chow De Faustina* (Linda Montano Episode, October 9, 1994), YouTube, March 5, 2007, http://youtu.be/qeRKDGAQY-0. Also see "Best of Austin '95."

35. Both the original and the remix are currently available on YouTube and on FeastofFun.com.

36. On queer Spanglish, see Lawrence La Fountain-Stokes, "The Queer Politics of Spanglish," *Critical Moment* 9 (March/April 2005): 5.

37. In 1994–95, when this episode was recorded, terms such as "trans" and "intersexual" were not widely used; for example, Cheryl Chase did not publish her groundbreaking essay "Hermaphrodites with Attitude" until 1998. See Cheryl Chase, "Hermaphrodites with Attitude: Mapping the Emergence of Intersex Political Activism," *GLQ* 7, no. 4 (1998): 189–211.

38. I thank Claire F. Fox for this insight.

39. Diana Taylor, "La Raza Cosmética: Walter Mercado Performs Latino Psychic Space," in *The Archive and the Repertoire*, 110–32.

40. See description in "Best of Austin '95."

41. See Fernós interview and "Ninth Annual Cleveland Performance Art Festival," Performance Art Festival 1997, http://web.ulib.csuohio.edu/PAF97/paf_index.html. Fernós performed on August 15 and 16, 1996.

42. The Chicago Radical Faeries organized a "Halloween Howl" at the Randolph Street Gallery on November 1, 1997; see Cara Jepsen, "Days of the Week," *Chicago Reader*, October 30, 1997. They also organized a "Faerie Frolic Arts Festival" on March 16–22, 1998 (Williams, "Faerie Frolic"). Fernós participated in both. Also see "Randolph Street Gallery Archives," http://libraryguides.saic.edu/rsga. Documentation of the December 1, 2004, show at Schubas Tavern appears at http://fausto.org/ under "Media."

43. See Obejas, "'Feast of Fools.'" On the Radical Faeries and its founder, see *Hope along the Wind: The Life of Harry Hay*, dir. Eric Slade (San Francisco: Frameline, 2005). Also see *The Cockettes*, dir. Bill Weber and David Weissman (Santa Monica, CA: Strand Releasing Home Video, 2002); *Dzi Croquettes*, dir. Tatiana Issa and Raphael Alvarez (Brazil: Imovision, 2009); Jean-Yves Le Talec, *Folles de France: Repenser l'homosexualité masculine* (Paris: La Découverte, 2008).

44. In *Drag Queens at the 801 Cabaret* (Chicago: University of Chicago Press, 2003), Leila J. Rupp and Verta Taylor discuss the centrality of drag names and how performers choose them.

45. St. Sukie de la Croix (born Darryl Michael Vincent) is best known for his book *Chicago Whispers: A History of LGBT Chicago before Stonewall* (Madison: University of Wisconsin Press, 2012).

46. Fausto Fernós, "The Fire Eating Drag Princess—Fausto Fernós—April 1, 2000," YouTube, June 6, 2009, http://youtu.be/J2xe7JgkiGg. According to Wikipedia, "The HotHouse is a celebrated cultural center last located in the South Loop, Chicago, United States, and known for its program of innovative jazz and world music concerts and as a central meeting place for a variety of community groups." See https://en.wikipedia.org/wiki/HotHouse_(jazz_club).

47. Scott Lauria Morgensen, "Ancient Roots through Settled Land: Imagining Indigeneity and Place among Radical Faeries," in *Spaces between Us: Queer Settler Colonialism and Indigenous Decolonization* (Minneapolis: University of Minnesota Press, 2011), 127–60.

48. Critiques of the contemporary Taíno movement by Dávila, Duany, and Jiménez Román appear in *Taíno Revival: Critical Perspectives on Puerto Rican Identity and Cultural Politics*, ed. Gabriel Haslip-Viera et al. (Princeton, NJ: Markus Wiener Publishers, 2001). For a sympathetic assessment, see Tony Castanha, *The Myth of Indigenous Caribbean Extinction: Continuity and Reclamation in Borikén (Puerto Rico)* (New York: Palgrave Macmillan, 2011).

49. See Sherina Feliciano-Santos, "Negotiating Ethnoracial Configurations among Puerto Rican Taíno Activists," *Ethnic and Racial Studies* 42, no. 7 (2019): 1149–67; Feliciano-Santos, *A Contested Caribbean Indigeneity: Language, Social Practice, and Identity within Puerto Rican Taíno Activism* (New Brunswick, NJ: Rutgers University Press, 2021).

50. See Monika Reinfelder, ed., *Amazon to Zami: Towards a Global Lesbian Feminism* (London: Cassell, 1996), 4.

51. See Philip J. Deloria, *Playing Indian* (New Haven, CT: Yale University Press, 1998); Maylei Blackwell, "Indigeneity," in Vargas, Mirabal, and La Fountain-Stokes, *Keywords for Latina/o Studies*, 100–105.

52. See Brian Eugenio Herrera, *Latin Numbers: Playing Latino in Twentieth-Century U.S. Popular Performance* (Ann Arbor: University of Michigan Press, 2015); Negrón-Muntaner, *Boricua Pop*; Román, *Performance in America*; Alberto Sandoval-Sánchez, *José Can You See? Latinos On and Off Broadway* (Madison: University of Wisconsin Press, 1999).

53. See Aparicio, *Negotiating Latinidad*.

54. Ragan Fox, "Sober Drag Queens, Digital Forests, and Bloated 'Lesbians': Performing Gay Identities Online," *Qualitative Inquiry* 14, no. 7 (October 2008): 1245–63, 1255.

55. Juan Flores, *Divided Borders: Essays on Puerto Rican Identity* (Houston: Arte Público Press, 1993); Zimmerman, *Defending Their Own*, 80–111.

56. Juan Flores, *The Diaspora Strikes Back: Caribeño Tales of Learning and Turning* (New York: Routledge, 2009).

57. Fernós interview. On Bluestein and podcasting, see Fox, "Sober Drag Queens."

58. Richard Berry, "Podcasting: Considering the Evolution of the Medium and Its Association with the Word 'Radio,'" *Radio Journal: International Studies in Broadcast and Audio Media* 14, no. 1 (April 2016): 7–22, 7–8.

59. Fernós interview. For a discussion of Internet search maximization and its links to race, racism, and capitalism, see John Cheney-Lippold, *We Are Data: Algorithms and the Making of Our Digital Selves* (New York: New York University Press, 2017); Astrid Mager, "Algorithmic Ideology: How Capitalist Society Shapes Search Engines," *Information, Communication and Society* 15, no. 5 (2012): 769–87; Safiya Umoja Noble, *Algorithms of Oppression: How Search Engines Reinforce Racism* (New York: New York University Press, 2018).

60. Fausto Fernós, "Forced Feminization—Feast of Fun," YouTube, June 3, 2009, http://youtu.be/7hdJioRGsYM. For legal feminist analysis of forced feminization in men's prisons, see Mary Anne Franks, "How to Feel Like a Woman, or Why Punishment Is a Drag," *UCLA Law Review* 61, no. 3 (2014): 566–605.

61. Lamarr died in 2013. See Fausto Fernós, "Farewell Victoria Lamarr—RIP," *Feast of Fun*, November 26, 2013, https://feastoffun.com/about-the-fof/2013/11/26/farewell-victoria-lamarr-rip/.

62. See https://feastoffun.com/author/saltina/. Marc Felion has clarified that the actual "Fruitcake Capital of the World" is Corsicana, Texas, not Caricola (personal communication, May 2013, Evanston, IL).

63. For analysis of YouTube, see Jean Burgess and Joshua Green, *YouTube: Online Video and Participatory Culture* (Cambridge, MA: Polity, 2009); Geert Lovink and Sabine Niederer, eds., *Video Vortex Reader: Responses to YouTube*, INC Reader no. 4 (Amsterdam: Institute of Network Cultures, 2008).

64. See *I Am Divine*, dir. Jeffrey Schwarz (Los Angeles: Automat Pictures, 2013); Frances Milstead, Kevin Heffernan, and Steve Yeager, *My Son Divine* (Los Angeles: Alyson Books, 2001); John Sanchez, "In Performance: Vaginal Davis Unplugged," *Chicago Reader*, May 15, 1997, https://chicagoreader.com/arts-culture/in-performancevaginal-davis-unplugged/; Hili Perlson, "Vaginal Davis Speaks," *Sleek*, September 30, 2011, https://web.archive.org/web/20120930013403/http://www.sleek-mag.com/berlin/2011/09/vaginal-davis-speaks-featured-in-sleek-31-xx-xy/.

65. Deborah R. Vargas, "Ruminations on Lo Sucio as a Latino Queer Analytic," *American Quarterly* 66, no. 3 (September 2014): 715–26; Muñoz, *Disidentifications*.

66. Cruz Miguel Ortiz Cuadra, *Eating Puerto Rico: A History of Food, Culture, and Identity*, trans. Russ Davidson (Chapel Hill: University of North Carolina Press, 2013).

67. Ana Teresa Toro, "La mancha que nos une," *El Nuevo Día*, December 25, 2012, http://www.elnuevodia.com/lamanchaquenosune-1414028.html.

68. Esther Newton, *Mother Camp: Female Impersonators in America* (1972; repr., Chicago: University of Chicago Press, 1979); Rosamond S. King, *Island Bodies: Transgressive Sexualities in the Caribbean Imagination* (Gainesville: University Press of Florida, 2014).

69. Philip Auslander, *Liveness: Performance in a Mediatized Culture*, 2nd ed. (London: Routledge, 2008).

CHAPTER 4

Finding MexiRican Placemaking in Michigan

DELIA FERNÁNDEZ-JONES

The smell of freshly made *arroz con gandules* overtook my parents' suburban backyard in Michigan amid the clanking of dominoes slammed on a table. Salsa boomed from speakers at the sixteenth annual Luísa and Pío Fernández Memorial Domino Tournament in June 2016. The yearly gathering brought together my father's seven siblings and their children and grandchildren to honor our late Puerto Rican grandparents. The 2016 tournament fell on my Mexican American mother's birthday. Well into this daylong tournament, my brother-in-law abruptly paused the salsa to introduce a mariachi singer for a surprise serenade for my mother. To honor her and her family, the mariachi sang "Mexico Lindo" and other songs that her father, also a mariachi, once sang to her. After he was done singing, my mother asked him for one last song. She requested "En Mi Viejo San Juan"—a tune we regularly sing at large gatherings and the only song capable of stopping a backyard full of three generations of Puerto Ricans playing dominoes. As the Mexican mariachi sang, a feeling of palpable nostalgia swept over the Puerto Ricans who had left their homes on the island more than fifty years ago, those who only know the island as adult visitors, and guest visitors from Puerto Rico. Mexican Americans, MexiRicans, and a host of other relatives who are Dominican, Honduran, and Colombian, among others, sang whatever words they knew to this song. This struck me as very tangible evidence of Latinx placemaking in the Midwest.[1]

It was no wonder that in the present we chose a private area for this festive but still intimate occasion. A suburban home in the middle of the twentieth century, when both my Mexican and Puerto Rican grandparents first arrived in Grand Rapids, would have been out of reach for most of the city's "Spanish-speaking," as they collectively referred to themselves. We created the tournament as a celebration that also served as a private way for us to remember our grandparents. The location of this tournament reflects the ways that Latinx communities have grown in Michigan over the previous decades. While the neighborhood my parents live in was still majority white, within the last ten years increasingly more Latinxs and African Americans moved in as white folks moved farther away or to the city's gentrifying center. On that day, everyone in my parents' neighborhood heard the salsa music, slamming dominoes, and a boisterous mariachi over loudspeakers. This was our way of saying that like Grand Rapids, like Michigan, and like the Midwest, this neighborhood was a place we could also call home.

This event emerges from decades of work by Mexicans and Puerto Ricans in the middle of the twentieth century to create places of belonging for themselves in Grand Rapids. As newcomers, they arrived in an environment that favored religious conservatism, privileged whiteness, and maintained a Black/white binary of racial categorization. All of those factors could have served to erase Mexicans' and Puerto Ricans' cultural identities and practices. Instead, in the 1940s and 1950s, they maintained their identities, formed relationships with one another, and engaged in placemaking to create their own home in Grand Rapids. This was not always a seamless process. There were disagreements, tensions, and negotiations, but despite these, the community ended up with tangible products of their interactions and relationships.[2] Latinx religious and recreational spaces, such as a Latinx Catholic church, baseball games, dance halls, movie theaters, and festivals, are just some examples of their cultural expression. This was proof that Latinxs, who came to the area for labor, were more than just workers. Rather, they were human beings willing to make a space into a place that met all of their needs.

The personal connection I have to this area intersects with the formal training I have as a historian. I grew up hearing stories of a vibrant Latinx community. My father passed down stories his parents told him of what it was like to live in Grand Rapids in the 1950s as Puerto Ricans. My maternal grandfather, from the stories told to me about him, stressed that his children never forget that they were both Mexican and American. He worked through the Mexican Patriotic Committee in Grand Rapids to provide programming that would achieve that. These stories inspired me to study this area formally as a historian.

My historical look at placemaking among Mexicans and Puerto Ricans fills gaps in the existing literature. A number of interdisciplinary scholars examine contemporary placemaking among Latinxs.[3] However, there have not been many projects that look at the historical process of placemaking among these two groups, and there are not many sources that look at this phenomenon in smaller cities.[4] In many cases, this gap in the literature speaks to the trends in labor migration and colonization that brought Mexicans and Puerto Ricans to separate areas of the United States. This, however, does not take into account those Mexicans and Puerto Ricans who moved to the Midwest, where they encountered one another as early as the late 1940s and early 1950s.[5]

Placemaking is the most accurate way to describe the way that Latinxs engaged with one another and with the area in which they lived. In this study, I borrow from social scientists Katia Balassiano and Marta María Maldonado's definition of when a space becomes a place: "when people become attached to a place . . . and when the place is used in pursuit of shared socially and culturally specific goals."[6] I find that Latinxs sought out public spaces that were not made for them, yet they assigned them value and cultivated feelings of belonging with one another as they met in those areas. For example, Rumsey Park was a baseball field, but when Latinxs met there every Sunday, it became part of their routine and their assurance that they could interact with their families and friends there on a regular basis.

Furthermore, I agree that placemaking transforms the "behavior of citizens from that of passive consumers of services to actors, co-creators, and agents of change" as described by urban planner Jesus Lara.[7] Latinxs in Grand Rapids took places that were not made to serve their needs and transformed them for their own uses. As they entered into a downtown city plaza that was mostly used by middle-class white Grand Rapidians and played mariachi music there, for example, they were agents of change. It is this power negotiation embedded in placemaking that I look at among Mexicans and Puerto Ricans as they created their relationships with one another in particular sites.

This chapter examines archival issues when researching placemaking, the earliest evidence of physical placemaking among Latinxs, the ways that leisure and placemaking intersected among the two groups of Latinxs in the area, and, finally, relationship building via intermarriages and friendships among Mexicans and Puerto Ricans that, in combination with physical placemaking, created a cohesive community that later fought for civil rights in the late 1960s and 1970s.

Finding Latino Voices in a Midwestern Archive

I began this research project after I tried to put my family's history in context but found that both histories of Latinos and histories of the Midwest did not include small cities with Mexicans and Puerto Ricans. From the 1920s to the 1970s, the period in which I was interested, Grand Rapids was a city of about 190,000 at its largest. Mexicans and Puerto Ricans made up no more than 5 percent of the population at any given time. Thus, the smaller community of Latinos did not garner the same kind of attention they did in places such as Chicago, New York, and Los Angeles. As such a small part of the general population, they were often overlooked by mainstream accounts of Grand Rapids as well.[8] As a researcher with insider knowledge of the city, I knew this history was there, but I needed to read the sources available against the grain.

Books on Latinas were the most effective at teaching me how do this. Historians such as Vicki Ruiz and Miroslava Chávez-García, for example, found the voices of women from the 1800s to the mid-twentieth century by reading traditional sources for what was not there and by using sources in a way that their authors did not intend for people to use them.[9] Patriarchal norms silenced women's voices in the mainstream, yet these researchers showed how to recover those voices from the archive. They looked at court records and other governmental documents and found women's agency. They also did so by carrying out oral histories with women themselves. Thus, I sought out the same type of records—ones that were not made to tell a history of Latinxs—and learned to read them.

Through this, I discovered that I too could reconstruct the process of placemaking that Latinxs used and recover a history that could be lost. Among other sources, I utilized jail records; court records; city directories; city assessor files; governmental reports; municipal correspondences; baptism, confirmation, and marriage records; photos; and oral histories. I found most of those sources at the Grand Rapids City Archives and the Grand Rapids Public Library. These sources were created to document the mundane responsibilities of city government. I went to individual parishes to access clerical records, which in many ways were also created to record the Catholic Church's responsibility of baptizing, confirming, and marrying the population. Read against the grain, those documents revealed demographic information about the Latino population that had not been recorded elsewhere. I was thus able to document the earliest Latino populations' birthplaces, birth dates, ages, genders, addresses, nationalities, races, whether or not they could speak English or Spanish, and occupations, among other information. I also accessed oral histories with the first Latinx residents in Grand Rapids that researchers collected long before I came to my project. I then carried out my own oral history interviews with over twenty-five people. Through this strategy, in effect, I have created an archive of information on Latinxs gleaned from both other sources and primary participants that has allowed me to reconstruct a history of Latinxs in Grand Rapids.

Latino Recruitment to Michigan and Grand Rapids

To many, Grand Rapids, a middling city in the Midwest, seems like an unlikely place for Latinxs to make a home for themselves. The city is situated about equidistant from Chicago and Detroit in western Michigan. It was not a typical Rust Belt city like Gary, Indiana, or Youngstown, Ohio. Instead, its earliest economic claims were in the furniture industry. Located on the Grand River and with access to lumber from northern Michigan, Grand Rapids produced a portion of the nation's wood furniture in the late nineteenth and early twentieth centuries. Anglo-Saxon Protestant men dominated in local politics prior to the 1950s. However, a smaller population of Dutch Christian Reformed followers began to influence the local culture and thus the politics.

The Dutch Christian Reformed Church (CRC) is a religious sect that in its strictest form prohibits dancing, drinking, and many forms of public entertainment. All of those activities created opportunities for temptation, doctrine argued. Instead, CRC members prided themselves on how honest, hardworking, and thrifty they were and fiercely kept to themselves. Their turn inward helped them to resist forms of assimilation that would take them further away from their religious devotion. By the 1950s, however, many of those Dutch CRC followers were considered white in the public sphere, with all of its privileges, regardless of how tightly they held on to their ethnic and religious identities in the private sphere. According to doctrine, the most pious of them would be actively engaged citizens in their community and engage in the public sphere.[10] Thus, when Latinxs began to arrive in the 1940s, they settled into an area whose residents disapproved of open celebrations, drinking alcohol, and dancing—celebratory acts that many Latinxs engaged in regularly during cultural events.

Beyond the Dutch CRC's specific cultural norms, Grand Rapids's race relations looked much like those of the rest of the urban North. The city subscribed to a Black/white dichotomous understanding of race. From the 1910s to the 1940s, the First and Second Great Migrations more than quadrupled the Black population in Grand Rapids. Though some Black migrants had settled in the area as early as the 1850s, it was not until the 1940s that the Black community in the county grew to over twenty thousand, about 10 percent of the total population.[11] There had also been European immigration during this time. However, African Americans were hardly equal partners in the city. Jim Crow–style restrictions dictated where Black folks could work, live, and spend their leisure time. Their living conditions were better than those in the Deep South, but they were still severely limited. Though World War II brought an economic boom, as it did to other northern cities, it only mildly improved the lives of African Americans. For many Grand Rapidians, nonwhite meant Black. When Mexican Americans and Puerto Ricans arrived in Grand Rapids in the 1940s and 1950s, respectively, they found a rigid Black/white binary and an uncertainty as to their place within it.

Colonialism, economic exploitation, and racism mitigated Latinxs' choice in picking Michigan as a place to make their home. When Mexican Americans from Texas were looking for work *al norte*, many desired an escape from a dual wage system, violence perpetrated against them, and a general discrimination that prevented them from equal access to quality schools, jobs, and housing.[12] In the 1920s, railroads were one of the most prominent ways Mexicans came to the Midwest. Rail lines went from central Mexico, to Texas, to Kansas City, to Chicago, and then to virtually anywhere in the Midwest. Those who took the lines to Grand Rapids found the reproduction of the dual wage system and that they were barred from the unions. Yet conditions were still better than they had been in Texas, and there were more opportunities to find other work.

Farmwork was the other way Mexican Americans came to Michigan. Since the 1920s, agricultural growers had sought workers to replace European immigrants who moved into industrial jobs. Growers began recruiting in Texas for people to work on sugar beet fields in eastern Michigan. Farmers in western Michigan also looked for people to plant and harvest apples, blueberries, and onions, among other crops. With few options in Texas, Tejanos came to Michigan and found arduous working conditions and low wages when they arrived.[13] During and after World War II, many Mexican American farmworkers across the country began looking for industrial jobs as well. This brought some folks to Grand Rapids. As some of them found low-skilled jobs in industry, a labor shortage emerged on Michigan fields.

Puerto Ricans filled that gap. By World War II, most of the island was in a desperate economic situation. The island's American administrators turned Puerto Rico, a colonial possession of the United States, into a sugar monocrop economy shortly after 1898. The Great Depression hit particularly hard, given the underdeveloped economy. Island administrators' plans for recovery were slow and uneven. Unemployment was close to 50 percent, and many people were threatened by starvation.[14] During World War II, Puerto Ricans successfully lobbied the War Manpower Commission to include them in its efforts to fill labor shortages around the country. Soon after, the Puerto Rican government engaged in a plan called Operation Airlift. Mainland growers, some in the Northeast and many in the Midwest, had labor needs to fill. In the early 1950s, planes full of Puerto Ricans made their way to the mainland. Workers who arrived in Michigan found the same poor working conditions as Mexican Americans did.[15] Like Tejanos, they left agricultural jobs in search of higher-paying industrial jobs. Some left Michigan and headed for Chicago, Cleveland, or New York, where many had family members. Some stayed in Michigan and went to Detroit and Grand Rapids.

When Mexicans and Puerto Ricans arrived in Grand Rapids, the economic environment offered more opportunities to them than in other places, but employers still assigned them the hardest, lowest-paying jobs. As the furniture industry waned, city planners worked to diversify their economic offerings. Grand Rapids, unlike Detroit nearby, never completely depended on auto manufacturing. There were several manufacturing companies that supported automotive production but could also be used to make other products. For Latinxs and for African Americans, the high-paying industrial jobs that were available during and after the war were largely off-limits. Compared to African Americans, who were strictly kept in "nonskilled" labor positions, such as janitors, there were a few Latinxs who were able to acquire some semi-skilled positions. However, those jobs had waned as well by the 1960s due to deindustrialization. The smaller size of the city also made accessing the rural peripheries a feasible option for people who wished to live in an urban area but still made their living doing agricultural work. Small nearby towns such as Hudsonville, Zeeland, Borculo, Grant, and Lowell offered agricultural work that many Latinxs used as a temporary way to earn money while dealing with layoffs or when in-between jobs. In some cases, women and children worked on fields all summer to make up for their family's budget shortfalls.[16] While not the best economic opportunities, there were enough job options for Latinxs to stay in Grand Rapids.

Racial and Social Obstacles to Living in the Midwest

Latinxs faced a number of challenges as they tried to settle into the Midwest that mostly rested on their racial ambiguity and clashes between their social norms and those that white Grand Rapidians practiced. Mexicans and Puerto Ricans, as well as African Americans, were often unwelcome in many of Grand Rapids's social spaces. They also faced difficulty in finding housing because of their racial and ethnic identity. White landlords, bar owners, and policemen scrutinized Latinxs' skin color, hair type, and accents to determine where they fit on a racial hierarchy that privileged whiteness and demonized Blackness and foreignness.

After companies recruited Latinxs to the area, the white majority tried to place them on the racial hierarchy. Examining police records of Mexican Americans from the 1940s illustrates this. Upon making an arrest, police noted the color (race) and complexion (skin color) of the detainee on the record. Albert Aguirre was described as being white in color but listed as having a "light chocolate" complexion. Other complexions listed for Mexican men included "medium copper," "light," "dark," "medium dark," "dark chestnut," "swarthy," "white," and simply "Mexican." After the cards only asked for the color or race of the arrested, the department listed them as "Brown" and "Mexican" and only occasionally as "Black."[17] All of this made it clear that the arresting officers were unsure exactly how Mexicans fit into their current understandings of race, but they knew Mexicans were not white in the same way that those of European descent were white.

Puerto Ricans with more apparent African ancestry found that they faced racism akin to that experienced by African Americans in Grand Rapids. My paternal grandmother, a Puerto Rican woman with light skin, and her husband, a Puerto Rican man who had dark skin, found their choices for apartments limited in Grand Rapids. De facto segregation meant that African Americans could only live in the southeast side of Grand Rapids. When my grandparents tried to find housing outside that area, they were rebuffed. This led my grandmother to take her light-skinned brother, who posed as her husband, and her light-skinned children with her to look for housing. She remarked that if you were "dark-skinned, you couldn't get an apartment" in 1955.[18] Other Afro–Puerto Ricans, such as the Sánchez family, who came to Michigan in the early 1950s, were often called "niggers" as they were turned away from potential houses.[19] Blackness was an indicator of inferiority in Grand Rapids. The Sánchezes' children also remembered that African American youth were confused as to why the Black newcomers did not speak English. When Mexican Americans and Puerto Ricans with lighter skin were turned away from housing it was due to xenophobia marked by their accents or inability to speak English. This discrimination led them to seek out places where they could avoid those kinds of interactions.

Limited housing options and a clash in social norms also made it difficult for Latinxs to enjoy themselves. For example, arrest records also reveal that leisure practices among Latinxs were not acceptable in Grand Rapids. Their racial and ethnic identity likely made them more of a target for policing as well. The majority of the arrest records for Mexicans and Puerto Ricans showed that the police arrested Latinxs for nonviolent crimes such as drinking in public and gambling. Since the first Latinxs often found housing in boardinghouses or by doubling up with relatives or new friends, living quarters were cramped and limited where people could spend leisure time together. Without many recreational spaces that welcomed them when they first arrived, many Latinx newcomers had to take their leisure practices to their porches and streets, making them more visible and vulnerable to policing. This furthered the need for these groups to have places for themselves outside of the purview of those who sought to relegate them to second-class citizenship.

Catholicism and Placemaking

Mexican and Puerto Rican Catholic devotion provided both a social space for Latinxs to interact and the beginnings of their own physical space in Grand Rapids. While the church has a history of encouraging immigrant assimilation, as recent research by Sergio González shows, it is also important to acknowledge the "power that religious devotion has had in fortifying struggles against the assimilatory pressures that nativist groups" deployed.[20] St. Andrew's Cathedral in Grand Rapids provided the space for Latinxs to reinforce their cultural identity. It was within walking distance of some of the first Latinx neighborhoods. By the mid-1940s, Mexican Catholics were holding their own services in the basement of St. Andrew's Cathedral.

Soon thereafter, the community started to create their own spaces and practices that catered to their needs. They raised funds to purchase a house next to the church to serve as the *capilla*, or chapel. At the urging of community leaders Daniel and Guadalupe Vargas, who came to Grand Rapids from Crystal City, Texas, and Daniel and Consuelo Vasquez, who were both Mexican and Mexican American, the diocese also formed an outreach branch called the Mexican Apostolate.[21] The Vargases and Vasquezes were some of the first Latinxs to settle in Grand Rapids and to take active roles in the community. Through securing a physical space and making their presence known to the diocese through the Mexican Apostolate, Mexican migrants shifted the landscape of Grand Rapids Catholicism to include them.

Eventually, in 1956, the diocese opted to call the capilla "the Mexican Chapel." Puerto Ricans arrived in the early 1950s, just a few years after the chapel opened. Some of them raised some opposition to naming their shared space after Mexicans only because it erased their presence and their cross ethnic cooperation. This did not stop Puerto Ricans from worshipping at the *capilla*, as Miguel Bérrios remembered during an oral history. He had arrived from Puerto Rico just a few years earlier as a child with his family.[22]

These types of negotiations did not negate their ability to engage with Latinx identity; instead, this discourse was a central part of the maneuvering of Spanish-speaking people in the United States as they formed new identities and maintained the identities with which they arrived.[23] Mexicans and Puerto Ricans went on to participate in dances and Christmas celebrations that the Mexican Apostolate held in the gymnasium at St. Andrew's School, located right near the church. The Latinx community also invited other non-Latinx Catholics and other Grand Rapidians to join them in dances that served as fundraisers. They ran ads in the *Grand Rapids Press* informing people about their upcoming cultural celebrations and the cost to participate.[24] Claiming physical space in Grand Rapids's Catholic landscape and inviting others to participate in it were signs that Latinos were invested in making a place for themselves in Grand Rapids.

Their daily interactions in the church and their choice to celebrate some of the most important parts of their lives within the church also show their commitment to transforming the space. The church's dedication to recording sacraments, such as those for marriage and baptism, has produced one of the richest archival databases on Latinx life in Grand Rapids. Marriage records hold a wealth of information that might not have been recorded elsewhere. For example, they include the date of a marriage, where the couple lived, the date and place of baptism, the pair's parents' names, and the names of their witnesses. In many cases, witnesses were usually friends or family of the couple, but some Mexican couples who migrated settled in areas without family members or friends nearby. Thus, they asked whoever was available in the church to serve as witnesses, and community leaders were often popular choices. For example, when Andrea Alvarado and Arturo Medina, a couple from Laredo, Texas, got married they chose Daniel and Guadalupe Vargas for witnesses. In fact, three other couples also chose the Vargases that year. In some cases, couples who were married on the same day served as witnesses for one another. When Florencio Paez of Flores, Mexico, and María Luisa Araisa were married, Gilberto García and Aurora González, who were also marrying that day, served as witnesses.[25] With a physical space to meet and forge bonds, Latinxs could formalize their friendships. This often served as the basis for deepening relationships with one another.

Reading baptism records against the grain revealed important demographic information about this budding community. Church officials recorded the location in which a child was born and when he or she was baptized. Knowing the location of where a child was born in the early 1950s helped me to deduce if the person being baptized was Mexican American or Puerto Rican. For example, if a child with a Spanish last name was born in Texas, I could deduce that he or she was Mexican American, given the history of the area. The insider knowledge that I have as a member of this community also helped me to determine if someone was Mexican or Puerto Rican. Various members of my family could confirm the ethnic identity of someone or put me in touch with someone who could help me based on the name of a particular historical actor I was researching. Understanding who was Puerto Rican and who was Mexican allows me to understand how these groups interacted with one another as well.

Baptism and godparent relationships in particular served as a formal way of creating new networks that reached across ethnic lines. In the Catholic tradition, a couple chooses godparents as a symbolic and meaningful gesture, since the parents and the godparents will become *compadres*.[26] This term describes the unique bond that links these two families in a semifamilial relationship. Social scientists have found that "choosing someone, especially a nonrelative, to serve as *compadre* or *comadre* [godparents] to one's child is considered a way to cement close friendships and make a public statement regarding the importance of the friendship."[27] This act also worked as an incentive for people to stay in Grand Rapids and to continue to shape it to their needs. As newcomers to an area, these types of bonds made living in an inhospitable location away from family and friends more endurable. Traditionally, godparents are supposed to help the parents ensure that the child learns the traditions and rules of the church. Whether or not this happened was not as important as the relationships that grew out of these arrangements, as they likely sustained these people as they continuously worked to make their new home more familiar.

Though it took some time to emerge, eventually Mexicans and Puerto Ricans saw the value in choosing cross-ethnic godparents. For example, baptism records also show how the Puerto Rican and Mexican communities slowly warmed up to one another. In the early 1950s, when Puerto Ricans trickled into the area, Mexicans chose Mexican godparents and Puerto Ricans chose Puerto Rican godparents for their children. Both groups chose well-respected people in the community. For example, Arnulfo and Josefina Colunga served as godparents for four Mexican American children unrelated to them. Though Puerto Ricans stuck to their Puerto Rican friends and family at first, they began to choose Mexican American godparents for their children. Mexican pioneer Daniel Vasquez was godfather to Puerto Rican Carlos Ayala. His parents, Santurino and Priscilla, chose a Puerto Rican godmother for him. In addition, Puerto Ricans Leopoldo and Guadalupe Figueroa chose Mexican Gregorio Chavez and Leopoldo's sister, Santa Sanchez, as godparents for their son. Chavez was very helpful in assisting Santa Sanchez and her husband, Paco, settle in Grand Rapids.[28] These godparent choices were evidence of the budding friendships people formed and the need for cross-ethnic networks in a place with a small Latinx population.

Leisure and Making Space into Latino Place

To live full lives in Grand Rapids, Mexicans and Puerto Ricans found themselves wanting more than just work and worship. For almost thirty years, a dance hall was home to Latinx celebrations and recreation, though it was not technically a space of their own. During oral history interviews, many Mexicans and Puerto Ricans alike remembered going to dances at the Roma Hall. The Italian-owned dance hall had long served the African American community and hosted jazz concerts as early as the 1920s and 1930s. By the 1950s, Latinxs were the next to find the Roma Hall a safe place for recreation. Located at Division and Wealthy, it was situated at the border of the southwest-side and southeast-side neighborhoods, making it easily accessible to most of the community. While African Americans and Latinxs might have attended each other's events at the Roma Hall with a date perhaps, many of the gatherings at this venue were specific to each community when the dances first began. Perhaps it was because the musical acts that Latinxs brought sang in Spanish or the communities were still figuring out how to interact with one another in a place that often saw them as separate, but Roma Hall events that Latinxs hosted often catered to Latinxs only, though this included Afro-Latinos.

To bring Mexicans and Puerto Ricans together also took some compromises, but learning new dances and dancing alongside each other contributed to building their intraethnic network. The very first dances relied on the talent within the community. Cruzita Gomez, who arrived in the early 1950s from East Chicago, remembers family bands as the only musical option available. The Ortega, Rincones, and Castillo families were largely responsible for bringing the population to their feet to the tunes of Tejano and *conjunto* music. While the crowd was both Mexican and Puerto Rican, the music did not reflect this mixture. At times, the bands could only play Mexican music. Cruzita, who was Mexican American but whose husband was Puerto Rican, recalls them trying "a little mambo."[29] They could not replicate the Puerto Rican music her husband, Pete, enjoyed. However, they both remembered a mixed crowd that tried to pick up the steps to the Mexican dances and have a good time. In the late 1960s and early 1970s, as the Puerto Rican population grew, the community was able to bring in Puerto Rican bands from Chicago and New York. Though Mexicans and Puerto Ricans had two different musical traditions, perhaps the rhythms and languages of the songs and likely a lack of other recreational activities brought them together on weekend nights.

Having an opportunity to hear Spanish in movies created another site of placemaking that Latinxs remembered fondly. Within a few years of settling in Grand Rapids, Mexican Americans began to find ways to bring Mexican movies to their new home in Michigan. Snippets from 1950s newspaper articles in the *Grand Rapids Press* revealed that Latinxs frequented theaters that showed films in Spanish. A small exposé-style piece on the "new" Mexican American community listed a number of amenities that the migrants had created for themselves in Michigan, including getting a movie theater to show Mexican films.[30] Oral histories with the community documented how María Aguilar's mother-in-law, Aurora Chavez, periodically ordered movies from Mexico to show at the Liberty Movie Theater.

While the difference in Spanish dialect and focus on Mexican culture in these films could have put off Puerto Ricans, many of them availed themselves of this cultural resource to enjoy themselves in a language they could understand. Many Latinxs had no choice in trying to learn English, given the limited availability of Spanish speakers in many of their daily interactions with people in Grand Rapids. For many, one to two hours of Spanish regardless of dialect might have been a welcome respite from having to translate all day long.[31] Puerto Rican Rosa Pérez, who came to Grand Rapids via Chicago, remembers frequenting the movie theaters with her female friends before she got married.[32] The Mexican American and Puerto Rican Gomez family usually went to the Town Theater on Grand Rapids's northwest side. The popularity of this pastime led other theaters to begin showing movies as well.[33] Though Grand Rapids was hardly like South Texas or Puerto Rico, these brief moments helped to make these communities feel at home.

Oral histories of baseball games in the Latinx community are some of the only documentation for one of the first organized Latinx sports leagues and another sign of placemaking. After mass at Our Lady of Guadalupe, many members of the congregation met at Rumsey Park, on the southwest side of Grand Rapids. Previously it was home to residents of the Dutch neighborhood, but as they left it became a visible Latinx recreational space. The "Spanish league," which was originally made up of all-male Mexican baseball teams, traveled to different areas in West Michigan to play against other Mexicans as early as the 1940s.[34] María Aguilar remembered watching her brothers and her in-laws play together. In the early 1950s, Puerto Ricans joined the other Spanish-speaking players on the Grand Rapids team.[35] The team was relatively open to accepting new players considering the talent that was coming its way. Many of the Puerto Ricans, including Juan Baez and Pete Gomez, had experience playing baseball competitively. For example, higher pay and less arduous work made Lake Odessa attractive, but the company baseball team also played a part in Baez's decision to leave the sugar-beet fieldsin Saginaw. Pete Gomez played in several leagues in East Chicago, Indiana, and he still boasts about his days playing against Orestes "Minnie" Miñoso, who later became a legendary Chicago White Sox player. As the Latino population grew, so did the team. Players were coming not only from the *capilla* but also through connections built at work or in the neighborhoods. Women carved out a niche for themselves at these games as well. There were no women baseball players, but many women used these games to earn money. An oral history with Juan Báez, who played in those games, revealed that my maternal grandmother, Luisa Fernández, who lived three blocks from the park, made and sold *alcapurrias*, a traditional Puerto Rican food, to the Puerto Rican and Mexican crowd.[36] Other women sold beverages and candies.[37] Through these baseball games people strengthened their communities by forming both economic and social bonds.

Lastly, photos, newspaper articles, and oral histories showed how Latinos occupied the most public and visible space in Grand Rapids through their celebration of Mexican festivals—though Puerto Ricans were a constant presence. From the organizers to the participants, these festivals were a pan-Latino event. The Mexican Patriotic Committee (MPC) was responsible for putting on celebrations of the feast day of Our Lady of Guadalupe and Mexican Independence Day held in downtown Grand Rapids. Although the name might suggest otherwise, Puerto Ricans were very much a part of this celebration. Julio Vega was one of the first Puerto Ricans to come to the area, and it is no surprise that he felt comfortable in spaces with Mexicans. They were probably the first ones to welcome him alongside other Puerto Ricans. Vega even joined the MPC.[38]

It is likely that he was not the only Puerto Rican to go to these events. It would have been commonplace for even the recently arrived Puerto Ricans to take part in Mexican celebrations as early as the 1950s in Grand Rapids. As the Puerto Rican community grew, their participation in these events only increased. Leah Tobar, a Puerto Rican woman who was married to a Mexican man, also joined the MPC in the late 1960s.[39] In addition, Puerto Rican girls learned both traditional Puerto Rican dances and Mexican dances. For example, my Puerto Rican aunts Nilda and Virginia Fernández danced to Mexican folkloric routines alongside their Mexican and Puerto Ricans friends in the mid-1960s during an independence parade. Puerto Rican festivalgoers even brought their Puerto Rican flags with them to this Mexican cultural event. With these celebrations, Mexicans and Puerto Ricans together created public displays that claimed Grand Rapids as their home.[40]

Intermarriage as MexiRican Placemaking

Time together at church, dances, and festivals allowed people to get to know each other and to develop romantic relationships. These Mexican–Puerto Rican marriages provide further evidence of the similar position that these two groups occupied in the local social and racial hierarchy.[41] The discourse around these marriages from the couples' families and friends reveals the negotiations behind the intellectual placemaking that happens when people come together and share their lives with one another. While this happened at a lesser rate than endogamous marriages, these examples had a profound effect on the dynamics among Latinxs in the city. These couples facilitated Latinx placemaking. By virtue of wanting places for their friends and family to hang out together, they created shared Latinx spaces.

Most of these romantic unions developed in the workplace. For example, Mexican Americans Angelita Arizola and Rosa Vasquez and Puerto Ricans

Marcial Hernández and Juan Vasquez met each other on farms in Lake Odessa, about thirty miles east of Grand Rapids. All four of them followed a similar migration pattern from the island or Texas to other Michigan agricultural towns and finally arrived in Grand Rapids. The women's families were originally from Texas and had come north as migrant workers.[42] For example, the Arizolas began bringing their nine children with them to Michigan in the 1930s and decided to settle in the North in the late 1940s, though many of Angelita's siblings continued to do migrant farmwork with their own families.[43] Marcial Hernández and Juan Báez came from Puerto Rico to harvest sugar beets in Michigan. Fields became shared spaces where these two groups encountered one another. Farms were not the only place where people met, however. For example, Amelia Silva and Juan Báez lived in a boardinghouse next to their manufacturing factory. Silva and other Mexican American women lived on the third floor, while Báez and other Puerto Rican men lived on the first floor.

Reactions to these relationships often rested on colorism among Latinxs. Amelia Silva's father, for example, never quite supported his daughter's choice in a husband. Perhaps Domingo Silva thought Juan Báez's clear African ancestry thwarted Silva's pursuit of whiteness and full acceptance of his Mexican American family. Though Amelia's MexiRican children never felt any particular poor treatment from their grandfather, this revealed the underlying tension that race played among Latinxs. Domingo Silva might have preferred that his daughter marry someone lighter in hopes that she would be able to get ahead because whiteness was so valued. Given the long history of *blanqueamiento,* or the pursuit of whitening, in a family over time among Mexican Americans and Latinxs in general and the better treatment that went along with it, these notions were commonplace at the time.[44] As well, during the 1950s, assimilation was the preferred method of social mobility among Mexican Americans, though later they focused on embracing indigeneity, or *mestizaje,* as seen in the Chicano movement. That Amelia did not hold these thoughts herself shows that some Mexican Americans made choices to not engage with the racial hierarchies that were so prevalent in the country. Labor migration, housing patterns, and recreational options put Amelia in regular contact with Puerto Ricans and other Mexican Americans in Grand Rapids, yet she still chose Juan. Their coming together is a testament to the bonds that these communities formed in the face of various factors that could have put distance between them.

These marriages only furthered the contact that Mexicans and Puerto Ricans had with one another and the friendships they formed. Angelita Arizola and Marcial Hernández's marriage is evidence of this. They belonged to large Mexican and Puerto Rican families in Grand Rapids. After they were married, their in-laws formed relationships and brought their other friends into

FIGURE 4.1. *From left to right*, the author's Mexican American aunt Lucinda Murillo sits with neighbors Wanda and Karen Vega, who are Puerto Rican. The author's Mexican American mother, Amelia Murillo, sits beside Karen on the far right. Wanda is holding the Murillo sisters' newborn niece, Priscilla, who happens to be MexiRican (1971). Personal collection of the author.

the fold, helping to shape the camaraderie that would further develop Latinx placemaking. Puerto Rican Pete Gómez, a close friend of Marcial, recalled that the Hernández-Arizola marriage allowed him to become close friends with Marcial's brother-in-law, Pete Arizola. They soon found themselves hanging out at bars or after community baseball games without Marcial or Angelita. These marriages were not always without protest, but the Arizola-Hernández children did not recall any lasting ill feelings about the intraethnic pairing.

These couples were important not only because they crossed ethnic lines among Latinxs but also because their children represented the forging of a new ethnic identity: MexiRicans. The presence of MexiRicans in Grand Rapids as early as the 1950s and early 1960s represents how West Michigan and the Midwest served as prime locations for intraethnic interaction. The relationships that Latinxs facilitated with one another at work, in their neighborhoods, and mostly at church helped to create these opportunities. Growing up, their families exposed their MexiRican children to both ethnicities, and as adults they continued to self-identify as MexiRican. "I don't feel more Mexican or Puerto Rican, I'm MexiRican," Rafael Hernández, Marcial and Angelita's son, explained. Juan and Amelia's daughter, Carolina Báez Anderson, also agreed that though she did not grow up in a Latinx neighborhood she felt equally Mexican and Puerto Rican.

Mexican and Puerto Rican couples also provided the structure necessary to unite the larger communities. For example, in organizing this community to fight against discrimination in the 1970s, the Mexican–Puerto Rican couple Cruzita and Pete Gómez played instrumental roles in accessing both Mexican and Puerto Rican social networks for voting drives and organizing boycotts. This became increasingly important as the city began to grow and the older, first-generation families were no longer the only Latinxs present. Both Pete and Cruzita bridged gaps and showed both groups what they had in common through their shared obstacles.

Conclusion

I am not sure if my grandparents ever intended on returning "home" when they left for Michigan. This is often a sentiment that many migrants and immigrants express. The conditions they left behind and the better but not perfect job opportunities in Grand Rapids gave them and people like them a reason to stay. The discrimination they faced in housing and recreation might have given them pause in regard to thinking about staying, but the community they helped to found might have also persuaded them to stay. Within a decade of their arrival, they and their compatriots created places in Grand Rapids to worship, dance, watch movies, play baseball, and enjoy each other's company. Through founding their own church, borrowing other spaces such as theaters and dance halls, and making claims on public spaces such as baseball parks, Mexicans and Puerto Ricans, my grandparents included, made Grand Rapids their home.

Surely, the circumstances in Grand Rapids helped to facilitate this process. The rigid cultural norms in the area helped Mexicans and Puerto Ricans see the similarities they had with one another vis-à-vis the differences they both had with the more reserved Dutch population and others who ascribed to their mores. However, Mexicans' and Puerto Ricans' agency in making these decisions also deserves attention in this analysis. The pan-Latinx sensibilities these individuals held allowed these types of arrangements to blossom. While national pride could have limited their interactions, Latinx identity actually makes room for the duality of holding both national identities and pan-Latinx identities. This is most easily seen in the MexiRican children of this generation and beyond, but we can also see glimpses of this as Puerto Ricans went to Mexican festivals or Mexicans volunteered to serve as *padrinos* for Puerto Rican children and become *compadres* with the children's parents.

The narratives of this early community were not readily available but instead needed to be excavated among larger histories of the Midwest and histories of Grand Rapids to show that Latinxs have long worked to make this area a home. This process would not have been possible without the deliberate acts of documenting Latinx lives in Grand Rapids. As a researcher, I am grateful to the historians and their students who carried out oral histories with Grand Rapids's first Latinx residents. The library volunteers who picked out newspaper articles on Latinxs and pulled together a sparse but growing Latinos in the Midwest Collection at the Grand Rapids Public Library have been incredibly important to this project. The archivists who saved jail records for future researchers have also made it possible to document this early community. Carrying out oral histories with migrants who remained to tell their story and the children of the first generation has saved a history that has been erased in the narratives of Grand Rapids, Michigan, and the Midwest. Lastly, I must also acknowledge that the very act of assembling and reading the archive and of writing this chapter and other written projects serves as another form of documenting and preserving a history that could easily remain hidden or even be erased. Moreover, these actions help to show Latinxs in Grand Rapids, in Michigan, and in the Midwest currently and those to come that they too have a claim to these areas and that they come from a long line of people who have worked to make that true.

The earliest generations of Latinxs built an environment where pan-Latinx relationships were welcomed and encouraged and that generally became the norm for more contemporary Latinxs living in Grand Rapids. This is evident in that the number of everyday acts of placemaking discussed in this chapter grew exponentially, as did the population of Latinxs in the late 1960s and 1970s to the present day. Though they numbered in the hundreds at midcentury, by the late 1980s, there were almost twenty thousand Latinxs in Grand Rapids.[45] Mexican Americans and nationals made up 60 percent of the Latinx population, followed by Puerto Ricans at 16 percent, Cubans at 7 percent, and a variety of other ethnic groups at 18 percent. In the present, Latinxs make up about 15 percent of the population in Grand Rapids. More interesting, however, is that Grand Rapids is home to at least a small percentage of Mexicans, Puerto Ricans, Cubans, Dominicans, and Guatemalans.[46] Midwestern destinations in general and Grand Rapids specifically have consistently been places that Latinxs transformed into home. In studying a diverse community of Latinxs in Grand Rapids, the second largest city in Michigan, we reshape the misconception that Latinxs are new to this area and are devoid of contributions to a place that is often billed as an up-and-coming city.[47] Examining this smaller city also allows us to see both the racialization and marginalization of Latinxs, as well as the tactics they used to create communities to combat such forces.

The bonds that Mexicans and Puerto Ricans forged in the 1940s and the 1950s sustained their shared efforts in the fight to create a place for themselves amid discrimination in Grand Rapids. As the community grew toward the end of the twentieth century, the work of earlier decades laid the groundwork for the community to now enjoy multiple recreational venues, churches, neighborhoods, sports leagues, and bars and clubs, among other spaces. Though all of these spaces exist, you can still find Latinxs in their backyards on suburban streets or on front porches in the city center during Michigan's warm summers. These not-so-public gatherings remain ways of reinforcing the idea that Latinxs belong there and wherever they settle. As chapters in this volume show, Latinxs in Grand Rapids are not alone. In East Chicago, Milwaukee, Ohio, and across the Midwest, Latinxs have persistently created ways of belonging and defending their communities. In the face of resurgent anti-Latinx sentiments, these human acts of joining one another in a backyard for dominoes in 2016 or watching a movie in a language they understood in 1957 hold the same capacity to give people dignity in a locale that affords them very little and to sustain them as they create a sense of belonging in a place that has become their home.

Notes

1. Portions of this chapter first appeared in Delia Fernandez, "Becoming Latino: Mexican and Puerto Rican Community Formation in Grand Rapids, Michigan, 1926–1964," *Michigan Historical Review* 39, no. 1 (2013): 71–100. Reprinted with permission.

2. Mérida Rúa, "Colao Subjectivities: PortoMex and MexiRican Perspectives on Language and Identity," *Centro Journal*, no. 2 (2001): 13.

3. Balassiano and Maldonado, "Placemaking"; Lara, *Latino Placemaking and Planning*.

4. See Frances Aparicio, afterword in Fox, Valerio-Jiménez, and Vaquera-Vásquez, *The Latina/o Midwest Reader*; and Aparicio, *Negotiating Latinidad*; both point to Chicago, a large urban metropolis, as a place that brings various Latino ethnic groups together. However, part of my argument is that labor recruitment is at the core of why people have come to share space. That can happen in both large and small areas alike, as it has in Grand Rapids and likely other smaller, more rural areas.

5. A selected list of Latinx Midwest histories includes Gabriela Arredondo, *Mexican Chicago: Race, Identity, and Nation, 1916–1939* (Urbana: University of Illinois Press, 2003); Fernández, *Brown in the Windy City*; Eileen Findlay, *We Are Left without a Father Here: Masculinity, Domesticity, and Migration in Postwar Puerto Rico* (Dur-

ham, NC: Duke University Press, 2014); Dennis Nodin Valdes, *Al Norte: Agricultural Workers in the Great Lakes Region, 1917–1970* (Austin: University of Texas Press, 1991); Rodriguez, *The Tejano Diaspora*; Felipe Hinojosa, *Latino Mennonites: Civil Rights, Faith, and Evangelical Culture* (Baltimore, MD: Johns Hopkins University Press, 2014). Relevant work in other disciplines includes Pérez, *The Near Northwest Side Story*; Rúa, *A Grounded Identitad.*

6. Balassiano and Maldonado, "Placemaking."

7. Lara, *Latino Placemaking and Planning*, 30.

8. David Gutiérrez, *Walls and Mirrors: Mexican Americans, Mexican Immigrants, and the Politics of Ethnicity* (Berkeley: University of California Press, 1995); George J. Sanchez, *Becoming Mexican American: Ethnicity, Culture, and Identity in Chicano Los Angeles, 1900–1945* (New York: Oxford University Press, 1993); Virginia Sánchez Korrol, *From Colonia to Community: The History of Puerto Ricans in New York City* (Berkeley: University of California Press, 1994); Valdes, *Al Norte*; Valdés, *Barrios Norteños.* Though there are not many historical studies on Mexicans and Puerto Ricans beyond Valdes's *Al Norte* and Fernández's *Brown in the Windy City*, there are many scholars who have looked at Mexican and Puerto Rican pan-Latino relations in the contemporary period. See Frances R. Aparicio, "Not Fully Boricuas: Puerto Rican Intralatino/as in Chicago," *Centro Journal; New York* 28, no. 2 (Fall 2016): 154–79; Angie Chabram-Dernersesian, "Growing Up Mexi-Rican: Remembered Snapshots of Life in La Puente," *Latino Studies* 7, no. 3 (2009): 378; De Genova and Ramos-Zayas, *Latino Crossings*; Lorena García and Mérida Rúa, "Processing Latinidad: Mapping Latino Urban Landscapes through Chicago Ethnic Festivals," *Latino Studies*, no. 3 (Autumn 2007): 317–39; Padilla, *Latino Ethnic Consciousness*; Rúa, "Colao Subjectivities."

9. Miroslava Chávez-García, *Negotiating Conquest: Gender and Power in Alta California, 1770s–1880s* (Tucson: University of Arizona Press, 2004); Vicki Ruiz, *From out of the Shadows: Mexican Women in Twentieth-Century America* (New York: Oxford University Press, 2008).

10. James D. Bratt, *Dutch Calvinism in Modern America: A History of a Conservative Subculture* (Grand Rapids, MI: W. B. Eerdmans Pub. Co., 1984).

11. Todd Robinson, *A City within a City: The Black Freedom Struggle in Grand Rapids* (Philadelphia: Temple University Press, 2012), ix. For more on African Americans in Grand Rapids, see Randal Maurice Jelks, *African Americans in the Furniture City: The Struggle for Civil Rights in Grand Rapids* (Urbana: University of Illinois Press, 2006).

12. William D. Carrigan and Clive Webb, *Forgotten Dead: Mob Violence against Mexicans in the United States, 1848–1928* (Oxford: Oxford University Press, 2013).

13. While repatriation threatened Mexicans and Mexican Americans alike around the country, including Detroit, the threat in Grand Rapids was not the same. I have found no evidence of Mexican repatriation in the city in jail records, deportation lists, newspaper articles, or oral histories. In fact, the only time there is a mention of immigration law and ethnic Mexicans came when a Mexican man cohabitated with a white woman in the 1930s. That man was held on an immigration violation in addition to a lewd and lascivious cohabitation charge.

14. James Dietz, *Economic History of Puerto Rico: Institutional Change and Capitalist Development* (Princeton, NJ: Princeton University Press, 1986), 111.

15. Findlay, *We Are Left Here*, 118–47.

16. Delia Fernández, "Rethinking the Urban and Rural Divide in Latino Labor, Recreation, and Activism in West Michigan, 1940s–1970s," *Labor History* 57, no. 4 (2016): 482–503.

17. Albert Aguirre, Ysmael Flores, Epitosio Duarte, Joseph Zaragosa, and Joseph Valdez, box 1–4, CA, 1924–61, 1913–74, Fingerprint Cards, Police Records Division, Grand Rapids City Archives (GRCA).

18. Luisa Fernández, interview with Kate Schramm, Grand Rapids, MI, 2001, Latinos in Western Michigan, Grand Rapids History & Special Collections, Grand Rapids Public Library (GRPL).

19. Ruben Sanchez, interview with author, Kissimmee, FL, 2017.

20. Sergio M. González, "Interethnic Catholicism and Transnational Religious Connections: Milwaukee's Mexican Mission Chapel of Our Lady of Guadalupe, 1924–1929," *Journal of American Ethnic History* 36, no. 1 (2016): 5. See also Anne Martinez, *Catholic Borderlands: Mapping Catholicism onto American Empire, 1905–1935* (Lincoln: University of Nebraska Press, 2014).

21. Guadalupe Vargas, interview with Gordon Olson, Grand Rapids, MI, 1997, Latinos in Western Michigan, Grand Rapids History & Special Collections, GRPL.

22. Miguel Bérrios, interview with author, Grand Rapids, MI, 2021.

23. For a discussion on how Latinxs maintain multiple identities that are not in conflict with one another, see Juan Flores, "Latino Imaginary: Dimensions of Community and Identity," in Aparicio and Chávez-Silverman, *Tropicalizations*.

24. "Mexicans Find a New Home," *Grand Rapids Press*, February 2, 1956, 13.

25. Mexican Apostolate, Marriage Records, April 1949, St. Andrew's Cathedral, Diocese of Grand Rapids (DOGR).

26. *Compadrazgo* has served as an effective way to build social networks since colonial Latin America to the present. In colonial Latin America, slaves used the practice of choosing godparents to connect their children to prominent members of their communities. For more information on godparents in colonial Latin America, see David Stark, "Parish Registers as a Window to the Past: Reconstructing the Demographic Behavior of the Enslaved Population in Eighteenth-Century Arecibo, Puerto Rico," *Colonial Latin American Historical Review* 15 (Winter 2006): 1–30; Stuart Schwartz, *Slaves, Peasants, and Rebels: Reconsidering Brazilian Slavery* (Urbana: University of Illinois Press, 1992). In the present, sociologists and anthropologists have examined how immigrants in the United States and communities around Latin America utilize *compadrazgo* to gain social capital. For more information on US immigrants, see Helen Rose Ebaugh and Mary Curry, "Fictive Kin as Social Capital in New Immigrant Communities," *Sociological Perspectives* 43, no. 2 (2000). For information on urban Mexican *compadrazgo*, see Robert V. Kemper, "The Compadrazgo in Urban Mexico," *Anthropological Quarterly* 55, no. 1 (1982): 17–30. Some sociologists have examined the impact of interethnic *compadrazgo* through examining Indigenous communities. See Jerome M. Levi, "Hidden Transcripts among the Rarámuri: Culture, Resistance,

and Interethnic Relations in Northern Mexico," *American Ethnologist* 26, no. 1 (1999): 90–113.

27. Ebaugh and Curry, "Fictive Kin," 196.

28. María del Carmen Chappa, Juan de la Cruz, Linda Monsalvo, María de Jesus Ruiz, Carlos Ayala, Santiago Figueroa, and Carlos Sanchez, Baptism Records, 1952–57, St. Andrew's Cathedral, DOGR.

29. "Roma Hall Story," West Michigan Music Historical Society: An Interactive Archival Database for West Michigan Music History, http://www.westmichmusic hystericalsociety.com/roma-hall-story/; Santos Rincones, interview with Gordon Olson, Grand Rapids, MI, Latinos in Western Michigan, Grand Rapids History & Special Collections, GRPL; Marilyn Vega, interview with author, Grand Rapids, MI, October 10, 2013; Cruzita Gómez, interview with author, Grand Rapids, MI, 2011; Simon Aguilar, interview with author, Grand Rapids, MI, 2014.

30. "Mexicans Find a New Home."

31. Rosa Pérez, interview with author, Grand Rapids, MI, 2011.

32. Pérez interview. See also Elizabeth Escobedo, *From Coveralls to Zoot Suits: The Lives of Mexican American Women on the World War II Home Front* (Chapel Hill: University of North Carolina Press, 2013); and Ruíz, *From out of the Shadows*, 51–71.

33. Pedro and Cruzita Gómez, interview with author, Grand Rapids, MI, 2013.

34. Ibid.

35. Maria Ysasi, interview with author, Grand Rapids, MI, 2012.

36. Juan Báez, interview with author, Grand Rapids, MI, 2011.

37. Ibid.

38. Photos, Latinos in Western Michigan Collection, GRPL; photos, collection of author.

39. Lea Tobar, interviews with author, Grand Rapids, 2012, 2015.

40. Photos, Latinos in Western Michigan Collection, GRPL; photos, collection of author.

41. It is also important to note that many of these marriages were between Puerto Rican men and Mexican American women. This gender and ethnicity pattern is likely due to these groups' migratory trends. Puerto Rican men often came to West Michigan as bachelors, while Mexican Americans came in a familial unit. Some of the earlier Puerto Rican–Mexican marriages were between Puerto Rican men and women who traveled to Michigan with their parents and siblings. Mexican and Puerto Rican marriages far outnumbered other endogamous unions. In comparison, Mexican and white intermarriage occurred at lower rates, and Puerto Rican and Black marriages occurred even less frequently.

42. "Year: 1940; Census Place: Gillespie, Texas; Roll: m-t0627-04040; Page: 10B; Enumeration District: 86-5"; Ancestry.com, 1940 United States Federal Census; United States of America, Bureau of the Census, *Sixteenth Census of the United States, 1940* (Washington, DC: National Archives and Records Administration, 1940), T627.

43. Rafael Hernández, interview with author, Grand Rapids, MI, 2013.

44. Carolina Baez Anderson, interview with author, Grand Rapids, MI, 2013. The long history of race and whiteness among Mexican Americans deserves a full review,

which is not possible in this chapter. Please see the following works that detail this dynamic, including my forthcoming book manuscript, which discusses this as it pertains to Grand Rapids. For a very detailed overview of this process in New Mexico immediately following the Mexican-American War, see Laura E. Gómez, *Manifest Destinies: The Making of the Mexican American Race* (New York: New York University Press, 2008). For other examinations, see Neil Foley, *Quest for Equality: The Failed Promise of Black-Brown Solidarity* (Cambridge, MA: Harvard University Press, 2010); and Foley, *The White Scourge: Mexicans, Blacks, and Poor Whites in Texas Cotton Culture* (Berkeley: University of California Press, 1997).

45. Jim Mercanelli, "A Story of Pride and Hope," *Grand Rapids Press*, July 27, 1986.

46. United States Census Bureau, Distribution of Hispanic or Latino Population by Specific Origin: 2010, September 30, 2013, https://www.census.gov/dataviz/visualizations/072/.

47. Ehren Wynder, "Grand Rapids Rates as One of the Best Places to Live in U.S.," *Grand Rapids Business Journal*, October 8, 2020.

CHAPTER 5

A Chicagolandia Zine Community

ARIANA RUIZ

Night winds scatter papers
like malignant leaves through gutters
broken glass glitters
like old discarded jewels
under harsh street lights
turning vacant lots
into treasure chests of debris
—Salima Rivera, "Pilsen"

In 1982 *ECOS: A Latino Journal of People's Culture & Literature* published the first of its series *Chicago: Nosotros/Nosotras*, which focused on literary work by Latinas/os in Chicago.[1] Inspired by and taking its name from *Revista Chicano-Riqueña*'s 1977 collection of Chicago-based Latina/o cultural production, the *ECOS* series aimed to "focus and foster Chicago perspectives and dimensions of Latinidad."[2] In their scope and dissemination, both projects sought to establish a Latinx literary and visual tradition rooted in Chicago and, in the case of *Revista Chicano-Riqueña*, inform a national readership of the diversity within Chicago's Chicano and Puerto Rican experiences. As *Revista Chicano-Riqueña* and the *ECOS* staff imply, Latinas/os in the Midwest were underrepresented within the larger Latina/o imaginary and thus in need of being not only written into but also circulated out to the national cultural landscape.

Chicago: Nosotros/Nosotras included the poetry of (now) widely recognized writer Sandra Cisneros and multimedia artist Carlos Cortez alongside writing by less well known artists including but not limited to Marcela Licea and Salima Rivera. With titles such as "South Sangamon" (Cisneros), "18th & Wood" (Licea), and "Pilsen" (Rivera), the contributors to *Chicago: Nosotros/ Nosotras* were not only writing as Latinas/os from Chicago but also mapping their *latinidades* onto specific Chicago neighborhoods.[3] Moreover, as is evident in the work of Salima Rivera referenced in the epigraph above, 1980s Black and Brown Chicago, including Pilsen, is socioeconomically neglected.

Nicholas De Genova and Ana Y. Ramos-Zayas note that in the 1970s (a decade before Rivera published "Pilsen") "Pilsen was the only Chicago neighborhood where Latinos constituted an absolute majority."[4] Pilsen was also among the most underresourced neighborhoods, ranking among the bottom fifth of the city's most impoverished areas at this time. And while city officials ignored the sizable Mexican community, the land that makes up Pilsen was seen (and continues to be seen) as prime property for city developers. As Wilfredo Cruz writes, "Since the 1970s . . . [r]esidents feared private developers were turning the neighborhood into an artists' colony for middle-class, white professionals who are displacing working-class Mexicans."[5] Salima Rivera reflects on these issues when describing families gathered on front stoops watching children play in open fire hydrants and goes on to exclaim: "Pilsen they say you're a slum."[6] The "they" Rivera refers to are outsiders to the community, those with the ability and power to name Pilsen a slum (landlords, land developers, city officials, etc.). As such, Rivera's personal observations are important counternarratives to these outsiders' assumptions. She is careful not to obscure or romanticize the socioeconomic hardships of the community and instead places their adversity among the quotidian practices of the neighborhood's residents. Writing from within, as Rivera and the other *Chicago: Nosotros/Nosotras* contributors do, offers firsthand accounts of Latina/o experiences and historicizes ongoing struggles for social justice and visibility in Chicago, the Midwest, and the United States at large.[7]

It is within this activist Latina/o literary tradition that I locate the contemporary Latinx zine community. I am specifically interested in placing Chicago's Latinx zine culture within a larger history of alternative Latinx print culture to address how it is informed by its precursors. Zines provide a unique space for Latinx recognition in that they connect individuals and their stories to a collective that reaffirms and reimagines the creative sites where Latinx cultural identity is lived. Such an analysis also renders the way Latinx trouble and constitute zine communities in Chicago and extend perceptions of Latinx activism through print. Indeed, Latinx zinesters not only create material worlds but also help shape the social character of their physical and print communities. While *Revista Chicano-Riqueña* and *ECOS* had institutional support and some financial backing (as opposed to a majority of self-financed zines), their inception in and engagement with the Midwest, promotion of Latina/o artists from Chicago, inclusion of activist-focused rhetoric, and modest circulation make them an apt entry point for analysis of Chicago-based Latinx creative placemaking practices in zine culture and community.[8]

I begin my analysis by describing the national (US) and regional (midwestern) Latina/o independent press tradition in which I see Chicago's Latinx zines thematically and aesthetically emerge. My guiding question is, How do Latinx zinesters and audiences claim and/or create space in Chicago's zine scene?[9] I address this by considering some of the creative placemaking practices of Latinx zinesters in Chicago, specifically through a case study on the work by Oscar Arriola and CHema Skandal!, co-organizers of Chicago-based zine festival #ZINEmercado. In doing so, I seek to portray the ways Chicago's Latinx zinesters contest, represent, and circulate local identity at various geographic scales (locally, regionally, nationally, and internationally) and thereby enrich and diversify the story of Latinx communities in the Midwest. Ultimately, I read zines (and zine communities) as material sites where placemaking occurs through networked communication; a conglomerate of rhetorical elements from disparate places/times/sources; sites of activity, such as the bookstores or archives, that activate practices of collecting and engagement with print culture; and festival sites that (if temporarily) amplify the reach of these print objects into expanded cultural platforms.

An Alternative Lens: Latinx Print Culture

Stephen Duncombe defines zines, which emerged out of the alternative press, as "noncommercial, nonprofessional, small-circulation magazines which their creators produce, publish, and distribute themselves."[10] And while technologies of print have given rise to digitally produced zines, they are still typically found in analog form. Furthermore, as Duncombe later notes, "any effort to classify and codify them [zines] immediately reveals shortcomings."[11] Nevertheless, he goes on to note a series of broad categories, including the usual suspects described below, as well as "fringe culture zines," "health zines," and "comix."[12] As such, rather than speak of categorizations or specific genre conventions that zines may or may not perform, zines are read as engagements in expression, sharing, and communication.[13] As illustrated documents, zines marry textual and visual forms of communication through a cut-and-paste photocopied aesthetic. In print form, they can be circulated at local, national, and international zine fairs or festivals, through the mail, or through distributors known as "zine distros." The cost of zines varies by creator, but the general effort to remain accessible and reach wider audiences means they are often offered on a sliding scale, for trade, or for free.

Traditionally, zines are understood as informed by three periods of alternative press production: 1930s sci-fi fanzines, 1970s punk (fan)zines, and (perhaps most popularly linked to) the 1990s riot grrrl movement. While zines produced by Latinx communities are no doubt in conversation with these periodizations, as Elke Zobl writes, this is "zine history from a (white) Anglo-American viewpoint."[14] Moreover, expanding on the observations of Chicana zinester Bianca Ortiz, Toronto-based zinester of color Leah Lakshmi Piepzna-Samarasinha notes, "One can draw a history of zines that sees them as coming out of riot grrrl, punk, and other usual (and majorly white) suspects, or look through an alternative lens that sees them equally birthed 'out of the self-publication methods utilized by Chicana, Latina, Black, Indigenous and APA [Asian Pacific American] artists, poets and writers during the '60s and '70s.'"[15]

As the work on print culture by Nicolás Kanellos, Kirsten Silva Gruesz, and Raúl Coronado shows, Hispanics have been writing and self-publishing as a way to create community and maintain connection with their homeland since the mid-nineteenth century.[16] In the mid-twentieth century, "the Chicano movement provoked an explosion of Chicano/a publications across the United States, each with its own regional focus, political agenda, and aesthetic."[17] However, as has been widely criticized within Chicanx (and the larger field of Latinx) studies, these periodicals of the *movimiento*, while aiding in the establishment of a Chicanx Latinx print community, tended to relegate women to its margins. Martha Cotera's, Alma M. García's, and Maylei Blackwell's projects on Chicana feminist print communities not only recover but, more importantly, incorporate the contribution of Chicanas to *movimiento* print culture of the late 1960s.[18] "Movement print culture [thereby] functioned as a mediating space where these debates [over gender and sexuality] circulated and where new ideas, theories, and political claims were forged."[19] Periodicals such as *El Grito, Consafos, Regeneración,* and *Hijas de Cuauhtémoc* were sites of ideological dialogue, contention, community formation, and a tool for political mobilization.

Not surprisingly, scholarship on Latinx print culture in the Midwest is relatively underexamined especially when compared to the Southwest. Mirelsie Velázquez has expanded on the work of Kanellos and Blackwell to analyze the contributions of Chicago's Puerto Rican community to the history of 1960s Latino/a print culture. Velázquez reads texts including *The Rican: A Journal of Contemporary Puerto Rican Thought* and *El Puertorriqueño,* as well as newspapers by the Chicago-based Young Lords Organization, "to acknowledge the critical historical importance of [these] particular publication[s] and the indispensable relationship [they] maintained with an otherwise silenced or misrepresented community."[20]

More recently, Sara A. Ramírez and Norma E. Cantú have explored the impact of Third Woman Press and *Third Woman* journal to Latina feminist print culture.[21] Founded by Norma Alarcón in 1979 at Indiana University, *Third Woman* journal, like *Revista Chicano-Riqueña,* has its roots in the Midwest. Significantly, the first issue, published in 1981, resulted from Alarcón's participation in the Midwest Latina Writers Workshop and was entitled "Of Latinas in the Midwest," with a photograph of Sandra Cisneros sitting to the right of her typewriter on the cover.[22] In the introduction to the inaugural issue, Alarcón acknowledged the work of *Revista Chicano-Riqueña* in circulating cultural production by Chicago's Latina artists. Moreover, along with other participants in the Midwest Latina Writers Workshop, she wanted "to overcome the dependency on the 'special-issue syndrome.'"[23]

The content of the first issue of *Third Woman* journal, like the periodicals examined by Velázquez, stakes claim to a politicized midwestern *latinidad* that demands recognition not as a special issue or to be read as a geographic anomaly but rather as representative of a Latina/o community with a rich history of cultural expression in the Midwest. I draw attention to the scholarship on Latinx print culture to establish a brief history of Latinx in self-publishing and to underscore the political and communal praxis that informed and continues to inform Latinx print communities. Additionally, this scholarship helps forge connections between early Chicana/o-Latina/o print culture aesthetic practices and contemporary Latinx zines.

The projects of Alma M. García and Maylei Blackwell on Chicana print communities of the late 1960s and 1970s are significant to the types of alternative print cultures from which I see Latinx zines emerging. Garcia's groundbreaking study emphasizes the circulation, mobilization, and articulation of Chicana feminist writing that responded to and contested the injustices that shaped Chicanas' everyday lives.[24] In medium, content, and design, I see the Latinx zine community informed by these material and cultural political practices. Take, for example, Blackwell's description of the first issue of the Southern California–based publication *Hijas de Cuauhtémoc* (1971): "The newspaper theorized and editorialized new forms of *feminismo* and began to name the interconnections of class and race through an innovative mixed-genre format that was equal parts journalism, poetry, photography, art, social critique, recovered women's history, and political manifesto."[25] In this depiction of the newspaper, I read a blend of what Tomás Ybarra-Frausto terms "rasquache sensibility" and what is considered zines' do-it-yourself aesthetics.[26] In each of these traditions, the (usually) working-class subject employs the resources available to them in order to achieve a desired goal or function. Moreover, Ybarra-Frausto notes, the act of being *rasquache* is "a bawdy, spunky consciousness seeking to subvert and turn ruling paradigms upside down—a witty, irreverent and impertinent posture that recodes and moves outside established boundaries."[27] The *Hijas de Cuauhtémoc* cull material from a variety of sources (poetry, recovered women's history, art, photography, etc.) to construct a politicized counternarrative to official histories that is driven by a gendered socioeconomic imperative. Moreover, in this case, it is a gendered sensibility that creatively deploys *feminismo* in response to multiple oppressions both in and outside the Chicano community. To read DIY and, more importantly, *rasquache* sensibility into these print practices underscores how these alternative periodicals destabilize power through transgressive articulations that question normalized views on gender, sexuality, race, class, and ethnicity.[28]

Furthermore, the cut-and-paste cultural expressions that are associated with mainstream zine culture have long been an aesthetic strategy in Latina/o print culture. One among various examples is the special issue of the newspaper *La Razón Mestiza II* (summer 1976), published by the San Francisco Chicana feminist organization Concilio Mujeres.[29] The publication title is centered in the header at the top of the black-and-white page. The title is bordered by an image of Frida Kahlo split in two. The left side of the header depicts Kahlo with her hair down and an image of a young female activist with her right arm raised in a fist and her mouth open as if caught in midshout. Above her flies the United Farm Workers' flag. To the right of the header, Kahlo's hair is braided and is surrounded by an image of a hand holding a pen, with a stenciled figure of an expressionless woman behind her. Below the header are an array of images, including photographs, sketches, and paintings. The illustration of Aztec serpent heads and a woman performing danza Azteca affirm ties to a Mexican indigeneity. Meanwhile, Ester Hernandez's "La Virgen de Guadalupe defendiendo los derechos de los Xican@s" (1975), sketches of fashionable women of the era, and photographs of Concilio Mujeres members acting, singing, and gathered around a guitar convey the organization's modern and diverse Chicana identity.

The cover of *La Razón Mestiza II* also exemplifies Michelle Comstock's observation of grrrl zine creators who "selectively cut and paste the styles and genres of popular and alternative culture and engage in writing as an intrinsically networked process of both consumption and production."[30] Concomitantly, the periodical performs what Laura E. Perez terms "aesthetic altarities."[31] Applying this concept to her reading of the zine *Flor y Canto*, created by the East Los Angeles collective Mujeres de Maíz, Norell Martinez describes how "art with an altar-like function can serve to invoke all those women who have gone unacknowledged, or whose pain has been ignored, or whose bodies have been abused, and thus, this [zine as] art-altar can in itself be seen as a political act."[32] Indeed, *La Razón Mestiza* can be read as both a conglomeration of Chicana Latina influences and an offering or commemoration to the precursors who illuminated the publication and identity of this Chicana Latina print community. While these examples primarily focused on Latina print culture, we can see the form of *rasquache*, DIY, cut-

and-paste, homemade aesthetic in a variety of Latina/o cultural expressions from this period.[33] These alternative periodicals are subversive in their ability to interpellate, initiate dialogue, and (in the process) transform communities around them.[34] That is, in their artistic material form and place-based archival function, I read these texts as a medium for individual agency and collective Latina/o action. They not only capture the Latina/o community in place and time but also provide resourceful strategies that are similarly observed in contemporary zine culture by Latinxs more broadly.

Social and Cultural Practices of Latinx Zine Culture

Zines have hastily been imagined as an exemplar of white liberal cultural expression, given their strong association with the punk and riot grrrl subcultures. Transnational feminist cultural studies scholar and zinester Mimi Thi Nguyen's compelling analysis of riot grrrl's and punk's "possessive investment in antiracist whiteness" shows how a desire for intimacy with (and over) a racialized Other yields "smothering love."[35] Accordingly, Nguyen emphasizes the need to observe contributions made by zinesters of color apart from riot grrrl and punk scenes: "We [artists of color] assembled compilation zines . . . made documentaries . . . traversing punk, hip-hop, and other scenes to trace their entangled genealogies. . . . In these other histories, other archives, race is not an interruption into a singular scene or movement but the practice of another, co-present scene or movement that conversed and collided with the already-known story, but with alternate investments and forms of critique."[36] This statement observes the inadequacies and short-sightedness of the dominant zine narrative. In positioning Latinx zinesters within a tradition of Latina/o print culture, I read them not as entering a predetermined white zine scene but instead as actively participating in multiple "co-present scene[s] or movement[s]."[37] Accordingly, Latinx zinesters' involvement in and practice of various art forms, political activism, and social justice affect the ways and degrees to which they engage with a larger (whiter) zine community.

Alternative print scholars overwhelmingly read zines as constituting what critical theorist Nancy Fraser terms as a counterpublic.[38] Like Fraser's counterpublics, zines function as "parallel discursive areas where members of subordinated social groups invent and circulate counterdiscourses to formulate oppositional interpretations of their identities, interests, and needs."[39] Zines are then understood as a disruptive force that provides a platform to affirm difference while establishing politicized forms of belonging and understanding the world. Exploring the oppositional possibilities of zines through the work of Gloria Anzaldúa, Adela Licona contends that "zines as il/legitimate and im/

pure third-spaces challenge sanctioned—authorized and expert—discourses in ways that redress the obfuscation of alternative, nondominant expressions and representation of self and Others. . . . The borderlands rhetoric they produce flourish in the fertile third space of the interstitial and the liminal."[40] Licona's use of third-space theory to describe the desire of zinesters of color to connect and act as agents of social change also calls attention to the intimate affective relationships that are formed and perhaps not as strongly articulated in the "imagined communities" of print culture described by Benedict Anderson.[41] Yet within Latinx print culture and zine studies, Anderson's *Imagined Communities* is often cited to articulate the strong bond among frequently dispersed zine audiences. This analysis joins the work of Fraser and Licona to offer a series of redefinitions that aim to address the numerous forms of affiliation that arise through printed forms of communication.

Useful to this analysis is Blackwell's attention to images in *movimiento* print media: "The concept 'image(d) communities' names how Chicanas/ activists produced visual images and new symbols as a political practice and collective conversation of reimagining historical subjectivity across temporal and spatial borders."[42] An analysis of Latinx zines must therefore address the interplay of words and images in cultivating and communicating within a print community. And whereas Blackwell is directed toward the image, Alison Piepmeier pays attention to one's relationship with the materiality of the zine itself: "The embodied community of the zine world is intimate rather than extensive, and linked to the body rather than simply to an imagined other."[43] In this model of community formation, the product or object is given precedence in its ability to transmit labor (from zinester to zine reader), feeling (in zines' content), and play on the senses (e.g., the smell of the zinester's home and the zine itself). The zine is given a life of its own (albeit short-lived, given the ephemeral nature of these publications) in its ability to engage a reader and elicit a variety of feelings, reactions, and responses. As a result, zines run the risk of being hailed as a site of uncritical utopian possibility. Consequently, in problematizing the historicization of the zine community, Nguyen asks us to reconsider how we remember and historicize the past in order to imagine a different, better, and more just future.[44] Similarly, in what follows, I seek to critically engage Chicago's established zine communities with the intent of highlighting limitations and possibilities for its Latinx participants.

As various texts on Chicago's long-standing underground and alternative print culture show, there are various threads of influence from which contemporary Chicago zine communities emerge.[45] However, for the purpose of this chapter, I begin in the 1990s with the establishment of Quimby's Bookstore and the archiving of zines at institutions of higher education.[46] Quimby's Bookstore provides a brick-and-mortar location in which to find zines, and it hosts space for zinesters to meet and carry out events. Independently owned and operated since 1991, the Wicker Park establishment is nationally recognized as an important fixture in the independent publishing and small press world. In that capacity and of interest to my discussion is its in-store decision to spotlight "P.O.C./Bilingual" zines as it provides an opportunity for publicity that may lead to wider exposure and readership.

Along with Quimby's Bookstore, support from universities and festivals has marked Chicago as a major hub for zine production and circulation. And given that Chicago is the third most populous metropolis in the country, it can be expected that, like Quimby's, these spaces attempt to engage the city's diversity. DePaul University and the University of Chicago house extensive zine archives and have partnered with local zinesters to provide educational programming that opens their collections to the community at large. Furthermore, the University of Chicago's zine collection guide states that it "collect[s] zines on important issues for people in Chicago, such as those of minority voices, people of color, migrant and LGBTQIA communities."[47]

Chicago also has one of the more established annual zine festivals among other major cities.[48] Founded in 2010, the Chicago Zine Festival is no different from the aforementioned bookstore and university archives in its attempt to showcase and promote local zinesters and cultivate an inclusive and diverse festival. Organizers have arranged a sliding registration fee, implemented a "safer spaces" policy, and planned a variety of inclusive workshops and panels with different zine communities.[49] Among the participation of Latinx zinesters from the Midwest and throughout the country, leading zinesters Cristy C. Road (*Greenzine* and *Indestructible*), Tomas Moniz (*Rad Dad*), and current Chicago resident Celia C. Peréz (*I Dreamed I Was Assertive*) have presented as part of formal panels and workshops at the Chicago Zine Festival.[50] Locally, Chicago Latinx collectives and individual zinesters that have participated in the Chicago Zine festival include but are not limited to CHema Skandal!, Curandera Press, Las Topo Chicas, marimacha monarca press, Vixtopher, and Xicx Zine Collective.[51] As zine production and consumption are fairly intimate and solitary practices, zine festivals offer a unique opportunity for zinesters (especially of color) to meet face-to-face and move the community from material object to public arena. However, even as Chicago's more established organizations aim to create a progressive and inclusionary zine scene (replete with *safer* spaces [emphasis added]), zinesters of color continue to experience the familiar feeling of "becoming a stranger," to borrow Sara Ahmed's phrase.[52]

California transplant and active Chicago zinester Luz Magdaleno Flores recalls attending national and international zine festivals with her collaborator, Alvaro Zavala, in order to showcase their series, *¿SERIO?* Zine: "It wasn't easy though. Not only was the profit non-existent, but being all up in white spaces can be exhausting. A lot of white folx would walk by our table and see that we were two brown kids selling social justice propaganda and kept on walking. That didn't bring us down though, because everywhere we went, we met other zinesters of colour!"[53] Magdaleno Flores's experiences—being seen and interrupted only to be passed by again, feeling tired as a result of this constant exchange—characterize Ahmed's theorization of "stranger making": "Strangers are not simply those who are not known in this dwelling, but those who are, in their very proximity, *already recognised as not belonging*, as being out of place. Such a recognition of those who are out of place allows for a demarcation and enforcement of the boundaries of 'this place.'"[54] The outcome is an exhaustive racialization of Magdaleno Flores, Zavala, and their zines and zine content *as strangers* and incongruous with their seemingly progressive surroundings. Yet as Magdaleno Flores states above, the opportunity to connect with other zinesters of color and allies is an important reason to be there. The exclamation in her statement is telling of a network of zinesters who are not easily located but can often be found dispersed among larger citywide festivals. There is a joy in the mutual recognition between zinesters of color and allies that underscores the need to claim the space of the exhibitor's table or risk further elision.

"¡Lee zines!" (Read Zines!): Latinx Zinesters Shaping the Chicago Zine Community

Among Latinx zinesters, taking up space operates as a tool to physically (with their bodies) and materially (through their zines) demand recognition while inscribing their existence and ties to the community. In an effort to "take up space" and thereby create new placemaking projects, artists and self-described zineophiles Oscar Arriola and CHema Skandal! organized Logan Square's independent zine festival, #ZINEmercado, in 2016.[55] I first came across #ZINEmercado while researching Latinx zines at the 2017 Chicago Zine Festival. Like Luz Magdaleno Flores's experience recounted above, I sought and found familiarity among a predominantly white zine community. As I walked by Arriola's table, the quintessential Spanglish play on words—in its combination of zine and *mercado* (marketplace)—caught my attention. Moreover, the use of the hashtag at the start of the festival name prompted me to think of the various user-generated tagging that was at work in their project. This includes placemaking in the realm of the virtual through a shared tag that is both fixed in content and host to a network of users in different sites who, like the zine, activate it in practice. As such, I have followed #ZINEmercado online through social media sites such as Instagram, Twitter, and Facebook.

I have also acquired zines from their participants, attended the festival, and interviewed Oscar Arriola.

While zine festivals continue to grow in number throughout Chicago, #ZINEmercado offered an opportunity for Arriola and CHema Skandal! to curate a smaller local festival with an objective to integrate zines and zine culture into the long-standing Logan Square community.[56] Little more is known about CHema Skandal!, who enters zine culture as a zinester and active participant in ska, punk, and reggae music scenes, than that he was born in Mexico City and trained at the National Autonomous University of Mexico's School of Art before relocating to Chicago. CHema Skandal! rarely takes pictures without, and is often seen at festivals in, his signature Mexican wrestler mask, which covers the entirety of his face. Additionally, when doing interviews, CHema Skandal! largely focuses on the projects he is involved in and promoting rather than providing any personal biographical information. As a result, Arriola tends to serve as the spokesperson for #ZINEmercado.

Born and raised in Chicago's Rogers Park neighborhood to Guatemalan parents, Arriola was introduced to the medium through an interest in photo documentation, graffiti zines, and Chicago's hip-hop scene.[57] Arriola states, "I started shooting graffiti in the late 80's when I realized how quickly the city of Chicago was buffing it out. I'd see the amazing pieces off the train lines and realized that there probably wasn't much documentation of it since they were disappearing so quickly."[58] This desire to document subcultures that especially run the risk of erasure is seen in his work with the hip-hop magazine *Chicago Rocks* in the mid-1990s to his solo exhibition *Fotoflow* (titled after his moniker) and his general passion for zines.[59] Arriola participated in the second annual Chicago Zine Festival of 2011 and served as a co-organizer for the festival the following year. Furthermore, given his cultural interests and current position as staff member for the Chicago Public Library, Arriola has also cofacilitated a panel entitled "On Speaking Terms: Zines, Librarians, and Communities" at the 2018 Chicago Zine Festival. It is a shared affinity for zines as political artform and community-making, as well as respect for one another's work, that brought Arriola and CHema Skandal! together and has resulted in a collaborative effort that sees #ZINEmercado having completed its fifth-year cycle in October 2020 with ongoing plans to continue the yearly festival.[60]

#ZINEmercado's first promotional activity was a post on the social media platform Instagram on September 30, 2016. The caption in the post states: "Zine Hobo has hopped a train and is heading to @comfort_station in Chicago for the ZINEmercado Sunday, October 23rd!"[61] Accompanying the description is a playful black-and-white, retro-styled cartoon of a stout burly man carrying a bindle over his right shoulder. Zine Hobo is rendered midwhistle and midstroll as he looks up to his left. The figure is drawn with heavy line, as if silk-screened onto the page, and is framed in a solid black round spotlight (see figure 5.1). Illustrated by CHema Skandal!, Zine Hobo is based on Oscar Arriola and is a fixture on the majority of #ZINEmercado advertising material. The decision to adopt Zine Hobo for the festival is very well an homage to Arriola's collection of zines themed around train monikers: "Tramps, hobos, and train workers traditionally marked their monikers (or nicknames) on the sides of freight trains with chalk or oil markers. That tradition has been carried on by present day artists and train hoppers . . . [the] contemporary hobos."[62] This form of graffiti relies heavily on images of artists' tags scrawled on the side of freight trains. Revealingly, this shows Arriola's interest in various forms of cultural expression that circulate either on paper or momentarily as they pass by on the side of a train.

The work of pioneering US sociologist Nels Anderson on hobos and homelessness helps to further entrench this mobile figure in the history of Chicago and concomitantly the *placeness* of Chicago onto the Zine Hobo. Anderson refers to Chicago as "Hobohemia" because by the late nineteenth century it had become an important city for homeless men who were drawn to the railroad industry.[63] For this group of "predominantly white and native-born [men] . . . homelessness was not so much a shelter condition, but a distinct way of life characterized by casual lodging, temporary labor, and frequent migration."[64] #ZINEmercado's production of a hobo character that is to be affiliated with zine culture highlights the transitory nature that is rooted in Chicago's hobohemia—the circulation of zines mimicking movement by railroad. Furthermore, if as Anderson suggests the "typical hobo" is emblematic of one form of US white masculinity at the turn of the twentieth century, then Mexican national CHema Skandal! and Guatemalan American Oscar Arriola's deployment of this image as symbol for their zine festival inserts them into this US experience.[65] Yet a discussion of labor and migration in Chicago's railroad history as related to contemporary Latinx placemaking practices would be remiss without addressing the significant role that Mexican track workers played in railroad construction.

The nineteenth and early twentieth centuries saw "Chicago quickly become an important (one might say inevitable) destination for Mexican migrant labor, the early patterns of which so thoroughly corresponded to the expansion of railroads. . . . At least as early as 1907, Mexican/migrant workers were employed by the railroads in Chicago."[66] It is important to underscore that the Zine Hobo is in no way a direct representation of Mexican or Latinx migration. In fact, while Anderson's view of homelessness as a "distinct way of life" motions toward a romanticization of conditions that denied workers stability, Mexican migrant labor was largely in response to economic needs and displacement because of these new industries. Nevertheless, Zine Hobo unearths a transborder history established on Chicago's railways and invisible labor that also invites the Anglo community to see these ties to gender, race, ethnicity, and nation-building.

The transitory theme of #ZINEmercado came up once again in another Instagram post. In October 2017 the group announced that the zine festival would now be described as "a roving Chicago #ZINE fest."[67] The plan was (and, as was evident in 2020, continues to be) to maintain a festival in Logan Square but, like their wanderlust cartoon, take the festival on the road. Arriola and CHema Skandal! continue to serve as curators by selecting the zines for their journey to new locations, and like the monikers on the side of passing railroad carts, the zines travel but are grounded in their Chicago identity. This is evident in a number of zines that were featured in the 2019 #ZINEmercado, such as Paloma Mercier's *Ten Letters: Belmont*, MANTIS's *FULL*, and Alexa Ramirez's *A CTA Love Letter*. Whether it be a zine made up of letters from a zinester's favorite signs down Belmont Avenue (Mercier), a photo collage book made up of scenic images that include Chicago's municipal flag and Metra trains in the background (MANTIS), or a long rectangular zine shaped like a CTA train that retells the zinester's school journey from the Addison Blue Line stop to Clark Terminal (Ramirez), these zines are quintessentially Chicago. Since that Instagram message went out to followers, #ZINEmercado has done zine festivals in, among other sites, Chicago neighborhoods beyond Logan Square, created a pop-up show in San Francisco, and exhibited at Mexico City's Rrreplica Art Book Fair. Zine Hobo is featured on advertisements for all appearances, as he is in other promotional material. For example, in the Bay Area, Zine Hobo is presented in the back of a San Francisco patrol car.[68] This tongue-in-cheek image suggests a carceral surveillance society in which the Zine Hobo (whether as hobo or as courier of nontraditional print) has been "caught" transgressing. Meanwhile, in Mexico City, he is once again center stage on a large poster along with the festival's social media account information and its capitalized self-description as "A ROVING CHICAGO #ZINE FEST."[69]

Although there are a number of zine collectives that exhibit their work at various festivals locally, nationally, and globally, what is unique about #ZINEmercado is its insistence on describing itself as a festival rather than a collective, even when attending a festival like the Rrreplica Art Book Fair. #ZINEmercado's decision to maintain this identity, which is linked geographically to Chicago (and thereby always taking Chicago with the festival), in turn often makes it *the* Chicago zine representative whenever it goes beyond city limits. For this reason, the zines the festival chooses to travel with and curate as part of the Chicago zine scene—including, among others, the work of Amara "Rebel Betty" Martin (*Mujer en Revolución, The Gentrification of*

Chicago, and *El Barrio No Se Vende*), Tom Guenther (*No Hands Western*), and James Liu (*Sonic Visual Graphics*)—become important place markers and a statement of Arriola and CHema Skandal!'s version/vision of Chicago.

For #ZINEmercado's inaugural festival in 2016, Oscar Arriola and CHema Skandal! posted what I interpret as their mission statement on the Facebook event page: "We want to be all inclusive with all types of zine makers, share our ideas / backgrounds / aesthetics / aspirations / dreams and engage in dialogue through our self-made publications. Kids and families are encouraged to attend :)."[70] Inclusivity is the overarching vision for the festival with the intent to build community. This is done first through the diversity in zinesters that exhibit their work and second in the hopeful attempt to influence future zinesters who may be in attendance with their families. This vision of diversity and communion around print may not seem overtly political, yet it runs counter to assumptions of Logan Square's historical ethnoracial population and to the erasure of the neighborhood's long-standing communities. Moreover, while Chicago's Puerto Rican population is commonly fixed in the Near Northwest Side (which includes West Town, Humboldt Park, and Logan Square), Gina M. Pérez's study of Puerto Ricans in the city finds that these communities "are actually quite mixed. . . . [In the 1990 census] Logan Square's Puerto Rican population is the largest in the city, but this community area is also home to . . . Mexicans and Chicago's largest Cuban and South and Central American populations."[71] #ZINEmercado, in inviting all in the neighborhood to participate, thus recognizes these long-standing community residents. However, #ZINEmercado is not an exclusively Latinx zine festival, as it welcomes and promotes the event to the community at large. The festival, therefore, attempts to rightfully showcase the different people who have made up this neighborhood and make up the neighborhood around the exchange of printed cultural expressions.

While emphasizing inclusivity, CHema Skandal! also expresses frustration when it comes to revitalization projects that purport to "build a new Chicago" but leave the long-standing communities vulnerable to the market pressures of gentrification. CHema Skandal! moved to Chicago in 2010 and by 2016 observed: "I've seen Logan Square change a lot. Now imagine people who have been living here 30 years, how fast it's changing for them, so I wanted to merge the different backgrounds that we *used* to have here, Polish people, Latino, Puerto Rican, Mexican, and of course, [Caucasian] in a cultural event."[72] The influx of different people to Chicago throughout the twentieth century has transformed the neighborhood and left a lasting impact on Logan Square that risks erasure. A neighborhood with German, Norwegian, Polish, and Russian Jewish roots in the early 1900s, by the 1970s "disinvestment and white flight left the least desirable sections of Logan Square, and other neighborhoods on the Near Northwest Side, to blacks and Latinos."[73] Like Pilsen, Logan Square is in a coveted location for real estate development and has significantly been marked by gentrification and a fight to maintain neighborhood diversity. Further, as Mérida Rúa notes, "a 2007 study that analyzed the remarkable changes in Chicago's housing stock over the last decade and a half, identified Logan Square . . . as [one of] the community areas that [has] experienced some of the most striking condominium growth and simultaneous apartment decline."[74] Urban renewal and redevelopment projects that price out local residents present a challenge to the diversity #ZINEmercado seeks to illuminate and honor.

Noticeably, CHema Skandal! as a recognizable, transnational, and cosmopolitan artist based in Chicago is himself an agent of change to Logan Square. Yet I would argue that his efforts to learn about and collaborate with the community through art and activism exemplify a self-awareness that challenges assumptions about new Chicago transplants. Moreover, as Oscar Arriola describes, "we wanted to bring . . . [Latinx] voices to Logan Square because it's changing so much."[75] He goes on to acknowledge that some of those same Latinx voices that assert *latinidades* in Logan Square through their participation in the #ZINEmercado are now moving to the South Side of Chicago, which in itself disrupts long-standing communities. In both of these instances we see that concerns regarding gentrification are striking but not so cut-and-dried, especially as Arriola and CHema Skandal! attempt to transform a cultural practice they are a part of through, among other things, the inclusion of diverse zine vendors, advertising, and attending public.

Representation of people who historically made up Logan Square is an important aspect of #ZINEmercado's work. One of the more apparent ways that this task is done is by keeping the event free and advertising in English, Spanish, and Polish (figure 5.1). The 2016 flyer that circulated in local alternative weekly newspapers and was posted around the city promotes the event in the three languages and states: "ALL ARE WELCOME TO PARTICIPATE IN THIS ART EVENT. FREE ADMISSION!"[76] In the short statement, #ZINEmercado welcomes those who may not be familiar with zine culture by describing it as an "art event" and articulates that all, regardless of English proficiency, are invited. This advertisement expresses solidarity and coalition-building through code-switching, a format that #ZINEmercado continues to use (although no longer translating to Polish). Adela Licona's work on zines and the act of code-switching as Anzaldúan praxis argues: "Third-space tactics and borderlands rhetorics are often comprised of code switching or bilingualism as a means of representing lived experiences and thereby resisting the limits of dominant discourse. . . . Code switching is identified in dominant contexts as illegitimate, impure, improper, and therefore invalid. As a practice,

FIGURE 5.1. Image of Zine Hobo as rendered on first Instagram post on September 30, 2016, and featured here on the #ZINEmercado 2016 promotional flyer with information about the event in English, Spanish, and Polish. Designed by CHema Skandal!

code switching demonstrates a commitment to the value of lived experiences and the validity and import of the (allegedly) impure in nondominant contexts."[77] In this manner, #ZINEmercado's use of English, Spanish, and Polish not only is a way to invite people into the festival but also serves as a linguistic signpost of Logan Square's diverse historical social and cultural practices. To those looking at the promotional material who may be familiar or unfamiliar with any of these languages, these words demand attention and participation, and they oblige us to consider the relationship among these languages and in turn the relationship between their histories. Moreover, in the circulation of the material at the national and global scales, English, Spanish, and Polish draw attention to a transnationalism that exists in the city itself.

While I have focused on the placemaking practices of #ZINEmercado through the festival and its promotional material, I would briefly like to turn to #ZINEmercado's own zine as a tangible manifestation of its mission statement. If, as Michel de Certeau stated, space represents a practiced place, then the zine represents practiced paper.[78] The annual #ZINEmercado *Compilation Zine* is a collaborative effort between the organizers and festival participants. All vendors are invited to contribute to the zine, which is released on the day of the festival and printed in small runs (the 2020 edition had sixty-nine runs, 2019 edition had seventy-four runs, 2018 edition fifty runs, 2017 edition seventy-five runs, and 2016 edition forty runs). As a "compilation" it performs similarly to a mixtape—exhibitors are asked to submit a sample of their work and thus collectively create that festival year's "greatest hits." Moreover, bound together, the pages are a conversation among artists in a particular time and space. The zine forms a textual community materially established and brought together by #ZINEmercado that marks the placemaking practices of the festival into the zine itself.

CHema Skandal! and Oscar Arriola design the covers of the *Compilation Zine* (and contribute a page as independent zinesters) that includes the festival year and, of course, has Zine Hobo incorporated into all issues. The back page includes #ZINEmercado's social media information, thanks the contributors in English and Spanish, and informs the reader what numbered copy of the run they are interacting with. The zine therefore enacts Piepmeier's embodied community among the contributors and among the small number of readers that engage the zine.[79] In this way, #ZINEmercado establishes a space for *its* Chicago physically through the festival and literally in the production and collaboration with zinesters, as well as the engagement with zine readers at large.

PAZ: Piñatas and Zines

In December 2017 Oscar Arriola curated an exhibit at the Logan Square performance space, Elastic Arts, entitled *PAZ: Piñatas and Zines*. The curatorial statement asks the audience to consider the "latent potentialities in a conceptual congruence between seemingly unrelated uses of paper . . . between piñatas and zines."[80] Among the various compelling connections that are made between the two seemingly incompatible paper objects is their need for people to make them active. I read the efforts of Latinx zinesters Oscar Arriola and CHema Skandal! functioning in a similar manner—ostensibly at odds with conventional zine culture, connecting people, activating community, and energetically occupying space. In #ZINEmercado's efforts to foster community it depicts the type of collective action or placemaking that Pérez describes as "grounded in a particular place, [but it] is not limited by neighborhood boundaries, but rather expands conventional ideas of community, place, identity, and belonging to include people who share common interests and concerns and who might otherwise be excluded."[81] Through their image(d) communities (Blackwell), roving festivals, code-switching, and the production and circulation of the *Compilation Zine*, Oscar Arriola and CHema Skandal! physically and materially create and claim space but do so in mutual recognition of other like-minded zinesters. Their ongoing contributions to the zine community usher in a contemporary way of understanding the collaborative placemaking processes that occur in Chicago. CHema Skandal! and Oscar Arriola's Chicago is one that is rooted in their experience as Latinx in the Midwest and is shaped by the Latino/a print communities that came before them, as well as a zine culture that they make their own.

Notes

1. I use "Latina/o" when the term is referenced in the source material that predates the use of the term "Latinx."

2. According to Marc Zimmerman, *Revista Chicano-Riqueña's Nosotros: A Collection of Latino Poetry and Graphics from Chicago* (1977) was the first collection focused on Chicago-based Latina/o writers and artists. See "Chicago and the Forgotten Poets of Aztlán (Part I): Introduction," in El Beisman, http://elbeisman.com/article.php?action=read&id=516. ECOS Staff, "The City & Our Lives," *ECOS: A Latino Journal of People's Culture & Literature* 2, no. 1 (Winter 1982): 10.

3. "South Sangamon" later appears in Sandra Cisneros's poetry collection *My Wicked Wicked Ways* (Berkeley: Third Woman, 1987).

4. De Genova and Ramos-Zayas, *Latino Crossings*, 39.

5. Wilfredo Cruz, *City of Dreams: Latino Immigration to Chicago* (Lanham, MD: University Press of America, 2007), 25.

6. Salima Rivera, "Pilsen," *ECOS: A Latino Journal of People's Culture & Literature* 2, no. 1 (Winter 1982): 13. For more on Salima Rivera's work, see Zimmerman, *Defending Their Own*.

7. *Chicago: Nosotros/Nosotras* contributors were heavily involved in community organizing efforts. For example, Rivera was an active member of local groups, including Mujeres Latinas en Acción and the Westtown Concerned Citizens Coalition. Similarly, Carlos Cortez drew inspiration from Mexican printmaker and anarchist José Guadalupe Posada, striving to integrate activism into all forms of artmaking. Cortez was a member of the Industrial Workers of the World and contributed to the union paper, the *Industrial Worker*. He also helped found the Movimiento Artistico Chicano (MARCH). See http://www.elbeisman.com/article.php?action=read&id=354 and https://www.chicagotribune.com/news/ct-xpm-2005-01-23-0501230040-story .html.

8. *Revista Chicano-Riqueña* was founded at Indiana University in 1972, and *ECOS: A Latino Journal of People's Culture and Literature* was housed at the University of Illinois at Chicago beginning in 1980.

9. I use "zinester" or "zinesters" to describe a person or people who make zines.

10. Stephen Duncombe, *Notes from Underground: Zines and the Politics of Alternative Culture* (Portland, OR: Microcosm Publishing, 1997), 10–11.

11. Ibid., 15.

12. Ibid., 15–17.

13. Ibid., 18.

14. Elke Zobl, "Cultural Production, Transnational Networking, and Critical Reflection in Feminist Zines," *Signs* 35, no. 1 (2009): 2.

15. Leah Lakshmi Piepzna-Samarasinha, "Brown Star Kids: Zinemakers of Color Shake Things Up," *Broken Pencil*, no. 24 (2004): 25–26, quoted in ibid., 3.

16. See Nicolás Kanellos and Helvetia Martell, *Hispanic Periodicals in the United States, Origins to 1960: A Brief History and Comprehensive Bibliography* (Houston: Arte Público Press, 2000); Nicolás Kanellos, "Recovering and Re-constructing Early Twentieth-Century Hispanic Immigrant Print Culture in the US," *American Literary History* 19, no. 2 (2007): 438–55; Kanellos, *Hispanic Immigrant Literature: El Sueño del Retorno* (Austin: University of Texas Press, 2011); Kirsten Silva Gruesz, *Ambassadors of Culture: The Transamerican Origins of Latino Writing* (Princeton, NJ: Princeton University Press, 2002); Raúl Coronado, *A World Not to Come: A History of Latino Writing and Print Culture* (Cambridge, MA: Harvard University Press, 2013).

17. Colin Gunkel, "Building a Movement and Constructing Community: Photography, the United Farm Workers, and El Malcriado," *Social Justice* 42 no. 3–4 (2015): 31–32.

18. See Martha P. Cotera, *Diosa y Hembra: The History and Heritage of Chicanas in the U.S.* (Austin, TX: Information Systems Development, 1976); Alma M. Garcia, ed., *Chicana Feminist Thought: The Basic Historical Writings* (New York: Routledge, 1997); Maylei Blackwell, *¡Chicana Power! Contested Histories of Feminism in the Chicano Movement* (Austin: University of Texas Press, 2011). As Maylei Blackwell argues, there is a misconception that Chicanas did not begin to articulate their political identities

until the 1981 publication of *This Bridge Called My Back: Writing by Radical Women of Color,* ed. Cherríe Moraga and Gloria Anzaldúa (New York: Kitchen Table Press).

19. Maylei Blackwell, "Contested Histories: Las Hijas de Cuauhtémoc, Chicana Feminism, and Print Culture in the Chicano Movement, 1968–1973," in *Chicana Feminism: A Critical Reader,* ed. Gabriela F. Arredondo et al. (Durham, NC: Duke University Press, 2003), 61.

20. Mirelsie Velázquez, "Solidarity and Empowerment in Chicago's Puerto Rican Print Culture," *Latino Studies* 12, no. 1 (2014): 88–110, 94.

21. Sara A. Ramírez and Norma E. Cantú, "Publishing Work That Matters: Third Woman Press and Its Impact on Chicana and Latina Publishing," *Diálogo* 20, no. 2 (2017): 77–85; see also Catherine Ramírez, "Alternative Cartographies: Third Woman and the Respatialization of the Borderlands," *Midwestern Miscellany* 30 (2004): 47–62.

22. See Norma Alarcón, ed., *Third Woman: Of Latinas in the Midwest* 1, no. 1 (1981).

23. Ramírez and Cantú, "Publishing Work," 78.

24. See Garcia, *Chicana Feminist Thought.*

25. Blackwell, "Contested Histories," 67.

26. Tomás Ybarra-Frausto, "Rasquachismo: A Chicano Sensibility," in *Chicano Aesthetics: Rasquachismo* (Phoenix: Movimiento Artistico del Río Salado, 1989).

27. Ibid., 5.

28. See Laura G. Gutiérrez, "Rasquachismo," in Vargas, Mirabal, and La Fountain-Stokes, *Keywords for Latina/o Studies,* 184–87.

29. See Concilio Mujeres, *La Razón Mestiza II* (Summer 1976).

30. Michelle Comstock, "Grrrl Zine Networks: Re-composing Spaces of Authority, Gender, and Culture," *JAC: A Journal of Rhetoric, Culture, & Politics* 21, no. 2 (2001): 394.

31. See Laura E. Pérez, *Chicana Art: The Politics of Spiritual and Aesthetic Altarities* (Durham, NC: Duke University Press, 2007).

32. Norell Martínez, "Femzines, Artivism, and Altar Aesthetics: Third Wave Feminism Chicana Style," *Chiricú Journal: Latina/o Literatures, Arts, and Cultures* 2, no. 2 (2018): 45–67, 48.

33. For a list of Chicano/a-Latino/a periodicals of the period, see Guillermo Rojas, "Chicano/Raza Newspaper and Periodical Serials Listing," *Hispania* 58, no. 4 (December 1975): 851–63.

34. A similar spirit of transformation informs *Third Woman* journal: "It is not enough to imitate the models that are proposed to us. . . . We have to invent ourselves. That is, our woman's history provides us with consciousness of our past, of the central agents we have been, as well as the central roles we have played in the construction of our world, but without woman's envisioning and invention of the self and the future, the former is not enough. If we ask ourselves what our condition or situation is or has been, we must also ask what we can do to transform it" (Alarcón, "Hay que inventarnos / We must invent ourselves," 4).

35. Mimi Thi Nguyen, "Riot Grrrl, Race, and Revival," *Women & Performance: A Journal of Feminist Theory* 22, no. 2–3 (2021): 186.

36. Ibid., 186–87.

37. Ibid., 187.

38. See Blackwell, "Contested Histories"; Comstock, "Grrrl Zine Networks"; Zobl, "Cultural Production."

39. Nancy Fraser, "Rethinking the Public Sphere: A Contribution to the Critique of Actually Existing," *Social Text,* no. 25–56 (1990): 67. See also Michael Warner, "Publics and Counterpublics," *Public Culture* 14, no. 1 (2002): 49–90. For examples of counterpublics and print culture in Latinx studies, see Blackwell, *¡Chicana Power!*; Urayoán Noel, *In Visible Movement: Nuyorican Poetry from the Sixties to Slam* (Iowa City: University of Iowa Press, 2014); Antonio López, *Unbecoming Blackness: The Diaspora Cultures of Afro-Cuban America* (New York: New York University Press, 2012).

40. Adela C. Licona, *Zines in Third Spaces: Radical Cooperation and Borderlands Rhetoric* (Albany: State University of New York Press, 2013), 13. Licona describes third spaces as "in between spaces that are created at virtual and material intersections" (ibid., 4).

41. See Benedict Anderson, *Imagined Communities* (London: Verso, 1983).

42. Blackwell, "Contested Histories," 109.

43. Alison Piepmeier, *Girl Zines: Making Media, Doing Feminism* (New York: New York University Press, 2009), 79.

44. See Nguyen, "Riot Grrrl."

45. Duncombe, *Notes from Underground.* See also John McMillian, *Smoking Typewriters: The Sixties Underground Press and the Rise of Alternative Media in America* (New York: Oxford University Press, 2011); Mary Ellen Waszak, *A Guide to Chicago's Zine Scene & Alternative Press* (Chicago: iWrite Publications Inc., 2006); James P. Danky and Wayne A. Wiegand, eds., *Print Culture in a Diverse America* (Urbana: University of Illinois Press, 1998).

46. DePaul University began collecting zines after hosting the inaugural Chicago Great Lakes Underground Press conference in 1994. http://depaulmagazine .com/2019/06/13/seen-in-zines.

47. "Zines," http://guides.lib.uchicago.edu/zines.

48. The San Francisco Zine Festival was established in 2001. The Los Angeles Zine Festival began in 2012. New York City's active zine festivals are tied to particular boroughs such as the Brooklyn Zine Festival (established in 2012).

49. The sliding scale for 2018 was $30 to $60. See Chicago Zine Festival, "Registration for CFZ 2018," http://chicagozinefest.org/2017/12/registration-for-czf-2018/. See also Chicago Zine Festival, "Safer Space Policy," http://chicagozinefest.org/safer -spaces-policy/.

50. Celia C. Peréz's recent publication *The First Rule of Punk* (2018) centers on a thirteen-year-old Mexican American girl named Malú. An avid zinester, Malú relocates with her mother to Chicago and draws on punk ethos to adjust in the new city. Cristy C. Road was a panelist on "Gender, Race, and Sexuality: A Discussion with Women in Self-Publishing" (2012), Tomas Moniz participated in "In it for the Long Haul: A Discussion on Longevity in Zines" (2014), Celia C. Pérez shared work as part of an organized youths and exhibitor reading (2015).

51. Chicago Zine Festival, "2018 Exhibitors," http://chicagozinefest.org/2018 -exhibitors/.

52. See Sara Ahmed, *Strange Encounters: Embodied Others in Post-coloniality* (New York: Routledge, 2000).

53. Anisa Rawhani, "Nos Apoyamos: ¿Serio? Zine, Brown and Proud Press & Beyond," *Broken Pencil*, November 14, 2017, http://brokenpencil.com/news/nos-apoyamos -serio-zine-brown-and-proud-press-beyond/.

54. Ahmed, *Strange Encounters*, 21.

55. CHema Skandal! is one of several variations of the artist's name. Others include Chema Skandal! and Chema Skandal. Early advertisements refer to the festival as #ZINEmercado; however, ZINEmercado and Zinemercado are also used as alternatives. CHema Skandal! and Arriola were initially approached to host a zine festival at Chicago's art center Comfort Station by programming directors Raul Benitez and Nando Espinosa. Arriola, interview with #ZINEmercado co-organizer, December 11, 2018.

56. You did not already have to be a zinester to take part in the festival. It was and continues to be an event for community members to learn about zines or connect with zine friends.

57. See Karina O. Alvarado, Alicia Ivonne Estrada, and Ester E. Hernández, eds., *U.S. Central Americans: Reconstructing Memories, Struggles, and Communities of Resistance* (Tucson: University of Arizona Press, 2017), 9. While California was and remains a significant port of entry, Guatemalans settled in many urban cities, including Chicago. Cruz notes that "many Guatemalans moved into North Side neighborhoods like Albany Park, Lincoln Square, Uptown, Edgewater, and Rogers Park" (*City of Dreams*, 139). Arriola briefly majored in photography at Columbia College Chicago but left before completing the degree. Arriola interview.

58. http://theonesheet.net/post/163695744372/oascar-arriola-aka-fotoflow-august -2017-vol2.

59. Arriola held his first solo show, *Fotoflow*, in 2008 at Chicago's Believe Inn.

60. The fifth annual #ZINEmercado was hosted on October 4, 2020, at Comfort Station in Logan Square. As a result of COVID-19, the festival implemented pandemic protocols, reduced the number of in-person exhibitors, and encouraged virtual participation during the festival weekend by using the hashtag #ZINEmercado2020.

61. https://www.instagram.com/p/BK_7YQLBrPF/?taken-by=zinemercado.

62. Kala Anderson, "Zineophile: Oscar Arriola," *SAIC-Engage*, February 2, 2017, https://engage.saic.edu/news/123708.

63. See Nels Anderson, *On Hobos and Homelessness* (Chicago: University of Chicago Press, 1998).

64. Todd DePastino, *Citizen Hobo: How a Century of Homelessness Shaped America* (Chicago: University of Chicago Press, 2005), xviii.

65. Anderson, *On Hobos and Homelessness*.

66. Nicholas De Genova, *Working the Boundaries: Race, Space, and "Illegality" in Mexican Chicago* (Durham, NC: Duke University Press, 2005) 113.

67. https://www.instagram.com/p/Bag90LYB1fg/?taken-by=zinemercado.

68. Undoubtedly, Zine Hobo's "arrest" speaks to a history of racially charged incidents involving the SFPD and directed at ethnic minorities.

69. https://www.instagram.com/p/Bbm7b7qBsby/?taken-by=zinemercado.

70. https://www.facebook.com/events/312141649151664/.

71. Pérez, *The Near Northwest Side Story*, 131.

72. Sabina Bhasin, "The First Logan Square Independent Zine Fest, #ZINEMercado, Is Sunday," *LoganSquarist*, October 20, 2016, https://logansquarist.com/2016/10/zine-mercado-logan-square/.

73. Rúa, *A Grounded Identidad*, 63.

74. Ibid., 74.

75. Arriola interview.

76. Ibid.

77. Licona, *Zines in Third Spaces*, 52–53.

78. See Michel de Certeau, *The Practice of Everyday Life* (Minneapolis: University of Minnesota Press, 1998).

79. See Piepmeier, *Girl Zines*.

80. "Oscar Arriola, PAZ: Piñatas & Zines," Elastic Arts, http://elasticarts.org/oscar-arriola-paz-pinatas-zines-dec2017-feb2018/.

81. Pérez, *The Near Northwest Side Story*, 161.

PART II

Practices of Placemaking

CHAPTER 6

Creating La Estación Gallery

SANDRA RUIZ

During the spring and summer months of 2018, a community of queer women of color, feminists of color, and feminists across the University of Illinois at Urbana-Champaign campus transformed an atypical space in the Department of Latina/Latino Studies into a self-sustaining art and performance gallery.[1] Ranging in age from twenty to fifty-seven and representing staff, advisors, student interns, alumni, and the featured artist herself, we collectively redesigned a copy machine / computer / waiting room into La Estación Gallery, a cultural, social, and educational space that showcases queer Latinx and Latinx performance artists who strategically place pressure on transparent categories of race, ethnicity, gender, and sexuality and popular aesthetic practices and genres. Contributing to and advancing multiple representations of *latinidad*, we gave particular attention to work derived from the experimental art tradition, art that deliberately modeled our inaugural artist's aesthetic practices. For six months we worked diligently to secure funding from across the university, reshape the room's architectural structure, establish and mount light and sound systems, build and assemble furniture, install technology, create on-site interactive installations, and curate the gallery's first show. In considering the relationship between the creation of space and aesthetic genre, our debut artist, avant-garde minoritarian performance artist Erica Gressman, guided and joined us in reconstructing the room while also preparing for her first solo exhibition in the gallery and live performance at the Krannert Art Museum (KAM).

Attempting to confer new meaning to both spatial politics and acts of collaboration, this case study charts how the repurposing of a small waiting room by a queer and feminist collective cultivated a Latinx commons by building an experimental art gallery from the ground up.[2] It follows this

FIGURE 6.1. La Estación Gallery, Department of Latina/Latino Studies, University of Illinois at Urbana-Champaign. Photo by Alicia P. Rodriguez.

(inter)discipline's journey to reimagine itself outside of its own ideological, epistemological, and methodological boundaries, in which the avant-garde aesthetic remains at the center of new Latinx placemaking endeavors. Additionally, this case study documents the synergies and dissonances between ethnic studies and aesthetic sites, particularly the gallery's collaboration with the KAM, "the second largest general fine art museum in Illinois."[3] Both places were compelled to contend with difference and representation by embracing the plurality of being, being-with uncomfortable art, culture, and politics. To initiate this undertaking, Gressman's art was placed on display, as her work is often described as troubling, unsettling, inharmonious—an artist training from "the violence of becoming" into the political domain of difficulty as a framework for experiencing art.[4] By difficulty, I am thinking of Jennifer Doyle's idea of contemporary art that "quite literally takes us out of our comfort zone," engendering a rush of emotional intensity that we might not immediately or even necessarily welcome. In reassessing the emotional tenets of the artist, Doyle interrogates the spectator's own feelings and sentiments, exposing how difficult art propels one into a deeper understanding of self that manifests a full sensorial experience.[5] Understanding the often inorganic and thorny project of collaboration, Gressman's compositions help us elaborate on and prepare for such moments of incongruity.

Gressman's body of work follows in a tradition of queer, Brown, Latinx, and minoritarian artists who rely heavily on both conceptual and dissonant aesthetic practices to relay the everyday sentiments of marginalized subjects under empire. While Gressman is certainly unique in her aesthetic elections and sonic dispositions, her oeuvre can be seen alongside disquieting but invigorating performance pieces by artists such as Andres Serrano, Ana Mendieta, Papo Colo, William Pope L., Adrian Piper, Ron Athey, Ryan Rivera, Autumn Knight, Linda Mary Montano, and Nao Bustamante, along with sound and noise artists who have reshaped our listening practices such as John Cage, Pauline Oliveros, and a score of punk musicians. In refusing the call to be a subject formed by transparent representations of race, gender, sexuality, nation, and medium, Gressman turns to the posthuman to facilitate ethical and political exigency. The content of her avant-garde art practices crystallizes the gallery's mission and exposes the complicated and interlaced exchanges fashioning collaboration.

These interwoven collaborative exchanges contribute to Erica Gressman as entity. She defines herself as a queer, Latinx, mixed-race, and Colombian avant-garde performance and sound artist, costume designer, and design engineer from Miami, Florida, living and working in Chicago.[6] For the artist, all of these identificatory markers contribute to her artistry, none inseparable from creative labor or acts of collective drive. Gressman is highly influenced by noise music, the punk aesthetic, queer camp and kitsch culture, Latinx everyday social scenes and religious iconographies, intercultural theater, science, and science fiction, and her posthuman entities restructure our understanding of existence and subjectivity, as her body of art consistently blurs the lines among the senses, sound, light, and embodiment. From cyborgs, queer monsters, disembodied aliens, occult witches, and shamans/sorcerers, Gressman utilizes sound, image, and theatricality to exact memory through these figures. Fusing noise music with analog technology, including handmade synthesizers, her art is an evolving interactive audible set that intermixes technology and various artistic methods from repurposed materials. She creates her own musical instruments (from hand drills to hair brushes), compositions, installations, hardware designs, and elaborate costumes, driving us to listen sharply as she creates new worlds out of reappropriated elements and methods.

Along with generating art that is challenging to endure, Gressman also produces sustainable performances that not only bear the hardships of quotidian life for marginalized subjects but also weather the precarity of artmaking, of being an artist. Using DIY tactics in all of her performances, the artist simultaneously recognizes the ephemeral life of her craft and the endurance of being resourceful; for Gressman, both are interwoven forms and practices of sustainability that are informed by her cultural upbringing. For this artist, every object can be transformed into an art object, and every space is a potential for mutual exchange whereby the only limitation placed on innovation is desire itself. Such invention through the appropriation of materials is never removed from everyday acts of survival, as Gressman's methodology mirrors the conditions of living on the margins.

So in thinking intently with the artist's style, this essay asks the following questions: How can we critically engage the experimental and DIY aesthetic to attend to matters of placemaking within already established institutions? What can space come to signify when one reshifts its inherent purpose within a field of study? How does a project involving educators, students, curators, and artists who collectively remodel atypical spaces into intimate and promising aesthetic repositories arouse new cultural and conceptual turns for ethnic studies? And how does difficult art help engender a collaborative synergy between ethnic studies and the world of aesthetics? Considering these questions, this essay argues two entwined points: the reappropriation of physical space has the ability to alter the internal life of a field of study, including those invested in its evolution, and experimental and DIY aesthetic practices have the ability to unite and transform us in our own anxieties, alienations, and biases about belonging across spatial repositories that are often seen as antithetical to one another. This is to also say that La Estación Gallery is concerned with how the internal reappropriation of space in a deliberate act of placemaking establishes bonds between subjects across identification while also pushing the boundaries of discipline, genre, media, and culture.

La Estación is a base, a place at an already designated location, a waiting station that generates experience through the ephemeral act of lingering and passing through. But this gallery is not always transitory; it is also a curricular, aesthetic, political, and cultural initiative that highlights emerging queer Latinx and Latinx performance artists within the space of an established academic discipline. By privileging this art form, the aim is to alter the internal architecture of Latinx studies while also holding accountable the KAM, "equally a university art museum—devoted to teaching and research—and a regional museum, serving audiences in East Central Illinois," that will in partnership open its doors to these artists. In this way, the gallery engenders new forms of collaborations across campus that privilege both aesthetics and politics as opposed to reinforcing the marginalization of the arts within less humanistic forms of study and the exclusion of culture and race within museums. This initiative also trains student interns in performance curation and arts management, with keen attention paid to racial formations produced by aesthetic sites. Many of our Latinx studies students learn how to work creatively, conceptually, and administratively, and they are hands-on during the entire exhibitionary process, working closely with the artist, staff, faculty, and KAM affiliates. For example, La Estación Gallery will receive approximately twenty thousand visits per school year, including students, alumni, and educators across disciplines, and community members from Champaign-Urbana, Chicago, and the surrounding midwestern areas. These visits will be organized and run by students; at other times, they will be guided by the artist herself. Funding provided, the gallery will house an artist-in-residence each school year working on diverse areas of Latinx cultural and aesthetic life with a profound investment in experimental art practices.

While working to build a commons and create sustainable means by which to represent community publicly and privately, the gallery was not established without tension. La Estación Gallery was created as a response to several interlocking concerns: faculty and students feeling the immediate burden of state-sanctioned violence under the current administration; students demanding a way to evaluate everyday life through the arts; a community-building effort in conversation with the KAM to reframe the representational models of people of color on display; a communal space for emerging experimental queer Latinx artists to share their often unassessed work; a space for public engagement within the university's internalized demise of and need for diversity. Although these seem like different political considerations, everyday sites such as fields of study and the university often reflect the policies of national governmentality. Latinx studies' preoccupation with empirical methodology as a prime way to share insight into the racialized and sexualized human often imitates national acts of governance, even if unconsciously. For instance, when a country is in a state of daily emergency, certain avenues of political thought overshadow aesthetic channels of expression, for the aesthetic becomes indexed as a luxury, an afterthought to politics. This gallery asks us to release ourselves from this trap, allowing both aesthetic and political life to emerge from a conservation with, as opposed to against, one another. Invested in how the very act of remaking space within Latinx studies might amend the field's own sense of self, we pushed past positivism, empirical evidence, and data analysis into the promising domain of the aesthetic—not as a signifier of beauty but as a common responsibility to one another. In this way, the aesthetic and our collective engendered new spatial turns in our Latinx studies by refusing the burden of empiricist representation and reshaping the contours of representation itself.

These new spatial turns include a series of ongoing challenges that rehearse some of the issues listed above. By its nature, space is never empty, politically neutral, or just a container for physical entities, as Henri Lefebvre contends. It is also always imbued with power relations that authorize our cultural interactions—dynamics that we must collectively change, even in the face of complication.[7] Thinking with Lefebvre, I hope to move away from a theoretical construction of space and into its practice in everyday life. Creating La Estación Gallery involved various demanding strands, from securing funding for equipment to paying our artist; to learning from scratch how to rebuild a material structure; to working for months during the weekends without pay; to dealing with the bureaucracy of building management; to accommodating statewide austerity measures; to listening to concerns from certain faculty about the communal value and use of the gallery space, with particular reservations given to the content of the aesthetic; to considering concerns about the governing role of the KAM. Bearing in mind that our unit "rents" already limited space from the university, I could understand these concerns, although they further solidify the feeling of my insider-outsider status both within Latinx studies and as a curator of minoritarian performance within a predominantly heteronormative museum. These concerns remained throughout the process, and I often wondered how best to negotiate the political objective of this gallery, treat ensuing epistemological patriarchy, consider the university's fiscal control over our unit's resources, and reaffirm the importance of a communal space in a department that focused on queer and experimental Latinx artists who turn to the posthuman to underscore colonial life.

Consequently, for our inaugural exhibition, I organized a retrospective of Gressman's work with the guidance of brilliant interns Jema Torres, Monica Alvarez, Chloe Nagle, Iris Hernandez, and Victoria Giesso; LLS colleagues M. Laura Castañeda and Alicia P. Rodriguez; KAM's contemporary curator, Amy L. Powell; a graduate student installation specialist, Katie Netti; and the artist herself. Convinced that the more difficult the art, the more chances for individual, institutional, and communal transformation under perilous national times, we devised a solo show, *Limbs, Ligaments, Parts: My Body Is There*, featuring Gressman's body of work since 2009. The show intermixes pieces on embodiment, sound, science, and technology, headlining how Gressman questions what it means to look and sound Latinx, queer, Brown, and Colombian in everyday life by reordering our conventional schemas of listening, seeing, touching, and moving. She breaks the spell that binds us to strict categories of race, gender, and sexuality while never entirely revealing her own flesh. Yet as the title of the exhibition shares, her body is *there*. In searching for her, the exhibition asks spectators to tap into their senses and do the difficult work of finding the artist through their own sensorially engaged bodies.

For Gressman, the world, like art, is a scientific experiment in which constant variables change at the line between the human and the humanoid. From sound and light installations to videos, photographs, and a reproduced touch center of one of Gressman's live performances, the exhibition underscores Gressman's refusal to give us her skin; instead, she covers up her body to witness it transform into another organism such as a monster, alien, cyborg, robot, or mythical shaman. Viewers are encouraged to touch Gressman's work, make noise on an interactive installation, and reenact Gressman's own performances with the very materials she uses to make her artwork. Throughout the exhibition the spectator notices how the artist embraces fantasy with deliberate political intent, creating live biofeedback performances in sound and light to present her body in discrete ways. From cyborgs (*Wall of Skin*) to queer monsters (*Monster Wedding*) to disembodied monster-aliens (*Full Frontal Biopsy*) to occult witches (*Circuit Witch*) to shamans/sorcerers (*Disco Butoh*), Gressman turns to the interconnection among sound, image, and theatricality and how these interlaced practices challenge, affect, and welcome, through disorientation, an audience.[8] Gressman's experimentation with her own body discovers new ways of doing politics, art, and culture. These cyborgs, aliens, monsters, witches, sorcerers, and speculative entities guide Gressman in challenging both heteronormative practices of art and the indexical markers that join and disjoin the human/posthuman within categories of race, gender, and sexuality.[9] By amalgamating the senses and genres, the artist expresses how to make it in a world that refuses people of color, women, queers: learn to listen against typical constructions of the human, particularly when these categories overburden the right to be more than a singular entity. Between the limits of the human and machine, being and alter ego, Gressman redeems our senses and reshapes our politics, gesturing ever so forcefully to what it means to be more than just one thing in the world, in a gallery, in an institution.

An example of this is seen in the video of *Full Frontal Biopsy*, where Gressman performs a "self-surgery" on her abdomen, using a Dremel drill to replace a real scalpel. She morphs into the character named Boogita, a "hyperfeminine Latina consumer" turned excessive monster. Boogita is layered in "frightening makeup, fishnet stockings, corsets, a lab-coat, and an untamed wig." By putting a plastic plate on her belly, which is also attached to a contact microphone, Gressman uses the "drill to operate on herself," exaggerating vocal noises from another contact microphone in her mouth.[10] Both her vocal noises and the sounds emitted from the drill on the plastic plate are looped with effect pedals, creating percussive vibrations through the layering of sound. Because the drill is in direct contact with the plastic, the contact microphone transduces the actual sound, and the contact microphone in her mouth amplifies her own biological noises. In this performance, the artist pushes noise music into the space of theater and science, displaying that she is both "the input and the output, the patient and the surgeon, the artist and the audience." This exhibition moves the spectator to question what happens when we change into something else and obscure the fine line between human form and posthuman desire.

In another video of a live performance for gallery spectators, Gressman is a human-like organism recently dropped on planet Earth. *Wall of Skin* is an immersive noise, light, and movement piece, revealing the sound of light, with the artist fully covered in cybernetic skin. Using homemade analog electronic instruments that are sensitive to light and reactive to movement, this performance represents an enlivened musical composition that explores the complexity of skin, both its psychological and its social effects. The viewer witnesses that Gressman begins her performance in the dark on a raised platform in front of a piece of drywall with cables attached to it. Dressed from head to toe in her snug white cybernetic skin, with her breasts taped against her chest and her face obscured, she erases any traditional markers of sex, gender, and race as she releases herself from her own cyborgian body.[11]

In yet another performance, *Monster Wedding,* the artist stages a theatrical scene of a queer wedding heralded and led by a live violinist. This performance is a response to Proposition 8 and the banning of gay marriage in California in 2008, as well as the continual violence against queers of color. This piece invites the audience to attend a freak show celebration in which Gressman is the costume designer, director, and vow master of the ceremony. And in *Circuit Witch*, also included in the exhibition, the artist creates a cinematic performance led by an occultist, mixing light and sound in a large cauldron. In this piece, the witch is trapped in a series of twigs and spider webs, and electronic noise is used to hypnotize audiences into a spiritual cleanse, an otherworldly sound-bath. Finally, the artist reimagines a queer and Brown rendition of *butoh* (an avant-garde Japanese aesthetic practice grounded in dance and silent theater). This performance, seen on video, involves a speaker that creates music when audience members gather closely and hold hands. Gressman suspends her body above a large speaker filled with glitter, which is then sprayed onto the artist's face through subsequent sound waves. The light simultaneously bounces off the movement of the glitter and onto the walls to create a full sound-based theatrical scene. All of her performances use everyday materials as art and present her body in discrete forms, expounding on notions of embodiment, sound, science, and technology.

On September 12, 2018, at least 125 people attended the gallery's two-hour inaugural exhibition opening. Students, community members, and visitors from Indiana, Florida, and Chicago and from across the college from departments such as anthropology, dance, theater, geography, English, psychology, social work, music, Asian American studies, African American studies, neuroscience, pathobiology, computer science, and advertising, along with alumni from Latina/Latino studies, just to name a few, packed the room and helped create joy, wonder, intrigue, and hope even in the face of uncomfortable artwork and national upheaval. As the doors opened to the public, Latinx studies colleagues, in a show of incredible support, flooded the room first, eager to see what had been transpiring within their walls throughout the past six months. One colleague described the creation as "a beautiful and inviting new space," while others praised its "authenticity," sharing how "the space looks like a real gallery in a large city." Still others commented on the good feeling the space generates, explaining how they felt like they had walked into another world. While many of our students felt "thankful," "seen," "heard," "allowed to be more than what's expected" as a queer and Latinx subject, some had slightly different reactions. One student from another unit described feeling "disturbed, but intrigued."[12] This student, with notebook and pen always in hand, remained for the entire two hours of the opening, writing and rewatching videos, talking with the artist and her mother about the meaning of it all.

The diversity of visitors was expansive, including deans, vice chancellors, chairs of several units, faculty across disciplines, family members of the artist and staff, many students across schools, art critics from out of state, members of the museum committee, curators, staff, design installers, and the director. Our committed interns, alongside the artist, directed viewers across the room, showing the audience how to engage with the touchable installations. Throughout this collaborative process student interns shared their demands for accessible art and why they refused to attend galleries and museums, especially on campus. They voiced concerns about the "coldness of art spaces," feeling watched by guards, having to be silent or to whisper while viewing work, and being unable to touch/engage with objects. Therefore, we collectively decided that there would be objects in the exhibition that would welcome and sustain touch, a rare find across campus. This added bonus to being-with art created a sense of wonder throughout the room that also transferred to the artist herself. At times, one could see the artist explaining her work, playing with her own sound installations, or watching her videos with a viewer. Throughout the evening, the gallery expanded into a space where bodies interacted, played with objects, and made noise together, enacting some of Lefebvre's ideas on how space is enlivened by the very bodies that collectively reshape its inherent social and cultural meaning.

If opening night was any indication of its success, we expect at least 150 visits to the gallery per week, since courses and lectures held within several departments and schools will attend the show. Gressman's solo exhibition will run for nine months, during which she will also conduct class visits in several departments and cultural houses. With the present financial support of the department, the gallery is quickly becoming a fierce collaboration among faculty, graduate and undergraduate students, staff, academic counselors, and community members, crossing boundaries between disciplines and methods. Gressman's work will be used to further promote this collaborative synergy, bringing aesthetics and politics into closer proximity across fields and schools.

At least 350 people, including students, staff, faculty, collaborators in Chicago, surrounding community members, and members from out of state, attended her solo performance, *Limbs*, at KAM on September 13, 2018, more than three times the expected amount, to a standing-room-only audience. Performed to one of the largest audiences in the museum's history, *Limbs* involved a metal cage shaped like a tripod and doubling as a large-scale sound instrument, which the artist made herself. Violin-like electronic sounds are controlled by Gressman's moving body within the cage. The cage, her instrument, is responsive to both her movement and light, using contact microphones and light receptors to exact feeling and sound. From head to toe, Gressman is trapped in a suit made of reflective material, glowing brightest as special lights from the audience shine on her self-made costume. At first, she appears like two enmeshed bodies, as five hanging limbs attach to her costume—all used to amplify sound. She stands still within the cage for approximately eight minutes, steadying her breath for any movement will create sound and change the score. Motionless and trapped before the audience enters, she carefully stages curiosity, suspense, anxiety, even fear. The audience members are then led into the long gallery alongside the same orchestral sound, violins repeatedly creating a sense of hypnotic splendor. The removal of her limbs engenders the evolution of a musical composition, and through a sense of controlled chaos, Gressman controls our sentiments. In yet another piece, the artist turns to the posthuman resembling, as she shares, "a bioluminescent alien, an aquatic multi-limbed creature that was underwater or in space" that could express the affective tenors of loss, losing family, friends, contact with those you dearly love.[13] In this sound-light-movement piece, Gressman once again rethinks deep feelings against ideological and political sentiment in the face of everyday subjugation, expressing how difficult aesthetics help us become human/humane in multifaceted ways.

As a curator and scholar of performance art, I have been following Gressman's work for four years now, trying to figure out the resonances among all of her aesthetic practices. I have come to know the work, human, and posthuman intimately, and as culturally counterintuitive as it may appear, given the tough layering of her pieces, Gressman's body of art offers hope during incredible loss and national peril. Her layers become a refuge, and that refuge lives across space, thought, art, discipline, and subjectivity. If we imagine a more dynamic future in which the minoritarian subject reshifts the management of life and death through art and space, Lefebvre's following idea reverberates profoundly: "In reality, social space 'incorporates' social actions, the actions

FIGURE 6.2. Erica Gressman, *Limbs*, performance at Krannert Art Museum, University of Illinois at Urbana-Champaign, September 13, 2018. Photo by Alicia P. Rodriguez.

of subjects both individual and collective who are born and who die, who suffer and who act. From the point of view of these subjects, the behaviour of their space is at once vital and mortal: within it they develop, give expression to themselves, and encounter prohibitions; then they perish, and that same space contains their graves."[14] Considering both the vitality and mortality of placemaking, it is evident that sustainability operates as an infinite temporal condition that carries the vestiges of those present and all their afterlives. In all social spaces there are ways to make place, either through new lines of invention or by tracing over already designated locations with repurposed meaning and vigor. If social space operates "as a tool for the analysis of society," as Lefebvre notes, then the feminist collective as both a concept and practice exposes itself as a prime example of a productive counterhegemonic strategy within a station lodged within a place located within a larger institution.[15]

This sense of placemaking stems from negotiating the boundaries between being a complicated and nuanced Brown subject with varying ideologies and one invested in experimental aesthetics as paramount to political life. This conveys that La Estación Gallery is generated and regenerated through the idea that the aesthetic reshapes existence and fosters building coalitions and making community even as the artwork pushes us to think beyond our normative worldmaking practices.[16] Reestablishing the parameters of infrastructure, labor, and curation was necessary in order to unite a respective community through both Gressman's avant-garde art and the conversion of space itself. By reshaping curation into an act of collective formation, I see its role as building insurgent networks and, as a result, collecting kin as opposed to objects neatly displayed against a wall.

Notes

1. This queer and feminist collective consisted of five interns who worked throughout the development of the project, me, and staff. Jema Torres and Monica Alvarez were our first interns, and they helped write grants and secure funding for our first exhibition. Chloe Nagle was our MFA intern from the Department of Dance, who focused on marketing and writing reviews; Victoria Giesso was our LLS alumni graduate in charge of all social media and promotion; Iris Hernandez is our current undergraduate Latinx studies intern and now in charge of marketing, social media, and graphic design. She also began leading tours to visitors of the exhibition in early 2019. Katie Netti is an MFA student in sculpture and served as our brilliant installation specialist. Alicia P. Rodriguez is the Latina/Latino studies academic advisor and administrative coordinator, as well as our resident photographer. M. Laura Casteñada is the LLS office support specialist, who was in charge of all supplies and funding.

2. By "a commons" I am thinking with José Esteban Muñoz's "The Brown Commons" located in his book *The Sense of Brown*, ed. Joshua Chambers-Letson and Tavia Nyong'o (Durham, NC: Duke University Press, 2020).

3. Citation taken from an email conversation with KAM contemporary curator Amy L. Powell conducted throughout February 2021.

4. After Gressman's live performance of *Limbs* at KAM, scholar, musician, and composer Fiona Ngô described the artist's piece as an example of art that shows us the violence embedded in becoming. For Ngô, Gressman's body of work exposes us to the inherent violence implicated in the act of subjectivity, whether in art or in everyday life.

5. In my assessment of difficulty and difficult art I turn to Jennifer Doyle's book *Hold It against Me: Difficulty and Emotion in Contemporary Art* (Durham, NC: Duke University Press, 2013), 5.

6. Gressman received her MFA from the School of the Art Institute of Chicago's Department of Performance and her BA from the New College of Florida, with a concentration in experimental music. She has performed at the Museum of Contemporary Art Chicago, the Royal Danish Art Academy, Pittsburgh's VIA Festival, New York's Grace Exhibition Space, Chicago's Defibrillator Gallery, Miami Art Center, the Channing Murray Foundation, and the Independent Media Center.

7. Henri Lefebvre, *The Production of Space*, trans. Donald Nicolson-Smith (Malden, MA: Blackwell Publishing, 1974), 1–67.

8. For full access to Gressman's documented performances, go to https://www.ericagressman.com.

9. Sandra Ruiz, "Organismal Futurisms in Brown Sound and Queer Luminosity: Getting into Gressman's Cyborgian Skin," *Performance Matters* 3, no. 2 (2017): 72–91.

10. Ibid.

11. Ibid.

12. Citations taken from gallery guest sign-in sheet where comments were solicited.

13. Sandra Ruiz, interview with artist Erica Gressman, September 15, 2018.

14. Lefebvre, *The Production of Space*, 33–34.

15. Ibid., 34.

16. María Eugenia Cotera, "El Museo del Norte: Passionate Praxis on the Streets of Detroit" in Valerio-Jiménez, Vaquera-Vásquez, and Fox, *The Latina/o Midwest Reader*, 197–210. Cotera's chapter provides critical inquiry into how one makes place through the aesthetic. I turned to her chapter throughout my writing for inspiration and political vision.

CHAPTER 7

Testimony

A Welcoming Spirit

CARMEN HERNANDEZ, PBVM

Brief Background

Born in Waterloo, Iowa, Sister Carmen Hernandez is a member of the leadership team of the Sisters of the Presentation of the Blessed Virgin Mary (also known as the Presentation Sisters), located in Dubuque, Iowa. In 2013 she became the founding executive director of La Luz Hispana community center in Hampton, Iowa, a position that she held for five years. Prior to her work with La Luz Hispana, she served as the Hispanic outreach coordinator of Mercy Medical Center North Iowa in Mason City and as a team member of Caminando Juntos, a Latinx-serving community center operated by the Aberdeen Presentation Sisters in Sioux Falls, South Dakota. Among her previous career experiences, she worked as an elementary school counselor and teacher and as a police department chaplain in various Iowa cities. In the fall of 2018, shortly after the fifth-anniversary celebration of La Luz Hispana, Sister Carmen returned to Dubuque to become the congregational leader of the Sisters of the Presentation of Dubuque, Iowa.

Meanwhile, La Luz Hispana continues to thrive under new leadership and a new name, La Luz Centro Cultural. Hampton, Iowa, a town with a population of approximately 4,231 in the north-central part of the state, and surrounding communities have witnessed a rapid increase in Latinx residents in recent decades. La Luz Hispana provides essential social services and support for Latinx Hamptonians, including translation, language and citizenship courses, transportation, cultural programming, and education.

The following was transcribed by Laura Fernández and Marie Lerma from a recorded presentation that Sister Carmen Hernandez made to the volume contributors on August 9, 2017.

Sister Carmen's Testimony

I am a Presentation Roman Catholic religious sister from Dubuque, Iowa, and I am half Latina and half German. My family says that I never really recognized that I'm German. I always say that I'm Mexican, and so they question, "Whatever happened to the other half?" We never spoke Spanish in our home. I took Spanish in high school, but I've always had a desire to learn Spanish and to do something with that language. After studying in Bolivia, where our sisters work, I decided that I wanted to get a job that would use my cultural and language background. I was hired immediately at Mercy Medical Center North Iowa in Mason City as their Hispanic outreach coordinator. I didn't care for the job. They employed me as a receptionist at a clinic to make appointments, and that's not what I was hired for.

From there, I decided that I wanted to start my own community center. As part of my job at Mercy, I traveled to Hampton, Iowa, once a week with the Namaste clinic for pregnant women, a mobile clinic that served Latinas, Anglos, and other patients so they didn't have to travel thirty-five miles north for services. They could receive health care locally. Over the course of my work in that position, I had the opportunity to build relationships with many Latinx families. I began to have conversations with them, asking, "Are you happy with Hampton? What is it that you'd like to see that would make it better?" And many responded that they wanted their own space, their own center. So I worked with some of the Latina women, and—this is the beauty of it—they are the ones that really came up with the ideas as far as programming for the center. One of the women said, "Oh, I'll do a survey, and I'll pass it out!" So together we conducted a survey. We circulated it to some of the families in town and decided that there were certain programs that they would like at a center. Meanwhile, I did research with my own community of religious sisters and associates. These initial steps in developing a mission and programming for La Luz Hispana were an effort in which everybody felt included, even though they were not actually involved in the groundwork. But everybody had some ownership in it. I then decided to go to Sioux Falls, South Dakota, to work in their Latinx community center [Caminando Juntos] for two years. I returned to Hampton after much research and decided to start there. There was no Latinx-serving community center there. The nearest ones were in Marshalltown, a little over an hour and a half away, and Webster City, about forty-five minutes away. But the Latinx population in Hampton seemed to be growing, and we found a place and began La Luz Hispana in 2013.

We've been running the center for four years now as a 501(c)(3) nonprofit organization. We are funded mainly by the Sisters of the Presentation, and that picture will change in the coming years. We are receiving the annuity of one of the sisters, and when she dies, the funding stops! Thank goodness, she's in great health! She is eighty-nine years old and still doing all the driving for the community. The other source of funding that we have is through grants. Sister Maura McCarthy, who works with me—God bless her!—she writes the grant proposals. She's going to be eighty years old in December. She worked in Bolivia for thirty-three years and has a real love for the Hampton Latinx community. In addition to grant funding, the other initiative that we started, now in its second year, is Gran Festival, and that is our annual fundraiser. We've raised quite a bit of funds through this event. We've got music, and we began our own cultural dance group featuring women who frequently come to our center. The dance group has been invited to a lot of different places to dance, and from those performances we receive donations also. Within the dance group, we have a small kids' group, a middle-aged group, and the women's group. The group always dances at the festival and at other events, too.

Hampton has a population of about 4,300, and the population of Franklin County, in which Hampton is located, is approximately 12 percent Latino and growing. Our philosophy at La Luz Hispana is that we are a welcoming spirit to anyone who walks through the door, offering support services not just to the Latinx population but to everyone. The largest demographic of Latinx people in Hampton comes from Veracruz, Mexico, so they call Hampton "Little Veracruz." We also have Guatemalans and Salvadorans that come to the center. The Honduran population is starting to grow because Prestage Foods [a hog-processing plant] is coming to Eagle Grove, and groundbreaking will occur soon. So we have seen an increase in numbers of Latinx people moving to the area. The challenge is that Hampton has a housing shortage. I'm not sure what we'll do about that; however, within a thirty-to-forty-mile radius there are small towns where people seem to be finding housing.

At La Luz Hispana, we do anything and everything! Until this last May, I was one of two people who worked there. With no salary, we offer our time, and we try to meet the needs that are not already being addressed by another organization or business in town. We find that one of the main things we provide is transportation: community members have a great fear of driving, especially long distances. Just Monday, I was in Omaha at the immigration office with someone at the consulate getting paperwork done for them, and I drove. We've also gone to Des Moines and Chicago. Translation and interpretation are also frequent requests. Until last May, when we hired a part-time staff member, I was trying to be the administrator and executive director, do all the budgeting and financing, and help Sister Maura with transportation. We were feeling the strain. It's supposed to be an eight-hour workday, but it often ends up being twelve hours.

Our programming comes from proposals submitted by community members. Aimee [the newest staff member of La Luz Hispana] has a Survey Monkey set up on our Facebook page that solicits programming suggestions. We've organized events such as computer classes and collaborations with local businesses. We've also had the chief of police and the sheriff come in and speak. La Luz Hispana is a wonderful environment, and it is the only center in town that really works with Latinx people. Thus, we are a point of contact for any organization that wants to communicate with local Latinx people. For example, the high school will call and ask, "Can we offer this program at your place?" The center is a safe place for Latinx community members. Some organizations have been holding events there since we were founded, such as the Iowa State Extension Office. Now, Latinx community members are actually going directly to that organization instead of having the Extension come into ours. Now that a relationship has been built through La Luz Hispana, communication between local residents and these organizations is occurring directly.

Sister Maura does all of the interpretation and translation. I don't feel that I'm completely bilingual yet, but rather, I'm still learning. However, both of us have received phone calls from local businesses in which someone asks, "Can you come now? We have somebody that's wanting to rent a house, and we don't understand a thing they're saying." US Cellular has called and said, "Can you come over? We're trying to get a phone for . . ." In this manner, we've built relationships with local organizations and businesses, and we assist in these situations when we are able to do so.

The primary reason that people come to Hampton and surrounding communities is because they know one another. Their family is there already—pretty soon the whole state of Veracruz will be in Hampton I think! Once someone arrives and becomes familiar with Hampton, one sees that it's a pretty calm and tranquil town. The police and the sheriff are good people. They know who has licenses and who doesn't, and unless someone is breaking the law, there are no problems with community policing to enforce immigration policy. In terms of job opportunities that draw Latinx people to Hampton, there are over three hundred hog confinements in the Franklin County area, and there are poultry-processing plants, and construction work, always a big employer. Those are probably the three largest labor sectors that employ Latinx people in the area. An immigration lawyer from Catholic Charities comes to La Luz Hispana quarterly. She does anything that she can as far as citizenship renewal and DACA status. We have a grant from the Presentation community that helps to pay half of the DACA or citizenship fees. The family pays the other half, which seems to work out well. We want community members to have some ownership in these legal fees, so we assist but do not cover the full cost. Likewise, sometimes people need help with gas, rent money, and so on. We offer financial assistance to support these requests to the extent that we can.

One of the initial barriers to our mission at La Luz Hispana is the fact that because we are Roman Catholic sisters, people perceived us to be a Catholic institution. We try to get out to the churches to talk about that. It has helped now that we have Aimee on staff, who is not Catholic. Hopefully, her presence will have some advantage for us also. We've started a group consisting of religious leaders of churches that serve the Latinx community. There are probably seven to nine different denominations, from Pentecostal to Mormons, Catholics, and others. We try to get them together to discuss "How can we work together?" This effort has not been very successful—I'm not sure why. I think everybody tends to stick to their own group. Even at the center, we've heard people say to us, "Well, I don't come to your center. I'd like to, but I don't get along with those people from Veracruz." There are some relational issues that occur among community members from different parts of Mexico or Honduras and Guatemala. That has sometimes been a struggle.

We work in great collaboration with the schools, and when parent-teacher conferences are held, if they need assistance beyond the school interpreters, we help with that. Twice a year the school administrators hold meetings where they explain to the Latino families the new rules for the school year, and we host those events. Our space is modest, consisting of four rooms: a front room, a computer room, a kitchen, and a back room, which was formerly a garage. Organizations like banks have generously let us use their basement space for large events. We have held some meetings on diversity-related topics. For example, Mark Grey from the University of Northern Iowa, Cedar Falls, who has done a lot of work with Iowa Latinx groups, came in to speak. Mark Prosser, the ex–police chief of Storm Lake, a diverse northern Iowa city, also came to speak, as well as Zadok Nampala, the international student advisor at North Iowa Area Community College. These speakers were funded by a grant from Franklin County, and we hope to continue that series this year. We have also organized immigration workshops on how to designate power of attorney and create a financial and child custody plan in the event that community members are arrested or deported. Those workshops have been highly attended. Any time we hold an event featuring an immigration lawyer, we get a big crowd. We are at a point where we are looking for a bigger space and actually are wondering if it would be better to work with like-minded nonprofit organizations. We might remain a cultural center or become part of a collective of nonprofit organizations. We are considering our options.

When I first started working at La Luz Hispana in 2013, the incoming kindergarten class was approximately 20 percent Latinx. This year, 2017, 50 percent of Hampton's kindergartners are Latinx. The Latinx population is growing, and the city knows that. This year we have our first ever Latina running for the school board, and that's pretty exciting. I hope she does well, but just the fact of having a Latina run for that office is impressive. She is a graduate from the high school in town. We had one of the high school graduates also do alley art on one of the buildings and did a wonderful depiction on the side of what Hampton represented, including the cornstalks, fairgrounds, and a little bit of Latinx imagery. In Hampton, there are approximately nine or ten Latinx-owned businesses, which sustain the Hampton economy. The city is hoping to add Spanish-language texts to its messaging system so that Spanish speakers can receive texts about snow removal and parking regulations, for example.

As for our current plans, we're discussing further fundraising and how to publicize who we are. La Luz Hispana has been here for four years, yet there still seem to be people who don't know that we exist. Some people think that we're a restaurant—yup! They come in and ask, "What are you serving today?" It's interesting: for all the advertising we've done, a small number of local residents still think this. But really, my personal priority is building a relationship with the Latinx population. Once that happens, you've got the world in your hands, because they'll do anything for you. When we talk about where we want to see La Luz Hispana go, we've held small-group meetings at community members' houses. A Latina community member will invite a group of approximately twelve women into her home, and Sister Maura and I are there to raise questions about what we can do to make things better for them.

One final comment I would add about funding is that we are considering requesting compensation from organizations that use our interpretation services. We're asking them, "Do you have some kind of funding that you could also give back to us?" Sister Maura does the translation for the Mercy Hospital newsletter in Spanish, and last year they began to give a donation to La Luz Hispana for her work. Sister Maura also does the translation for all the Crisis Intervention domestic abuse cases, and last year they said that they had a small amount they could commit for this service. As I said previously, the funding from our congregation won't last forever. The big question that will come up is whether the city of Hampton will help to sustain us.

CHAPTER 8

Creating Latinx Arts Networks in Chicago

J. GIBRAN VILLALOBOS

Brief Background

J. Gibran Villalobos was the partnerships and public programs manager for the Chicago Architecture Biennial and is faculty lecturer at the School of the Art Institute of Chicago. He was born in Los Angeles and raised in Glendale, Arizona. He has managed collections for municipal public art collections and has advocated for the arts with congressional officials. His work focuses on civic engagement and the administration of cultural practice. He is presently an assistant curator of performance and public practice at the Museum of Contemporary Art in Chicago.

The following testimony was transcribed by Laura F. Fernández and Marie Lerma from a recorded presentation that J. Gibran Villalobos made to the volume contributors on August 9, 2017.

Testimony

I am very happy to be here at a time when conversations like these are critical. My name is Gibran Villalobos, and I am currently the partnership and public programs manager for the Chicago Architecture Biennial. This is the biennial's official second year, and I say that with a little bit of a funny tone because I think every time I see Ramón [H. Rivera-Servera], I have a new position to announce. In a way, this relates to the urgency and the speed of the work that I do, moving between multiple organizations, all in different capacities. A lot of my work rests on the opportunities and needs of major arts and cultural organizations to reach different parts of the city. Also, the work I am building relies on Chicago's history as a city deeply steeped in social action, particularly within cultural institutions. Take, for example, the Chicago Cultural Center, originally a public library once dubbed "the People's Palace." The Chicago Architecture Biennial exhibition, held within this building, recognized its responsibility to work with organizations outside of the city center in order to ensure we live true to the motto of the regal building.

In the past I've worked for the Chicago Park District as the cultural liaison for the Culture, Arts, and Nature Department. I've worked for the MCA as their community liaison also, where I am tasked with going into Chicago communities and neighborhoods, and I've worked for the Art Institute of Chicago in the Department of Architecture and Design as a program manager. To me, it is funny how I always work in this realm of community outreach and within my title I always find the word "liaison," which always makes me very suspicious, but at the same time, I've learned to use that to my advantage. Now I tend to play with it as a way to develop my personal practice. The ambiguity allows me to practice administration while at the same time observing and researching institutional structures. I'm also faculty at the School of the Art Institute of Chicago in the Department of Arts Administration and Policy, and I will touch on the curricular work that I do there, but for the most part, my academic work is in art history and arts administration. I have learned a lot about using that duality and how I think about the work that I do as something that does not just happen in the classroom. It is actually happening across art institutions and at the same time shapes my engagement with the public.

I am originally from Arizona, where I was working with the Public Art Collection in the City of Glendale, as well as the grants program at the Arizona Commission on the Arts, where we supported artists across the state. In those meetings, I also developed a very close relationship with the National Association for Latino Arts and Culture (NALAC). I had the opportunity to participate in NALAC's Advocacy Leadership Institute in Washington, DC. The institute was a four-day engagement with the White House, where we sat with the Hispanic Caucus, the White House Office of Public Engagement, and we brought our talking points and statistical information on an index card. Speaking with legislators and senators underlined for me the critical urgency and need to directly communicate issues affecting Latinos. It is the direct contact with elected officials that raises the urgency of impact and makes community engagement work real. I came back from that experience very inspired to perform more direct work here in Chicago not just with the Latino community but also specifically with arts administrators and artists.

Some of you are familiar with an artist named Theaster Gates?[1] Maybe you're familiar with the Black Artists Retreat and the work that he was doing with Black artists and administrators? In the summer of 2011 he established a retreat to look at Black cultural environments here in Chicago. I became very jealous of not being able to attend my own version of a Black Artists Retreat, an inability to participate in a cultural environment catering to the needs of my community, so I created a retreat that was open to Latinos, Latinas, and Latinxs. I recently launched what I am calling LARD, the Latino Artists Research Division. The name, of course, is on purpose: it is the ingredient that you want in your food because it makes it taste "authentically" good but the thing that your doctor tells you not to eat, right? I mentioned this as a joke to a friend, and he said, "Actually, that works perfectly." Lard is the solvent that greases up, that thing that lubricates the inside of a machine. As I thought more about institutions, questions became increasingly necessary: Who's doing the work inside of these institutions? Who doesn't get the visibility or doesn't get the attention for the work within institutions?

I'm proud to say that we got funding through the Propeller Grant, which is a local small grant given to start-up organizations by the nonprofit Threewalls. On May 19–21, 2017, we made LARD happen. We brought together over sixty artists not just from Chicago but from San Antonio, Philadelphia, New York City, Tucson, and Los Angeles. I am also happy to report that it was really exciting to see how cross-generational this event became. It was not the echo chamber of just a couple of grad students talking about art—which is great and critically important too. I wanted to break out of this pattern, to bring visibility to the people that are doing the work: educators, writers, administrators. Also, it was very important for us to make this event appealing and inviting. We paid for food. We paid speakers. We paid for a party. It was, thinking about the ethos behind the work that happens here at the National Museum of Mexican Art where we are meeting right how, a way of making things accessible for our community. This might be critical for Latinos who, like myself, are first-generation college graduates.

I was the first in the family to ever venture into art as a profession. My parents almost had heart attacks when I told them that I would go from the ideal of medical school into art history! Now they laugh about it, but I think that it is still a very scary thing for a lot of young Latina/o/x academics. How do you negotiate, being first generation, going into a field that is not always the most profitable or even able to sustain the basics of living? This issue of affordability to even venture into the field is another unspoken visibility question as we set our aims toward questions of diversity, access, and inclusion. Who and how do we prepare institutions to listen deeply and look for voices that haven't been historically represented within leadership staffing? Who do we include in those conversations, and how do we invite them in?

From our LARD summit we came out with a few main goals of what we want our annual retreat to do. We want to establish a set of curricular topics that others can utilize to augment their academic lesson plans. We want plans that invite Latina/o/x artists across history but also across disciplines, so that if an institution, specifically in the arts, wants to start developing a curriculum and needs Latina/o/x photographers in the 1800s or 1900s, they have a resource available. We want this to be prepackaged so that there is no excuse for them to say, "We don't know where to find these resources" or "We don't have these resources available to us." So it has a muscular arm to really push curricular development toward inclusivity.

Second, we want to develop mentorship and visibility by actually bringing attention to a lot of emerging arts administration practitioners. What I noticed when I first came to the School of the Art Institute of Chicago is that in Chicago, less than 7 percent of our student base is Latinx. That is a grave issue that I had a huge problem with. How can we be in the Midwest, how can we be in Chicago, a city that is comprised of nearly one-third Latinx population, and have our student base be less than 7 percent Latinx? Especially when we have Pilsen, an epicenter of great art happening. I am certainly suspicious.

Today, we have a growing base of Latinx faculty at SAIC. The next step for us is to figure out how to bridge them to institutional leadership. Because speaking from my own experience, my own hunger for leadership, and my own need for mentorship, I know that when I would walk into institutions, I always want to know: Who looks like me that is going to eventually mentor me or take me under their wing to tell me what I am doing wrong, what I am doing right? Or to help me orient my next step and figure out how to move upward?

Recently, I was having a conversation with a real estate agent as part of the Chicago Architecture Biennial programs. One of the things he said was, "Well, as an arts administrator, clearly you must have a passing of the baton system, right? Something that teaches you the ropes of your field? We do, in the real estate business." I said, "Actually, we don't, we're emerging, it's a very new field." If you look at the history of arts administration, formal programs had not really started until the late sixties or early seventies, and even that's questionable. As a formal course of study, arts administration is still emerging, it is still being defined as a practice. Who are the existing organizations that are connecting young arts administrators to positions of leadership? To me this is second nature in how other fields operate. I'm now very happy to say we have been funded by the Chicago Community Trust with an Act Up Award, so we are hoping to replicate a lot of what we did this year and retaining it as a free and accessible program. Our goal is to put into action a lot of these goals and deliverables that emerged in the urgency of our conversations.

I would like to momentarily think about the curatorial work I have been doing across Chicago to highlight emerging artists. I have another Latinx art historian with whom I collaborate frequently: William Ruggiero. We have executed public art installations for the Chicago Park District and exhibitions for the Chicago Artist Coalition and with the School of the Art Institute of Chicago. Most recently, we were resident curators at the Chicago Cultural Center. Much of the work we are doing is to bring into visibility Latin American / Latinx art history. We have been thinking about the relationship between the Casas de Cultura found across Latin America as collective institutions for art and culture and our perception of shared public space. We want to learn how notions of shared space for culture can shape our understanding of community engagement. How do we invite those administrative practices that center collectivity into the work we aim to do within a culture that centers individualism? I want to take this moment to recognize Professor Claire Fox in the room. The research found in her work into Latin America and its articulations of cultural policy is at the forefront of administration. Claire, I am excited to be in this room with you.

I think that now the work is moving us to figure out how we might make this not solely an institutional need but an actual change in the culture of institutions. Many of the lessons that we learn about administration as policy can actually direct things, create mobility, circulate funding. Now our challenge remains to make Latinxs visible in those conversations by either invitation or demand. In class, one of the things that surprises incoming students into our arts administration program is that we don't center our teaching around budget sheets, marketing campaigns, or development strategies. Yes, these are valuable subjects and are present in many aspects of our curriculum. However, we encourage our students first and foremost to listen. To first identify the voices that have not been represented and to construct the values and ethics of the work to be done to bring them into the space and the conversation. I hope we can start asking some really interesting and urgent questions about the state of arts administration, specifically as it relates to challenging funding and leadership practices that have kept us out of place.

Note

1. https://www.theastergates.com.

PART III

Scale and Place

CHAPTER 9

Festival de las Calaveras and Somatic Emplacement in Minnesota

KAREN MARY DAVALOS

I carry my roots with me all the time
Rolled up I use them as my pillow.
—Francisco X. Alarcón

Growing up in southern California and living for two decades in Los Angeles, a city recognized as a "continuous community" because it predates the formation of the United States, I intimately knew Chicana/o/x places and placemaking.[1] In fabricated but beloved commercial zones such as Olvera Street, in neighborhoods such as Boyle Heights, the epicenter of Chicana/o/x art and activism since the 1960s, and in public schools such as Grand View Elementary School, with its growing Oaxacan and Zapotec-speaking population, spatiocultural claims throughout the Los Angeles metropolitan region were empirically registered, even if contested. I understood place as central to belonging.[2] When I moved to the Twin Cities in 2016, a metropolitan region with less than 12 percent Latina/o/x residents, most of whom are Mexican origin, arrived after 1965, and live in heterogeneous communities, I was skeptical about Latina/o/x placemaking.[3] I did not understand the body as the site of transit for belonging. My expectations forced me to conceptualize corporeal emplacement in the Twin Cities and to emphasize the body as an ephemeral space of belonging.

In Minneapolis and St. Paul, Latina/o/x residents live alongside whites, Blacks, American Indians, and Asians. Only one short commercial zone, Cesar Chavez Street on the West Side of St. Paul, is recognizably Chicana/o/x with the successful business El Burrito Mercado, which operates a restaurant, gift shop, and grocery store. Although the West Side of St. Paul, established in the 1920s, is one of the oldest ethnic Mexican enclaves in Minnesota, its historical longevity makes it distinctly Mexican, not its demography.[4] Similarly, Minneapolis witnesses "multiethnic adaptive streetscapes" where "multiple groups" coalesce on a "commercial street" such as East Lake Street.[5] In South Minneapolis, East Lake Street is anchored by Mercado Central, a thriving "permanent entrepreneurial cooperative space" with "forty-three businesses" that cater to people from Latin America and the Caribbean and often conduct business in Spanish.[6] The multistoried mercado is part of an urban corridor with *taquerías, tortillerías, panaderías, música latina,* shoe stores specializing in cowboy boots, and Mexican and Salvadoran restaurants, as well as a Scandinavian gift shop and deli, the Somali Museum of Minnesota, restaurants with Ethiopian and southern cuisine, hipster coffee shops, and "corporate fast-food restaurants and liquor stores."[7] However, Latina/o/x "presence along Lake Street is fairly recent," and outside of a few census tracts adjacent to East Lake Street cutting east–west across contiguous neighborhoods of Phillips, Whittier, Corcoran, and Powderhorn Park, residents of Latin American and Caribbean heritage do not enjoy demographic majority status in any community of the Twin Cities.[8] Even in those neighborhoods closest to East Lake Street, Latina/o/xs do not exceed 25 percent of the total population.

Without a recognizable Latina/o/x place in Minneapolis, I became interested in emplacement as it is produced somatically, through bodily registrations of belonging immediately and temporarily felt between bodies. Two scholars inspired my attention to the soma, defined as "the intelligent, communicative body."[9] Elaine A. Peña's description of a pilgrimage to the basilica in Mexico City alerted me to the ways *las peregrinas* find connection to Our Lady of Guadalupe and their spiritual world through their blistered feet and other involuntary bodily expressions. Their blisters, thirst, and exhaustion become source material for collective spiritual engagement and intersectional identities.[10] Stephanie Fetta's transdisciplinary study of racial shaming allowed me to diverge from Cartesian thought and empiricism to document the soma as an expressive and perceptive "response to our place in the world."[11] Fetta's definition of the soma is helpful. As an embodied register of our lived reality, the soma exists "at the organismic level—at the level of musculature, organs (such as the stomach and the bladder)," to which I add lungs and skin.[12] Somatic expression may include muscular states of relaxation or tension, the pace or depth of breath, tingling on the skin, swaying to music, belching, sighing, and a vocalization of wonderment ("ooh" or "aah"). Powerful and fleeting, the soma is "a core constituent of subjectivity and interpersonal relations," and thus, I suggest, it operates in placemaking.[13] For Cartesian thinkers and empiricists, the soma is a paradox because it communicates outside of awareness. As Fetta argues, the soma is "clear and decipherable" to and by individuals, but it is not always recognized.[14] Moreover, somatic expression is ephemeral, yet it can linger and transfer through the body to other spaces, particularly as multiple people experience the somatic effects of emplacement. It is real, but it is also illusive and temporary. Since it is embodied belonging, it supports a sustainable sense of place beyond external forms or forces.

This chapter calls attention to belonging enlivened within and between bodies through El Festival de las Calaveras in Minneapolis. Somatic analysis is an important method because somatic emplacement may precede Latina/o/x civic participation, commercial zones, or built environments. It is also an ideal method for understanding placemaking when populations are migratory, reside in heterogeneous neighborhoods, or have not reached majority status. El Festival de las Calaveras engages the body, the site in which placemaking occurs, and produces Latina/o/x somatic emplacement, a temporary but potent and corporeal political sociality referred to as "belonging."

Somatic emplacement may also be useful for scholars wishing to explore placemaking outside of "material objects, expressions, and traditions that can be contained, studied, or exhibited."[15] It allows scholars to heed Arlene Dávila's warning about "cultural objectification" and its tendency to "contribute to ahistorical and essentialist definitions that limit culture to particularized material objects or embodiments" that service exclusion and judgments of authenticity.[16] In contexts of invisibility and erasure, such empirical spaces or expressions may appeal to a politics of representation and sustainable structures, but they may also stifle or delegitimize flexible, porous, contested, and mysterious qualities of cultural belonging among diasporic, intersectional, and marginalized communities. More critically, by residing in the body, somatic emplacement need not be anchored to the physical environment, and it may not impact material realities, only perceptions of space. Because it is not attached to a physical site, Latina/o/x somatic emplacement may overcome invasive settler-colonial logics that use displacement to foster inclusion and exclusion. Following M. Bianet Castellanos and Luis Urrieta, who expose Chicana/o/x studies' limited views of indigeneity yet refuse to abandon the field, I suggest that somatic emplacement can dislodge investments in origins and tradition, spatial and temporal expectations that reify a political and social configuration of Mexicans, particularly Indigenous Mexicans, as premodern.[17] Such investments in space and time can stifle migrants' claims to cultural authority or homeland, but fidelity of their emplacement cannot be denied by their somas.

Feeling at Home at El Festival de las Calaveras

El Festival de las Calaveras plays an important role in engendering Latina/o/x somatic emplacement because it emerges from "relational aesthetics," a term coined to describe a genre of visual arts practice dependent upon social inter-action for full realization of the artwork.[18] Chicana/o/x art historians perceive relational aesthetics, although named differently, as a political sociability that extends beyond art forms.[19] Through the relational aesthetics of El Festival, not only art exhibitions and *ofrendas* (offerings) but also danced and drummed *ceremonia* (ceremony), poetry, and music, participants engage with art forms and each other, supporting a transformation of social life and experience. As I describe below, participants somatically experience music of El Festival and do so with awareness of each other as they dance across the floor or stand on the edges of the crowd and rhythmically jut their chins to the beat of the music, smiling when they catch the eye of another person whose neck and head also keep rhythm. Thus, while ephemeral, somatic emplacement allows for affective belonging that informs complex and "oppositional consciousness" of Latina/o/x subjectivity.[20]

El Festival de las Calaveras is similar in form to any number of multimedia, locally produced festivities that commemorate the dead in the style modified by California Chicana/o/xs in the early 1970s and throughout the Southwest and Midwest since the 1980s.[21] Over multiple days and nights leading up to November 2 and across a variety of rented locations in Minneapolis, the festival offers music, Mexica *danza, ceremonia*, poetry, arts workshops, art exhibitions, and community-built and artist-designed *ofrendas* to honor the dead. Produced by Tlalnepantla Arts since 2013, an organization founded by artist Deborah Ramos that operates without a brick-and-mortar facility, this homage to the dead engages "Indigenous and traditional arts," namely, the centrality of corn in the Americas.[22] In fact, the festival originated as a fundraiser for Ramos's urban community garden, Zenteotl Project, which had entered its fifth growing season.[23] From a South Minneapolis garden, Zenteotl Project produces blue corn for communal meals and organizes art-making and Nahua and P'urhepecha spiritual practices tied to harvest. After the inaugural celebration for the dead in 2013, Tlalnepantla Arts committed to producing El Festival de las Calaveras independently of the urban garden to "create and present multiple art forms . . . and to promote cultural identities and transform community."[24]

El Festival de las Calaveras is playful, joyous, critical, spiritual, and com-munal in its remembrance of the departed. Similar to the Zenteotl Project, it reaches ethnic Mexicans, Indigenous North Americans, and Latin Americans, a phenomenon also found in annual Cinco de Mayo parades in San Fran-cisco's Mission District, which include Central Americans, and in Mexican independence parades in Chicago, which include Puerto Ricans.[25] Similar to a hybrid *latinidad* generated by Fausto Fernós's cabaret performances, which use emotion rather than nationalist affiliation to generate belonging (see Lawrence La Fountain-Stokes, this volume), the pan-*latinidad* sensibility supports a sustainable practice that emphasizes temporary and ephemeral registers of belonging without specific geographic mooring, whether a homeland or a physical neighborhood. Ramos does not include a procession to a cemetery, common among Chicana/o/x Día de los Muertos celebrations in California. She explains, "We are not from Minnesota." Although Mexican migrants settled in Minnesota in the first decades of the twentieth century, Ramos and many of her collaborators are recent arrivals. "Our relocated [Latina/o/x] community [commemorates] dead relatives not buried [in the Twin Cities]." As such, the festival pays homage to the dead across vast territories, bridging families who are living in Minnesota to those in Latin America, the Caribbean, or the American Southwest.[26] The festival, therefore, calls on "the spirits" to join us in this place "from a geographic long-distance," and in turn, it does not emphasize a territorial sense of land and belonging.[27] While this contrasts with Indigenous identities that are tied to place, it allows migrants from Latin America and the Caribbean to avoid colonial logics of land encroachment.[28]

With broad inclusion of "Latinx/Indigenous artists" and relational aesthetics that emphasize somatic emplacement rather than built environments or homeland territories, El Festival subordinates ethnic nationalism common in the American Southwest's homage to the dead.[29] It validates Latina/o participants and, more recently, Latinx, the gender-nonconforming, nonbinary, and intersex term that references people living in the United States with Latin American and Caribbean heritage. This notion of *latinidad* supports a growing recognition of "multiple colonialities," migration experiences, and residency on Dakota land, topics to which I return in the conclusion.[30]

Descriptions of the event rhetorically emphasize the agency, voice, and presence of Latina/o/x residents, and these texts further suggest why it is necessary to focus on the inexplicable rather than the empirical forms of placemaking. "As the Twin Cities Latino population continues to grow," states Ramos, "cultural institutions and community organizations scramble to keep up with its demands. This growth brings a need to create spaces to celebrate our traditions, our cultures, and our beliefs. [El Festival de las Calaveras] creates such a space, a sense of feeling 'at home' in a terrain that is foreign and often uninviting."[31] Ramos's attention to the ineffable—"feeling 'at home'"—syntactically structures "space" as a sensibility, not a physical location. I became attentive to the indescribable, the affective, and the ephemeral that Ramos imagines when I attended the 2017 opening event of El Festival de las Calaveras at the Cedar Cultural Center, an all-ages, nonprofit music venue in the Cedar-Riverside neighborhood of Minneapolis. I was perplexed by a sudden feeling of belonging, even though the Cedar-Riverside neighborhood, near the University of Minnesota, is home to "the nation's largest Somali diaspora."[32] There was nothing particular about the Cedar Cultural Center, a large auditorium similar to the style found in public schools: a shallow, raised thrust stage and an open, rectangular auditorium without seats. Don't ask me to describe it, but I can say I felt at home, profoundly and viscerally, within the festival. "The potency of the soma" generated my emplacement.[33]

Other locations for El Festival de las Calaveras also offered little physical evidence for *latinidades* and placemaking.[34] For example, the family-centered event in 2016 at Intermedia Arts, a multicultural arts center located in Lyn-Lake, one of Minneapolis's hottest real estate and nightlife neighborhoods, is removed from the Latina/o/x commercial zone of East Lake Street. During its heyday, Intermedia Arts was known as a multicultural arts center that privileged queer, immigrant, and artists of color, signaled by the wild-style art painted on the exterior surface of its building. But in 2016 Intermedia Arts could not rely on its immediate neighbors for programming, because the area to the east has increasingly experienced gentrification, and residents of color were displaced by rising rents.[35] Families in attendance could have been the newly settled whites or displaced Latina/o/xs. Outside of explicit claims of cultural pride and the Chicana/o/x friends and colleagues I recognized, it was impossible to determine the identities of the participants. To this newcomer, the bodies themselves could not register *latinidad*. In the following section, I employ autoethnography, a Chicana feminist methodology of personal narrative for counterhegemonic knowledge production, to describe the festival and the making of Latina/o/x somatic emplacement.[36] The chapter also documents my somatic knowledge and expression, records the mundane interactions of somatic emplacement, and explores the significance of these forms of emplacement for Latina/o/x residents, especially those living among American Indian communities.

Enlivening the Soma and Emplacement

For the 2017 multigenre performances at Cedar Cultural Center, El Festival de las Calaveras began without a formal introduction. Danzantes of Mexica Yolotl walked into the open-floor auditorium and positioned themselves in a circular line in front of the raised stage. Their drummers gave some cue to the audience by placing their instruments to the left of the stage and facing the open floor. From their location among the audience, the *danzantes* proceeded with *ceremonia*—they ritually danced and drummed prayers to the four directions, the heavens, and the earth that link pre-Cuauhtémoc Mexica movement and contemporary Chicana/o/x and Mexica meaning.[37] The event unfolded, opened, but without a demarcated start; the ceremony inhabited the space, and we, the audience members, were forced to adjust our bodies—moving to another spot on the floor or gathering up the young children who had been playing and running throughout the crowd—to see or avoid collision with the *danzantes* and with each other.

Our movement brought to somatic awareness our relationality; we were here together, adjusting to each other's presence, and moving to the drum beat, which made our chest cavities resonate. Sonically, we were participants in the ceremony whether or not we joined the *danzantes* as they turned to face the four directions. Breadth was informed by the intense reverberations of the drums, and sound waves generated our somatic inclusion and relational aesthetics. This sociality of the art practice could have happened in any crowded auditorium. It was the seamlessness of the event—the sudden presence of the *danzantes*—and the venue's size that forced audience members to become aware of each other. As we moved across the floor and into active participants, a somatic relationship developed and continued after *ceremonia* came to an end.

When the troupe completed their ritual dancing, Ahmed Anzaldúa, conductor and trained pianist, led what he terms a "community sing," a performance in which audience members and rehearsed singers join in song.[38] Similar to the *danzantes*, Anzaldúa staged the work to enhance audience participation. He entered the raised stage and gestured to those of us congregating in the house of the theater to come closer. As he silently hailed the room to gather near the stage, a group of approximately fifty people poured into the theater from the lobby and encircled the *danzantes*, who had taken up the front area of the auditorium after finishing their ceremonial movement. Those entering the auditorium handed sheets of paper to us. As he continued to gesture to people with the wave of his hand, it became more and more ambiguous whom he was calling forward, the rehearsed singers or the spectators. With this deliberate act, all present were invited into the ritual of gathering and singing.

Before he began conducting the a cappella compositions, Anzaldúa spoke the first words of the evening and explained the vocal performance of *canto cardenche*, "a traditional Mexican musical style based on songs sung a cappella by [rural] people from Sapioriz, Durango and La Flor de Jimulco."[39] He also noted that *cardenche* is a type of cactus with a claw-like spine that "pulls out flesh from the body." Referencing this specific cultural form of a cappella music and its index of the body, Anzaldúa tacitly invited the community to become physically and spiritually present in their singing about death and melancholia. Without knowing what was coming or why he summoned people to the stage, the audience's generosity in moving toward Anzaldúa established a mindful and bodily interaction and exchange. Those who opened their mouths, lungs, and hearts to sing furthered their interaction with the music, the space, and each other. But even as we sang words in Spanish—some simply following the phonetically designed sheet music, a format that allowed non–Spanish speakers to participate—the melody engulfed the space and enlivened a somatic response as we swayed to the music or breathed with the rhythm of the song. The community sing moved toward the inexpressible, slipping into incommensurable qualities of somatic emplacement.

This mode of direct address, immersion, and the inexplicable that dissolves the distance between audience and performer was also used at Modus Locus, the Powderhorn Park gallery selected for the 2018 festival's art exhibition. In the garden of this flex-use arts organization (it functions by day as a real estate business), the *danza* troupe Kapuli Huitzilli opened with *ceremonia*, moving around the circular space without acknowledging those present. Eyes cast down, they drummed and danced around the center platform of the garden, which was walled on three sides. The surface of each wall was filled with murals in the style of contemporary graphic street art. Although somatic emplacement is difficult to describe, I knew as we stood among the circle of trees at the garden's edge with our backs to the murals that we were more than witnesses. Our relationship to the ceremony became clear after the completion of the ritual dance and remarks by Ramos and others. At that moment, the audience/participants were summoned into the garden's center to inhabit the area sanctified by the *danzantes*. Our bodies served as the conduits for collective spatial and temporal emplacement: our companionship became apparent as we moved among each other, each attuned to our gathering, and we adjusted our bodies to make room for strollers, small children, and the elderly. It was one spiritual encounter at the festivals I witnessed, but I suggest that relational aesthetics engage the spiritual realm when the political sociability of art is present. The acknowledgment of that which is between us and the worlds beyond us requires an oppositional consciousness that rejects Cartesian thought and the Western hegemonic logic of individualism.

Once we had gathered to the garden's center, artist Dougie Padilla invited us to write the names of our departed loved ones on slips of paper and then toss the papers into a campfire that had been burning at the farthest edge of the garden. That is, everyone had to pass through the center of the garden to reach the fire pit, reinforcing our participation in the ritual and physically passing through the porous space between audience and participant. As Erin Manning declares, "Potentiality is called forth every time language exceeds its syntax, every time an other exceeds any reach, every time I sense more than I comprehend."[40] Our gathering and reaching toward the fire held the potential for aesthetic relationality and Latina/o/x somatic emplacement.

These interactions are intentional for Ramos. She insists that El Festival de las Calaveras is "not a typical concert where people sit or stand and watch." Her goal is to stage more than "an event" with music, dance, poetry, and visual art exhibitions. She does not want people to "consume the experience, [she] wants them to be part of it" as they "enter the space." In my experience, El Festival generates Latina/o/x somatic emplacement at the threshold. While I could not explain my sense of belonging in 2017 at the Cedar Cultural Center, the unfolding and immersive program moved me.

Scholars of performance and dance are attuned to the inexplicable gestures between bodies that generate and exceed the political and cultural domains of Western thought.[41] Music is a relational aesthetic, as the song is expressed in the dancers' movement. At the same time, Ramos's selected musical performers insist on engagement, hailing audiences to the dance floor or calling for a raised fist in solidarity with the disappeared forty-three Ayotzinapa youth, the enslaved living among us, or Salvadoran, Guatemalan, Honduran, and Dominican refugees migrating to the United States. For Ramos, musical performances "set the tone" for the festival by "sending energy out to the ancestors, collectively sending energy out." She reports that the music opens for her "an energetic gateway" to those who have passed away, expanding relational aesthetics to the otherworldly.[42] Furthermore, dancing among a crowd requires a keen awareness of one's body (proprioception) and those also on the floor. One's sociality is enlivened through dance. Even if dancers do not touch, the gesture that Erin Manning argues rethinks the political, their movement and awareness generate a potentiality for exchange, community, and somatic emplacement. We move not in unison or from a common identity but to a shared sound and rhythm, and this brief moment of somatic awareness offers a sense of belonging. Yet "to sense, we must cut through time and space, moving, challenging both semantic and geographical boundaries . . . [w]hen we sense we are not producing a map that will lead us back to an 'origin.'"[43] It is a perception alive in that moment that repeatedly dissipates and reemerges as dancers or participants change their visual and corporeal focus from one person to the next. Somatic emplacement is temporary, fleeting, fragile, and incommensurable.

Somatic Knowledge

While I was initially unable to describe my corporeal perception and response to belonging in 2017, over time I learned to catalog somatic information. Sadly, my first attempts to describe the soma led me to embodied racialization. It was easy for me to access the somatic expression of intersectional racial exclusion.[44] I am a short, brown-skinned, cisgendered woman who has worked in predominantly white institutions; I daily encounter oppressive microaggressions. They make my head throb, my stomach burn, my gut churn, and I find my shoulders slouched and vision restricted. Sometimes I feel heat on my cheeks, close to the eyes, or at the hairline on the back of my neck. Muscles grip, tighten, and strain, even when no additional weight is placed on them. When forced to inhabit a space of intersectional racialized exclusion, say, for three or four hours, I become numb. I physically feel less, recall less, and engage less with others. I do not look too hard. DO NOT STUDY THE SIGNS OF EXCLUSION BECAUSE IT HURTS. In predominantly white spaces, I take in the minimal visual information to remain safe. All this and more change with somatic belonging.

Typically, the lungs are the first somatic attribute to shift; the breath relaxes and smooths out so that it escapes and appears without awareness. Yes, yes, elementary knowledge of human biology tells me that breathing is involuntary, automatic, and continuous, but I *hold* my breath when I am within spaces of racial and gendered exclusion. It is biologically illogical to deny the body oxygen, but ironically and tragically, holding the breath is an *involuntary* response to exclusion. When I feel a sense of belonging, I am completely unaware of my chest's rising and falling. The breath returns to the involuntary flow of unrestricted inspiration and expiration. The lungs expand as the parasympathetic nervous system activates. If the space is defined, such as an auditorium, gallery, or enclosed festival grounds, the soma responds at the threshold, just as Ramos intends. It is triggered by familiar faces, language, or other cultural cues, but it may also register my interaction with those present. When we were invited to add our ancestors' names to the fire at Modus Locus in 2018 and those present had to adjust their bodies in the space, I felt a lightness in my chest cavity.

My body surrendered to its own knowledge. The space behind my eyes opened. Indeed, my facial muscles and body relaxed. My ears lifted, expanding the space behind them. My muscles surrendered to gravity. Motion was more fluid. Proximity or personal space expanded, and fear of encroachment dissipated. When I recall the 2017 festival, I realize that as the event unfolded into ritual dance, I moved easily with and against the people in the auditorium to find a place on the floor where I could see the action. As the community sing blended into a ritualized creation of *la ofrenda* built across the entire house of the theater, I adjusted my body to accommodate the four artists, including Ramos, who dropped rose petals onto the floor. Simultaneously, I moved my body among other people near me. "Excuse me." "No problem." "Con permiso." "Pásale." These words were whispered with confidence, stated firmly, but without anger, shame, or insult. The registration of our humanity is the register of belonging, and this shared somatic experience is the site in which emplacement is found.

As I watched the designs created by the rose petals and smelled the burning *copal*, a swelling originating from an unnamed place inside me—perhaps behind the breast bone—became a fullness of emotion that moved to my head. A pressure increased at my forehead's center and pushed back and down through my diaphragm. I cried. I recognized the staged movements. Their actions—the rose petals sprinkled across the floor, the dangling fingers and pendulous slow motion of arms and hands from which petals fell, the silent gestures with the smoke and *copalero*—I knew *this* as ritual. Their careful and slow motions had not been performed by my family, nor was it something I had learned at Self Help Graphics and Art or the Mission Cultural Center, the two places in California where I had participated in public celebrations for the dead, but it was familiar. I knew spirits were being gathered. The affective and indescribable experience and the aesthetic performance invoked memories of my Mexican elders, all dead and buried in Los Angeles. I cried for the feeling of what might be termed "their presence"—again a somatic and inexplicable quality that occupies your thoughts so strongly that the effect is visceral ("ah, she is here with me, now she is present"). I cried for the loss—my *nana* has been dead for over thirty years—and for her incommensurable presence.

Mundane Somatic Emplacements

If I have lost readers who recoil at the spiritual or who fear I have reduced "'lo indio' to the ephemeral" and aligned with the tropes of European Enlightenment, such as the "magical negro" or Noble Savage, then I turn to the mundane to provide clarity.[45] The festival's *mercaditos* also produce Latina/o/x somatic emplacement. These *mercaditos* are staged at various locations, depending on the venue's size and configuration, and artists are invited to them to market their work: printed T-shirts, jewelry, small-batch lotions and soaps, artisanal food products, hats, and sugar skulls, as well as paintings, offset and fine art prints, cards, stickers, and poetry booklets. This informal economy provides more than transactional exchange, as the objects are infused with and generate belonging.[46] Inspired by anthropologist Mary Douglas, who examines the social purpose of goods; Theresa Delgadillo, who in this volume explores how the *rebozo* creates belonging and relationships among the characters of Sandra Cisneros's *Caramelo*; and my own analysis of Chicana/o/x art collectors; I focus on the affective and productive processes at play in commerce, in this case, the *mercaditos*.[47]

The sighs, lingering touches, and slowness with which people peruse the merchandise create a somatic expression of emplacement. Touching of and drawn-out looking at the items for sale can affectively inspire memories of home and family, the places and people that engender belonging. These pauses and encounters with objects can mobilize memory for political ends and cultural nostalgia. We gather around the small tables that display the merchandise, and we take our time together, waiting patiently for more room to observe. The modulation of time breaks with capitalism's rapidity, and slow shopping is out of sync with normative expectations of consumption.[48] In other contexts, our closeness might turn to voyeurism, but at the festival, we closely witness the details of the exchange, encouraging each other with compliments and gestures of familiarity. "That necklace is perfect on you." "Ooh, I love that T-shirt. Does he have one in my size?" We form immediate bonds through the shopping experience because of our perceptions of objects as "our own." As one participant observed in 2018, "This is not Target selling our culture back to us." Even shopping can produce somatic solidarity.

From the Soma to Latina/o/x Solidarity

This companionship was repeated throughout the festival. As I stood among a crowd of strangers, I felt the political efficacy of my emotions. The affective response was not nostalgia or melancholia. The wetness in my eyes, the opening of and pressure on my chest cavity, and the expansion of my vision conjure relationships that imagined a larger world, one beyond myself. The people around me were transformed into something else, no longer strangers but witnesses to our shared experience. We became companions, my Latina/o/x community. My soma moved me from a single spectator into a Twin Cities Latina. The body was the transit for belonging, and the relational aesthetics of the festival allowed the sense of emplacement to travel outside of the walls of the theater or gallery. I felt connected to others, and my own imagined Latina sensibility bridged Indigenous Mexican ways of knowing about life and death with Chicana/o/x aesthetic expression, including *calaca* attire.[49] My somatic experience enlivened solidarity with other Twin Cities Latina/o/x residents.

"Latina/o/x" is not used euphemistically for "Chicana/o/x." The festival includes Chicana, Mexican, Puerto Rican, Afro-Latino, Tejano, and Guatemalan artists—among others. Participating artists insist that the commemoration for the dead is itself transnational, as Spanish colonialism appropriated Indigenous epistemologies throughout Latin America and the Caribbean and rerouted them onto the Catholic calendar for All Souls' and All Saints' Days in November. Poet Teresa Ortiz lyrically provided this lesson about our transnational Latina/o/x imaginary in 2018 when she recited prose about contemporary celebrations for Día de los Muertos that she witnessed in Guatemala and Colombia. As a survivor of the 1968 Tlatelolco Massacre in Mexico City, Ortiz intimately understands the politics of solidarity, and her prose identified her mutuality with others.[50] In 2017 and 2018, Maya Calendar Keeper Gina Kanbalam Miranda of Guatemala and Honduras revealed to multiple audiences that the homage to the dead is thousands of years old, predating Spanish colonization of the Americas. While the event appeared to echo the inclusive cultural politics of San Francisco's Mission District and Chicago's ethnic festivals, for some participants the homage to the dead is associated with places other than Mexico or the Chicana/o/x communities of the American Southwest. El Festival de las Calaveras is not an *expansion* of a Chicana/o/x and Indigenous Mexican celebration but an admission that many Latin Americans commemorate the dead.

Thus, Twin Cities Latina/o/x solidarity does not travel along routes of ethnic nationalism, citizenship, or language, although these are aspects of the festival. It simultaneously holds cultural specificity and complexity. For instance, Ramos deliberately orients the festival toward "Indigenous and traditional art" by promoting Nahua and Chicana/o/x indigeneity through spiritual, cultural, and aesthetic practices. It features Mexica *danza* with Nahuatl incantations and traditional Mexican music sung a cappella in Spanish along with contemporary hip-hop and other fusion styles popular among urban youth. Latina/o/x emplacement is flexible and capacious. Indeed, I find this ambiguous and expansive quality of Latina/o/x emplacement more difficult to describe than the soma because it extends "national optics" beyond the "referential homeland."[51]

This capaciousness also supports what Michael Hames-García refers to as "original relation . . . a new way of relating to the past [that] responds to the needs of the present and remains dynamic, rather than traditional or custombound."[52] For example, Mexica *danzantes* are recognized for their interracial coalitional politics, which need not be directly enunciated at the festival. Kapulli Yaocenoxtli, a dance and drumming troupe, is known for supporting political mobilizations that cross racial communities, such as the Black Lives Matter Movement and justice for Philando Castile.[53] This group was invited to perform at the inaugural festival at the Parkway Theatre and again in 2014 because of these intersectional political affiliations that contribute to "the needs of the present."

Other artists reinforce an original relation that honors intersectional politics, contemporary Indigenous cultures, and their histories and epistemologies. For instance, in 2017 Star Girl Clan, an arts collective comprised of Rebekah Crisanta de Ybarra ("enrolled Maya-Lenca"), an interdisciplinary artist who describes her work as "rooted in Latinx Indigenous *artesanías* of Mesoamerica and Liberation Theology of El Salvador," and Magdalena Kaluza, a young Guatemalan American woman raised by activist parents, performed shadow puppet theater for children and adults at Intermedia Arts.[54] The artists used music that was sonically rooted in Indigenous drum and flute instrumentation and poetry that was spoken in Spanish and projected on a screen in English to tell a contemporary story about a young girl who learned to honor corn and the dead from her Maya grandmother. The girl's transformation from shame to pride is a lesson about Indigenous cultural resilience and the festival's antiassimilationist thread. Ramos also challenges colonial narratives of Indigenous extinction through the inclusion of Mexica *danza* and the creation of *ofrendas* as expressions of contemporary Indigenous knowledge and arts. Additionally, Ramos is cognizant that the festival is produced on the traditional Dakota homelands and home to Ojibwe (or Anishinaabe) people. The urban garden was built with the direction and support of local American Indians and Mexican Indigenous elders, and these communities continue to inform Ramos's studies of the corn cycle as emblematic of human connections to land and decolonial thought. Latina/o/x somatic emplacement can shift settler logics among diasporic Latina/o/x residents in Minnesota by generating new forms of belonging through, between, and within bodies.

Expressing this broad range of intersectional *latinidades* and their constitutively communal, relational, and plural qualities was Maria Isa, the 2017 headline performer and at two 2016 festival events. Isa is a singer-songwriter who describes herself as a "Boricua . . . born in Minnesota and raised on St. Paul's West Side barrio."[55] Her claim to the West Side of St. Paul is a marker of her cross-cultural capacities, as it signals her political affiliation with this Mexican community. Similarly, her music blends Afro-Latino rhythms, hip-hop, and reggaetón with Spanish and Spanglish lyrics, which frequently appeal for justice and liberty for Puerto Ricans and Latina/o/x residents of the Twin Cities. In 2017 she asked those present to pay homage to Puerto Rico's dead and suffering in the aftermath of September's devastating Hurricane Maria. Between songs, she spoke in English and called on the audience to join her in the street to honor Dennis J. Banks, a cofounder of the American Indian Movement in Minnesota and leader in the liberation of Wounded Knee in 1973 who passed away on October 27, 2017. A mix of Indigenous drummers were scheduled to close down Cedar Avenue, and their brief, insurgent occupation inspired a large crowd that danced, clapped, and recorded the moment before the sound of police sirens dispersed the ensemble.

A speaker's comments in 2018 at Modus Locus further support somatic emplacement as a methodology that expands an overemphasis on built environments and territory to comprehend placemaking. That year, Ramos invited a survivor of the September 26, 2014, mass disappearance of forty-three male students from Ayotzinapa Rural Teachers' College in Iguala, Guerrero, Mexico. Speaking in Spanish at the opening ceremony at Modus Locus, he identified himself as a survivor and cousin of one of the disappeared.[56] He acknowledged the beautiful celebration in the art garden but reminded us that the parents and families of the disappeared have no burial site, no body to recover, and no earthly space to which they can orient their homage. Theirs is a commemoration for a death that has no home. His sad narrative provides a lesson for Latina/o/x emplacement in the Twin Cities: the origins and roots are elsewhere. Belonging is felt in the soma and through relational expressions such as dancing, singing, *ceremonia*, and shopping. These interactions between performers and audiences, as well as among audience members, produce a political sociability, a space and temporal emplacement that is more than a geographic foothold. Expressed somatically through sighs, muscular relaxation, touch, reach, tingling on the skin, or swaying to music, this embodied form of community may be temporary, but its power and potential are expansive. His comments remind us that "the bond between community and land is very different than the association between citizenship and territory," as full citizenship was withheld from the living and dead of Ayotzinapa, as it is from many Latina/o/x migrants.[57] We turn our attention to multiple sense registries when the land cannot offer us roots.[58]

Speculation

Yet somatic Latina/o/x emplacement is precarious. Once the jubilation subsides or is interrupted by the force of intersectional racialization, it can easily dissipate. But its capacious and ambiguous qualities are also a source of potential creativity.[59] Borrowing from José Esteban Muñoz's future-oriented queerness, it is useful to understand Latina/o/x somatic emplacement as a potentiality rather than an "inert category."[60] Indeed, several scholars who grapple with theorizing Latina/o/x imaginary find that it is not "a static or unifying formation but a flexible category that relates to a plurality of ideologies of identification, cultural expressions, and political and social agendas."[61] The complexity and inexpressibility of Latina/o/x somatic emplacement can generate a mobile condition, and if it fails to congeal, its ephemerality brings new possibilities that mitigate appropriation.[62] By extending beyond colonial time frames (origins) and space (territoriality), Latina/o/x somatic emplacement pushes against the normalizing strategy of neoliberal multiculturalism and its mythos of inclusion and commonality. It does so by operating *with* national, ethnic, and racial categories *and* simultaneously beyond them. Latina/o/x somatic emplacement resists neoliberal "accommodationist politics that erase history and occlude difference."[63]

Within this expansive and corporeal sense of belonging is a potential to reconsider settler colonialism and American Indian displacement in Minnesota. An embodied belonging holds the opportunity to negotiate the multiple colonialities that divide northern and southern indigeneities. In this somatic form, emplacement has the capacity to acknowledge Dakota and Ojibwe stewardship of the land, support transnational solidarities, and illuminate Afro-Latina/o/x and African American coalitions. At the festival, this plurality is articulated through Indigenous Mexican and Chicana/o/x forms of homage to the dead, intersectional politics, hemispheric indigeneity, and multiple identifications of the artists. The multimodal and intersectional politics holds the potential for what Chela Sandoval identifies as differential consciousness, as participants shift and negotiate a variety of positions to suit their context.[64]

Indeed, this embodied emplacement was tangible for those who refused to vacate the excessively crowded art gallery at Modus Locus in 2018. Hundreds of people stood body to body, nearly immobile, for over two hours in a storefront room approximately fifteen by twenty-five feet to see the visual art and hear the music. Somehow Minnesotan personal space was thrown out the window. A mass of people slowly moved inch by inch around the gallery. I found a spot near the wall with art by Olivia Levins Holden, Minnesota-born Puerto Rican muralist who apprenticed under Chicana artist Juana Alicia in Oakland, California, for several years before returning home. I was confused by the persistence of the crowd. Later, it occurred to me that it was the crowd itself—the gentle touch on one's arm or back, the subtle shift from one foot to the other that caused a ripple in the gathering, and the willingness to follow the current of the throng—that generated somatic emplacement. It was the lack of distance between our bodies that provided our Latina/o/x belonging, a corporeal and sustainable form of placemaking.

Notes

The Borders and Bodies (B2) Writing Group at UMN provided unconditional support during a critical moment in the writing. I am grateful for David Melendez, Naimah Petigny, Elizabeth Wijaya, Emily Mitamura, Saya Bhattacharya, and Jennifer E. Row. Jessica Lopez Lyman helped me find my way in the Twin Cities. I am also grateful for the labor of the UMN student research assistants: Jeffrey O'Brien, Olivia Marti, Alison Kraemer, and Katherine Swartzer. Deborah Ramos was generous with her time and documentation, especially during the months of planning for the festival. I turned to specialists—Carla Hill, endy trece, and CatherineMarie Davalos—who helped me understand that somatic awareness might be unconscious initially, but once recognized, it is conscious, and to friends—Roberta Tinajero-Frankel and Todd Frankel—to develop an awareness of my own somatic emplacement. I am grateful for the collaboration of Team Midwest Latinx Placemaking and the comments of Stephanie Fetta, CatherineMarie Davalos, and Lettycia Terrones, who read an earlier version of this essay.

1. "New communities" are distinct from the "continuous communities" or ethnic

enclaves that emerged during Spanish colonization of the American Southwest. See Arreola, *Hispanic Spaces*; Villa, *Barrio Logos*; Lara, *Latino Placemaking and Planning*; Daniel D. Arreola, *Tejano South Texas: A Mexican American Cultural Province* (Austin: University of Texas Press, 2002); and Pérez, *The Near Northwest Side Story*.

2. Yi-Fu Tuan, "Space and Place: Humanistic Perspective," *Progress in Geography* 6 (1974): 211–52.

3. Mexican-heritage residents are 72 percent of Minnesota's Latin American-descent population. "Demographic and Economic Profiles of Hispanics by State and County, 2014," Minnesota, Pew Research Center, 2014, https://www.pewresearch.org/hispanic/states/state/mn. Following the coeditors of this volume, I understand *latinidad* as a "productive friction of difference and familiarity" not "universally welcomed or rejected." When describing this population, I use "Latina/o/x."

4. St. Paul's West Side is largely white (45 percent) with 30 percent Latino, 14 percent Black, 6 percent Asian or Pacific Islander, 1 percent Native American, and 4 percent two or more races. "West Side Neighborhood Data, Race and Ethnicity, 2015–2019," Minnesota Compass, https://mncompass.org.

5. Inés M. Miyares, "Changing Latinization of New York City," in Arreola, *Hispanic Spaces*, 157.

6. Jessica Lopez Lyman, "Revitalizing Poetics: Latin@s Reshape South Minneapolis," *Chicana/Latina Studies* 15, no. 2 (2016): 39.

7. Ibid., 34.

8. Ibid., 40. The western region of Powderhorn has clusters of predominantly Hispanic residents. "55407 Zip Code (Minneapolis, MN) Detailed Profile," City-Data.com, http://www.city-data.com/zips/55407.html. My analysis focuses on Minneapolis because in the 1980s it "surpassed [the West Side of St. Paul] as home of the largest Mexican population in the state" (Valdés, *Barrios Norteños*, 224).

9. Stephanie Fetta, *Shaming into Brown* (Columbus: Ohio State University Press, 2018), xiii. While readers may desire a reference to phenomenology, its debates about intentionality lure me toward other methods, such as ethnography and performance studies.

10. Elaine A. Peña, *Performing Piety: Making Space Sacred with the Virgin of Guadalupe* (Berkeley: University of California Press, 2011), 11.

11. Fetta, *Shaming into Brown*, xiii.

12. Ibid., 7.

13. Ibid., 23.

14. Ibid., 45.

15. Arlene Dávila, "Culture," in Vargas, Mirabal, and La Fountain-Stokes, *Keywords for Latina/o Studies*, 41.

16. Ibid.

17. M. Bianet Castellanos, "Rewriting the Mexican Immigrant Narrative: Situating Indigeneity in Maya Women's Stories," *Latino Studies* 15, no. 2 (2017): 219–41; Luis Urrieta Jr., "Identity, Violence, and Authenticity: Challenging Static Conceptions of Identity," *Latino Studies* 15, no. 2 (2017): 254–61.

18. Nicolas Bourriaud, *Relational Aesthetics*, trans. Simon Pleasance and Fronza

Woods (Dijon: Les Presses de Réel, 2002); Anthony Downey, "Towards a Politics of (Relational) Aesthetics," *Third Text* 21, no. 3 (May 2007): 267–75.

19. For Chicana/o/x art histories that examine relational aesthetics by other names such as "community art," "political art," and "spiritual aesthetics," see Karen Mary Davalos, *Yolanda M. López* (Los Angeles: UCLA Chicano Studies Research Center Press, 2008); Ella Diaz, "The Necessary Theater of the Royal Chicano Air Force," *Aztlán: A Journal of Chicano Studies* 38, no. 2 (2013): 41–70; C. Ondine Chavoya and Rita Gonzalez, eds., *Asco: Elite of the Obscure, a Retrospective, 1972–1987* (Ostfildern, Germany: Hatje Cantz Verlag, 2011); Guisela Latorre, *Walls of Empowerment: Chicana/o Indigenist Murals of California* (Austin: University of Texas Press, 2008); Pérez, *Chicana Art*.

20. Chela Sandoval, *Methodology of the Oppressed* (Minneapolis: University of Minnesota Press, 2000).

21. Lara Medina and Gilbert R. Cadena, "Días de los Muertos: Public Ritual, Community Renewal, and Popular Religion in Los Angeles," in *Horizons of the Sacred*, ed. Timothy M. Matovina and Gary Riebe-Estrella (Ithaca, NY: Cornell University Press, 2002), 69–94. See also Regina M. Marchi, *Day of the Dead in the USA: The Migration and Transformation of a Cultural Phenomenon* (New Brunswick, NJ: Rutgers University Press, 2009).

22. Deborah Ramos in "MSAB [Minnesota State Arts Board] Festival Support FY2015: *Baile de las Calaveras* Day of the Dead Festival 2015," private collection of Deborah Ramos. While the use of Nahuatl in Minnesota aligns with Chicana/o/x indigeneity and its privileging of the Mexica empire, Ramos is actively studying in Mexico with living Nahua and P'urhepecha elders and elders "initiated into the Chalca tradition." Some of her teachers recognize their *mestizaje*, complicating criticism of Chicana/o/x indigeneity. Personal communication 12 August 2019.

23. Deborah Ramos and the volunteers who produce the festival use the term "Latinx." The demography of the audience is unknown, although a small sample survey reveals they identify as Latino, Chicano, and Indigenous. Audiences overwhelmingly comprehend Spanish and recognize the cultural forms of *danza*, *la ofrenda*, and *la calavera*.

24. The website announces additional Indigenous epistemologies. For example, it states that Tlalnepantla is Nahuatl for "between the earth" and "signifies the space created by the fusion of worlds: a place of creativity, exploration, and transformation" (Tlalnepantla Arts-Zenteotl, http://www.zenteotl.org/english/art.html).

25. Regarding Cinco de Mayo parades, see Brian J. Godfrey, "Barrio under Siege: Latino Sense of Place in San Francisco, California," in Arreola, *Hispanic Spaces*, 94; regarding Chicago's Independence Day parades, see Lorena Garcia and Mérida M. Rúa, "Processing *Latinidad*: Mapping Latino Urban Landscapes through Chicago Ethnic Festivals," *Latino Studies* 5, no. 3 (2007): 317–39.

26. Other Minneapolis celebrations include processions, but not to a cemetery.

27. Unless otherwise noted, quotations in this paragraph are from Deborah Ramos, interview with author, July 4, 2018.

28. Mishuana Goeman, "Land as Life," in *Native Studies Keywords*, ed. Stephanie

Nohelani Teves, Andrea Smith, and Michelle H. Raheja (Tucson: University of Arizona Press, 2015), 71–89.

29. "History," http://festivalcalaveras.com/.

30. Maylei Blackwell, "Indigeneity," in Vargas, La Fountain-Stokes, and Mirabal, *Keywords for Latina/o Studies*, 101.

31. Ramos, "MSAB Festival Support FY2015."

32. Allie Shah, "Go Inside 'Little Mogadishu,' the Somali Capital of America," *Star Tribune*, March 2, 2017.

33. Fetta, *Shaming into Brown*, 7.

34. I did not witness the inaugural festival at Pepitos Parkway Theater, the only Chicano-owned theater in the Twin Cities. Its official name, Parkway Theatre, reveals only its geographic location.

35. Edward G. Goetz, Brittany Lewis, Anthony Damiano, and Molly Calhoun, *The Diversity of Gentrification: Multiple Forms of Gentrification in Minneapolis and St. Paul*, Center for Urban and Regional Affairs, University of Minnesota, 2019.

36. I identify this method as a trend of Chicana feminism. Karen Mary Davalos, "Sin vergüenza: Chicana Feminist Theorizing," Chicana Studies special double issue, *Feminist Studies* 34, no. 1 & 2 (2008): 151–71. See also Bernadette Maria Calafell and Shane T. Moreman, "Envisioning an Academic Readership: Latina/o Performativities per the Form of Publication," *Text and Performance Quarterly* 29, no. 2 (2009): 123–30.

37. Ernesto Colín, *Indigenous Education through Dance and Ceremony: A Mexican Palimpsest* (New York: Palgrave Macmillan, 2014).

38. On the festival's website, he is introduced as Egyptian Mexican. He did not know that Gloria Anzaldúa, his aunt, was prominent in academia until he was a young adult.

39. These words are found on social media platforms and in promotional materials for the 2017 El Festival de las Calaveras.

40. Erin Manning, *Politics of Touch: Sense, Movement, Sovereignty* (Minneapolis: University of Minnesota Press, 2007), 6.

41. Ibid.; Cindy Garcia, *Salsa Crossings: Dancing Latinidad in Los Angeles* (Durham, NC: Duke University Press, 2013); and Jill Dolan, *Utopia in Performance: Finding Hope at the Theatre* (Ann Arbor: University of Michigan Press, 2005).

42. Unless otherwise noted, quotations in this paragraph and the preceding are from Deborah Ramos, interview with author, July 4, 2018.

43. Manning, *Politics of Touch*, 20.

44. José Esteban Muñoz specifically addresses somatic countenance or bodily composure, arguing that racialization is the result. José Esteban Muñoz, "Feeling Brown, Feeling Down: Latina Affect, the Performativity of Race, and the Depressive Position," *Signs* 31, no. 3 (2006): 675–88. In *Shaming into Brown*, Stephanie Fetta refers to this bodily experience as racial shaming.

45. Blackwell, "Indigeneity," 104.

46. For a discussion of the false binary between art and commerce in Chicana/o/x arts organizations in Los Angeles, see Karen Mary Davalos, *Chicana/o Remix: Art and Errata Since the Sixties* (New York: NYU Press, 2017). It should be noted that

El Festival de las Calaveras does not produce a large profit. While it originated as a fundraiser for the community garden, the net profit is minimal.

47. Karen Mary Davalos, "A Poetics of Love and Rescue in the Collection of Chicana/o Art," *Latino Studies* 5 (2007): 76–103.

48. I acknowledge Jennifer E. Row, who encouraged me to consider the temporal aspects of these shopping moments. It is an analysis that resonates with the work of Vincent Duclos, Tomas Sanchez-Criado, and Vinh-Kim, "Speed: An Introduction," *Cultural Anthropology* 32, no. 1 (2017): 1–11.

49. *Calaca* attire refers to the "ornately designed calaveras painted on [one's] face and . . . improvised costumes that echo pop culture, high fashion, and Mexican tourism" (Karen Mary Davalos, "Innovation through Tradition: The Aesthetic of *Día de los Muertos*," in *Día de los Muertos: A Cultural Legacy; Past, Present, and Future*, ed. Mary Thomas, curators, Linda Vallejo and Betty Ann Brown [Los Angeles: Self Help Graphics and Art, 2017], 24).

50. Lopez Lyman, "Revitalizing Poetics," 52.

51. Juan Flores, "The Latino Imaginary: Dimensions of Community and Identity," in Aparicio and Chávez-Silverman, *Tropicalizations*, 188.

52. Michael Hames-García, "How to Tell a Mestizo from an Enchirito®: Colonialism and National Culture in the Borderlands," *Diacritics* 30, no. 4 (2000): 113.

53. Philando Castile was an African American male shot by a police officer who had pulled him over for a traffic violation. The violence was caught on video by his girlfriend and witnessed by her four-year-old daughter. "After Philando Castile's Killing, Obama Calls Police Shootings 'an American Issue,'" *New York Times*, July 8, 2016, https://www.nytimes.com/2016/07/08/us/philando-castile-falcon-heights-shooting.html.

54. "Bio," Rebekah Crisanta de Ybarra, http://www.rebekahcrisanta.com/.

55. "Home" and "Bio," Maria Isa, https://www.iammariaisa.com/. Not ironically, Isa became the headline performer when the band Maria Moctezuma from Mexico was unable to obtain visas in 2017.

56. Ramos invited three speakers to the circular clearing. First, she asked Gina Miranda, keeper of the Maya calendar, to teach those gathered about the Indigenous origins of Día de los Muertos and the Maya twenty-day cycle of remembrance. The curator, Ana Laura Juarez, also spoke, and established artist Dougie Padilla, who describes himself as a "literalist" for Día de los Muertos, declared the feminine leadership and wisdom as central to the future of the "Latinx community."

57. Goeman, "Land as Life," 85.

58. In this way, Latina/o/x somatic emplacement is not producing what Yi-Fu Tuan theorizes as a topophilia, "an affective bond between people and place" (*Topophilia: A Study of Environmental Perception, Attitudes, and Values* [Englewood Cliffs, NJ: Prentice-Hall, 1974], 4).

59. Fetta, *Shaming into Brown*, xvi.

60. José Esteban Muñoz, *Cruising Utopia: The Then and There of Queer Futurity* (New York: NYU Press, 2009). For quotation, see Flores, "The Latino Imaginary," 187.

61. Agustín Laó-Montes, "Niuyol: Urban Regime, Latino Social Movements, Ide-

ologies of Latinidad," in Laó-Montes and Dávila, *Mambo Montage,* 8; see also Nicole M. Guidotti-Hernández, "Affective Communities and Millennial Desires: Latinx, or Why My Computer Won't Recognize Latina/o," *Cultural Dynamics* 29, no. 3 (2017): 141–59; and Richard T. Rodríguez, "X Marks the Spot," *Cultural Dynamics* 29, no. 3 (2017): 202–13.

62. Muñoz, *Cruising Utopia*, 65–82.

63. Rodríguez, "X Marks the Spot," 205.

64. Sandoval, *Methodology of the Oppressed.*

CHAPTER 10

Refugees, Religious Spaces, and Sanctuary in Wisconsin

SERGIO M. GONZÁLEZ

On May 23, 1983, the congregation of St. Francis House Episcopal Student Center on the campus of the University of Wisconsin–Madison became the first church in the city and the first Episcopal church in the country to offer sanctuary to undocumented refugees fleeing political persecution from Central America. Reverend Thomas Woodward, pastor of St. Francis, explained that the congregation had made the difficult decision to open its doors to Central Americans in spite of potential legal consequences for two main reasons. The first was a matter of humanitarian compassion: the religious community sought to offer safe harbor to asylees fearing detention and deportation at the hands of the US government. The second, however, was political. Sanctuary offered Central Americans the chance to perform what the pastor referred to as "an act of public witness against really a kind of demonic situation" and to provide a personal story of migration in a broader discussion on US immigration and foreign policy.[1]

That spring evening, St. Francis House's parishioners invited four Salvadoran refugees into their parish. Congregants sat intently in the church's pews as they listened to stories of persecution under the rule of a repressive military dictatorship. Eliza and Angel (pseudonyms to shield their identities), students and workers at a medical clinic, narrated their account of torture at the hands of government police who had erroneously branded them guerrillas. Their daughter, Noemi, was forced to watch as officers brutally beat Eliza. Standing in front of the congregation and speaking with the aid of a translator, Eliza decried corruption in her home country, explaining that her government was "good for nothing but killing people, extorting bribes, robbing, raising prices on the necessities of life, and freezing wages." Her face covered with sunglasses and a bandana to protect her family's identity, she explained that this corruption was only possible with "the help of the United States," which supplied millions of dollars "for arms to destroy families." Amos, a law student and the fourth refugee to enter into sanctuary that night, echoed Eliza and exhorted the Madisonians in attendance that evening to demand that their government cease military support to Central American governments.[2] Believing that sharing their stories might raise the political consciousness of Americans and help to shift the country's policy toward Central America, Eliza, Angel, and Amos made more than one hundred presentations across southeastern Wisconsin over the next year, meeting with congregations, organizations, and even presidential candidate Walter Mondale.[3]

The May 1983 vigil was a spark in a decade-long campaign in Madison to aid the hundreds of thousands of undocumented Central American asylees fleeing civil war. With its roots in the medieval tradition of churches providing safe harbor for those escaping extrajudicial persecution, the sanctuary movement sought to provide refuge for Central Americans evading political repression and violence in their home countries. Refused asylum in the United States because of the government's support for anti-Communist regimes in El Salvador and Guatemala, exiles faced the prospect of detention and deportation to their war-ravaged home countries. The movement, launched in the spring of 1982 with the declaration of sanctuary in congregations in the US Southwest, grew to include nearly five hundred faith communities across the nation within just five years. Of the hundreds of thousands of Salvadorans and Guatemalans fleeing their homes, hundreds risked deportation by publicly sharing their stories of war, repression, flight, and a search for a safe haven. Faith communities in places as geographically dispersed as the US Southwest, Pacific Northwest, and Upper Midwest heard asylees' stories and opened their congregational spaces in defiance of federal immigration policy. Functioning in concert with secular humanitarian and progressive movements against US intervention in Central America, this transnational solidarity movement became the largest and most sustained protest movement against US foreign policy since the campaign against the Vietnam War.[4] Understanding that their protests against the government's treatment of asylees might place them outside the bounds of legal activity, activists in the United States cited a higher moral mission in opening their congregational doors to undocumented asylees. Reverend Ted Seege of Madison's Lutheran Memorial Church explained this calling in 1983: "When there is a choice, we must obey God rather than human beings."[5] Throughout the 1980s, asylees and Americans alike made this choice and worked together to shift US foreign and immigration policies and, in the process, reorient the moral compass of the nation.

Through an examination of the 1980s sanctuary movement and the contemporary immigrant justice campaigns that have followed in the twenty-first century, this chapter argues that religious sites have been crucial locations for a form of sanctified Latinx placemaking in the US Midwest. Like workplaces and recreational settings, religious institutions are contested spaces made by the people who create, inhabit, maintain, and challenge them. An analysis of the organizational records of the activist organizations and parishes that joined the sanctuary movement, as well as the testimonies of asylees arriving in the Midwest, reveal how these sites offer the *potential* for active cross-cultural and interethnic engagement, opening avenues for Latinxs to engage society, as historian Gerald Poyo has noted, with "a sense of purpose, self-confidence, and security."[6] Through a practice of *religious placemaking*, midwestern Latinxs have participated in faith communities to meet economic and social needs, foster relationships, reinforce customs, and validate individual and communal identity, all while also working to create fellowship with other congregants. The sanctuary movements that Latinxs and their allies cultivated both in the 1980s and in the twenty-first century reveal this active process of religious placemaking, demonstrating how sacred spaces and the religiosity practiced within them have been significant in shaping the experiences of Latinxs in the Midwest. This chapter uncovers a history of how Latinx communities and their allies have turned to their faith to find moral validation for movements for social and immigration justice. Through movements built around sanctuary, Latinx communities have thus, in the words of performance studies scholar Elaine Peña, looked to "the sacred to address the secular," crafting responses grounded in shared religious values to address the racial discrimination and economic exploitation they face in their daily lives.[7]

States in the Upper Midwest displayed an early and vigorous level of support for the movement during the 1980s despite being thousands of miles removed from the southern border where thousands of Salvadorans and Guatemalans arrived every year.[8] Across the region, congregations engaged in sanctuary became crucial spaces not only for placemaking amongst Latinxs but also for creating a sense of fellowship with and among communities that were often predominantly white. The movement propelled residents of different racial backgrounds, faith beliefs, immigration statuses, and economic classes to acknowledge the role they might play in creating more just national immigration policies. Collaboration between Latinx and white congregants proved crucial for creating the spark needed to initiate change in parishes across the Midwest as activists invoked and reinterpreted theological practices to defend their decision to aid Central Americans. By transforming religious spaces into incubators for refugee justice, sanctuary allowed activists to articulate a shared moral consciousness built upon a publicly expressed and politicized devoutness in support of Central American asylees.

Churches can demonstrate a commitment to their newest congregants in a way that supersedes cultural accommodation. Scholars have noted the role faith communities have served in integrating Latinxs in cities and towns across the Midwest as early as the first decades of the twentieth century. The forms of hospitality midwestern parishes have extended to newly arriving Latinxs, as Delia Fernández-Jones and Claire Fox note in their contributions to this volume, have been complex and not always altogether inviting, often marked by struggles over assimilation, language use, and control of faith-based community institutions.[9] As Latinxs have constituted a rising share of the population in a region with declining native-born and white demographics, they have also accounted for the largest and most rapid growth in faith communities, including Catholic, mainline Protestant, Pentecostal, and other Christian congregations.[10] In response to these demographic shifts, many midwestern religious communities have expanded the inclusion of Latinx ethnoreligious traditions into church life. The infusion of Spanish-language masses and the incorporation of celebrations such as *las posadas* and *quinceañeras*, for example, have served as significant indicators that churches mean to incorporate these growing populations, important as they are for the very long-term viability of congregations in the region, into their communities. The political tenor and weight of this commitment, however, have evolved over the last four decades as the number of undocumented Latinx congregants in midwestern church pews has grown. These new parishioners have pressed their churches to move further than simply honoring familiar religious practices or altering worship schedules and have in the process pushed religious bodies to increasingly become some of the most vocal advocates for the rights of migrants, immigrants, and refugees.[11] This contemporary attention to immigration activism and solidarity with Latinxs represents a succession of the politically inflected fellowship of the 1980s sanctuary movement, one that recognizes the well-being of Latinx parishioners as constitutive of the larger community's health and its religious and social sustainability.

Through this practice of sanctified Latinx placemaking, a growing contingent within immigrant rights movements has endeavored to shift the moral consciousness of its fellow parishioners and community members. As part of the larger constellation of organizing for justice for immigrant communities, midwestern clergy and laity have centered their concern for Latinx communities and their battles to define belonging in the region in scripture, papal and church encyclicals, and larger calls for attentiveness to those who have been pushed to the margins of society. Sanctuary activists in both the 1980s iteration and the renewed movement of the twenty-first century believe that remonstrations infused with the language of religious morality offer a larger resonance for religious communities that is missing from broader political contentions. Activists have sought to engage in a form of consciousness-raising across divisions of race and class by utilizing a common moral language—in the tradition of liberation theology, a process known as *concientización*—that might then become part of the central mission of a congregation.[12] This attention to the connections between placemaking, hospitality to immigrants, religious social teaching, and the political responsibilities of faith communities, then, has never merely involved applying the "inflection" of religion into immigration activism. By turning to scripture, sanctuary activists created the moral foundation for organizing through their religiosity and centered their activism as fundamental to their identity as people of faith.

The Formation of the US Sanctuary Movement

The 1980s sanctuary movement developed as part of a broader transnational solidarity movement in response to an escalating exile crisis caused by political revolutions, mass migrations, and US foreign policy in Central America. Revolutions in Guatemala (1960–96) and El Salvador (1979–92) destabilized governments and economies and led to the deaths of more than a quarter of a million people. The United States, in its efforts to stave off the spread of Communism in countries near its southern border, played a key role in these conflicts by supporting military dictatorships and covertly supplying weapons and training to paramilitary forces. The conflicts correspondingly created massive migration northward. During the second half of the twentieth century, nearly two million individuals fled their homes for safe haven in Mexico, the United States, and Canada. Between 1980 and 1984 alone, more than five hundred thousand Salvadorans and Guatemalans entered the United States via border states. By the end of the decade, more than one million exiles had settled across the country.[13]

Central Americans arriving in the United States found limited safe harbor through federal immigration channels. Arrivals sought political asylum via protections offered by the Refugee Act of 1980, which afforded refugee status for those demonstrating "well-founded fear of persecution on account of race, religion, nationality, membership in a particular social group, or political opinion."[14] From 1983 to 1990, however, while the overall approval rate of asylum applications for asylees from across the world stood at 24 percent, US immigration officials approved only 2.6 percent of Salvadoran and 1.8 percent of Guatemalan claims. Federal administrators instead deemed the Central American arrivals "economic migrants" who were unlawfully present in the country and thus susceptible to removal. Beyond denying them asylum, Immigration and Naturalization Services (INS) on average deported one thousand Salvadorans and Guatemalans every month throughout the decade.[15]

Despite escalating civil wars and the arrival of increasing numbers of refugees at the US southern border, most Americans remained unaware of events in Central America through the late 1970s. The vicious murders of clergy and American missionaries in El Salvador in 1980, however, moved citizens to question their country's expanded military involvement in the region. In March 1980 the archbishop of San Salvador, Óscar Romero, an outspoken prelate who railed against poverty, extralegal killings, and corrupt government in his country, was brutally assassinated while delivering a Sunday mass. American public attention and outrage returned to the region with the murder of four churchwomen stationed in El Salvador in December 1980.[16] An increasing number of US religious communities and politicians laid these murders squarely at the feet of the country's right-wing military dictatorship. Historian Amanda Izzo notes that the murders of Romero and the churchwomen "provided a symbolic touchstone" that linked secular liberal-leftist protest movements for peace in Central America with rising "peace and justice wings" within Catholic, Protestant, and Jewish religious communities.[17]

Along the US-Mexico border, the confluence of increasing public attention to US involvement in Latin American revolutions, an uneven application of asylum requests, and the rising detention of asylees prompted religious communities to more assertively consider their role in assisting Central Americans. Faith communities along the borderlands offered new arrivals humanitarian and legal aid, contending that the federal government actively misclassified Central Americans as economic migrants instead of political refugees to conceal the US government's support of military dictatorships in El Salvador and Guatemala.[18] Increasingly frustrated with the ineffective protections offered by US refugee law, members of Tucson, Arizona's Southside Presbyterian Church voted to house undocumented Central Americans within the confines of their church building in March 1982. Understanding that harboring unauthorized asylees could be interpreted as a violation of federal law, the church community turned to the biblical practice of sanctuary to justify the opening of congregational doors to those fleeing persecution.[19] The call for sanctuary issued in Tucson spread across the country over the next decade as hundreds of Protestant, Catholic, and Jewish communities in nearly every state opened their doors to asylum seekers. At the height of the movement in the mid-1980s, an estimated thirty thousand faith members belonging to nearly five hundred churches and synagogues offered physical sanctuary to or support for Central Americans.[20]

Movement participants envisioned sanctuary as prophetic action not simply protecting individuals but also sounding public alarm to alert Americans of their country's complicity in the suffering of Central Americans. They utilized press conferences and a protracted media campaign to both shield themselves from retribution from the federal government and amplify the voices of asylees themselves. Religious communities relied upon the biblical exhortation to "welcome the stranger" without qualification, thus accusing the government not only of breaking international and federal human rights law but also of violating the moral law of God.[21] From the movement's inception, then, two central aspects of sanctuary ministry were inextricable: humanitarian assistance and resistance to US foreign and immigration policy. Faith communities resisted asylees' deportation because they opposed the conditions of terror in El Salvador and Guatemala from which asylees fled. As their government aided authoritarian governments in the region by supplying training and supplies to militaries implicated in death squad activities, sanctuary workers implicated US foreign policy in Central America in creating the circumstances forcing refugees northward.[22]

As a form of public action, the sanctuary movement blurred the margins of public and private space that often distinguish churches and temples in the popular imagination. Scholars have long shown how faith spaces have historically served as incubators for practices of morally infused social protest in the United States, whether in the efforts of antislavery abolitionists in the nineteenth century, the social gospel crusade of the Progressive Era, or the civil rights movements of the mid-twentieth century.[23] As another chapter in this history, sanctuary activists of different religious beliefs, racial backgrounds, and documentation statuses interrogated the extent to which personal faith, often considered an intimate and private affair, might be explored, questioned, and amplified in a larger communal and political manner. The movement demonstrated that placemaking manifests not only in built environments but also through movements for social and political change. Urbanism scholar Jesus Lara notes that placemaking can be more than the "physical manipulation of spaces." It can include the social networks and relations individuals create within corporeal locations.[24] The churches and synagogues in which sanctuary coalitions developed an ethos of religious placemaking thus became places where congregants could cultivate a sense of community and bonds of solidarity crossing denominational lines, political boundaries, and barriers marked by race and ethnicity. As Jim Corbett, a Quaker leader of the Tucson movement, explained to Madison congregations in 1983, "Churches are not just buildings, they are people."[25] By understanding "church" as more than a physical space, the movement moved to extend the morality and spirituality professed within religious locations beyond the physical boundaries of places of worship. Activists sought to turn moral teaching into public action, mobilizing to support and protect Central American asylees. As it spread across the United States, sanctuary demonstrated the ways in which religious sites could be places of imagined religious placemaking, positions from which Latinx communities and their allies can develop strategies to curtail hardship and organize for change.

Developing a "Midwest Praxis": The Sanctuary Movement in the Midwest

Organizing an interregional movement, specifically one capable of transporting asylees from border states to areas around the country, required broader resources and coordination than individual congregations or coalitions could muster. Activists in Tucson turned to the Chicago Religious Task Force on Central America (CRTF) in the spring of 1982 for assistance in establishing the infrastructure for such a network. While at first glance Chicago may have seemed like an unlikely locus of sanctuary activism, separated as it is from the border by hundreds of miles, a vibrant century-long history of Latinx migration to the region, as well as the imprint of decades of interracial political activism, primed the city to become a hub for the movement. Clergy and activists, many of whom had experience in the city's civil rights activism and in missionary work in Latin America, had founded the ecumenical CRTF in late 1980 following the murder of Romero and US missionaries in El Salvador. Before the start of the sanctuary movement, the coalition had worked to turn public attention toward and opinion against US interventionist policies in Central America. This nascent Central American peace and solidarity movement in Chicago, meanwhile, had also begun to extend support to a growing undocumented Central American population; by 1982 an estimated twenty thousand Salvadoran and Guatemalan refugees had settled in the city, many of whom required aid in securing employment, housing, and basic social services.[26] Heeding the call from Tucson, the CRTF expanded its footprint beyond the Midwest by serving several organizational roles in building sanctuary across the country, including coordinating correspondence between local parishes, regional coalitions, and national religious bodies; publishing a monthly periodical called *Basta!*; and distributing sanctuary "how-to" manuals and guidebooks for faith communities undertaking the discernment process of deciding whether to join the movement. Structurally, the coalition also assumed responsibility for managing aid for refugees and organizing their travel arrangements from border states to congregations across the country.[27]

Before the end of 1982, the CRTF had become the national clearinghouse for the movement. Beyond its capacity for organizing, the coalition moved to open congregational doors across the Midwest as spaces of sanctuary for Central Americans. The CRTF initially envisioned its Sanctuary Project as an organizing tool for its broader solidarity work. Within a few months, however, offering safe harbor to Central Americans and thus engaging in the process of religious placemaking became the coalition's primary mission.[28] In the summer of 1982, Chicago's Wellington Avenue United Church of Christ inaugurated the first public sanctuary for refugees in the Midwest, welcoming Juan, a twenty-three-year-old Salvadoran man, and the Vargas family, a Salvadoran family of six, into the church's community. Over the next five years, more than ten Chicago congregations would join the movement, hosting hundreds of asylum seekers in Protestant, Catholic, and Jewish houses of worship.[29]

Activists in southeastern Wisconsin began planning for sanctuary sites in Wisconsin shortly after the founding of the Chicago Wellington sanctuary in the fall of 1982. Milwaukee's Latinx community, the third largest Latinx community in the Midwest, had grown dramatically over the previous two decades and had demonstrated a robust capacity for political organizing in prior years.[30] In the fall of 1982, white and Latinx lay members of religious organizations in the city formed the interfaith and interracial Milwaukee Sanctuary Coordinating Committee (MSCC). The coalition coordinated efforts across several southeastern Wisconsin cities, including Milwaukee, Racine, and Kenosha. It was led by Milwaukee's lay and clerical Catholics, a denominational characteristic that distinguished it from every other Protestant-led sanctuary coalition in the country. Like their Chicago counterparts, the MSCC worked in concert with a vibrant local Central American peace and solidarity movement, one that predated the sanctuary movement. The coalition of secular organizations organized weekly protests and sponsored lectures from displaced Central Americans who denounced increasing US military intervention in their home region.[31] MSCC leadership corresponded with the CRTF for assistance in developing the structure of Milwaukee's program and recruiting Central American asylees to Wisconsin.[32] Perhaps most importantly, the coalition obtained the blessing of Milwaukee archbishop Rembert Weakland, the first Catholic bishop in the nation to support the movement, securing a pivotal endorsement for their efforts. With momentum in the city growing, three churches declared themselves sanctuaries on December 2, 1982, becoming the first Catholic sites to join the movement beyond the borderland region. The MSCC's declaration, along with the archbishop's support, initiated what CRTF leaders referred to as "a Midwest *praxis*," an invitation to the broader North American religious community "to join a national campaign for sanctuary sponsorship."[33]

The CRTF's invocation of the term "praxis" in the winter of 1982 underscored the importance of sanctuary as both a temporally placed location—in this case, the US Midwest—and an active and liberatory process. Liberation theologians understand praxis as the conversation between doctrine and doing, a method of translating intention into movement. When understood as a physical space, sanctuary could create a safe harbor for Central American asylees seeking respite from persecution in their home countries and the encroaching power of US immigration enforcement. As a *process* of religious placemaking and movement formation, sanctuary required coequal collaboration between refugees and midwesterners, a partnership that depended on the power of Central Americans' voices and their personal histories, as well as the social and political capital of US faith communities. The process and praxis of creating sanctuary, defined as both a place and a movement for refugee justice, thus required all members of the movement, in the words of liberation theologian Gustavo Gutiérrez, to take on an "active presence in history" to mitigate the potential harm that might be caused if Central Americans were to be returned to their war-ravaged homes.[34]

Among those original southeastern Wisconsin sanctuary sites engaged in creating this "Midwest praxis" was Cristo Rey Parish. The Catholic congregation in Racine, situated just forty minutes south of Milwaukee, became the first predominantly Latinx church in the country to join the movement. Many in the Cristo Rey congregation had once been migrants and asylum seekers, and several of those who had voted for sanctuary were presently undocumented immigrants. Rachel Parra, the self-identified Chicana secretary of Cristo Rey's parish council, stated that undocumented parishioners who had voted in favor of sanctuary, despite holding a tenuous legal standing in the United States themselves, were the most daring members of the movement. According to Parra, the parish considered their entry into the sanctuary movement as "small and insignificant when compared to the courageous action taken by the refugees who are willing to risk deportation and death that their people might live."[35] Parra's comments highlighted the importance of asylees' voices and their personal stories in the expansion of sanctuary across Wisconsin and the Midwest. The church's Capuchin pastor, Glenn Gessner, a former missionary in Nicaragua, noted that congregants, upon hearing from asylum seekers arriving in the city, expressed disgust with the US government "backing military dictatorships in Central American countries where there is persecution, war, and killing."[36] According to Gessner, parishioners voted to support the movement in part to break out of a feeling of political hopelessness and instead "protest the injustice our military arms are producing."[37] Expressing their obligation to defend the human rights of Central American asylees, the pastor told the *Milwaukee Sentinel*, "We say we are not revolutionaries. We are just defending our Spanish brethren. We have the right in the name of God to protect these people."[38] In referring to

Salvadoran and Guatemalan asylees as "our Spanish brethren," Gessner—a Bulgarian American priest who traced his kinship to asylees to his own multi-decade missionary work in Central America and Latinx Wisconsin—defined a sense of religious placemaking that imagined the church of Cristo Rey not merely as a physical building but also as a fount for transnational fellowship created by the Latinx congregants who constituted its community.

While the Milwaukee area's nascent sanctuary movement drew in large part from the city's growing Latinx population, nearby Madison's mobilization grew initially from the city's progressive white religious and student community.[39] A history of leftist politics, as well as a vibrant antiwar protest culture at the University of Wisconsin–Madison, made the area a central midwestern hub for Central American solidarity work throughout the decade.[40] Madisonians first experimented with the practice of sanctuary in the midst of virulent anti-Vietnam protests in the late 1960s, when a university student sought asylum in a city church for nearly two weeks in opposition to draft orders.[41] As US involvement in Central America accelerated throughout the 1980s, university students expanded the scope of both humanitarian and nonviolent political actions against militarism in the region. Student organizations such as Movimiento Estudiantil Chicano de Aztlán (MEChA), the Union for International Action, and the Progressive Student Network held rallies, marches, and candlelight vigils against what they called "another Vietnam" brewing in Central America. They took particular aim at the presence of Wisconsin reserve troops in Nicaragua and protested against CIA recruiters on campus.[42] The city's congressional representatives echoed fears that US involvement in El Salvador would result in cascading entanglements that would devolve from supplying weapons and military advisors to the deployment of American soldiers to the region.[43]

Madisonians' opposition to their country's Central American policies grew to include a vibrant refugee justice movement in the spring of 1983. Within a year of the initiation of sanctuary at St. Francis House, fifteen area congregations representing Protestants, Catholics, and Jews had joined the movement. The rapid growth of sanctuary in the city prompted the editorial board of the local *Capital Times* to note that the "scene" of Central American families, their faces covered by masks and standing before a religious congregation promising solidarity, had become "a familiar one" in Madison.[44] These religiously affiliated activists worked closely with their secular counterparts in student movements and community coalitions. While most students at the university may have perhaps demurred at the overtly religious nature of sanctuary, they certainly understood the moral weight that faith-based arguments could hold in US society. Working in consultation with these secular and devout activists in the spring of 1984, the city's Common Council passed a resolution forbidding public employees and police from cooperating with federal immigration officials, a symbolic act that nonetheless gave efforts for immigrant justice wider visibility in the state.[45] Just one year later, Wisconsin governor Tony Earl announced his administration's support for the movement by declaring Wisconsin a "state of sanctuary" for Guatemalan and Salvadoran refugees. Not intended as a legal challenge to federal immigration policies, Earl's statement instead served as a political declaration and a "strong statement of values" for the state.[46]

Political action in support of asylum seekers at the local, state, and federal levels, symbolic or otherwise, was spurred on primarily by the work of Central Americans. The principal objective of the movement was for asylees themselves to offer living testimony, or *testimonio*, about the war's effects on individuals' lives. This practice served to amplify refugees' voices in national political conversations regarding immigration and refugee policy and the role of the United States abroad. Interactions between Central Americans and communities of faith within religious spaces also served to invoke a moral dilemma that invited, indeed required, a decision from Americans: Would they stand by their complicit federal government, or would they open the doors of their churches and synagogues as spaces of sanctuary to refugees in defiance of immigration enforcement? *Testimonios* offered the potential of constructing empathy and identification between individuals, forcing listeners, as literary scholar Marta Caminero-Santangelo has proposed, to "feel a sense of obligation and responsibility for what [was] happening elsewhere."[47] The decision to broadcast their personal and often traumatic narratives to midwestern religious communities and thus speak "not for the individual but for the experience of a community," however, required that Central Americans take on a considerably draining role as spokespeople for the movement.[48] Eliza, living in sanctuary at Madison's St. Francis, relayed her story to congregation after congregation in her first few months in Wisconsin. She explained to church members that she was haunted daily by the memories of her family's escape: "It is difficult to explain. One lives with so much fear that you wake up in the middle of the night and hear somebody."[49] Working to raise Wisconsinites' awareness through the process of consciousness-raising (*concientización*), those living in sanctuary took on the considerable task of recounting the stories of assault, rape, and murder at the hands of military forces in their home country, harrowing accounts of their migration across Central America and the US-Mexico border, and the difficulties of living undocumented in the United States.

As asylum seekers arrived in midwestern parishes, their *testimonios* recounting violence and migration became fundamental for placemaking in religious spaces. *Testimonios* provided a counternarrative to the US media's depiction of revolutions in Central America. As legal scholar Sophie Pirie has noted, they brought home for congregants the realities of rising violence and Salvadoran and Guatemalan death squads in order to "arouse Americans' suspicions about government honesty" and equip them with the "information—the power—to question and rebut government accounts."[50] Antonio, living in sanctuary in Madison, believed that a personal testimony could force midwesterners "to know more deeply the necessity of our people and advance more the protest against the American government and form small groups to conscienticize the American people." While sanctuary was fundamentally a collaborative process between asylees and Americans, full consciousness-raising required that refugees lead the movement. Antonio believed that in order to combat a sense of paternalism that would force those seeking asylum to share their stories just to then become passive recipients of American religious hospitality, "we [Central Americans] must play a role" in leading the creation and proliferation of sanctuary.[51]

Those living in sanctuary in a particular midwestern congregation found that their *concientización* efforts could take them on speaking tours across the region. Central Americans shared their individual stories and connected them to larger national and international histories of imperialism and violence in order to create a stronger interregional Central American solidarity network. Rene Hurtado, a former solider in the Salvadoran army who had fled his regiment after receiving commands to commit atrocities against his fellow countrymen, had originally entered sanctuary at Cristo Rey in Milwaukee in December 1982 before moving on to a permanent residence in a Twin Cities church in early 1983. Over the next year alone, he spoke to more than 140 organizations in three states, at times speaking to three different groups in a day.[52] Teresa Lopez, a Guatemalan refugee living in sanctuary in Minnesota, visited the University of Wisconsin–Milwaukee in the spring of 1984, where she delivered a lecture detailing her country's political history and argued for the importance of solidarity among all Latin Americans resisting against military dictatorships and US intervention.[53] The lecture circuit took Salvadoran José Sánchez, living in sanctuary in Iowa, across rural Wisconsin in 1985 to discuss his own migration history and the impact of continued US support of repressive regimes in his home country as he visited high schools and churches in the small Wisconsin towns of Cuba City, Viroqua, and Gary Mills.[54]

In touring the Midwest and speaking in even the most remote congregational spaces, Central Americans and sanctuary workers sought to put face and voice to the civil wars that the US media was making increasingly visible to more Americans. They also hoped to expand the coalitional capacity of their movement beyond progressives or immigration activists. Movement members sought, in effect, to reach beyond their church choirs. Outside of Chicago's growing undocumented Central American asylee population, most midwestern states were home to a relatively small number of Salvadoran and Guatemalan communities during the 1980s. Sanctuary members thus aimed to raise the consciousness of middle-class Americans who professed faith and might be appalled to learn of US involvement in the violence and wars that had caused the flight of Central Americans northward. This was an explicitly political objective articulated by the Chicago Religious Task Force and most midwestern sanctuary coalitions, all separated from the border geographically. Through religious placemaking, the concept of sanctuary forced congregations to wrestle with the meaning and scope of their faith as it might extend beyond the walls of the physical spaces in which they prayed and joined in fellowship. Those churches and synagogues that voted to declare themselves sanctuaries and join the movement engaged in a life-changing decision, what some members referred to as a "conversion process." Sanctuary workers forged what they referred to as a "covenant of solidarity with the oppressed," amplifying the concept of solidarity beyond a relationship not only with asylees arriving at the border or those living in asylum in midwestern congregations but also with all people struggling and dying in Central America.[55]

One such midwestern convert was Mary Collet, a Madison Quaker who was stirred to join sanctuary work in 1983. The formerly politically inactive Collet had been "moved by conscience" after hearing an asylee living in sanctuary share their story. Especially troubled to hear of her own country's role in accelerating Central American revolutions, she had grown even more "ashamed for the way the [Reagan] administration" had treated arriving asylees. A mother of three and homemaker, Collet committed herself to raising Wisconsinites' awareness of asylum justice. She pushed back against the idea that sanctuary movement members were merely "rabble rousers" or that their activism was "an isolated phenomenon," instead noting that the movement included "everyone from college kids to white-haired ladies," or, as she noted, "a lot of people like me." Collet's role in the movement evolved beyond congregational sanctuary throughout the 1980s. She traveled to Brownsville, Texas, in 1984, where she served as a representative for twenty-six Madison congregations and lay organizations in conducting solidarity work along the US-Mexico border.[56] Other Madisonians began their Central American advocacy in sanctuary work before joining the Madison Border Support Group, a small but dedicated organization founded in 1983 to aid Central American asylees arriving in southern Texas. The group raised thousands of dollars, collected more than two tons of clothing, and gathered food and medical supplies in the Madison area to be sent to the border region where religious organizations ran refugee projects.[57]

Sanctuary participants' decade-long activism in the Midwest and across the country spurred substantial legal victories for Central American refugees in 1990. Federal legislators supportive of expanding asylum opportunities successfully included provisions in the Immigration Act of 1990 to allow Salvadorans to apply for eighteen-month protections under temporary protected status (TPS). This novel legal arrangement proved significant for other displaced populations from across the world, as over the next three decades individuals affected by natural disaster or armed conflict from Central America, the Caribbean, the Middle East, Africa, and eastern Europe successfully found reprieve in the United States through TPS. The legislative codification of refugee protections was followed by a significant court decision known as the ABC Settlement Agreement. Led by a coalition of more than eighty religious and refugee organizations, activists secured an out-of-court settlement with the federal government in the civil suit *American Baptist Churches et al. v. Thornburgh*, allowing Salvadorans who had been present in the United States since September 1, 1990, and Guatemalans who been in the country since October 1, 1990, the right to apply anew for asylum interviews.[58] These legal achievements at the federal level, along with the reduction of migration from Central America with the beginning of peace processes in El Salvador and Guatemala, brought the national sanctuary movement to a slow end by the early 1990s.

Beyond these significant judicial and legislative victories, efforts to reorient the country's moral compass had long-standing effects on midwestern religious communities and their commitment to Latinx populations. Joining in solidarity with Central American refugees served as what Reverend Joseph Ellwanger of Milwaukee's Cross Lutheran Church referred to as an "experiential baptism" for many activists into social and political organizing for immigrant and refugee justice. Just as critically for members of Christian and Jewish congregations, these mobilizations functioned as an awakening of religious consciousness, a form of *concientización*, that made concrete their faiths' call to "welcome the stranger."[59] Participants involved in sanctuary continued transnational efforts connected to Latin America in the decades following the end of the movement, including engaging in humanitarian aid at the US-Mexico border, protesting persistent US military support and training for paramilitary forces in the region through School of the Americas Watch, expanding medical and religious missionary work in the region, and eventually helping restart the movement decades later in the early twenty-first century.[60] Ultimately, congregants of different ethnic, racial, class, and denominational backgrounds came to understand their local and regional sanctuary efforts as part of broader struggles to expand the bounds of hospitality toward immigrants and refugees across the country.

Conclusion

Decades removed from the original sanctuary movement, midwestern Latinx communities continue to navigate the complex relationship between immigration, placemaking, and activism into the twenty-first century. For many Latinxs, the church serves as a vital institution within which to organize community and, when necessary, movements for social change. It is a space where, as Roberto Treviño notes, Latinxs have "countered inequality . . . by claiming legitimacy," a legitimacy to envisage community, cultivate modalities of collective organization, and reimagine identities in an effort to define their sense of belonging in the Midwest.[61]

The spirit of sanctuary that flourished in midwestern religious spaces in the 1980s found renewed energy in the early twenty-first century as local and national political leaders advanced immigration policies that further thrust undocumented immigrants into the nation's shadows. Punitive immigration enforcement first accelerated under the administration of George W. Bush and then ramped up under Barack Obama, in effect creating what historian Rachel Buff refers to as a "deportation terror" among immigrant communities, forcing individuals and families to live in constant fear of detention and deportation.[62] In response to these policies, congregations remobilized to support immigrants such as Elvira Arellano, who in August 2006, fearing detention and deportation to Mexico, took sanctuary along with her US-born son in a Chicago Methodist church. Arellano's decision to seek refuge in a religious space garnered national attention and transformed her into a leader in a growing immigrant justice movement.[63] Spurred on by mobilizations in Chicago, lay and religious activists from cities across the country convened to establish the New Sanctuary Movement in early 2007, a loose coalition of faith communities that professed a commitment to engage in public ministry in support of immigrant communities. Religious leaders such as Reverend Alexia Salvatierra, director of Los Angeles' Clergy and Laity United for Economic Justice, pledged to offer sanctuary and spread "the living story of the families broken by a broken system."[64]

If the light of sanctuary was rekindled in response to expanding immigration enforcement in the first decade of the twenty-first century, its flame burst to a searing brightness following the 2016 presidential election. The xenophobic rhetoric espoused by Donald Trump throughout his campaign placed Latinx immigrants again in the center of conversations regarding belonging and placemaking. Facing the threat of potential large-scale deportation raids, religious communities across the country answered the call of immigrant rights organizations to fortify sanctuary efforts. Activists expanded the number of congregations committed to offering sanctuary to undocumented immigrants across the country from four hundred to more than eleven hundred within one year of the election. By January 2018 thirty-six individuals were living in public sanctuary, supported by sanctuary coalitions across forty states. The expansion of sanctuary networks steadily progressed in the Midwest, with coalitions including the Chicago Religious Leadership Network, the Iowa Sanctuary Movement, the Immigrant Justice Advocacy Movement (Kansas City), the St. Louis Inter-Faith Committee on Latin America, the Ohio Interfaith Immigrant and Migration Justice Coalition, the Omaha Area Sanctuary Network, the ISAIAH/Sanctuary Coalition (Minneapolis), the Dane Sanctuary Coalition (Madison), and Milwaukee's New Sanctuary Coalition.[65]

The spirit that moved in churches and synagogues during the 1980s sanctuary movement—a coupling of faith with political and social consciousness—is alive again in religious spaces in the Midwest and across the country. There are distinctions to be made between these movements: the countries from which asylees are arriving today in some cases are different, the policies that have prompted mass exiles abroad and detention and deportation in the United States are unique, and many of the policymakers and movement participants have changed. Perhaps most notably, unlike the 1980s iteration, which aided newly arrived asylees from Central America, the New Sanctuary Movement seeks to address the concerns of undocumented immigrants from around the world who have lived within their communities in the United States for extended periods of time, some even for decades. If the guiding scriptural backing for the original movement drew from Leviticus's and Matthew's exhortation to "welcome the stranger," this new movement follows the United States Conference of Catholic Bishops and Conferencia del Episcopado Mexicano's 2003 joint pastoral letter's call to embrace these communities as "strangers no longer."[66] Churches engaged in sanctuary work in the twenty-first century acknowledge their primary responsibility to develop an ethic of placemaking of hospitality and communion with immigrant and migrant communities, regardless of their documentation status. In this way, these religious communities counteract immigration policies that undermine the human dignity of undocumented persons and their right to pursue a full life in the United States.

Notes

1. "Local Church to Offer Asylum for Latin American Refugees," *Capital Times* (Madison), May 13, 1983.

2. "Salvador Refugees Find Sanctuary," *Wisconsin State Journal*, May 24, 1983.

3. "Salvadoran Finds Haven in Madison," *Wisconsin State Journal*, March 8, 1987.

4. Margaret Power and Julie A. Charlip, "Introduction: On Solidarity," *Latin American Perspectives* 36, no. 6 (November 2009): 3–9.

5. "Salvador Refugees Find Sanctuary."

6. Gerald E. Poyo, "'Integration without Assimilation': Cuban Catholics in Miami, 1960–1980," *U.S. Catholic Historian* 20, no. 4 (Fall 2002): 92.

7. Elaine Peña, "Beyond Mexico: Guadalupan Sacred Space Production and Mobilization in a Chicago Suburb," *American Quarterly* 60, no. 3 (September 2008): 740.

8. By 1987 three out of ten of the most active sanctuary states were in the Midwest, with Illinois home to twenty-six sites, Wisconsin hosting eighteen, and Minnesota with ten. "Summary of Sanctuary Sites," *Basta! National Newsletter of the Chicago Religious Task Force on Central America*, December 1987, Chicago Religious Task Force on Central American Records, 1982–92, Wisconsin Historical Society, Madison (hereafter WHS).

9. David Badillo, "The Catholic Church and the Making of Mexican-American Parish Communities in the Midwest," in *Mexican Americans and the Catholic Church, 1900–1965*, ed. Jay P. Dolan and Gilberto M. Hinojosa (Notre Dame, IN: University of Notre Dame Press, 1994), 223–308; Robert Orsi, *Thank You, St. Jude: Women's Devotion to the Patron Saint of Hopeless Causes* (New Haven, CT: Yale University Press, 1998), 1–39; Deborah Kanter, "Making Mexican Parishes: Ethnic Succession in Chicago Churches, 1947–1977," *U.S. Catholic Historian* 30, no. 2 (2012): 35–58; Martinez, *Catholic Borderlands*; Sergio M. González, "Interethnic Catholicism and Transnational Religious Connections: Milwaukee's Mexican Mission Chapel of Our Lady of Guadalupe, 1924–1929," *Journal of American Ethnic History* 36, no. 1 (Fall 2016): 5–30.

10. Pew Research Center, "The Shifting Religious Identity of Latinos in the United States," May 7, 2014, https://www.pewresearch.org/wp-content/uploads/sites/7/2014/05/Latinos-Religion-07-22-full-report.pdf.

11. Stephen P. Davis, Juan R. Martinez, and R. Stephen Warner, "The Role of the Catholic Church in the Chicago Immigrant Mobilization," in *¡Marcha! Latino Chicago and the Immigrant Rights Movement*, ed. Amalia Pallares and Nilda Flores-González (Urbana: University of Illinois Press, 2010), 79–96; Hinojosa, *Latino Mennonites*; Amalia Pallares, *Family Activism: Immigrant Struggles and the Politics of Noncitizenship* (New Brunswick, NJ: Rutgers University Press, 2015).

12. Sanctuary's doctrinal underpinnings and ethos for political engagement drew in large part from liberation theology. First developed in the late 1960s and early 1970s as a response to the Catholic Church's centuries-long colonial relationship with Latin America, this form of understanding of the Christian faith called on clergy and laity to more closely connect scriptural teaching with temporal action, charging believers to adopt a "preferential option for the poor" and radically reorder the social and economic structures of their communities. See Leonardo Boff and Clodovis Boff, *Introducing Liberation Theology* (Maryknoll, NY: Orbis Books, 1987); Gustavo Gutiérrez, *A Theology of Liberation: History, Politics, and Salvation*, 15th anniversary ed. (Maryknoll, NY: Orbis Books, 1988); Christian Smith, *The Emergence of Libera-*

tion Theology: Radical Religion and Social Movement Theory (Chicago: University of Chicago Press, 1991).

13. Gil Loescher, "Humanitarianism and Politics in Central America," *Political Science Quarterly* 103, no. 2 (Summer 1988): 296; María Christina García, *Seeking Refuge: Central American Migration to Mexico, the United States, and Canada* (Berkeley: University of California Press, 2006), 13–43.

14. Public Law 96-212 (Refugee Act of 1980), 8 USC § 1521 (1980).

15. García, *Seeking Refuge*, 90.

16. Matt Eisenbrandt, *Assassination of a Saint: The Plot to Murder Óscar Romero and the Quest to Bring His Killers to Justice* (Berkeley: University of California Press, 2017), 1–37.

17. Amanda Izzo, *Liberal Christianity and Women's Global Activism: The YWCA of the USA and the Maryknoll Sisters* (New Brunswick, NJ: Rutgers University Press, 2018), 191.

18. Geraldo L. Cadava, *Standing on Common Ground: The Making of the Sunbelt Borderland* (Cambridge, MA: Harvard University Press, 2008), 198–206.

19. Five churches in Berkeley, California, publicly joined the Tucson church in declaring their support for undocumented asylees that spring. See Van Gosse, "'The North American Front': Central American Solidarity in the Reagan Era," in *Reshaping the US Left: Popular Struggles in the 1980s*, ed. Mike Davis and Michael Sprinker (New York: Verso, 1988), 27–28.

20. Ignatius Bau, *The Ground Is Holy: Church Sanctuary and Central American Refugees* (Mahwah, NJ: Paulist Press, 1985), 75–123.

21. John Fife, "Civil Initiative," in *Trails of Hope and Terror: Testimonies on Immigration*, ed. Miguel A. de la Torre (Maryknoll, NY: Orbis Books, 2009), 172.

22. Hilary Cunningham, *God and Caesar at the Rio Grande: Sanctuary and the Politics of Religion* (Minneapolis: University of Minnesota Press, 1995), 38–43; Susan Bibler Coutin, *The Culture of Protest: Religious Activism and the U.S. Sanctuary Movement* (Boulder, CO: Westview Press, 1993), 174–92. See also "Some of the Differing Philosophies on What Sanctuary Should Be" (1985), box 4, folder 61, Chicago Religious Task Force on Central American Records, 1982–92, WHS.

23. See, for example, Paul Harvey, *Freedom's Coming: Religious Culture and the Shaping of the South from the Civil War through the Civil Rights Era* (Chapel Hill: University of North Carolina Press, 2007); David Chappell, *A Stone of Hope: Prophetic Religion and the Death of Jim Crow* (Chapel Hill: University of North Carolina Press, 2005); Christopher Cantwell, Heath W. Carter, and Janine Giordano Drake, eds., *The Pew and the Picket Line: Christianity and the American Working Class* (Urbana: University of Illinois Press, 2016).

24. Lara, *Latino Placemaking and Planning*, 30.

25. "Quaker Listens to His Conscience, Not INS," *Capital Times* (Madison), August 13, 1983.

26. Summary proposal, undated, box 3, folder 20, Chicago Religious Task Force on Central America Records, 1982–92, WHS.

27. Jennifer Lynn Murray, "The Chicago Religious Task Force on Central America:

Moral Defiance in the Face of U.S. Policy, 1980–1992" (MA thesis, University of Wisconsin–Eau Claire, 2012), 19–42.

28. "Working Paper: Sanctuary Project as CRTF Central Organizing Tool," undated, box 3, folder 20, Chicago Religious Task Force on Central America Records, 1982–92, WHS.

29. Summary proposal, CRTF, undated, box 3, folder 20, Chicago Religious Task Force on Central America Records, 1982–92, WHS; "Sanctuary Movement Hanging On," *Chicago Tribune*, January 31, 1985.

30. By the early 1980s Milwaukee trailed only Chicago and Detroit in the Midwest in the size of its Latinx community. The city had witnessed a rapid growth of its population due to both the transformation of a migratory Tejano labor into permanent settlers and a boom in new Mexican and Central American immigration. Elisa Basurto, Doris P. Slesinger, and Eleanor Cautley, "Hispanics in Wisconsin, 1980—a Chartbook," University of Wisconsin Department of Rural Sociology's Applied Population Laboratory (Madison, 1985). For more on Milwaukee Latinxs' activism, see Rodriguez, *The Tejano Diaspora*.

31. "Festival Marks Revolution," *Milwaukee Journal*, July 19, 1981; "Policy on Latin America Denounced," *Milwaukee Sentinel*, July 20, 1981; "Play by Guatemalan Theater Group Tells Story of Repression," *Milwaukee Journal*, October 27, 1982.

32. Notes regarding December 2, 1982, sanctuary announcement, undated, box 1, folder 1, Chicago Religious Task Force on Central America Records, 1982–92, WHS.

33. Renny Golden and Michael McConnell, "Sanctuary: Choosing Sides," *Christianity and Crisis*, February 21, 1983, box 3, folder 54, Chicago Religious Task Force on Central America Records, 1982–92, WHS.

34. Gutiérrez, *A Theology of Liberation*, 6.

35. Renny Golden and Michael McConnell, *Sanctuary: The New Underground Railroad* (Maryknoll, NY: Orbis Books, 1986), 12.

36. Father Glenn Gessner, interview with author, November 21, 2016.

37. "Two Parishes Offer Sanctuary to Refugees," *Catholic Herald* (Milwaukee), November 18, 1982.

38. "Weakland to Let Catholic Churches Harbor Refugees," *Milwaukee Sentinel*, November 12, 1982.

39. By the late 1970s, Dane County's Latinx population stood at approximately fifty-three hundred, a combination of settled-out migrant workers from surrounding rural areas and a growing Latin American contingent enrolled at the University of Wisconsin–Madison. "Información del Lunes," *Capital Times* (Madison), January 3, 1977.

40. For more on Madison peace and solidarity efforts in Central America, see Molly Todd, "'We Were Part of the Revolutionary Movement There': Wisconsin Peace Progressives and Solidarity with El Salvador in the Reagan Era," *Journal of Civil and Human Rights* 3, no. 1 (Spring/Summer 2017): 1–56.

41. In September 1969 Ken Vogel took sanctuary in Madison's First Congregational Church after refusing induction into the armed forces. He lived in the church for twelve days before turning himself over to federal agents. "Young Draft Resister Takes

Sanctuary in Church Here," *Capital Times* (Madison), September 17, 1969; "Vogel Arrested and Awaits Trial," *Wisconsin State Journal,* October 4, 1969.

42. "1,000 at UW Protest Latin Policy," *Wisconsin State Journal*, April 22, 1983; Progressive Student Network (University of Wisconsin–Madison), "Central America . . . Another Vietnam!" (1986), Pamphlet Collection, WHS; Progressive Student Network (University of Wisconsin–Madison), "U.S. War on Nicaragua" (1986), Pamphlet Collection, WHS.

43. Representative Robert Kastenmeier criticized the Reagan administration's hawkish thrust in Central America and what he referred to as a "Dr. Strangelove mentality" evolving in Washington military circles. Throughout the 1980s, the Madison representative voted against continued military spending in the region and led investigations into the FBI's surveillance of Central American solidarity organizations. Quoted in "'Perilous Push for Arms' Worries Kastenmeier," *Capital Times* (Madison), March 28, 1981. See also "Kastenmeier: House to Investigate FBI," *Capital Times* (Madison), January 29, 1988.

44. "Sanctuary from Oppression," *Capital Times* (Madison), February 21, 1984.

45. "Little Expected of 'Sanctuary' Motion," *Wisconsin State Journal*, March 9, 1985. The Madison resolution was largely symbolic, as the city's police chief had previously expressed no desire to deploy local law enforcement as immigration officers. That same spring, Chicago mayor Harold Washington signed an executive order ending the city's policy of asking employment and license applicants about their citizenship status and halting city agencies' cooperation with federal immigration authorities. See City of Chicago, Office of the Mayor, "Executive Order 85-1 (Equal Access to City Services, Benefits and Opportunities)," March 7, 1985, http://www.chicityclerk.com/legislation-records/journals-and-reports/executive-orders.

46. Earl quoted in "Haven Declared for Latin Refugees," *Milwaukee Sentinel*, September 20, 1986. See the proclamation from Governor Anthony S. Earl, State of Wisconsin, September 1986, box 6, folder 27, Darlene Nicgorski Papers on the Sanctuary Movement, Special Collections, Honnold Mudd Library, Claremont University Consortium, Claremont, CA.

47. Marta Caminero-Santangelo, "Documenting the Undocumented: Life Narratives of Unauthorized Immigrants," *Biography* 35, no. 3 (Summer 2012): 450.

48. The Latina Feminist Group, "Introduction: *Papelitos Guardados*: Theorizing *Latinidades* through *Testimonios*," in *Telling to Live: Latina Feminist Testimonios* (Durham, NC: Duke University Press, 2001), 20.

49. "Refugee Family Recalls Life in El Salvador," *Wisconsin State Journal*, June 25, 1983.

50. Sophie H. Pirie, "The Origins of a Political Trial: The Sanctuary Movement and Political Justice," *Yale Journal of Law & the Humanities* 2, no. 2 (1990): 394.

51. "Refugees Speak Out about Direction of the Sanctuary Movement," *Basta! National Newsletter of the Chicago Religious Task Force on Central America*, January 1985, Chicago Religious Task Force on Central American Records, 1982–92, WHS.

52. "Wayzatta Church Shelters Salvador Refugee," *Minneapolis Tribune*, December 12, 1982; "City Church to Give Refugee Sanctuary," *Minneapolis Tribune*, June 19, 1983;

"Groups Say Minnesotans among Those Investigated by FBI," *Albert Lea Evening Tribune*, January 28, 1988; "Hunger Strike Ends; Fighting Aid Continues," *Wisconsin State Journal*, December 12, 1989. Hurtado remained in the Twin Cities throughout the 1980s, becoming a leader in the midwestern Central America solidarity movement.

53. "Exiled without Identity: Refugee Tells Story of Poverty and Brutality in Guatemala," *UWM Post* (Milwaukee), March 6, 1984.

54. "Central American Refugee Speaks at Gays Mills," *Crawford County Independent-Scout*, April 11, 1985.

55. Chicago Religious Task Force on Central America, "Sanctuary: A Justice Ministry (Revised)" (1985), Pamphlet Collection, WHS.

56. "Local Woman Spreads Word on Sanctuaries," *Capital Times* (Madison), December 15, 1984.

57. "Miracle of Hanukkah Story Is One Life Helping Others," *Wisconsin State Journal*, December 11, 1982; "What Leads Activists to Help Refugees," *Capital Times* (Madison), May 5, 1986; "Madisonians Put Refugee Action First," *Wisconsin State Journal*, March 8, 1987.

58. The ABC Settlement Agreement allowed for the readjudication of nearly 150,000 asylum requests and opened the door for more than 350,000 asylees who had previously never applied for refugee status to seek hearings. Susan Bibler Coutin, "From Refugees to Immigrants: The Legalization Strategies of Salvadoran Immigrants and Activists," *International Migration Review* 32, no. 4 (Winter 1998): 901–25.

59. Reverend Joseph Ellwanger and Joyce Ellwanger, interview with author, January 5, 2016. See also Joseph Ellwanger, *Strength for the Struggle: Insights from the Civil Rights Movement and Urban Ministry* (Milwaukee: Maven Mark Books, 2014), 153–57.

60. Gessner interview; Ellwanger interview; Sister Barbara Kraemer, interview with author, January 22, 2016; Ruth Chojnacki, interview with author, January 7, 2016; Carolyn Jackson, interview with author, February 4, 2016.

61. Roberto R. Treviño, *The Church in the Barrio: Mexican American Ethno-Catholicism in Houston* (Chapel Hill: University of North Carolina Press, 2006), 8.

62. Rachel Ida Buff, *Against the Deportation Terror: Organizing for Immigrant Rights in the Twentieth Century* (Philadelphia: Temple University Press, 2017).

63. Grace Yukich, *One Family under God: Immigration Politics and Religion in America* (New York: Oxford University Press, 2013), 13–38; Pallares, *Family Activism*, 38–61.

64. Alexia Salvatierra, "Sacred Refuge," *Sojourners* 36, no. 9 (September/October 2007): 12–20.

65. Myrna Orozco and Reverend Noel Anderson, "Sanctuary in the Age of Trump: The Rise of the Movement a Year into the Trump Administration," Church World Service, January 2018, https://www.sanctuarynotdeportation.org/sanctuary-report-2018.html.

66. United States Conference of Catholic Bishops and Conferencia del Episcopado Mexicano, *Strangers No Longer: Together on the Journey of Hope* (Washington, DC: United States Conference of Catholic Bishops, 2003).

CHAPTER 11

The Ratio of Inclusion in East Chicago, Indiana

EMILIANO AGUILAR JR.

Northwest Indiana is situated at the southernmost tip of Lake Michigan in Chicago's shadow. Drawn to the region to work in the steel industry, a diverse array of southern and eastern Europeans, African Americans, and Latinx populations settled in cities such as Gary and East Chicago. Under East Chicago's motto of *Progredemur* (Latin for "we progress"), thousands of families found employment within the region's steel mills at the turn of the century. From the perspective of many of their neighbors, African American and Latinx communities, for much of the late twentieth century, organized against their treatment as second-class citizens. The city of East Chicago neglected to include the Latinx Fifth District when the city decided to create three new recreational centers, depriving the youth of a central place to gather.[1] In the fall of 1970, Washington High School administrator Mitchell Baran allegedly referred to Mexican Americans as "lazy, and ignorant."[2] When the East Chicago School Board reinstated Baran, Latinxs protested in front of Mayor John B. Nicosia's residence. The mayor responded by calling the protestors "pigs" and demanding that police remove them from his property. When a young photographer attempted to take a photo of the scene, Mayor Nicosia struck him.[3] With these clear slights, nearly three dozen Mexican American and Puerto Rican community organizations came together as the Concerned Latins Organization (CLO). This group fought for inclusion within politics, the labor force, and the city.

Set against the backdrop of this broader context, this chapter explores the work of one prominent group of Latinx community members to combat discrimination against them: the Concerned Latins Organization (CLO), which pressured the city of East Chicago, Indiana, to adopt an affirmative action program in its fire department that would require it to hire more African

Americans and Latinxs. The CLO targeted discriminatory policies, such as exorbitant physical exam fees, height requirement, and promotion through seniority, as policies that barred minority firemen from advancing in the fire department. Advocacy by the CLO was an important part of the pursuit of an affirmative action program in East Chicago, Indiana, but the effort was also aided by a dozen minority firefighters who were already employed by the East Chicago Fire Department (ECFD) and who initiated a class-action lawsuit against the department.[4] The case, *Dawson v. Pastrick* (1977), began in 1971, before the CLO was incorporated and nearly a year before East Chicago elected Robert Pastrick as mayor.[5] The case would become one of the longest in the history of the Northern District of Indiana, US Circuit Court.

East Chicago was just one place in the United States where affirmative action in government employment was being hotly contested in the 1960s and 1970s. Lawsuits such as *Dawson v. Pastrick* highlighted the tension between the federal and district court orders for workplace equality, on the one hand, and local resistance to affirmative action policy, on the other. Ira Katznelson described affirmative action as a policy "used to compensate members of a deprived group for prior losses and for gains unfairly achieved by others that resulted from prior governmental action."[6] Although governmental action required fair representation of underrepresented minorities, the ECFD utilized avenues to prevent both the hiring and promotion of minority firefighters. East Chicago's delay in hiring minority applicants, or the city government's utilization of seniority to prevent young minority firefighters from earning promotions, makes the city an important site for exploring the affirmative action battles of the era.

The growing presence of the Latinx community in Northwest Indiana gave its members the confidence to demand inclusion in municipal employment, political office, educational opportunities, and much more. The region became populated during the 1910s as the lakefront became transformed into an industrial powerhouse. African Americans, ethnic Europeans, and Mexicans and Mexican Americans served as laborers for area industries. However, when jobs became scarcer in the 1970s, the region underwent a period of white flight. Demographics changed, and Latinx and African American communities became more prominent.

In the entire county, the steel mills employed 66,600 workers in 1979, but this number had dwindled to 38,300 by 1985.[7] This period of deindustrialization coincided with the growing call for affirmative action within East Chicago and Northwest Indiana. Several East Chicagoans left their jobs in the steel mills and sought employment with the fire department. Many of them claimed they experienced discrimination in the hiring process.[8] Despite becoming a more visible presence in the city, Latinx and African American communities did not gain equal treatment in education, housing, or employment. As Jefferson Cowie observed in his important study, *Stayin' Alive: The 1970s and the Last Days of the Working Class*, "The new occupational opportunities for women and minorities arrived just as the call for broad economic justice was in decline." The result, he continued, was "heightened competition for dwindling opportunity."[9] For the Latinx and African American communities in East Chicago, municipal employment seemed to offer a solution to the decrease in industrial jobs.

These shortcomings led to grassroots activism to advocate for a place in the city's workforce. For the Latinx community, the Industrial Areas Foundation (IAF), which was affiliated with the CLO, became an important voice for equality. Scholarship on the work of IAF-affiliated organizations with Latinx communities has focused on the Community Service Organization (CSO), Communities Organized for Public Service (COPS), and United Neighborhood Organizations (UNO). The scholarship pertaining to the Concerned Latins Organization in the Midwest is minimal. Often the organization is briefly mentioned and footnoted; however, these citations stem from the early research of Carl Allsup appearing in the edited volume *Forging a Community: The Latino Experience in Northwest Indiana, 1919–1975*. This chapter expands on the research initiated by Allsup, whose work aimed to outline the entire history of the organization by exploring the pursuit by the CLO of affirmative action legislation at various levels of government.[10] Through expanding Allsup's initial research, this chapter will explore how minority communities gained municipal employment. The CLO and minority firefighters believed that creating a place for themselves within the ECFD would provide a significant steppingstone toward placemaking in the city as a whole.

In this chapter, examining Latinx involvement in affirmative action battles of the 1970s allows us to understand how Latinx communities in the Midwest pursued policies to make a home for themselves and their descendants. The pursuit of affirmative action in the ECFD was undertaken through mutually reinforcing episodes of activism by the Latinx and African American citizens of East Chicago in the streets and in the courtroom. One of the plaintiffs associated with the class-action lawsuit, James Dawson, an African American pipeman in the ECFD, became a prime example of what was at stake for minority firefighters in the city.[11] His actions reinforce a point already made in *The Latina/o Midwest Reader*, that "placemaking is not necessarily the domain of architects and city planners, but rather refers to the collective, everyday forms of communication and community formation" enacted by the region's African American and Latinx residents.[12] The CLO and minority firefighters believed that the opportunities denied them in the ECFD would open the door for further placemaking both in the workplace and outside of it.

The ECFD offered a unique avenue for employment within the deindustrializing community. The integration of fire departments offered historically underrepresented groups stable employment in municipal government and an entry into the middle class. In his study *Black Firefighters and the FDNY: The Struggle for Jobs, Justice, and Equity in New York City*, David Goldberg explored how Black New Yorkers, firefighters, and members of the fraternal organization of Black firefighters, the Vulcan Society, "built, sustained, and advanced the struggle for racial representation, equal opportunity, and racial equity in the FDNY for more than a century despite facing staunch 'massive resistance' from whites within and outside the fire department who fought to protect their jobs."[13] Goldberg's account of African American firefighters in New York emphasized the connection between the pursuits of civil rights, upward economic mobility, and municipal employment. Although Goldberg effectively demonstrated the importance of the case in New York, extending this history to East Chicago offers a more complicated and prolonged legal battle. The pursuit for employment within the ECFD highlights the struggles of Latinxs and African Americans both within and outside of the fire department. These actors engaged in a grassroots campaign in East Chicago and in federal courts with the class-action lawsuit *Dawson v. Pastrick*, initiated in 1971.

From the courtrooms to newspaper articles to municipal politics, men were the dominant actors in this story. There were a few notable exceptions, of course. Irene González served as the chairperson for the Concerned Latins Organization. As a leading member of the Youth Advisory Board (YAB), González was an instrumental voice in one of the region's most active civil rights groups in the coalition. Although women were not directly mentioned in the federal case, East Chicago's city council records note their presence during the debate over local ordinances. The presence of women at these meetings showed that the issue at hand was not simply a fight for affirmative action but also a struggle for municipal employment for all genders in general, which would grant historically disenfranchised communities (both Latinx and African American) an opportunity to enter the workplace at positions that would guarantee them greater socioeconomic opportunities.

This chapter seeks to explore the struggle against discriminatory policies aimed at limiting minority employment in the ECFD as a form of placemaking by the CLO and minority firefighters. The CLO and minority firefighters engaged in two separate and slightly overlapping struggles for affirmative action in East Chicago. Although the class-action lawsuit began in 1971, a few years before the CLO formed, the two episodes—the establishment of the CLO and the firefighters' lawsuit—overlapped during the CLO's push for affirmative action ordinances at the city level. Each struggle, in the streets and the courtroom, is representative of how Latinxs fought for inclusion and employment equality at the municipal level throughout the Midwest. Whereas the minority firefighters sought a district court decision, the CLO desired the commitment of the East Chicago City Council through a municipal ordinance, City Ordinance 3083, which established an affirmative action hiring program for municipal employment.

Latinx and African American communities sought to gain influence through employment opportunities that had previously rested with European ethnics. I include the class-action lawsuit, *Dawson v. Pastrick*, in this discussion of the Concerned Latins Organization's process of placemaking for two reasons. First, the common actors among the CLO and minority firefighters help explain why the CLO made employment one of their three primary concerns. Edward Egipciaco, a Puerto Rican firefighter in East Chicago, served as one of the initial officers for the CLO and the head representative of the Minority Fireman and Supporters group in the coalition. John Gomez, an applicant for a position with the ECFD and fellow plaintiff in *Dawson v. Pastrick*, was also a member of the CLO and a representative from the Northside Chapter of East Chicago.[14] Second, the CLO and Latinx community itself blurred these struggles. The bilingual newspaper *Latin Times* makes little mention of City Ordinance 3083 but covered several events concerning the decisions in *Dawson v. Pastrick*. However, the grassroots activism of the CLO and its calls for affirmative action hiring shaped the community's views of the issue both at the municipal level and in the district court.

This story is also one that is of personal importance for my family. My stepfather's dad, David Castro Sr., was a member of the CLO. I hope that exploring the city council minutes, newspaper articles, and archival material has allowed me to give my youngest brother, David Castro III, an idea of who his grandfather was and what he and many like-minded individuals accomplished for their community and families. But this project also builds upon my interests in studying Northwest Indiana, my home. After many years studying the Southwest and Chicano communities, I have returned home to delve into the untold stories of my community, to write and rewrite our history. The struggle of the CLO decades before my birth created a place for me and my generation within our community. The CLO and minority firefighters through protest politics in both the streets and the courtroom and with the institutionalization of affirmative action legislation created place for Latinx and African American communities. It is my sincere hope that this project and future research help illuminate the legacy that Mr. Castro and the activists of the CLO left for my hometown.

Politics of Protest: The CLO Confronts Inequality

The CLO formed after Ernesto Cortés and Peter Martínez, organizers for the IAF, proved the need for an organization in the county to organize at the community level to incorporate the neighborhood into local political decisions. This occurred after the firefighters had already begun their lawsuit in 1971; however, the two struggles would overlap. The executive director of the IAF, Edward T. Chambers, signed a contract between the IAF and the CLO on July 28, 1973, for a year-long training agreement between the two organizations. The IAF agreed to provide eighteen to twenty-four days of leadership training for officers and leaders (not to exceed twenty-five individuals) for a fee of $3,000.[15] By the end of the 1970s, this contract fee was raised to $8,000 and included additional benefits such as weekly reports and consultation with a lead organizer, training seats at IAF training sessions in Chicago, and consultations with leadership.[16] According to memos from Martínez, the CLO raised funds to pay this fee from fundraising events and large donations from local churches.[17] These training sessions with IAF organizers allowed representatives of community organizations across the country to meet with each other and discuss their respective struggles.

The CLO was dedicated to three major issues affecting the Latinx population in the region: housing, jobs, and education.[18] The issue of discrimination in municipal employment presented the CLO with a significant hurdle to overcome. David Castro Sr. recalled his time on the jobs committee of the CLO: "The way we were taught by Saul Alinsky's group—they would send us organizers—was to go for the easiest first." He continued: "Affirmative Action wasn't easy but [it was] easier than urban renewal."[19] Castro's claim reflected a priority system. Without representation in municipal sectors of employment and politics, Latinx and African American communities could not efficiently confront urban renewal. By confronting the easiest of the two, the CLO hoped to garner more visible success and in return more community support. Carmelo Meléndez, the cochair of the organization with Irene González, noted that "city hall used employment as a way to employ cronies."[20] The patronage system of city employment allowed public officials the autonomy to hire close friends and family into well-paid city positions. The involvement of CLO members such as Egipciaco and Gomez, two of the parties involved in the *Dawson v. Pastrick* case, influenced this decision to focus on affirmative action as well. Egipciaco also served as one of the representatives for the minority policemen and firemen group within the CLO coalition.

Whereas the class-action lawsuit allowed racial cooperation between Latinx and African American firemen, the formal incorporation of the CLO in 1974 restricted its scope and membership to the Latinx community. The coalition organized with the purpose "to promote the public welfare, health, and safety of the Latin Community in Lake County in a non-profit, non-political, and non-sectarian manner, and to unite all Latin organizations in Lake County."[21] Article V of the CLO's bylaws defined the membership of these Latinx populations as "one class and open to all persons and organizations (consisting of more than ten members which meet on a regular basis) who have exhibited an active interest in the purposes of this organization, paid their dues, and agreed to abide by the By Laws and policies of this organization."[22] The articles aimed to unite the thirty-five Latinx organizations in the city under a single board of directors, which would consist of a member from each organization, as well as an alternate.[23] The representatives of their respective organizations and Latinx communities dedicated their energies "towards alleviating discrimination and oppression of Latinos and others in three major areas: Employment, Housing, and Education."[24] These issues were central points of contention for the community prior to the CLO organizing.

Members of the Latinx community began articulating their grievances through the pages of the *Latin Times* as early as 1970. Discrimination within city government, specifically in the ECFD, was clear to many of the activists. In a series of articles and letters to the editor in the *Latin Times*, the Youth Advisory Board, which would become a vital organization under the CLO, used the ECFD as a prominent example of discrimination in the East Chicago Latinx community: "You are ignorant and lazy. You are socially inferior. And you won't do anything about it. Accept it. That's what the power structure believes about the Latins in Central Harbor. . . . This is why the Fire Department has 175 Anglos, 9 Blacks, and 7 Latins. . . . This is why the current price for a job in the Fire Department is $3,000."[25] Future CLO member John Gomez's essay "Sleeping Giant" captured the frustration of a community: "We can no longer tolerate a system that employs a fraction of a percent of our people in city jobs, then to keep us quiet will appoint one of our people as Chief of Police or Fire Department or will appoint our people as Asst. Superintendent of this or that department. . . . We Latins (the sleeping giant) are finally waking up, but remember that's not enough. Action speaks louder than words."[26] These claims proved not entirely unfounded, as CLO members later highlighted corrupt practices of cronyism and patronage politics within city government. A more representative municipal workforce should have been one result of the changing demographics of the city. Between 1960 and 1970, the City of East Chicago's "white" population decreased from 34,410 to 19,235, whereas Latinxs increased from 9,421 to 14,384.[27] Yet the employment of Latinxs by city government did not keep pace with their growing numbers. Acting on these changing demographics and Latinxs' anger with the status quo, the

Alinsky Institute would provide the burgeoning Latinx activists an ideology for action against discrimination in East Chicago.

Recognizing past and present discrimination by the ECFD, the CLO initially demanded that only Latinxs and African Americans fill the twelve vacancies in the department, which initiated a discussion concerning a new hiring policy. This demand by CLO members Tony Rodriguez and John Gomez led Councilman-at-Large John D. Klobuchar to make a motion that Mayor Robert Pastrick "appoint one third black, one third white and one third Latin" workers to the ECFD. However, the councilman received no second.[28] CLO members highlighted numerous policies designed to limit minority firemen from gaining employment in the fire department. Under the illusion of a "color-blind" system, these policies emphasized "the promulgation, normalization, and standardization of American myths of exceptionalism, meritocracy, and 'color blind' neutrality—myths that, in turn, are used to rationalize, codify, and maintain structural racism while advancing the false narrative that America is 'beyond race.'"[29] Aside from the lack of representation, the CLO targeted two policies as discriminatory and constricting for the hiring of Latinxs and African Americans to the fire department: the twenty-four hours on / forty-eight hours off work schedule and the exorbitant price of physical examinations.

Members of the CLO claimed that "the present system of working 24 consecutive hours and 48 hours off allows the majority of the Anglo firemen to hold two jobs."[30] This practice allowed the department to retain members who would typically retire because they were able to collect two salaried positions. The *Latin Times* followed this up with a suggestion that "for safety regulations and for a first rate performance while doing their job all the East Chicago firemen with twenty years of service should submit themselves to a physical examination to see if they are still in good condition to perform their duties as firemen."[31] This policy would also force current firefighters to realize how expensive the fee for a physical exam—ranging from $200 to $400—would be for those interested in city employment.[32] The policy would also present conditions for older members of the fire department to retire instead of holding a position that they might not be able to perform. According to the 1971 annual report of the ECFD, some members of the department in 1971 included men appointed nearly thirty years prior, many of them still retaining the rank of "Firefighter."[33] Due to the policy in place, these members could realistically work two or three days a week and moonlight at other positions.

Beginning in 1973, members of the CLO engaged in confrontational protests to pressure the city's administration into passing an affirmative action program based on a ratio of "four-four-one" for the hiring of firemen. Through this ratio, the CLO hoped that the inclusion of four Latinxs and four African

Americans for each new white recruit would create a ECFD that more accurately represented the near even three-way split of the city's demographics. Castro noted the dilemma of this cause: "Who were we to say we represented the community? We had to make them deal with fifty of us. That meant going to council meetings, pressuring businesses, banks, to get credibility."[34] Meléndez referred to this as "ping-pong." The "CLO hit the bank, school, city government," he said, "all with the goal of getting somebody to get a reaction. The focus of an action is to get a reaction."[35] Meléndez stated that "Hispanics while large in numbers could not convince powers that be to listen to them."[36] Two key events were the Summer Protests of 1973 and the continued public conflict at city council meetings with City Attorney Jay Given.

The most important protest occurred when the CLO targeted Irv Lewin's clothing store. The City of East Chicago administration responded negatively to the proposed ratio and methods of the CLO. Eddie Egipciaco, a CLO member and one of the seven Latino firemen on the payroll in East Chicago, was suspended. Accusing him of threatening the politician, businessman, and radio announcer Irv Lewin, the City of East Chicago placed Egipciaco on probation in November 1973.[37]

According to *The Times* (published in Hammond, Indiana) reporter, Egipciaco entered the store with fellow members and allegedly commented that "there would be a fire sale next week."[38] Egipciaco participated in the struggle for affirmative action hiring in the city and was a block organizer along with Castro. In response to the case against Egipciaco, sixty members of the Latinx community demonstrated outside of Mr. Lewin's business.[39] Councilman Jesse Gomez, the first elected ethnic Mexican councilman in Indiana, denounced the police officers who signed a letter accusing Egipciaco of offering "a fabricated lie," adding that it was "a conspiracy to discredit Egipciaco for his involvement in the struggle for the recognition of the civil rights of the Latin people."[40] The Civil Service Commission investigated the matter and forwarded Egipciaco's disciplinary case to the Board of Public Safety for an administrative hearing in September.[41]

The board concluded its case after a two-day hearing in September, but Given decided to delay a decision.[42] On October 25, 1973, the board found Egipciaco guilty and sentenced him to probation.[43] Commenting on his probation, Egipciaco questioned the verdict against him: "Am I guilty because I'm involved in the civil rights movement or am I guilty because I refused to become property of the city?"[44] Given ruled that the punishment "was not severe enough" for the activist.[45]

Egipciaco's probation occurred after the city agreed in August 1973 to implement an affirmative action program for hiring firefighters. The East Chicago Board of Safety agreed to fill nine vacancies with four African Americans, four

Latinos, and one white applicant. After this was fulfilled, the next forty-five hires would be hired along with a 2:2:1 ratio and a 1:1:1 ratio for the next ten. Once the fifty-fifth position was filled, the hiring process would default to the highest scores on civil service listings.[46] This decision came only months after two of the three members of the Board of Public Safety, Henry Lopez and Dr. E. L. Broomes, supported the ratio against Given, the lone holdout.

The CLO was renowned for its public presence at city meetings, and one of the organization's frequent targets was Given, whom they accused of running the political machine in East Chicago. Members of the CLO attended city council meetings en masse and were often escorted out or asked to leave these meetings. Castro recalled: "We had a prepared text and three or four people ready to read it. They wouldn't recognize us so one guy stood up and started reading as loud as he could. A cop came over and escorted him out. Another person started where he left and he was escorted out. I got up and I got escorted out. When we got outside, we saw that they had a line of police cars directing us out of town."[47] Getting kicked out of meetings was a common occurrence for the CLO activists. When city administrators filibustered meetings or refused to recognize their right to speak, members broke protocol and interrupted the councilmen. CLO member John Gomez, who was also an applicant to the ECFD, said that "somebody must be getting a kickback" from the physical examination fees. This claim of corruption garnered a reaction from Attorney Given, who told the members of the CLO, "I am tired of your smart ass remarks."[48] The barrage of interruptions and accusation of corruption forced the outburst from Given and provided the CLO supporters with a new talking point. This comment made Given the subject of ridicule the following week by the *Latin Times*, which ran a gossip column that said: "Our City Attorney Jay Given really overwhelmed us with his eloquent vocabulary this week. His parents must really be proud of him, spending all that money to send him through law school to learn such three letter words. If they would have invested a little more money, Mr. Jay Given might have come out with a four letter word. Here's to education."[49] This quip in the gossip column only continued the *Latin Times*' tradition of targeting Attorney Given. The gossip column afforded the Latinx community an opportunity to construct their narrative and retain their confrontational demeanor. In response to Given's claims that the firemen's issue could not be solved "overnight," an anonymous editorial reminded Given that the "firemen's issue is not something new"; instead, it was an issue the community had posed to the city administration since 1967.[50] However, according to the minutes of the city council and the East Chicago newspaper, the *Calumet News*, this incident never occurred. The CLO and the *Latin Times* even critiqued Given's claim to Mayor Pastrick that the ratio was "illegal." They said it was a reason that the issue was not solved sooner.[51]

Given's criticism of affirmative action made sense in the context of the broader opposition to affirmative action nationally. In an example of the backlash to affirmative action nationally, Given repeated the criticism that preferring minority groups over white candidates perpetrated a new form of discrimination, but this time against whites. Given's unfavorable legal opinion further encouraged the CLO to target the attorney. When meeting to discuss the proposed ratio, Given's every action proved fair game for criticism. In a meeting concerning the ratio and whether or not the Board of Public Safety would endorse it, Given arrived twenty-five minutes late. When members criticized his tardiness, Given stated, "As soon as you get appointed to this board and become chairman you can begin the meetings anytime you want." The attorney then walked out of the meeting for a few minutes to get a cup of coffee.[52] The antagonism to affirmative action at the municipal level complemented the prolonged legal struggle in the district courts to force change within the ECFD.

Dawson v. Pastrick (1977): The Issue Is Taken to Court

Beyond community protests, the issue of discrimination in the ECFD and the implementation of an affirmative action program resulted in one of the longest civil lawsuits in the history of the US District Court, Northern District of Indiana. Before the CLO made affirmative action one of the three pillars of their activism, minority firefighters already were engaged in fighting discrimination through the courts. The initial complaint, filed by James S. Dawson, Edward H. Egipciaco, and Xavier Becerra on August 3, 1971, set into motion a case that the courts did not completely resolve until December 10, 1986.[53] In 1977 the district court ruled in favor of CLO and the plaintiffs concerning discrimination in ECFD's hiring practices. However, the court continued to debate other aspects of the initial complaint until 1986, such as the issue of whether plaintiffs were entitled to back pay, if the plaintiffs were entitled to costs, such as the attorney fees, and if the city's proposed reorganization of municipal employment is discriminatory. The documents produced amounted to more than a thousand pages of complaints, orders, minutes, reports, and much more. For brevity, I refer primarily to the materials filed after the "Supplementary and Third Amended Complaint," from May 23, 1973. However, the whole range of material warrants further attention. Regardless of promises by the city, including by the up-and-coming young Democrat Robert Pastrick, who had recently been elected mayor, the affirmative action hiring program was not implemented until a US District Court ruled in favor of the CLO and against the City of East Chicago in 1975.[54] But the case did not end there. The city continued to appeal the lower court's decision until 1986. *Dawson v. Pastrick* therefore offers scholars insight into the changing politics and discussions surrounding a contentious period in the history of affirmative action.

The cast of characters within the courtroom ranged from the controversial lawyer, Jay Given, to the newly elected mayor, Robert Pastrick, who was the main defendant in the case. It also involved minority firemen and union representatives for the ECFD. Recently appointed judge Allen Sharp, named to the US District Court for the Northern District of Indiana by President Richard Nixon in 1973, presided over the case. The most important members of the case were the plaintiffs, who were nineteen Latino and African American men between the ages of twenty-four and thirty-six. Each man brought to the case his own story, a vignette in comparison to the thousands of pages the class-action suit produced. Many degrees of commonality exist between these men's stories. At a time when the ECFD did not have a residency requirement (and a growing number of white firefighters lived outside of the city), sixteen of the plaintiffs resided in East Chicago. All expressed an interest in applying for a job with the ECFD when they turned eighteen. Many of the men noted the corruption involved in gaining employment. Rubén Ceja claimed that his precinct committeeman said that "he could not have such employment unless he would pay at least $2,000." After passing the physical examination, Shannon Landers claimed that a councilman told him the job would cost $1,400. The necessity for political support and a bribe, although not listed on the application, was a requirement that some applicants knew about, causing them to delay their decision to apply. Men like the CLO member John Gomez and Carlos Ventura applied despite their uncertainty, and neither of them were offered jobs.[55]

James Dawson, whose name became attached to the title of the case, best made the case in support of affirmative action and an inclusive labor force. The debates at the heart of the case solidified Dawson's reputation as a champion of the would-be firefighters. A veteran of the US Navy (1961–65), Dawson became tired of working the swing shift in the industrial sector and decided to apply for the ECFD in July 1965. However, the ECFD delayed hiring Dawson until December 1, 1968, unlike its response to many of the Anglo applicants at the time.[56] Several of the plaintiffs listed were employed firefighters, primarily in the lowest ranks of pipeman and driver. At the time of the initial complaint, Dawson held the rank of pipeman.

Before filing the class-action suit, Dawson said that talks with the fire department's chief were "to no avail." The department suggested various proposals to Dawson and the minority firemen. At the time, the department consisted of five stations with three shifts. One proposal suggested placing a person of color at each station for each shift. However, this total of fifteen was less than the already employed seventeen firemen. Dawson noted his outrage that the proposed solution "would be going backward." According to Dawson, "most proposals we ignored" because "they didn't make sense." He concluded, "We eventually quit entertaining that nonsense."[57]

Once the plaintiffs filed the lawsuit, Dawson noted that "some of the people quit talking to us," especially "the older guys," he said. "The younger guys," he continued, "these are people we went to school with."[58] They supported the plaintiffs. This generational tension led to one altercation when Dawson wanted to raise the flag at Station Four, a task reserved for the lowest-ranked firefighter, which he was, but he was challenged by another firefighter. The other man claimed that Dawson was "doing unpatriotic things," to which Dawson responded with a question: "How much time did you spend in the service?"[59] The man had spent none. Although this quieted some of the backlash against them, the minority firemen experienced an internal conflict with their colleagues as the lawsuit and grassroots activism continued.

Judge Sharp declared that the plaintiffs had proven discrimination in the hiring process. Although John Gomez of the CLO and his fellow plaintiffs had filed their initial complaint on August 3, 1971, the City of East Chicago did not admit to discriminatory hiring practices against Latinos and African Americans until 1975. Despite Judge Sharp's ruling that East Chicago "shall conduct affirmative recruitment of minorities," it declined "to impose mandatory quotas as a remedy in this case."[60] If East Chicago refused to submit a report detailing the number of vacancies, the number and racial composition of applicants for those vacancies, and the number and racial composition of hired candidates, the court reserved the numerical quota as a possible future measure.[61] However, it was now within the city's best interest to grant minority firemen a place within the department before further court intervention.

With this first verdict, the members of the CLO took to the *Latin Times* to reflect on the verdict and their work with the case. In a press statement supporting the court's ruling and the progression of the case, CLO president Irene González stated, "For months we talked, demonstrated, and fought with the city fathers to admit that what they were doing to Latinos and Blacks in the Fire Department was clear and overt discrimination." But, she said, "from the mayor on down they denied it and would not come to terms."[62] Her comment echoed a previous statement made by Carmelo Meléndez at a city council meeting in which he likened attending the meetings to therapy, stating that "all we do is let out steam and all you see is them [the city council] looking at you but nothing is done."[63] Tony Rodriguez added to this sense of pessimism by stating, "Even our own representatives in the council would not help."[64]

The comments by González and Rodriguez and the *Latin Times'* portrayal of the court case as tied to the CLO instead of the ordinance push reflected the parallel and contemporary struggles that the group took at the municipal and district court levels. Through their grassroots advocacy, common actors in the push for the ordinance and the class-action lawsuit felt pressured (and incentivized) to acquiesce to their position. However, the coverage of the case by the *Latin Times* failed to mention James Dawson and the African American community, erasing the multiethnic push by and for minority firemen.

Although the CLO and the minority division of the ECFD rejoiced over this decision, there was backlash over the possibility of court-mandated diversification in the region. The potential ruling of Judge Sharp on *Dawson v. Pastrick* could pave the way for further affirmative action and support of the Equal Employment Opportunity Act of 1972. The act granted the Equal Employment Opportunity Commission (EEOC) the right to sue in district courts when it found that an employer had discriminated in its hiring based on race, color, religion, sex, or national origin.[65] Recognizing the ramifications of Judge Sharp's ruling, a letter from Stephen B. Fowdy, the superintendent of schools in Whiting, Indiana, to Judge Sharp expressed dissatisfaction with the verdict. Primarily bashing the "quota system" behind affirmative action, Fowdy questioned Sharp:

> How many "minority" judges are there in the federal system? Would you want to stand trial where your liberty, property, rights or life was at stake by a minority judge that was not qualified and only guilty of bribery? Or would you rather stand trial before the most competent judge that was available? Would you want to be operated on by a surgeon that was at the bottom of his class because he got into medical school on the "quota system," or would you rather have the best qualified one, regardless of race or color, perform the operation? The answers are obvious to 75% of the people of the nation. Why do judges have such a difficult time understanding these truths?[66]

Fowdy's letter to Judge Sharp stated many of the common arguments against affirmative action hiring. It repeated the idea that hiring "qualified" candidates and hiring diverse candidates were necessarily at odds. It also repeated stereotypes about what kind of jobs Fowdy considered applicable to this decision. These two critiques of the policy were reflected in Harvard law professor Randall Kennedy's conclusion that "racial affirmative action is limited in that it often directly assists only those who are already positioned to take advantage of enlarged opportunities."[67]

Judge Sharp's ruling in favor of the plaintiffs gave the CLO momentum in pushing for a broader municipal ordinance. Although the prolonged legal battle within *Dawson v. Pastrick* remained incomplete, Sharp's decision in

1975 provided a necessary boost to the CLO as the organization prepared to rewrite municipal ordinances that best combatted racial discrimination. Whereas members such as Egipciaco and Gomez were direct participants in the class-action lawsuit at the district level, many other CLO members simultaneously engaged at the local level to create a municipal ordinance.

After Judge Sharp announced his decision, the city council agreed to work with the CLO in forming an ordinance to combat discrimination in East Chicago. The city council read an affirmative action ordinance, City Ordinance 3083, on April 28, 1975. At this meeting two opposing groups presented two possible futures for the proposed legislation. Puerto Rican councilman Isabelino Candelaria and Councilman George Cvitkovich offered opposing plans for the document. Candelaria proposed that the "proper committee" take the ordinance for "further study and amendments." However, Cvitkovich proposed that the entire city council meet with the CLO, the Chamber of Commerce, and other interested groups to discuss the ordinance. Furthermore, forwarding the document to a committee would keep the ordinance there for a minimum of thirty days before a second reading.[68] During the second reading of the ordinance, Human Rights Commission director Leo Miller accurately summarized the proposed change:

> We have Ordinance 3026 that is now in effect; if every Contractor and Sub-Contractor did what they were suppose[d] to do under the present ordinance, we wouldn't need the new amendments, we wouldn't need a new ordinance[.] [A]ll they would have to do is what the old ordinance said to do. We are not asking, under the existing ordinance, for unqualified people to be put to work in East Chicago, we are not asking for blacks and browns to be put on just because they are black or brown, we are asking for equal opportunity, we are asking for a set of guidelines that they could follow very easily under good faith efforts.[69]

Miller emphasized that this ordinance would pertain to an "equal opportunity" and wasn't intended to "discourage and keep contractors out of the city," as Councilman Gus Kouros feared.

Prior to the vote, the city council received letters of support from the parish at Our Lady of Guadalupe Church; the Bishop's Committee on Spanish Speaking People of the Gary Diocese; Edward Sadlowski, director of the United Steelworkers of America, District No. 31; the American Legion Post 508; the League of United Latin American Citizens Post 259; the Chamber of Commerce; and Local 1010.[70] To emphasize the stakes of the ordinance, David Castro read a letter from Architect & Engineers, Inc., that implied that minorities could not do the work. Castro stated that "if the Council goes against the ordinance then they are saying the same, that the minorities cannot handle the job; in order to have better opportunities for the young and the minorities every facet of the ordinance must be approved."[71] Councilman Kouros asked, "Ten years from now when the minorities will be White, will this ordinance apply for them?" David Castro and Susan Roque responded to Kouros. Castro stated that "we are dealing with the problem today and not ten years from now," whereas Roque stated that "if a person is qualified and meet [*sic*] the criteria it applies to all people."[72] The ordinance, deemed the Affirmative Action Ordinance, passed on July 28, 1975, by a vote of eight to one, with Kouros abstaining.

Although the members of the CLO won their battle for representation in the municipal workforce, the organization ceased to operate by the end of 1977. It successfully created municipal legislation, City Ordinance 3083, that allowed for a more representative racial composition of city employees. This broader municipal legislation, in conjunction with the court-approved plan stemming from *Dawson v. Pastrick*, offered minorities a degree of inclusion into municipal employment.

Conclusion

Although City Ordinance 3083 was developed independently of the court's mandated program, the two solutions (the ordinance and the class-action lawsuit) constituted a form of placemaking within the workplace and in the Midwest more broadly for East Chicago's Latinx communities. Despite this splintering of onetime colleagues in pursuit of civil rights, the tenure of the CLO reflected a dismissal of placation in favor of confrontational tactics and relentless pressure. Through tackling the issue of affirmative action in the ECFD, the CLO gained the support for a citywide ordinance (City Ordinance 3083) to combat the admitted discrimination against minorities in municipal employment in the ECFD and beyond.

The complexities and interweaving of the local community protest and internal division in the ECFD present a community confrontation with structural discrimination. Regardless of national legislation aimed at prohibiting discriminatory hiring policies, local and state actors established criteria meant to discredit historically marginalized groups and prevent them from gaining employment. The popular mobilization of the community by the CLO and the internal conflict at the level of the district court allowed the Latinx community to legally structure their place within East Chicago.

The last mention of the CLO in the minutes of the city council in East Chicago came on January 12, 1976. Three separate times the record noted that an "Outburst by the CLO followed."[73] These five words accurately convey the spirit of protest espoused by the organization against the status quo they confronted. Paired with the legal battle by minority firefighters, who sought affirmative action in hiring, the Latinx community, outraged by discrimination in their city, took to the streets, city hall, and the courts to voice their disdain for a system that neglected them and to gain opportunity for themselves and future generations.

Notes

1. "Latins Invade City Hall," *The Times*, August 9, 1970; "E.C. Agrees to Youth Center Request," *The Times*, August 13, 1970.

2. See "Mexican American: Lazy, Ignorant," *Latin Times*, September 25, 1970; "Latin Bias Protested," *The Times*, September 29, 1970; "WHS Latins Boo Apology," *The Times*, October 1, 1970; "Students Say: An Apology Not Enough," *Latin Times*, October 2, 1970.

3. "Mayor Explodes at YAB Protest," *The Times*, October 30, 1970; "Nicosia Hits Latin Youth as YAB Demonstrates," *The Times*, October 30, 1970; "Protests at Mayor's Home," *Indianapolis Star*, October 30, 1970; "E. Chicago Mayor Attacks News Photog," *Chicago Tribune*, October 30, 1970.

4. Identity politics for the community remain a complicated matter. Throughout this chapter the reader will note that I make use of three terms: Latins, Latinos, Latinx. The Concerned Latins Organization refers to themselves as "Latins," a term rooted in its time period. This term is used in this chapter to refer to the organization, and I use it when engaging with its use in the primary sources. "Latinos" appears because of the nature of the affirmative action case. Focused primarily through the lens of the male-only East Chicago Fire Department, "Latinos" will appear when discussing the men who were hired into the fire department or who wanted to be. Finally, I prefer the use of "Latinx" as a more inclusive term for discussing the organization and community at large. Refer to Concepción de León, "Another Hot Take on the Term 'Latinx,'" *New York Times*, November 21, 2018.

5. There are several decisions decreed during the case's tenure from the initial complaint on August 3, 1971, to the resolution over disputed fees on December 10, 1986. This chapter will primarily deal with the 1977 decision.

6. Ira Katznelson, *When Affirmative Action Was White: An Untold History of Racial Inequality in Twentieth-Century America* (New York: W. W. Norton & Company, 2005), 149.

7. "Industry Defines Northwest Indiana, Then and Now," *The Times*, March 12, 2017.

8. Brief sketches of each of the nineteen plaintiffs in the class-action lawsuit concerning discriminatory hiring processes are included in the "Plaintiffs' Motion for Leave to File Supplementary and Third Amended Complaint," May 23, 1973, United District Court for the Northern District of Indiana, Hammond Division, *Dawson et al. v. Pastrick et al.*, civil no. 71-H-215, National Archives and Records Administration (NARA), Chicago. Although the docket number refers to the case as one from 1971, this chapter will reference a 1977 decision as key for pushing the affirmative action case.

9. Jefferson Cowie, *Stayin' Alive: The 1970s and the Last Days of the Working Class* (New York: New Press, 2010), 239.

10. Carl Allsup, "Concerned Latins Organization," in *Forging a Community: The Latino Experience in Northwest Indiana, 1919–1975*, ed. James B. Lane and Edward J. Escobar (Chicago: Cattails Press, 1987), 251–62.

11. James Dawson would rise to become fire chief of the East Chicago Fire Department before his retirement in January 2001. "Fire Chief Hangs Up His Ax after 32 Years of Service," *The Times*, January 27, 2001.

12. Omar Valerio-Jiménez, Santiago Vaquera-Vásquez, and Claire F. Fox, introduction to Valerio-Jiménez, Vaquera-Vásquez, and Fox, *The Latina/o Midwest Reader*, 11.

13. David Goldberg, *Black Firefighters and the FDNY: The Struggle for Jobs, Justice, and Equity in New York City* (Chapel Hill: University of North Carolina Press, 2017), 17.

14. "Concerned Latins Organization, Inc," Articles of Incorporation, March 29, 1974, box 1, file 8, Nicolás Kanellos Papers, Calumet Regional Archives (CRA), Indiana University Northwest (IUN).

15. "Letter of Agreement," July 28, 1973, box 55, folder 743, Industrial Areas Foundation (IAF) Records, Special Collections and University Archives, University of Illinois at Chicago.

16. "Letter of Agreement," September 1, 1976, box 55, folder 743, IAF Records.

17. Martínez noted that the CLO received donations from the Methodist Church and the Disciples of Christ. The memo also noted that the organization went to the Catholic bishop for funds. Later memos note funds received from Bishop Andrew Grutka. The CLO also used a Catholic church, Our Lady of Guadalupe, for its meetings. "Memo to Chambers and Harmon from Martínez," September 14, 1973, box 55, folder 743, IAF Records.

18. Interview with David Castro Sr., *Steel Shavings: Latinos in the Calumet Region* 13 (1987), courtesy of David Castro Jr. private collection. *Steel Shavings* is a regional magazine published annually by Dr. James B. Lane through the Calumet Regional Archives at Indiana University Northwest.

19. Interview with David Castro Sr., *Steel Shavings*.

20. Interview with Carmelo Meléndez by the author, February 2, 2018.

21. "Concerned Latins Organization, Inc.," Articles of Incorporation, March 29, 1974, box 1, file 8, Kanellos Papers.

22. Ibid.

23. The full list of organizations included in the Concerned Latins Organization included Apostolicos and Guadalupanos, Block and Pennsylvania Chapter, Black Oak Chapter, Calumet Boycott Committee, Christian Family Movement, Borinque Unidos de Norte Indiana, Calumet Homes Chapter, Youngstown Steel Chapter, Concerned Citizens Group, Concerned Latins Boosters, Drummond and Parrish Avenue Chapter, Enchanters and Friends, Inland Galvanizer Dept. Chapter, La Liga Latina, La Raza de Bronce, Latin American Students League, Latins for Progress, Northwest Latin Chamber of Commerce, Lincoln Street Chapter, Mexican American Parents Association, Minority Fireman and Supporters, Northside Chapter of East Chicago,

Southside Chapter of East Chicago, Operation March, Our Lady of Guadalupe Church, Primera Iglesia Christiana de Gary, The Gypsies, Youth Advisory Board of East Chicago, United Latin Teachers' Aides, Bishop's Committee on Spanish Speaking People of the Gary Diocese, Holy Angels' Mothers, 139th Street Group, East Gary Workers at US Steel Chapter, E&J&E Workers Chapter, and Latinos de Gary.

24. "Historical Information, Concerned Latins Organization," n.d., box 1, file 7, Kanellos Papers.

25. "Open Letter to the Community from the Y.A.B.," *Latin Times*, October 30, 1970.

26. "Sleeping Giant," *Latin Times*, November 20, 1970.

27. "Population 1970," November 7, 1972, p. 9, box 97, folder 1064, IAF Records.

28. "Regular Session of the Common Council, Monday, May 31, 1973," East Chicago City Ordinances book 18, pp. 261–62, maintained by the City of East Chicago, Indiana City Clerk Office.

29. Goldberg, *Black Firefighters*, 7.

30. "Ask Eight Hour Fireman Day," *Latin Times*, July 20, 1973.

31. "Physical Exam for Firemen," *Latin Times*, August 10, 1973.

32. "I Am Tired of Your Smart Ass Remarks . . .," *Latin Times*, August 10, 1973.

33. "1971 Annual Report, Fire Department and Fire Prevention Bureau for the City of East Chicago," box 1, file 18, East Chicago Collection, CRA, IUN.

34. Interview with Castro Sr., *Steel Shavings*.

35. Meléndez interview.

36. Ibid.

37. "Egipciaco on Probation?," *Latin Times*, November 2, 1973.

38. "Racial Quota Urged," *The Times*, July 12, 1973.

39. "Harbor Whispers," *Latin Times*, July 20, 1973.

40. Ibid.

41. "Concerned E.C. Latins Again Clash with Board," *The Times*, July 26, 1973.

42. "Hearing Concludes," *The Times*, September 14, 1973.

43. "Fireman Is Guilty," *The Times*, October 25, 1973.

44. "Egipciaco on Probation?"

45. "Fireman Is Guilty."

46. Allsup, "Concerned Latins Organization," 256.

47. Interview with Castro Sr., *Steel Shavings*.

48. "I Am Tired."

49. "Hello! My Name Is Tillie," *Latin Times*, August 10, 1973.

50. "Atty. Given Is Right . . . but . . .," *Latin Times*, August 3, 1973.

51. "Harbor Whispers."

52. "Concerned E.C. Latins."

53. Civil docket for *Dawson et al. v. Nicosia et al.* and *Dawson v. Pastrick* 71 H 215, case no. 2:71CV215, session no. 021-85-0179, box 3, NARA, Chicago.

54. Dawson v. Pastrick, 441 F. Supp. 133 (United States District Court for the Northern District of Indiana, November 15, 1977), no. 71 H 215; "Judge Sharp Rules for C.L.O.," *Latin Times*, February 7, 1975.

55. "Stipulation of Facts," filed September 12, 1974, Dawson v. Pastrick, case no. 2:71CV215, session no. 021-85-0179, box 3, location 466 960, BAN, NARA, Chicago. The plaintiffs in the case were Xavier Becerra, William Mackey, Edward Egipciaco, James Dawson, John Thomas, John Luellen, William Turner, Sanford Spann, Soloman Ard, Sandy Harrel, William Chavis, Ray Anguiano, Charles Orange, Thomas Brannon, Lorenzo Munoz, Ruben Ceja, Shannon Landers, John Gomez, and Carlos Ventura.

56. Interview with James Dawson conducted by author, October 23, 2018.

57. Ibid.

58. Ibid.

59. Ibid.

60. *Dawson*, 441 F. Supp. 133.

61. Ibid.

62. "Judge Sharp Rules for C.L.O."

63. Regular Session of the Common Council, Monday, November 11, 1974, East Chicago City Ordinances book 18, p. 545.

64. "Judge Sharp Rules for C.L.O."

65. Equal Employment Opportunity Act of 1972, approved March 24, 1972.

66. Stephen B. Fowdy to Judge Sharp, February 7, 1975, on file within *Dawson v. Pastrick,* case no. 2:71CV215, session no. 021-85-0179, box 3, location 466 960, BAN, NARA, Chicago.

67. Randall Kennedy, *For Discrimination: Race, Affirmative Action, and the Law* (New York: Vintage Books, 2015), 89.

68. Regular Session of the Common Council, Monday, April 28, 1975, East Chicago City Ordinances book 18, p. 623.

69. Regular Session of the Common Council, Monday, June 23, 1975, East Chicago City Ordinances book 19, p. 3.

70. Regular Session of the Common Council, Monday, July 28, 1975, East Chicago City Ordinances book 19, pp. 18–19.

71. Ibid.

72. Ibid.

73. Regular Session of the Common Council, Monday, January 12, 1976, East Chicago City Ordinances book 19, pp. 146–49.

CHAPTER 12

Ohio Latinx Festivals
Create New Publics

THERESA DELGADILLO, LAURA FERNÁNDEZ,
MARIE LERMA, AND LEILA VIEIRA

In this chapter we offer a discussion of the ways that Latinxs engage in the complex process of creating meaningful places for themselves in Ohio through participation in public summer ethnic festivals in 2017.[1] Our research examines the cultural, social, economic, and political dimensions of these events in the lives of participants at a moment of heightened xenophobic and racist discourse in the United States that has created fear among Latinx communities as it also considers our roles as participant observers and collaborators in research. Our research questions include the following: Does the political context of 2017 impact Latinxs' sense of belonging in Ohio? How do cultural events such as Latinx festivals contribute to placemaking and belonging? What can we learn about the experiences of Latinx people and their sense of belonging in Ohio through participating in and observing these events?

Our observations of the festivals revealed multiple expressions of *latinidad*, whether through dance, music, or food.[2] Ohio Latinx festivals are places where Latinxs (ourselves included) demonstrate that Latinx, Ohioan, and midwesterner are not incompatible identities. These festivals reveal Latinx populations engaged in carving out both a material and a sociocultural place for themselves through events that appear ephemeral yet accrue permanence in their repetition over time. We find that the history of each event and participant's length of residence in the state matters in their experience of the ethnic festival. We also note several Latinx expressions of interethnic coalition with other racial/ ethnic groups and intraethnic coalition among varied Latinx groups. Taking cues from Olivia Cadaval's research on the Washington, DC, Latino festival, Geraldo L. Cadava's work on Mexican and Native Americans negotiating changing social and cultural landscapes through participation in cultural festivals, and Ramón Rivera-Servera's scholarship on public performance, we consider each element of these events and how these reveal Latinx Ohioans generating meaning about their experience and their relation to other groups or other homes in ways that demonstrate an evolving community responding to the social, cultural, and political challenges of the era.[3]

From June until September of 2017 we traveled to ten different festivals across six cities in Ohio, from major urban cities such as Cincinnati, Columbus, and Cleveland to smaller towns such as Campbell and Springfield.[4] We surveyed over 120 participants at the festivals; collected materials from the events (such as pamphlets, sponsored memorabilia, trinkets, etc.); and walked, observed, and participated in the festivals.[5] As participant observers we took in as much of the festival's presence as possible; even when we were not doing interviews, we interacted with other attendees and volunteers at booths and under festival tents, ate, watched the parades and performances, and enjoyed a place where *latinidad* is celebrated. Although we wore our Ohio State University nametags and carried consent forms and information with us for possible interviews, we dressed in casual summer clothing, as did most participants. In this work, we also made a small contribution to creating greater knowledge about Latinx people among those who attended the festivals by sharing information on Latina/o studies at OSU and, in some cases, educational resources we developed on Latinx communities in the Midwest. Teachers and community leaders took multiple copies of fliers we had prepared with suggested readings on Latinxs in the Midwest.[6] While we each had moments of connection and belonging at the events in which we participated, we also experienced moments of disconnect. For example, only two festivals were explicitly inclusive of Latinx LGBTQ communities. Our pan-Latinx research team also noticed that half of the festivals welcome multiple ethnicities, while the other half are primarily geared to the dominant populations of Mexicans and Puerto Ricans. Therefore, we felt differing degrees of belonging at each event. These reactions heighten our awareness of the differences among ourselves, or perhaps the multiplicities, which are echoed by groups who remain drawn to the wider umbrella of Latinx as a signifier of both commonality and variation among peoples with distinct ethnic/national backgrounds.

We observe the power of Latinx public cultural expression to create place at these festivals.[7] Through their participation in ethnic festivals, Latinxs in Ohio assert themselves in the public sphere and create multiply defined communities. While a significant body of scholarship now exists about Latinxs in the Midwest, very little has been written about Latinxs in Ohio. The general perception of Ohio and of the Midwest is that this region is primarily defined by an imagined homogeneous white majority population and the rustiness of its industries and job opportunities, as Sujey Vega notes in her discussion of Latinxs in Indiana.[8] This popular narrative glosses the old and new Latinx populations in Ohio, encouraging us to "forget" the Mexican and Chicanx populations that migrated to Ohio's northern counties in the early twentieth century for industrial work and those that arrived at midcentury to harvest crops, as well as Puerto Rican migrants who began arriving in the mid-twentieth century in search of industrial work and continued to arrive for both professional opportunities and agricultural and industrial labor.[9] Indeed, significant Latinx settlement in Lorain, Ohio, in both the 1920s and then again in the 1940s and 1950s challenged the Black/white binary of racial relations and led to the emergence of a self-proclaimed "International City" by Latinx communities that sought legitimate inclusion in the civic life of Lorain.[10]

Our research, therefore, aims to contribute to our knowledge of the Latinx experience in Ohio by focusing on the space of contemporary Latinx cultural communities that come together around summer ethnic festivals in Ohio. In working to understand these public cultural expressions, we draw from Latinx studies scholarship in cultural studies, history, life story / oral history, performance, and ethnography. This chapter examines the significance of public cultural expression in Latinx placemaking in Ohio and derives from our observations and physical experiences of the festivals and our analysis of key themes in interviews.

A Sensory Alternative Public Space

Festivals provided a platform for public Latinx cultural expressions—music, dance, dress, art, and food—while also addressing the broader cultural and political contexts of Ohio and the United States. Our study found that Ohio ethnic festivals, in an era of growing insecurity for Latinxs across the nation, functioned as an alternative social and cultural space outside of home and work necessary for daily life and social interaction, not unlike other "third places" of sociality that help to make a community.[11] At the festivals we attended, spaces that were usually white and absent of Latinxs became sites for the assertion of Latinx cultural citizenship, which, as Renato Ronaldo states, "implies the notion of a polyglot citizen."[12] Latinx placemaking unfolded at these events through the reproduction of "sights, sounds, smells, and tastes" unique to Latinx cultures.[13] The social claiming of an "alternative public space" manifests in Latinx festivals in Ohio through the performances of *latinidad* that engaged with different sensory dimensions.[14]

The festivals, especially their parades, visually claim space and celebrate culture, not unlike the use of color, symbols, flags, and religious iconography to make place in Latinx business and residential areas, though in this case for limited duration.[15] Yet these events also enact community and belonging in multiple ways. At the Dayton festival parade, national floats ranged from a small family in traditional dress waving a Colombian flag to a large float with large graphics, traditional dancers, and a banner with "Amigos Panameños" (Panamanian friends). Latinx participants in the parades assert their varied cultural identities in the public sphere to educate other Latinxs and non-Latinxs about the diversity of *latinidad*. In the Cleveland Puerto Rico and Youngstown/Campbell parades, Latinx counterculture was represented by the large presence of motorcycle clubs such as the Taíno Club and Latin American Motorcycle Association. Visually, the forms of dress, national symbols, and flags that participants in the parades employed effectively communicated their cultural distinctiveness.

Flags and banners from countries across the Americas are among the most visible signals of individual and group belonging and identity at these events and are often incorporated in articles of clothing worn by Ohio Latinx festival participants that vividly convey their connection to places outside of the United States. At the Youngstown/Campbell festival, a Latinx place is visually created in an otherwise majority neighborhood by the display of flags. This is most common at both the Columbus Festival Latino, where flags from multiple Latin American countries appear on T-shirts and accessories of participants (including El Salvador, Colombia, Mexico, Puerto Rico, Honduras, Dominican Republic) and serve to connect people of similar national backgrounds, and the Cleveland Puerto Rican Parade, where both apparel emblazoned with the Puerto Rican flag and the presence of many Puerto Rican flags demonstrate national and social solidarity and pride. We suggest that the appearance of the Puerto Rican flag in these contexts functions as a decolonial symbol, given that, for almost a decade in the mid-twentieth century, the Puerto Rican flag was banned in Puerto Rico, and displaying it was a criminal offense.[16] In other cases, we suggest that the act of "being [insert nationality/ethnicity] in Ohio" by wearing this apparel also works to assert a transnational and borderland life in the Midwest.[17]

As Vega notes in her analysis of Latinx communities in Indiana, the distance between the Midwest and the actual US-Mexico border does not minimize the sense among Latinxs in the Midwest that they inhabit a borderlands where they must endure "spatial surveillance and linguistic assaults."[18] However, Vega notes that by their presence in public spaces and displays of cultural identities, Latinxs in Lafayette navigate the limitations on their social inclusion imposed by the borderlands and claim their ethnic belonging.[19] The display and wearing of flags at Ohio festivals is a way that Latinxs announce complex affiliations to both here and there (see figure 12.1). Likewise, the prominence of signage in Spanish was another way Latinxs visually created a place in the festivals, one that pushes back against an "English-only" attitude

FIGURE 12.1. Festivalgoer wearing Puerto Rican flag at the Columbus Festival Latino, August 12, 2017. Photo by authors.

or priority in the mainstream. Spanish-language menus were common, as were Spanish-language signs with photos rather than English translations. This display of Spanish in public spaces in Springfield, Dayton, Columbus, or Cleveland asserts the right for Latinxs to speak Spanish and know Spanish in public, especially in locations with small Latinx populations. The ability to enjoy the Spanish language in public was a significant reason for attendance by roughly a quarter of those we interviewed.[20]

The festivals also claimed place through the broadcast of sound, especially distinctly Latinx sounds. J. Lacey discusses how social interconnection helps create placemaking through sound, because "when the senses and imagination merge with place, [it causes] full integration between listener(s) and city. . . . [A] sense of belonging has been achieved."[21] In the festival contexts, space and Latinx listeners become integrated to create a new place, however ephemeral it may be. Though the Youngstown/Campbell festival is the smallest one we attended, its parade is the loudest. People on motorcycles, in cars, and on floats made as much noise as possible in the sleepy neighborhood by honking horns, revving engines, playing music, and cheering loudly. The sound of the parade can be heard well before the parade is seen, and the sounds echo. The Cleveland Puerto Rico parade is just as sonorous. In every single festival we attended, music—whether recorded or live—was a major feature and sometimes major reason for gathering, often sending Spanish-language sounds into the public ear.[22] To be heard and to hear was an important aspect of celebrating *latinidad* and attending the festival. The combination of impossible-to-ignore vocal and sonic aspects of the festivals—live bands, emceeing, music, singing, chanting, cheering, cars honking, motorcycles revving, loud conversations in both English and Spanish—could all be heard blocks away. To do this in spaces that—with the exception of the Cleveland Puerto Rican Parade—normally are not full of these sounds is a significant gesture in laying claim to space and gathering new publics.

Food vendors use bright, colorful images and graphic design to attract people to their stalls, along with descriptions such as "authentic," which conveys to both Latinxs and non-Latinxs that they "would get a 'real taste'" of Latinx cuisine.[23] Michael Hawkins aptly calls our attention to the ways that public ethnic festivals run the risk of reinforcing both uncritical national affinities among Latinxs and uncritical perceptions of the exotic for non-Latinx audiences, as well as the uninformed notion that diversity can be consumed.[24] However, for Latinx participants in Ohio festivals, the aroma of many different kinds of food at the festivals creates an olfactory landscape that echoes the visual transnational borderland of the festival and the sense of belonging both there and here. For Latinx and non-Latinx festivalgoers alike, food is a major attraction to the festivals, as one-third of our interviews shows.[25] Cuisines from different Latinx ethnic groups feature at most every event, with the exception of the Cleveland Puerto Rican Parade. In Springfield, Ohio, the festival features cuisine from Colombia, Honduras, and Venezuela, as well as almost every region of Mexico. By providing varied regional offerings—for example, pozole, pibil, and banana-leaf tamales versus tacos and burritos—the festival strives to create a place that conveys the complexity and diversity of Mexico and Mexicans while also offering a unique eating experience to non-Latinx audiences. And not unimportantly, each individual booth representing a specific region is generally staffed by a group of women who are themselves the cooks (see figure 12.2). Meredith E. Abarca's discus-

FIGURE 12.2. Booth featuring food from Honduras at the Springfield
Latino Festival, September 9, 2017. Photo by authors.

sion of how food preparation can convey social and conceptual knowledge
allows us to see festival hosts/cooks as agents of change in their communities,
spreading another kind of knowledge through food and perhaps changing
the space of Ohio in creating a place for themselves.[26] For Latinxs in Ohio,
having a multitude of food options in the festival is another way of making
place through taste and through the aromas in the air.

Even the sense of touch is a part of Latinx placemaking at these events.
At the festivals in Campbell, Cleveland, Dayton, Springfield, and Columbus,
people are encouraged to dance and move their bodies to the rhythm of reggaetón, mariachi, norteño, merengue, or salsa. Both Latinxs and non-Latinxs

danced at various times in the festivals, performing and moving to music in Spanish. At Dayton, one of the dance performers noted that dancing is when she feels she can most express herself.[27] When the audience joins in the dancing, they might well feel a similar expression of self not available to them in other places. The Dominican Republic group in the Dayton parade featured a green-and-yellow *diablo* who held the national flag in one hand and a whip in the other.[28] The *diablo* whipped the audience members, making them part of a Dominican tradition in downtown Dayton. While some of the audience members reacted negatively to being whipped (recoiling, taking a step back), others danced, clapped, and accepted being brought into this tradition. Regardless of the audience's response, however, the *diablo*'s whip was not explained, it simply was. The presence of the *diablo* and its whip and its invitation to the audience to be part of this Dominican tradition evokes Ruby Danta and Milagros Ricourt's notion of *convivencia diaria*.[29] Whether the audience embraces and accepts the *diablo* and its whip or not, they are collectively sharing that event and are participants in a performance of *latinidad*, and we see, as Ramón H. Rivera-Servera notes, that "*latinidad* may result from circumstantial encounters."[30]

At Ohio Latinx festivals in 2017, people participated in proud and public performances of their *latinidades* in the midst of an overtly hostile national political climate. While there were educational elements of several festivals—signs about regional cuisine at Springfield, dancing lessons at Columbus, descriptive introductions of folkloric dance performances at Dayton—aimed at both Latinx and non-Latinx audience members, in general, Latinx identities at the festivals we attended did not have to be explained. For a few days, Latinxs in Ohio claimed public spaces as Latinx places and danced and clapped and moved in ways they wished while also insisting on the complexity of their affiliations and enjoying the diversity of their expression.

Feeling Like You Belong

As participant observers in Ohio Latinx ethnic festivals, we are often reminded of Latinx community cultural events that form part of our own experience. The older, racially mixed, and economically challenged urban neighborhood of one festival reminds Lerma, who is Chicana, of her hometown in California.[31] One of our undergraduate researchers, Delacruz, is delighted to meet someone else with family origins in Oaxaca at a Cleveland festival.[32] Vieira, who is Brazilian, feels a strong sense of belonging at the Columbus Festival Latino because it involves multiple Latinx groups.[33] Fernández feels welcomed by her fellow Colombian Americans at the Festival Latino, who embrace her as a *paisana* when she introduces herself.[34] Delgadillo, a Chicana from the Midwest, relishes the summer festival experience and parades that remind her of similar events growing up in Milwaukee. These varied experiences of place, belonging, and *latinidad* contribute to each of our unique insights on the events we attend and observe, underscoring the many ways that Latinx ethnic festivals in Ohio create a sense of belonging for participants.

The festivals often draw a majority or large Latinx audience, including Latinx people from other parts of the state, making the festivals unique public events of cultural expression and importance in building community and making place in Ohio for those involved. As a way to gauge how Latinx ethnic festivals contribute to placemaking in Ohio, we query participants about where they feel at home and what places constitute home for them. Of the 120 brief interviews we conducted, 90 respondents identified Ohio as home, but for the majority, Ohio was not their exclusive home.[35] The twenty interviewees who did not consider Ohio their home were split between another US location and another Latin American location as their primary home.[36] While the vast majority of the majority Latinx audiences we interviewed indicated that Ohio was their home, a majority of these also suggested significant and ongoing connections to other US regions and Latin American places, indicating a population whose sense of belonging is not restricted to Ohio but definitely includes Ohio. In some cases, this sense of multiple belongings may be facilitated by dual citizenship status in other nations.[37] We see and hear evidence of these assertions of belonging at the festivals, indicating how individuals themselves create place and endow it with new meaning.

Latinx Ohioans who participate in organizing and staffing the festivals convey a strong sense of making place for themselves and for other members of their community through their gestures, actions, and postures. Our observation of La Placita festival in Cleveland bears this out: "People who were there felt it was important to be there. Even the teenage assistants who wandered around and lent a hand here and there, moved with purpose and authority, aware that they were doing something important. People greeted each other and commented on or celebrated the fact that the event was happening—it mattered that they were there."[38] Though the forms of organization and grassroots community involvement in running the festival on the days of the events varied across the state, we noted many echoes of the above scene at every event, including emcees guiding the schedule of events in Dayton, volunteers making seating areas at Calle 33 Festival in Cleveland, vendors inviting people into booths at Columbus, and volunteers proudly sharing their cuisine at Springfield. The physical movements of organizers and volunteers in hosting these events conveyed both belonging and welcome.

Several participants commented on the many years and ways that they have built home in cooperation with other Latinxs. One woman in Dayton told us that she and her husband had been in Dayton for nearly thirty years and that since they arrived her husband "ha participado con grupos culturales, tocando música, instrumentos" (has worked with cultural groups, playing music, instruments).[39] This participant expressly valued customs of including extended family and neighbors in social life, enjoying humor and fraternity together in addition to language and music and food customs.[40] A teenager at the Cleveland Puerto Rican Parade described it as only one of many where people routinely "get together for many different occasions."[41] A participant in the Columbus Festival Latino from Lebanon, Ohio, noted that she attends every year because she likes "la cultura latina." She describes her home as "donde yo esté," highlighting her flexibility in making place.[42] Given the smaller numbers of Latinxs in Ohio in comparison to other states, that flexibility may be crucial.

The lack of a sizeable or visible Latinx presence in their daily lives or neighborhoods, especially in comparison to other US locations, prompts appreciation among some Latinxs for ethnic festivals as an opportunity for enjoying culture, community, and a site for networking that participants do not otherwise experience. This observation emerges among participants who have migrated from New Jersey, Texas, Florida, North Carolina, New York—though no particular state or region seemed to predominate.[43] So many people we spoke to said they made sure to attend the festival every year. A festivalgoer noted that in Latinx-majority regions such as California, "La gente allá está bien. Pienso yo como ellos son la mayoria, son bastantes hispanos [allá] entonces ellos se sienten más apoyados, sienten más fuerza," versus in Ohio, where "acá como está apenas, estamos creciendo, entonces pienso yo que se sienten un poco con mucho miedo, pero poco a poco vamos a salir adelante" (Latinx over there are fine. I think that because they are the majority, there are many Latinx [there], then they feel more supported, they feel the strength of their numbers. Here, since we are just beginning to grow, I think that we feel a little more fear, but slowly but surely we will get ahead).[44] His sense of the fear felt by some resonates with us as we notice some apprehension among people we approach for interviews. A couple at the Columbus Festival Latino also noted the relative isolation of the few Latinxs they have come across: "Lo poquito [de comunidad latina] que hemos conocido se mantiene separada. No sé por qué razón, qué evento social o qué, pero está [la gente] muy separada" (The few that we have met keep apart. I don't know for what reason, what social event or whatever, but they are very separated).[45] For this reason, the couple decided to attend the festival, which they learned about from other Latinxs in Ohio: "Nos enteramos a través de otros latinos y queríamos ver, conocer porque llegamos recientemente a esta área y nosotros queríamos conocer a otros latinos" (We learned about this event from other Latinos, and we wanted to see and learn more because we recently arrived in this area and want to meet other Latinos).[46] An elderly woman also in Columbus told us that she attends Festival Latino in order to meet fellow Panamanians, since the town where she has lived for twenty years has a very limited Latinx population: "Bueno, es que la verdad, no tengo mucho contacto con latinos. Hoy conocí a tres panameñas. . . . Allí donde yo vivo no vivimos muchos latinos, así que, para conocer, yo tengo que venir como a festivales, lugares así" (Well, it's that honestly, I don't have much contact with Latinos. Today I met three Panamanian women. . . . Where I live we are not many Latinos, so to be able to meet [Latinos], I have to go to festivals, places like this).[47] In general, individuals from ethnic/national backgrounds in South America express this lack more often than do those of Mexican or Puerto Rican background; however, even those in the latter groups see the festivals as offering a unique kind of communal experience. As one woman noted while attending the Puerto Rican–focused Calle 33 Festival in Cleveland, "I feel like when we have these festivals we really come together and support each other and show what we're about. It gets better every year."[48] Another young woman at the Dayton festival told us about an annual indoor Latinx festival in Lima, Ohio, of which we were unaware: "There's always been a bit of community, so you locate that community."[49] Another young woman who identified as a midwestern Latina mentioned that she appreciated the differences between Latinxs in different parts of the country and felt most at home in the Midwest.[50] These placemaking efforts speak to "the way all of us as human beings transform the places in which we find ourselves into places in which we live."[51] As we demonstrate in this analysis, Ohio Latinxs cross many borders—cultural, linguistic, national, state, occupational—to make a life in this state, but their enjoyment of the Latinx ethnic festival derives from the fact that these differences are accepted at the festival and contribute to the shared enjoyment of the festival.

Ohio Latinx ethnic festivals attract Latinxs from small towns and from suburban and urban areas as members of this population seek out opportunities for forging communal relationships in a state with a smaller Latinx population, though this also reveals a dark side to the Latinx experience in the state. Two of the participants quoted above took notice of the fear among Latinx communities in Ohio, as well as the practice of actively keeping to oneself. Nearly a third of interviewees mentioned isolation, with several commenting on the lack of Latinx communities in rural parts of the state, as well as the sense that one is viewed with suspicion in those places. Others noted how Latinx people are limited to certain neighborhoods and few cultural events in larger urban centers. One person even noted active hostility directed toward Latinx people: "Ya nos están sacando de todos lados" (Now they are coming for us everywhere).[52] Beyond the bounds of the festival, Latinx festivalgoers' efforts to create place face contestation that the festival itself and on its own cannot resolve, though it clearly serves as an important location for experiencing community by providing affective and cultural sustenance.

Of More Than One Place:
Transnational and Translocal Experiences

A large number of festival participants we interviewed (sixty-three) indicated that they belong to a place other than Ohio, sometimes mentioning another US location or another Latin American location as also home. The incorporation of cuisine, artisanal crafts, and cultural performances from other Latin American locations into Ohio space at the festival provides strong material evidence of this phenomenon, as do the oral expressions among festivalgoers of also feeling connected to another location besides Ohio. The strong expressions of multiple sites of belonging among Latinx people in Ohio is, in many ways, not new or unique, as researchers have long identified transnational dimensions of *latinidad* and the ways they contribute to both "mobile livelihoods" and "civic binationality."[53] As a young man in his thirties at the Cincinnati festival described it,

> Yo creo que ambos lugares son mi casa ya. Yo tengo constante contacto con mi familia en México, regreso en los veranos, a veces voy en Navidad, toda mi familia está allí. . . . Me casé aquí, mi esposa es hispana también, pero su familia está aquí. . . . Pero yo creo que, a estas alturas, ya me hice a la idea de que siempre voy a extrañar algo, ¿no? Y no es porque haya perdido una casa, sino porque ahora tengo dos, y no puedo estar en ambas al mismo tiempo, eso es.

> I think that now both places are my home. I'm in constant contact with my family in Mexico, I go back during the summers, sometimes I go for Christmas, all of my family is there. . . . I got married here, my wife is Hispanic also, but her family is here. . . . Either way, there are people that are very important to me here and there. . . . But I think that, at this point in my life, I've reconciled with the fact that I'll always miss something, no? And it isn't that I've lost a home but instead I now have two, and I can't be in both at the same time. That's it.[54]

The recognition that he will always miss something from another place no matter where he is indicates a respect for cultural difference and uniqueness of place.

Translocal rather than transnational terms emerge in festivalgoer descriptions of their attachment to place in Ohio and elsewhere. For example, one young woman at the Cleveland Puerto Rican Parade identified herself as someone from the Clark and Fulton neighborhood of Cleveland rather than Ohio and from San Lorenzo in Puerto Rico rather than Puerto Rico generally.[55] This translocality illustrates how communities that were once "relatively localized become internationalized" while still retaining a sense of identity as "place-based rather than exclusively mobile, uprooted, or 'travelling' . . . [and] asserting the importance of local-local connections."[56] The young woman's commitment to the Clark and Fulton neighborhood and San Lorenzo, Puerto Rico, specifically, highlights "the fidelity and commitment that most migrants continue to feel towards family, friends, and community in particular locations."[57] This fidelity to the "local-local" is also evident in the highly localized identities of the parade princesses, each of whom bears a sash representing a particular municipality in Puerto Rico. Overall, what we find in these festivals is an opportunity for Latinxs from various nationalities to create a place for themselves in Ohio, as one attendee noted of Dayton's Hispanic Heritage Festival: "This is the biggest [Latinx festival] in the Dayton community, this is the biggest one, the one that all Latinos mostly come to, all the vendors, resources, everybody knows everybody's right here. So this is our home, no matter where you're from—Puerto Rico, Guatemala, wherever, it's still home."[58]

Recognizing Multiplicity and Building Coalitions

At the Columbus festival, artist Abraham Cordova's booth embodies the complex affiliations that Latinxs in the Midwest express at these events. Cordova displays designs that bilingually claim Ohio and transnationality. Cordova's "mi hogar" (my home) graphic sticker assembles the names of multiple countries in the Americas intermixed with the place-names "Ohio," "Columbus OH," and the words "mi hogar" in the shape of Ohio. Cordova's artistic vision asserts a bilingual Ohio, the land of "mi hogar," and constructs a transnational Ohio, creating a new Latinx homeland. By also including Guadeloupe, Martinique, and Haiti, Cordova gestures to a *latinidad* that is cognizant of the "historical struggle with European colonialism and US imperial expansionism."[59] This *latinidad* rejects a transnational white supremacy that erases Blackness. The Columbus Festival Latino typically has a strong Caribbean flavor, and there we meet many African American and

Black Latina/o participants. At La Placita in Cleveland, where we began our research, cultural performances included an Afro-Latinx dance performance that also brought local Black Latinx community members out for the festival; the salsa band Tumbaó, which has a strong percussion section; and later a Puerto Rican jazz band from Lorain, Ohio, who commented on the multiple ethnic/racial roots of the music they performed. La Placita also included among its vendors an African American small business. These observations and conversations suggest that Black Latinxs participate in Latinx ethnic festivals and that organizers of these events consciously include Black Latinx music, dance, and food.

The festivals show that making place in Ohio involves building relationships and coalitions. These events provide an opportunity for interethnic interaction, sometimes on the basis of the multiethnic and multiracial character of Latinx populations discussed above and sometimes through the concerted efforts of organizers to attract multiple audiences. African Americans and Black Latinxs participate in the Dayton Hispanic Heritage Festival and the Caribbean-focused Columbus Festival Latino, which features prominent Dominican and Puerto Rican musical acts. Significant numbers from the majority white population also attend many of these events, particularly in Cincinnati, Columbus, Dayton, and to a smaller degree Springfield. We did not notice or identify many Asian or Native American attendees on the days we attended. Nonetheless, our research concurs with that of Gerardo Francisco Sandoval that events such as these create "opportunities for interaction and adaptation between existing residents and the new Latino immigrants."[60]

Several African American and Black Latinx participants we interviewed in Dayton indicated that their residence in the area is owing to their work at nearby Wright-Patterson Air Force Base, the military being one institution where Black Americans have provided significant service.[61] In Dayton, therefore, the festival contributes to building bridges between these communities. As an African American man explains, "As a fellow minority, I feel inclined to support, come out, and experience a new culture that I'm not familiar with. . . . It kind of tears down preconceived notions. I think that's a good thing. . . . a peaceful, you know—festival, where people don't perpetuate negative stereotypes. I think it's good, even if you just meet someone and have a casual conversation."[62]

Individuals and vendors at several events also recognize Latinx interconnection with Indigenous peoples. We encountered a Mexican visitor from Pittsburgh at a Latin jazz performance who expressed pride and interest in her Indigenous heritage.[63] Another Ohio-born Puerto Rican man at the Campbell festival spoke about his and his daughter's involvement in a Taíno dance group and its extended networks in Puerto Rico, Florida, New York, and Ohio, expressing a strong identification with his Taíno heritage and with both Native American nations in the region and throughout the Americas.[64] Another man at the same festival identified as "mixed, I'm Latino and African American" and indicated that he participated in events in both communities.[65] These exchanges suggest that the festival space is one where Ohio Latinx communities celebrate multiple kinds of *latinidades.*

Festival organizers indicated that they create opportunities for Latinx peoples and other populations to interact. An organizer of the Springfield festival described the five-year-old event as an effort "to bring the Latinos and non-Latinos together. That way the non-Latinos could get to know our culture and get to know different Latino cultures."[66] The Columbus Festival Latino also targets and draws multiple audiences through advertising, including African American media outlets and mainstream media, as well as Latinx media and businesses, as festival organizer Diana Pagán explains.[67] In Dayton, the Hispanic Festival was cosponsored by both the Puerto Rican, American, and Caribbean Organization (PACO) and the United Rehabilitation Services (URS), which held its annual Rubber Duck Regatta on the Great Miami River adjacent to the site of the festival at RiverScape MetroPark. The marshal for the regatta was Eden, a disabled Latinx child. Eden's participation in the Hispanic Festival, as well as the collaboration between an organization that provides services for individuals with developmental and acquired disabilities (URS) and Dayton's leading Latinx organization (PACO), not only helps bring awareness to the growing numbers and visibility of Latinxs with disabilities but also demonstrates Latinx communities in the Midwest engaging in intersectional advocacy and collaboration. Given that Latinxs have largely been absent from the narrative of disability activism, we take one overheard comment—an older white man speaking negatively to his female partner on the emcee's use of Spanish in the bilingual program introducing the regatta—as a sign of the work that remains to be done in bringing together these two different audiences. On the other hand, at the Springfield festival, sponsored by a Catholic church, an older white parishioner of Czech, German, and Irish background told us that there are some folks in town who are accepting of Latinx immigrants and some who are not, but he takes issue with the latter, asking: "How could you not want to help or put your hand out to the next guy or gal standing next to you?.... If your neighbor is doing well, then you're doing well."[68] The festivals, therefore, show groups of people throughout the state working to enact Renato Rosaldo's notion of cultural citizenship, a status that "refers to the right to be different and to belong in a participatory democratic sense," and in the next section we examine the link between festivals and Latinx participation in democratic society.[69]

FIGURE 12.3. Support for DACA at Cincinnati Hispanic Fest, September 9, 2017. Photo by authors.

How the Political Climate of 2017 Impacts Latinx Festivals

As Latinx researchers, we all feel the need to *be with* Latinx communities at these events for solidarity with the many undocumented in our communities who face banishment to the shadows, as well as disruptions to their families and lives, and for sustenance in the face of overt racism. When the political winds shifted in 2015 with Donald Trump's campaign calls to "build a wall" and his assertions that Mexican migrants are rapists and drug dealers, all manner of ugliness gained an open platform. Long unspoken or unconscious biases manifested in open expression. To name just a few of the issues that by June 2017 were on our minds and also on the minds of those we interviewed: Trump issued various executive orders meant to ban Muslims from traveling to the United States, Trump attempted to bar transgender people from serving in the military, and Trump rescinded the Deferred Action for Childhood Arrivals (DACA) program in early September.[70]

The degree to which an anti-Latinx discourse permeates public life in the United States and Ohio became apparent when the emcee at the Campbell-Youngstown Latino Heritage Festival commented in his welcome address that "[this festival] is not discriminating against any race but showing Latinos are here, that we're part of this world, that we should not be taken out just because we are called Latino," before also adding that Latinx people have been present on this land much longer than others.[71] His comments, in attempting to answer both the misguided discourse of reverse racism in relation to Latinx gatherings and the anti-immigrant politics that have become a stand-in for anti-Mexican and anti-Latinx prejudice, insist on the longer historical presence of Latinxs in the United States. They also reveal both the contemporary pressure on Latinxs not to assemble and not to be seen, as well as the lack of education about Latinx peoples that has fueled the emergence of a discourse of ignorance. The social climate had shifted dramatically enough in the United States that organizers of the Columbus Festival Latino were prompted to consider contingency plans in case of an anti-Latinx protest at the 2017 festival, even though they viewed these as purely precautionary measures.[72] These episodes confirm that the climate we were noticing and feeling was also being felt and noticed by Latinxs throughout Ohio in 2017, its presence made more visible by the inescapability of political campaigns at every event.

We were struck by the prevalence of political candidates and campaigns at Ohio Latinx parades and festivals in 2017 yet noticed few who addressed anti-immigrant discourse. Some of the candidates campaigning at the festivals were themselves Latinx, and their presence conveyed a strong sense of the growing voting power of Latinx communities. A 2013 study on Latinx eligibility, participation, and voting preferences finds that Ohio is the "19th largest Hispanic eligible voter population nationally."[73] A 2014 *Columbus Dispatch* article reports that the state's "population growth is being driven by people who identify as Hispanic."[74] As Ramona Hernández noted in her study of the relationship between social and cultural organizations (such as those involved in the planning and maintaining of the Latinx festivals), "membership in cultural or affective organizations influences the likelihood of integration into society through social involvement . . . [including] high interest in political involvement."[75] This helps us to understand the presence of political candidates at these events, from the multiple candidates for local and state office marching in the Cleveland Puerto Rican Day Parade, to those mingling with crowds at Springfield, to the large screen broadcast of a speech by the Columbus mayor at the Festival Latino, to one candidate/politician leading a large group of followers dancing the Wobble at the Youngstown/ Campbell event. Postcards, fliers, and campaign paraphernalia are widely distributed at every event. On the day we attended the Youngstown/Campbell festival, four of ten booths were candidates hoping to get the Latinx vote. At the Cleveland Puerto Rican Parade, several contingents marched in support of their respective candidates, the largest made up of over twenty individuals marching in support of a Latina candidate while also sporting the only social justice–related signs in the parade—one condemning the alt-right protests and violence in Charlottesville, Virginia, and another in solidarity with the victims of the terrorist attack in Barcelona earlier that summer. These signs point to the importance of these festivals as sites for political action.

We did not ask anyone directly about their immigration status or views on current anti-immigrant politics and policies, but we understood many comments as retorts to the general political climate and heard many expressions of unease and discontent with the discourse emanating from the White House. One schoolteacher at the Cincinnati festival noted that he had students whose parents had been deported: "El día siguiente de la elección, fue uno de los días más tristes de mi carrera como maestro porque doy clase en una escuela en donde casi todos son hispanos o negros y unos y otros sienten que eso está en contra suya y había niños llorando en los pasillos" (The day right after the election was one of the saddest days in my career as a teacher, since I teach in a school where almost all [the students] are Hispanic or Black, and some of them feel that [the election] is against them, and there were kids crying in the hallways).[76]

At least four of the festivals included booths featuring immigration lawyers advertising their services and distributing information on basic civil and legal rights. The Columbus festival featured a "DACA Time" online platform booth in support of DACA applicants, which was strangely situated next to the county sheriff's booth. The Cincinnati Hispanic Fest on September 9, 2017, occurred just a few days after the Trump administration ended the DACA program, prompting many festivalgoers to openly express their dismay, fear, and anger.[77] A legal consulting service handed out information to Latinx attendees on their civil and legal rights should they be subjected to deportation raids while displaying a poster that said, "They tried to bury us, but they didn't know we were seeds." Indeed, on the heels of the DACA revocation, this poster reflected the general atmosphere of the Cincinnati festival. During the festival, a member of the United Food and Commercial Workers Union gave a speech calling for all Latinxs who could be impacted by the policy change to get informed, organized, and unified to overcome the political hardships they would face. His speech, just like our interview with him, reflects the growing awareness among Latinxs of the need to organize in defense of their communities.[78] A young woman at the Springfield festival also commented on the importance of the event given the political climate: "Right now we are struggling a lot with the political things and what's going on with DACA. . . . I feel like we need to come together as one and be more united and show that we're, that we can be who we want to be and strive to be best. . . . We also deserve to live our dreams."[79] One person at the Youngstown/Campbell festival, a smaller and more rural location than the other festivals we visited, noted the political climate of 2017 as one major difference between that year's festival and those held previously: "There's more political things here than in the past."[80]

Another noticeable presence at all these festivals was the police, who sometimes appear to go out of their way to maintain friendly bonds of communication with Latinxs and other times inspire ambivalence. At Cincinnati, a white police officer sported a *lucha libre* mask and interacted with Latinx children. He explained to us that he was a liaison with the migrant community, and his purpose was to highlight how "our role as the law enforcement has nothing to do with immigration enforcement."[81] Similarly, another officer in attendance at the Springfield festival chatted with festivalgoers, enjoyed the food, and spent time interacting with the many children at the festival. More and more police departments are engaging in this kind of work precisely because of the increased "threat of deportability" that Latinx migrants face today across the country.[82] In Cleveland, police and fire units actually participated in the Puerto Rican Day Parade with their motorcycles and fire engines, in addition to providing key traffic support. However, at Dayton, as at other festivals, we did not notice much interaction between police officers and festival attendees beyond their roles in providing traffic support. In Columbus a slight shift in location led to police stationed at two entrances to the festival grounds, unfortunately appearing to be gatekeepers and inspiring ambivalence.

Despite the generally positive, proimmigrant, and pro-Latinx stance that permeates the festivals and those who attend them, not everyone who attends these events feels kinship or solidarity with all others in attendance. We noted a small number of respondents expressing grievances against Latinx people, some of them being Latinx themselves. While these are a minority of the sentiments we heard expressed at these events, they do reflect the pervasiveness of a neoliberal discourse that assigns blame for structural economic inequalities to individual immigrants, criminalizing them, especially Mexican immigrants, without regard to an examination of US immigration and economic policies and practices.

Mapping the Dual Character of Latinx Placemaking: Ephemeral and Established Places

The festivals prompted us to consider the impermanence of Latinx place-making in Ohio. Unlike studies of the creation of Latinx residential areas or business corridors, which might represent a more established form of place-making or a more easily recognizable place through the use of semifixed or fixed features, festivals are impermanent and ephemeral.[83] They exist for a few days and then they disappear, yet during those days they make Latinx people in Ohio hypervisible to others, bring individuals and groups together to create temporary community with longer-lasting impact, and reflect the ongoing grassroots organizing of Latinxs in Ohio. The people who come together to organize these events create community together, often relying on their own efforts to make these festivals happen. In this way, the events bring together Latinxs in local communities and across the state who do not necessarily know each other in advance but join together within the space of the festival.

Location matters, and the location of Latinx ethnic festivals might be an indicator of a community's "manifestations of authority and claims of legitimacy as celebrations reflect a community's notion of its power (or lack of power) and its prerogatives."[84] Festivals in Columbus and Dayton are hosted in prime downtown space, while the Puerto Rican Parade in Cleveland takes over a major street in the neighborhood with city support, each reflecting a significant claim to legitimacy in that city. While we attended some events that were relatively new, only three years old (La Placita), others have a twenty-one-year (Columbus) or forty-nine-year (Cleveland) history, suggesting a long-standing and continuously renewed Latinx population in Ohio with the wherewithal, in locations across the state, to mobilize community and resources in celebration of ethnic/racial identity.[85]

The physical location of each festival may also reflect varied levels of engagement with municipal entities as residents and citizens. The Dayton and Columbus downtown festival locations indicate sustained resource mobilization by festival organizers and strong working relationships with city and state departments and their resources not unlike that of other cultural/festival organizations in those cities. The Columbus festival organizing committee works with multiple agencies to ensure their participation in the festival, which furthers Latinx inclusion in and knowledge of resources.[86] The Youngstown/Campbell festival took place in a small park in Campbell in 2017, in contrast to a previous year when they enjoyed a more central location.[87] The differences between Columbus or Dayton, on the one hand, and Youngstown/Campbell, on the other, are perfectly illustrated by the case of bad weather in 2016. Because of the festival's established power, the 2017 Columbus Festival Latino remained in the prime downtown recreation space despite the drop in the previous year's attendance due to rain and wind. In Youngstown/Campbell, the 2016 rain meant that the festival "ended up losing a lot of money," which led to a change in venue for 2017, as one organizer said they could no longer afford the Youngstown location.[88]

Another limitation in access to public resources arose for the 2017 Cleveland Puerto Rican Parade, previously scheduled for a central downtown recreational space but moved to the Clark-Fulton Street area, in the heart of the Puerto Rican neighborhood. In our interviews, we learned that the parade was forced to change location due to violence that erupted in the previous year. The move sparked debate. One participant felt that this change in location is like "shoving the Puerto Rican community back into a small corner of the city, whereas other ethnic/national parades get the entire city's attention."[89] Another attendee noted the importance of moving the parade back into the community because "it has more of a sense of a Hispanic feel to it."[90] For this individual, the festival's location added authenticity that was lacking when it was held in the primarily white downtown area. This person's support of the move is echoed by another attendee, who, when asked about the parade's importance, stated that it "makes me feel like I'm part of a community and the community is still alive and strong. And it's very important that they have it here on Clark Avenue today. This is like the center of the community. Especially for Hispanics of all kinds. Not only just Puerto Rican, but Dominican, Mexican, Guatemalan. We all reside here in this area."[91] We observed the use of more central municipal spaces for festivals in the southern part of the state versus neighborhood, smaller, or less central spaces for festivals in the northern part of the state, but further research is needed to determine whether this signals a difference in legitimacy for Latinx populations in the state.

Expanding Definitions of *Latinidad*

We met a number of Brazilians at Latinx festivals and with them considered whether Brazilians count in the "Latinx" panethnic label. Brazilians are "'in and out' of the Latino community" since they share characteristics with others from Latin America but also experience cultural, linguistic, and educational differences from them.[92] One Brazilian interviewee explained: "I don't see myself as Hispanic or Latino, because we don't speak Spanish pretty much. Um, we are in-between white and, and Latino, maybe, but it's hard to define."[93] Another woman stated: "I don't identify as Latina. . . . because I think Latinos are Hispanics . . . and you see that in the festival here, they yell the name of all of the countries, except Brazil."[94] In a study of Brazilians in Newark, Ana Ramos-Zayas found that Brazilians know that mainstream Americans would label them as "'Hispanic' or, depending on the phenotype, Black, but not white," which suggests that the Brazilians we encountered at festivals also recognize this mainstream perception, which perhaps prompts them to join the festivals.[95] We saw efforts by the organizers and vendors of two festivals to include Brazil in their promotional materials, art, and music, which suggests some awareness among Latinx Ohioans about including Brazilians.

We did not see as strong of an awareness about including Latinx LGBTQ communities in the festivals. Two vendors who sold rainbow flags alongside national flags at the Cleveland Puerto Rican Parade were the only open hints that "Latinx" and "LGBTQ" are not mutually exclusive identities. We did not witness any openly LGBTQ booths, community organizations, or acknowledgments within the festivals in 2017, although we did note one table at the Columbus event with information on a new medication to prevent contraction of HIV, as well as a booth dedicated to education on violence against women.[96] As a result, one of our team feels wary about entering some spaces or disclosing her lesbian identity. She feels a pressure to act straight at these events, particularly those marketed as "free, family-focused" events.[97] In only one of our interviews did we encounter anyone openly discussing queer identity, same-gender partners, or queer family members.[98] As Richard Rodríguez writes, the family in Latinx spaces is an "often-taken-for-granted, naturalized site, where cohesion presupposes not only the fixity of gender roles but, by extension, a continuum between male authority and heterosexual presumption."[99] The advertisement of festivals as family friendly easily taps into the naturalization of heteronormativity, yet we see some potential for a more inclusive *latinidad* in the small ways that LGBTQ Latinxs were acknowledged.

Conclusion

As we attended the festivals in 2017, we noticed the sheer joy of people gathered to celebrate, party, relax, meet new people, hear great music, cheer on their relatives and friends who were performing, and eat good food despite the national political climate. So many of those whom we interviewed expressed their sense of feeling at home at these events. One young woman in Springfield described the festival experience as "maravilloso," noting that Springfield had been her home for six years, and she regularly participates in celebrating Mexican cultural events at her children's school.[100] For us, attending the festivals and actively engaging with the various Latinx communities across Ohio became extremely meaningful learning opportunities where we could consider the power of place and interrogate it through our own intersectional identities. We learned that these events enable affective and social bonds even as they also serve to query Latinx positionality and belonging in local and larger spheres. Our work, therefore, resonates with that of Karen Mary Davalos on the Festival de las Calaveras and the work of Ariana Ruiz on the Latinx zine festivals earlier in this volume in recognizing the power of seemingly ephemeral events. This chapter also joins in attending to the playful and sensory dimensions of varied *latinidades* that Lawrence La Fountain-Stokes considers in his chapter in this volume.

Ultimately, these festivals are uniquely midwestern and Latinx. Lilia Fernandez underscores the importance of local origin to Chicano and Puerto Rican activism in Chicago, one that is shaped by the experience of being in the Midwest and is not transplanted from the Southwest or Northeast.[101] Likewise, Latinx communities in Ohio exist in a unique borderland where day-to-day placemaking is shaped by the specific experiences within the state and region, as well as connections to other localities and nations. While they may also claim other homelands, Ohio Latinxs at the festivals in both large urban centers and small towns assert that Ohio is "mi hogar" and demonstrate this with sensory celebrations in public spaces that reflect their diversity, their claims to representation, and their growing alliances with others in the state. In 2017 Ohio Latinx festivals also emerged as a site where exclusionary anti-Mexican, anti-Latinx, and white nationalist discourses were contested. Nonetheless, these celebrations revealed different degrees of belonging among Latinx participants. In the midst of a challenging political climate, these gatherings also offered a much-needed respite and space for recharging and likely paved the way for further community organizing and building beyond the ephemeral place of the festival. In downtown Dayton or Columbus, an everyday Latinx presence is minimal or even hidden, but for a few days each year Latinxs take center stage in Ohio cities and towns, and year by year we build new publics in each of these locations.

Notes

1. As Katia Balassiano and Marta Maria Maldonado note, "A physical area becomes a 'place' when it is regarded by the people who use it as different from other areas, i.e. when people become attached to a place, and when the place is used in pursuit of shared socially and culturally specific goals" ("Placemaking," 646). Initially viewed as a topic for urban planners and geographers, placemaking research has shifted to examine how individuals create appropriate spaces and embed (and embody) them with new meaning.

2. For more on the multiple intersecting identities that fall under the umbrella term "Latinx," varied *latinidades*, and the intraethnic relationships among varied Latinx groups in the Midwest, see Theresa Delgadillo, *Latina Lives in Milwaukee* (Urbana: University of Illinois Press, 2015); Rivera-Servera, *Performing Queer Latinidad*; and Aparicio, "Latinidad/es."

3. Cadaval focuses on how sectors of the Latinx community come together in the festival and on the internal organization of festival committees and their concerns in shaping these events. In contrast, we focus on the experience of those attending festivals. We also draw from Geraldo L. Cadava's examination of Mexican American participation in the mainstream Fiesta de los Vaqueros in the 1940s and 1950s, as well as later Mexican-organized *charrería* events, as these reflect Mexican American efforts to claim place and assert belonging. See Olivia Cadaval, *Creating a Latino Identity in the Nation's Capital: The Latino Festival* (New York: Taylor & Francis, 1998), 12, 56–57, 160, 130, 96, 102; Cadava, *Standing on Common Ground*; Rivera-Servera, *Performing Queer Latinidad*.

4. Our research team of six included two undergraduate researchers in the summer of 2017, Sophie Delacruz in literature and Genevieve Arce in public policy. We thank them and undergraduate Sonia Rayka for work on this project.

5. The questions we asked festival attendees in a sample survey were: (1) How do you identify yourself? (2) Why are you attending XX festival? (3) How would you describe the life of a Latina/o in Ohio? (4) How does the event relate to your life in Ohio? (5) What is your age group—twenties, thirties, forties, etc.? (6) Which ethnic/racial group do you most identify with and why? (7) Where is home for you? We asked festival organizers additional questions on the histories of these events, the organizing for them, and the changes in them over time.

6. Field notes, Theresa Delgadillo, August 12, 2017. For example, one woman asked Vieira for a selfie with her after the interview and followed up by email to learn more about our project. Field notes, Leila Vieira, August 12–13, 2017.

7. Vega, *Latino Heartland*.

8. Ibid., 4–5.

9. Nicolas J. Zentos and Wendy Marley, "Hispanic Community," *Encyclopedia of Cleveland History*, https://case.edu/ech/articles/h/hispanic-community; Vargas, *Labor Rights*; Western Reserve Historical Society, *Mexican Community in Lorain, Ohio* (Lorain, OH: Western Reserve Historical Society, 1999); Maria Elena Lucas, *Forged under the Sun / Forjada bajo el sol*, ed. Fran Leeper Buss (Ann Arbor: University of Michigan Press, 1993); Michael Grabell, "Sold for Parts," ProPublica, https://www.propublica.org/article/case-farms-chicken-industry-immigrant-workers-and-american-labor-law; Arreola, *Hispanic Spaces*.

10. Pablo Mitchell and Haley Pollack, "Making 'The International City' Home: Latinos in Twentieth-Century Lorain, Ohio," in *Beyond el Barrio: Everyday Life in Latina/o America*, ed. Gina M. Pérez, Frank A. Guridy, and Adrian Burgos Jr. (New York: NYU Press, 2010), 149–67.

11. Lara, *Latino Placemaking*. Michael Innis-Jiménez notes that early Mexican migrants to Chicago "brought a common culture with them that could be used collectively to transform their environment" (*Steel Barrio*, 84).

12. Renato Rosaldo, "Cultural Citizenship and Educational Democracy," *Cultural Anthropology* 9, no. 3 (1994): 402–11.

13. See Michael Hawkins's discussion of festival as ethnic performance in public space ("Ethnic Festivals, Cultural Tourism, and Pan-Ethnicity," in Airriess and Miyares, *Contemporary Ethnic Geographies*, 115–38).

14. Rivera-Servera, *Performing Queer Latinidad.*

15. Inés M. Miyares, "Changing Latinization of New York City," in Arreola, *Hispanic Spaces*, 145–66.

16. As Gerardo Francisco Sandoval notes, "Use of public and private spaces where they could openly practice their transnational ethnic identity without compromising their local belonging" matters. ("Transnational Placemaking in Small-Town America," in *Diálogos: Placemaking in Latino Communities*, ed. Michael Rios, Leonardo Vazquez, and Lucrezia Miranda [Milton Park, Abingdon, UK: Routledge, 2012], 50–66, 61).

17. Antonio Sotomayor, *The Sovereign Colony: Olympic Sport, National Identity, and International Politics in Puerto Rico* (Lincoln: University of Nebraska Press, 2016).

18. Vega, *Latino Heartland*, 149, 111.

19. Ibid., 75.

20. Twenty-seven interviewees mentioned Spanish as their reason for attending.

21. J. Lacey, "Sonic Placemaking: Three Approaches and Ten Attributes for the Creation of Enduring Urban Sound Art Installations," *Organised Sound* 21, no. 2 (2016): 147–59.

22. Thirty-three interviewees mentioned music as their reason for attending.

23. Field notes, Leila Vieira, August 12–13, 2017.

24. Hawkins, "Ethnic Festivals."

25. Thirty-nine interviewees mentioned food as the major reason for attending; thirty-three of these were Latinx, and six were non-Latinx.

26. Meredith E. Abarca, *Voices in the Kitchen: Views of Food and the World from Working-Class Mexican and Mexican American Women* (College Station: Texas A&M University Press, 2006).

27. 170916_002, interview by Marie Lerma and Leila Vieira, September 16, 2017. Interview numbers indicate the date of the interview: YearMonthDay_Number of Recording, so second interview recorded on September 16, 2017.

28. Field notes, Marie Lerma, September 16, 2017.

29. Rivera-Servera, *Performing Queer Latinidad*, 38. *Convivencia diaria* is from Ruby Danta and Milagros Ricourt, *Hispanas de Queens: Latino Panethnicity in a New York City Neighborhood* (Ithaca, NY: Cornell University Press, 2003).

30. Rivera-Servera, *Performing Queer Latinidad*, 38.

31. Field notes, Marie Lerma, June 10, 2017.

32. Field notes, Sophie DeLaCruz, June 10, 2017.

33. Field notes, Leila Vieira, August 12–13, 2017.

34. Field notes, Laura Fernández, August 12–13, 2017.

35. Twenty-seven exclusively identified Ohio as home, twenty-four indicated that Ohio and another US location is home, and thirty-nine stated that their home is both in Ohio and in another Latin American location.

36. Eleven named another US location, and nine named another Latin American location. Eleven respondents did not discuss home at all.

37. We did not ask questions about citizenship status.

38. Field notes, Theresa Delgadillo, June 10, 2017.

39. 170916_005, interview by Theresa Delgadillo, September 16, 2017.

40. Ibid.

41. 170820_001, interview by Leila Vieira, August 20, 2017.

42. 170812_012, interview by Laura Fernández, August 12, 2017.

43. Field notes, Leila Vieira, September 9, 2017.

44. 170909_005, interview by Laura Fernández and Leila Vieira, September 9, 2017.

45. 170812_011, interview by Laura Fernández, August 12, 2017.

46. 170313_004, interview by Laura Fernández, August 13, 2017.

47. 170813_004, interview by Laura Fernández, August 13, 2017.

48. 170820_003, interview by Laura Fernández, August 20, 2017.

49. 170916_004, interview by Theresa Delgadillo, September 16, 2017.

50. 170812_011, interview by Leila Vieira, August 12, 2017.

51. Schneekloth and Shibley, *Placemaking*, 1.

52. 170820_005, interview by Laura Fernández, August 20, 2017.

53. For more on this, see Jorge Duany's discussion of "mobile livelihoods" as "the spatial extension of people's means of subsistence across various local, regional, and national settings." As Duany observes, "The constant displacement of people—both to and from the Island—blurs the territorial, linguistic, and juridical boundaries of the Puerto Rican nation" (*The Puerto Rican Nation*, 210–11). See Aparicio's discussion of Dominican American connections to both the Dominican Republic and the United States in Ana Aparicio, "Translocal Barrio Politics: Dominican American Organizing in New York City," in Pérez, Guridy, and Burgos, *Beyond el Barrio*, 253–71; and Bada's discussion of transnational civic binationality: "In practice many Mexican migrants are becoming full members of both U.S. and Mexican civil societies at the same time, engaging in practices of civic binationality that have a great deal to teach us about new forms of Latino immigrant integration into the United States" (in Xóchitl Bada, *Mexican Hometown Associations in Chicagoacán* [New Brunswick, NJ: Rutgers University Press, 2014], 138).

54. 170909_002, interview by Laura Fernández and Leila Vieira, September 9, 2017.

55. 170820_002, interview by Leila Vieira, August 20, 2017.

56. David Conradson and Deirdre Mckay, "Translocal Subjectivities: Mobility, Connection, Emotion," *Mobilities* 2, no. 2 (2007): 167–74, 168; Ayona Datta and Katherine Brickell, *Translocal Geographies: Spaces, Places, Connections* (London: Taylor and Francis, 2016), 3.

57. Ibid., 168.

58. 170916_001, interview by Leila Vieira, September 16, 2017.

59. Lorgia García-Peña, *The Borders of Dominicanidad: Race, Nation, and Archives of Contradiction* (Durham, NC: Duke University Press, 2016).

60. Sandoval, "Transnational Placemaking," 61.

61. See Debora Duerksen, "Executive Order 9981," in *Encyclopedia of African American History, 1896 to the Present*, ed. Paul Finkelman (Oxford: Oxford University Press, 2009); Maggi M. Morehouse, "Racism in the Military," in ibid.

62. 170916_001, interview by Theresa Delgadillo, September 16, 2017.

63. Field notes, Sophie Delacruz, July 21, 2017.

64. 170826_005, interview by Marie Lerma and Laura Fernández, August 26, 2017.

65. 170826_009, interview by Marie Lerma, August 26, 2017.

66. 170909_002, interview by Theresa Delgadillo, September 9, 2017.

67. Diana Pagán interview by Theresa Delgadillo, May 29, 2018.

68. 170909_003, interview by Theresa Delgadillo, September 9, 2017.

69. Rosaldo, "Cultural Citizenship," 402.

70. "Trump Administration Civil and Human Rights Rollbacks," Leadership Conference on Civil and Human Rights, https://civilrights.org/trump-rollbacks/.

71. Field notes, Marie Lerma, August 25, 2017.

72. Pagán interview.

73. Nolan Stevens, Megan Uhrig, and Paola McDowell, "Ohio Hispanic Voters: Eligibility, Participation, and Preferences," PDF, Ohio Commission on Hispanic/Latino Affairs, April 15, 2013.

74. "In all but one of Ohio's 88 counties, population growth is being driven by people who identify as Hispanic" (Jennifer Smith Richards, "Hispanics Lead Population Growth in Ohio," *Columbus Dispatch*, June 26, 2014, http://www.dispatch.com/content/stories/local/2014/06/26/hispanics-lead-state-population-increases.html).

75. Ramona Hernández, "The Latino Paradigm: The Struggles Within and the Need for National Identity," in *Mapping Latina/o Studies: An Interdisciplinary Reader*, ed. Angharad N. Valdivia and Matt Garcia (New York: Peter Lang, 2012), 311–33, 315.

76. 170909_002, interview by Laura Fernández and Leila Vieira, September 9, 2017.

77. Michael D. Shear and Julie Hirschfeld Davis, "Trump Moves to End DACA and Calls on Congress to Act," *New York Times*, September 5, 2017, https://www.nytimes.com/2017/09/05/us/politics/trump-daca-dreamers-immigration.html.

78. Field notes, Laura Fernández, September 9, 2017.

79. 170909_007, interview by Marie Lerma and Theresa Delgadillo, September 9, 2017.

80. 170826_008, interview by Marie Lerma, August 25, 2017.

81. 170909_010, interview by Laura Fernández, September 9, 2017.

82. Adela C. Licona and Marta Maria Maldonado, "The Social Production of Latin@ Visibilities and Invisibilities: Geographies of Power in Small Town America," *Antipode* 46, no. 2 (2014): 517–36, 522, doi:10.1111/anti.12049.

83. Albert Benedict and Robert B. Kent, "The Cultural Landscape of a Puerto Rican Neighborhood in Cleveland, Ohio," in Arreola, *Hispanic Spaces*, 187–205.

84. Ramón A. Gutiérrez and Geneviéve Fabre, "Feasts and Celebrations: Introduction," in *Feasts and Celebrations in North American Ethnic Communities*, ed. Ramón A. Gutiérrez and Geneviéve Fabre (Albuquerque: University of New Mexico Press, 1995), 1–9, 9.

85. Interviews with organizers, materials provided by organizers, and previous news coverage of these events revealed a history of events. Community cultural organizations are key organizers, although two are hosted by churches, and two were formerly church-organized festivals. La Placita, in Cleveland, is technically not a festival but a Hispanic-themed open-air market organized by La Alianza Hispana for the third year in 2017 to promote local Hispanic businesses. The Annual Hispanic Heritage Festival & Parade in Dayton held its seventeenth event in 2017, organized by the Puerto Rican

American and Caribbean Organization (PACO) and the Five Rivers Metro Park, being held in conjunction with the United Rehabilitation Services' Rubber Duck Regatta. The Festival Latino in Columbus had its first event in 1996. The 2017 edition, which had 205,000 attendees, took place at Genoa Park, by the Scioto River, in downtown Columbus and is sponsored by well-known national companies, as well as local businesses, TV, and radio stations. The Cleveland Puerto Rican Heritage Parade held its forty-ninth event in 2017. It is organized by the Julia de Burgos Cultural Arts Center. The celebration after the parade, Calle 33 Festival, is organized by the only two Latino / Puerto Rican social clubs of Cleveland, Alma Yaucana and San Lorenzo. The Sagrada Familia Latin American Festival in Cleveland is a church festival in a Latinx parish with a thirty-year history. The only other explicitly church festival was the fifth Springfield Latino Festival at St. Teresa's Church, in a predominantly white neighborhood and parish in the city. Events in Cincinnati and Campbell/Youngstown exhibited ties to local Catholic churches, where they were formerly held. Today, the Hispanic Culture Society of Cincinnati hosts the festival in partnership with the community and local businesses and is in its twenty-fourth year of existence. After a long hiatus, the Campbell/Youngstown region had its seventh festival in 2017, organized by the community.

86. Pagán interview.

87. 170826_010, interview by Marie Lerma and Laura Fernández, August 26, 2017.

88. 170826_001, interview by Marie Lerma and Laura Fernández, August 26, 2017.

89. Field notes, Laura Fernández, August 20, 2017.

90. 170820_007, interview by Theresa Delgadillo, August 20, 2017.

91. 170820_002, interview by Leila Vieira, August 20, 2017.

92. Antonio Luciano de Andrade Tosta, "The Hispanic and Luso-Brazilian World: Latino, Eu? The Paradoxical Interplay of Identity in Brazuca Literature," *Hispania* 87, no. 3 (2004): 576–85, 578.

93. 170916_003, interview by Marie Lerma and Leila Vieira, September 16, 2017.

94. 170813_005, interview by Leila Vieira, August 13, 2017.

95. Ana Y. Ramos-Zayas, "Between 'Cultural Excess' and Racial 'Invisibility': Brazilians and the Commercialization of Culture in Newark," in *Becoming Brazuca: Brazilian Immigration to the United States*, ed. Clémence Jouét-Pastré and Leticia J. Braga (Cambridge, MA: Harvard University, David Rockefeller Center for Latin American Studies, 2008), 271–86, 280.

96. Field notes, Laura Fernández, August 12–13, 2017.

97. Festival Latino Columbus, "History." This reaction illustrates the relationship between the field researcher and the people observed, since "the ethnographer needs to become sensitive to, and perceptive about how she is seen and treated by others" (Robert M. Emerson, Rachel I. Fretz, and Linda L. Shaw, *Writing Ethnographic Fieldnotes*, 2nd ed. [Chicago: University of Chicago Press, 2011], 4).

98. 170812_007, interview by Leila Vieira, August 12, 2017.

99. Richard T. Rodríguez, *Next of Kin: The Family in Chicano/a Cultural Politics* (Durham, NC: Duke University Press, 2009), 2.

100. 170909_004, interview by Theresa Delgadillo, September 16, 2017.

101. Fernandez, *Brown in the Windy City*, 210.

CHAPTER 13

Is the Chicago Latino Film Festival a Latinx Place?

GERALDO L. CADAVA

When I moved to Chicago in 2008, I hadn't heard of the Chicago Latino Film Festival. Pilsen and Little Village and Humboldt Park loomed in my mind as the beating hearts of Latinx Chicago, and I recognized the National Museum of Mexican Art as an important cultural institution that rivaled Spanish Harlem's Museo del Barrio as the foremost museum of Latinx and Latin American art in the United States. As a student of Latinx and US-Mexico borderlands history, which I'd learned firsthand as a child in Tucson, Arizona, and in a more scholarly way in college and graduate school, I'd come to think of Chicago's Latinx communities as incredibly diverse, dominated by Mexican Americans and Puerto Ricans but also shaped by Cubans, Guatemalans, Colombians, Ecuadorians, and others. They had lived in and around the city for more than a century as workers in railyards and factories and as central figures in the region's steel strikes. They were northbound migrants from Mexico, Puerto Rico, and Cuba and refugees of wars in South and Central America.

I was struck by the fact, though, that Chicago was also home to one of the oldest and largest Latinx film festivals in the United States. The Chicago Latino Film Festival was founded in 1985 and had grown from a few films and a few hundred attendees watching movies projected on the wall of a church to an international film festival with hundreds of films and thousands of attendees watching movies screened at an AMC theater in River North, right downtown, not far from the Loop and Chicago's main business district.

I attended my first Chicago Latino Film Festival a few years after moving to the city, and two things in particular caught my attention: the great diversity of the films that claimed to represent *latinidad*—more than half of them from Latin America—and how the festival itself was a vibrant pop-up space for social, cultural, and political debate about almost every topic related to the concerns of Latinxs and Latin Americans in the twenty-first century. On back-to-back nights, I saw a Mexican sci-fi film haunted by the disappearance and murder of Mexican women *maquiladora* workers and a documentary about the crisis in Venezuela during and after the leftist leader Hugo Chávez's regime. In both cases, and in Spanish as much as in English, the directors of the films answered audience questions afterward. That these films were screened and debated at a Latinx film festival in Chicago seemed provocative, since they promoted an especially expansive understanding of what Latinx film, identity, and geographies were.

As I read more about the Chicago Latino Film Festival, I learned that others had already thought deeply about the festival's meaning and strategies of representing *latinidad*, and they picked up on many of the same themes that I did. Roger Almendarez, who received a PhD in screen cultures from Northwestern University, wrote a terrific dissertation titled "Representational Scales: Latinx Media Production in Chicago, 1953–2012," which includes a chapter about the Chicago Latino Film Festival. He demonstrates how the film festival was part of an incredibly diverse Latinx media landscape that stretched back to the establishment of radio and television stations in the mid-twentieth century. Unlike the Chicago Latino Film Festival, these radio and television stations were rooted in Pilsen because their shortwave frequencies did not reach far beyond the neighborhood's Mexican and Mexican American communities. The film festival, by contrast, was attended by Latinxs not only from Chicago but also from across the United States and many different countries. Almendarez used the phrase "mixed mandate" to describe the festival's aspiration to simultaneously have a positive impact on Chicago's Latinx community and project a truly hemispheric understanding of *latinidad*.[1]

Both Almendarez and Elizabeth Barrios, a scholar of Latin American literary and cultural studies who has also written about the Chicago Latino Film Festival, further observed that there have been tensions between the festival's purported goals and what it has actually accomplished. The film festival claimed that Chicago's Latinx community was one of its main audiences, but very few movies by Latinx filmmakers from Chicago have been screened each year.[2] Similarly, while the festival strives for the uplift of Chicago's Latinx communities, it does so, first and foremost, discursively by seeking to change the minds of non-Latinx individuals—or perhaps even of Latinxs who see *latinidad* as limited to particular class backgrounds, national groups, or political views—about who Latinxs are. Moreover, the vast majority of the films are screened outside of the neighborhoods where Chicago's Latinx communities live. According to Almendarez, it has been necessary for the Chicago Latino Film Festival to screen films outside of Latinx communities as part of its effort to shape and reshape understandings of *latinidad*.

The projection of a hemispheric and cosmopolitan *latinidad*—sophisticated, open-minded, worldly, artsy, with high-brow tastes—and the possible disjuncture between the aims of the film festival as stated by the main organizer, Pepe Vargas, who founded the festival and serves as the executive director of the International Latino Cultural Center of Chicago, may well be the most important observations to be made about the annual event.

But in the context of this volume about Latinx placemaking in the Midwest, there are other considerations that deepen what Almendarez and Barrios have already written about the film festival. First, the Chicago Latino Film Festival is only one example of Latinx placemaking in Chicago from 1985 to the present, and in order to understand the film festival as an example of Latinx placemaking—both its accomplishments and its shortcomings—it should be viewed alongside other Latinx-identified places. Second, to understand what kind of Latinx place the film festival has made, we also need to understand it alongside the other examples of placemaking addressed in this volume, because they operate on different scales, take place in different moments, and appeal to different audiences. Third, it is important to spend a little more time evaluating the critique that there is a disjuncture between the Chicago Latino Film Festival's claim to represent Chicago's Latinx communities and the possibility that it may not, in the end, deliver on this promise.

Film festivals are only partially for the cities where they are located. They are also businesses and part of a global network of filmmakers, critics, and audiences, and in this sense their main interest is to highlight developments within the film industry and perhaps even shaping its future. This is what Cindy Wong reminds us in her book *Film Festivals: Culture, People, and Power on the Global Screen*. And to the extent that they are rooted in a particular place and a benefit to it, Wong argues, it is because they celebrate and reinforce the vision of the host city as a leading city of the world.[3] The Chicago Latino Film Festival is therefore like many other film festivals: it is a celebration of *latinidad* perhaps even more than it is a celebration of Chicago's Latinx communities. If the mandate of the film festival is mixed, as Almendarez argues, it may prioritize one part of the mandate over the other.

As Arlene Dávila demonstrated in her book *Latino Spin: Public Image and the Whitewashing of Race*, Latinxs were simultaneously more influential and more marginalized in the United States during the late twentieth century, when the Chicago Latino Film Festival was established. They were an increasingly powerful group of consumers, opened new businesses, held elected office, and were gaining clout in media and advertising industries through the growth of Spanish-language radio and television. At the same time, they were seen as dangerous threats to the United States—more as invading illegals than as full citizens.[4] The same was true in Chicago. Their numbers were growing, and they were part of a multiracial coalition that helped elect the first Black mayor of the city, even as their neighborhoods were gentrified and they were pushed out to suburbs, and as they continued to be the victims of economic and educational inequities.[5] The Chicago Latino Film Festival—through the fact of its existence and the stories told there—was meant to represent both sides of this paradox: the growing influence of Latinxs in the city—and their diversity and cosmopolitanism—and the continued injustices they faced, as depicted on the screen. The film festival is in its fourth decade, yet the challenges faced by Latinxs have not dissipated, suggesting the limited ability of representation to bring about change in the absence of other forms of mobilization.

The Chicago Latino Film Festival has grown dramatically since its founding in 1985. For the first several years it was held during Hispanic Heritage Month, in late September and early October, but now thousands of moviegoers gather for two weeks every April to view more than one hundred films from the United States, Latin America, and, intriguingly, Portugal and Spain. By its own account, it is "the largest, most comprehensive and best Latino film festival in the United States"—larger, more comprehensive, and better, one would have to assume, than its rivals in New York and Miami, although these, too, have made claims to being the premier Latinx film festivals.[6]

Considering the festival's impressive growth, it is hard to imagine its humble beginnings. In the festival's first year, it was called the Chicago Hispanic Film Festival. In April 1985 fourteen films were screened on the blank wall in the Charlie Chaplin Auditorium at St. Augustine College, founded just five years earlier, in 1980. In the Chicago Hispanic Film Festival's second year, nineteen films were shown, this time on a screen.[7] In 1987 the Chicago Latino Festival, as its organizers, Armando Afanador and Vargas, had begun to call it, gained citywide attention and attracted its first corporate sponsors. By 1990, only five years after its beginning, the festival lasted for ten days and showed films from sixteen Latin American countries, Spain, and the United States. That year, more than twelve thousand viewers attended the festival, and movies were screened throughout the city, at the Three-Penny Cinema and Facets Multimedia, both in Lincoln Park, at Columbia College in the loop, and at Roberto Clemente High School in West Town.[8] By the early 2000s, the film festival reached beyond Chicago, extending into suburbs such as Wheeling, River Forest, Lake Forest, and Palo Hills, just as many Latinxs increasingly moved outside of Chicago's city limits.[9]

By the second decade of the twenty-first century, the festival's offerings were shown primarily at the AMC River East 21, one of the biggest cinemas in Chicago. At first, the festival had no sponsorships. But over time the Chicago Latino Film Festival has counted among its sponsors the Illinois Humanities Council, the MacArthur Foundation, Corona beer, Univision, Mexicana Airlines, and American Airlines, which for several years donated airfare for filmmakers traveling to Chicago to attend the festival from abroad. When the Chicago Latino Film Festival began to broaden its cultural offerings to include music, dance, and food, in addition to a year-round calendar of events, its organizers created an umbrella for it called the International Latino Cultural Center (ILCC). The new name more accurately reflects the broad range of the center's offerings. The ILCC eventually began to plan for the building of the "first Pan-Latino cultural facility" in the United States, which would host all of its events, including the film festival.[10]

Vargas was interested from the beginning in representing the diversity and transnationalism of Latinxs in the United States and in Chicago specifically. He moved to Chicago in 1975, and his plan was to study and learn English. He was born in Colombia and educated in Argentina, receiving his first bachelor's degree in law from the Universidad Nacional del Centro de Buenos Aires. Vargas worked in Argentina before he moved to the United States. Once in Chicago, he shifted course and decided he wanted to pursue a career in journalism. In 1985 he received a second bachelor's degree from Columbia College, this time in broadcast journalism and television and film production. The diversity of his own background is mirrored in the festival organizers' decisions to screen films that focus on culture, love, and politics made in Mexico, Argentina, Chile, Guatemala, Peru, and every other country in Latin America, in addition to Spain and Portugal. It is also mirrored in the growing diversity of Chicago's Latinx community in the late twentieth century.

While Vargas was a student at Columbia College, he worked alongside filmmakers and became increasingly interested in film. That's when he linked up with people who were plotting to show a few movies from the United States and Latin America on the walls of St. Augustine College in Uptown. The college was interested because it saw the festival as a way of increasing enrollments. The plan didn't work for the college, which decided to pull its support, leaving the organizers to decide whether or not they wanted to continue the festival. Afanador did not, but Vargas did, so he stepped in and took over. He has organized the Chicago Latino Film Festival for the past thirty years and has in many ways become synonymous with the festival itself.[11]

When Vargas moved to Chicago, Chicago's Latinx communities were undergoing dramatic transformations that demonstrated the many meanings of Latinx placemaking in Chicago. Mexicans had first settled in Chicago during the late nineteenth and early twentieth centuries to work for the railroads and in the city's meatpacking factories. Puerto Ricans first moved to the city in large numbers in the mid-twentieth century as participants in the US Department of Labor's Puerto Rico Migration Division, which matched workers with employers on the mainland. Mexicans settled primarily in the Pilsen neighborhood, and Puerto Ricans settled north of downtown in Lincoln Park. But by the mid-1970s, when Vargas arrived in Chicago, many Latinxs in these communities had been displaced by urban renewal and an influx of upwardly mobile, mostly white professionals. One predominantly Mexican and Mexican American neighborhood near the South Loop was razed so the University of Illinois at Chicago's campus could be constructed. Latinx placemaking in the Midwest, that is, was often the result of the unmaking of places where they had lived for a long time. The establishment of the Chicago Latino Film Festival as a virtual space for Latinxs from Chicago and beyond came at the same time that historically significant physical spaces were diminishing and Latinxs were being squeezed out of their neighborhoods.

In the thirty-plus years that the Chicago Latino Film Festival has been around, examples of Latinx placemaking in the city have proliferated quicker and spread farther. Like many cities in the Midwest, Chicago had experienced a version of the "urban crisis" that Thomas Sugrue and a generation of historians after him have written about: chronic underemployment, increased crime and policing, blighted neighborhoods, and health inequities.[12] As the city's economy transitioned from industry to service, finance, and tourism, homes in the city center became more expensive, so Mexicans moved from Pilsen to the suburbs, and Puerto Ricans moved to neighborhoods such as Humboldt Park and South Lawndale. Andrew Sandoval-Strausz, in *Barrio America: How Latino Immigrants Saved the American City*, has argued that Latinx communities have in fact revitalized Chicago. Their activity in support of their communities provided a model for how urban spaces could become vibrant again. Latinx individuals started businesses, purchased homes, became citizens when the Immigration Reform and Control Act of 1986 afforded them the opportunity, and inhabited public space in a way that resembled or even emulated the public squares of their Latin American homelands.[13] They displaced African Americans as the city's largest minority community and helped stabilize the city's population decline. In Sandoval-Strausz's telling, Latinx placemaking in Chicago had meant the remaking of the city itself.

Since the 1980s, when the film festival was founded, Latinx communities remade Chicago by expanding into corners of the metropolis they hadn't inhabited previously. In addition to suburbs such as Cicero and Waukegan, they moved in increasing numbers into neighborhoods within the city, such as Rogers Park, which by the late twentieth century had become the neighborhood with the fastest-growing number of immigrants from Latin America.[14] Pilsen and Little Village and Humboldt Park maintained their Latinx character and remained home not only to large cultural institutions such as the National Museum of Mexican Art, which was founded in 1987, just on the heels of the film festival, but also to vibrant subcultures of mural artists and the producers and consumers of zines of the sort that Ariana Ruiz writes about in her contribution to this collection.

Yet Latinxs and Latin American immigrants also opened restaurants (all up and down Clark Street in Rogers Park, for example), built religious shrines, and established hometown associations (HTAs) that eased the settlement of immigrants and collected remittances to be sent back to Mexico and other Latin American homelands. They organized other celebrations of Latinx and Latin American culture such as *fiestas patrias*, held every September during Hispanic Heritage Month, which coincided with celebrations of the independence anniversaries of several Latin American countries. These took place in Little Village and Pilsen, as well as in the Loop and on Michigan Avenue. All of these examples together, of course, represent the wide range of Latinx placemaking in Chicago. The Chicago Latino Film Festival should be understood alongside them as one more example, but one that is different because of its ephemerality, the fact that it targets non-Latinxs as much as it targets Latinxs, and the limitations of changing the minds of non-Latinx festivalgoers through representation alone.

The advent of the Chicago Latino Film Festival was of a piece with the broader changes in Chicago's Latinx community. The films screened at the festival aimed to depict the diversity of Latinxs; their humanity and growing cultural, economic, and political influence; and their transnational roots and enduring connections with Latin America. A professional from Colombia, Vargas was himself representative of the diversification of Chicago's Latinx population. Colombians, Ecuadorians, Guatemalans, and immigrants from other Latin American nations joined the already established Mexican and Puerto Rican communities. Some came as refugees from war-torn countries in Central America. The religious leaders who offered them sanctuary made Chicago one of the first and biggest cities to participate in the national sanctuary movement that Sergio González writes about in this volume. The engaged community members who founded Centro Romero, named after the martyred archbishop Óscar Romero, shot and killed in El Salvador in 1980, also helped to make Chicago a Latinx place. But others, like Vargas, were doctors, lawyers, and other sorts of professionals, and they also made important contributions to Latinx placemaking in the city with their health clinics, law offices, and, yes, film festivals.

Like other Latinx events in the city, the Chicago Latino Film Festival is intended, in large part, to create a sense of belonging for Latinxs in Chicago. But it accomplishes this goal rhetorically, visually, and representationally, unlike some of the more tangible physical examples of placemaking, such as restaurants, neighborhoods, schools, shrines, hometown clubs, and others.

Whereas these places host or are home to Latinxs day in and day out, the film festival is a physical space for only two weeks every year. Thousands of viewers inhabit the space and then go home. For the rest of the year, the theater returns to screening summer blockbusters, Oscar bait, and other new releases, and it is unclear what permanent traces the Chicago Latino Film Festival leaves behind. The most permanent marker of the film festival doesn't seem to be the festival itself but rather the endurance and even growth of the Chicago Latino Film Festival as an institution—raising funds, soliciting submissions for the following year's festival, forming partnerships with other city institutions.

None of this is intended to underplay the festival's significance. Even for two weeks a year, the Chicago Latino Film Festival is symbolically important to claim as Latinx space the city's downtown business and tourist district, areas not typically associated with Chicago's Latinx communities. The festival's thousands of attendees, approximately half of whom are Latinx, as well as the powerful marketing muscle and corporate sponsorship that the festival has developed over the years, in some ways mark the rising influence of Latinxs in Chicago, whose numbers have grown steadily from the late twentieth century forward. The organizers of the film festival have also demonstrated a remarkable ability and willingness to adapt to a particular historical and political moment, reflecting their belief that what it means to be Latinx in Chicago and in the world is constantly changing. Finally, the establishment of the International Latino Cultural Center, which was an outgrowth of the film festival and now runs it, has meant a more regular calendar of events—including concerts, film screenings, and other gatherings—that represents Chicago's Latinx communities year-round.

For two weeks each year, the Chicago Latino Film Festival becomes a hub for powerful debates about issues of social and political importance in the United States and Latin America. This has been a goal for Vargas and Lilia Delgado, chair of the board of directors for Chicago Latino Cinema. The films are chosen in large part, they said, because of "how accurately they reflect current or historical situations" throughout the hemisphere.[15] In the festival's early years, there were films about immigration that referenced the Immigration Reform and Control Act, the civil wars in Central America that led hundreds of thousands of Central Americans to seek refuge in the United States, and the AIDS crisis ripping through Latinx communities. In the early twenty-first century, there have been films about border enforcement, the construction of a wall between the United States and Mexico, the multiplying understandings of Latinx identity, the financial crisis of 2008, and the impact on daily life of cell phones.

It is without a doubt energizing to experience and participate in these social, political, and historical debates in a public venue in the middle of Chicago.

For the two weeks of the festival, it is possible for the Latinx and non-Latinx attendees of the film festival to feel that Latinx culture and communities are the center of city life. Relatedly, the fact that approximately half of the festival's films are from Latin America, along with many of its attendees, highlights the hemispheric and transnational origins of Chicago's Latinx community, which challenges stubborn ideas that Latinxs are provincial or that they are all the same and come from the same place. Films that offer a quotidian display of a broad range of Latinxs producing and enjoying creative endeavors are part of how the film festival fights these common misperceptions.

Displaying the diversity of Chicago's Latinx community and of Latinxs in the United States and around the world more generally has been the most consistent objective of the Chicago Latino Film Festival from the very beginning. Through comedy, documentaries, romances, animation, political satire, and other genres, festival participants, Vargas has believed, would come to better understand who Latinxs were. He didn't know any better way than film, he said, "to let people know who we are and what are our values."[16] His mission to capture hearts and minds therefore was geared as much toward non-Latinxs as Latinxs themselves, and his desire for the films to portray the full humanity of Latinxs and Latin Americans implied his belief that at least some festivalgoers saw them as less than that. Screening films that addressed the human dilemmas faced by Latinxs and Latin Americans and selecting only films that captured their humanity have been two more constants of the festival since its founding in the mid-1980s.

What were the films charged with this burdensome task of changing how Americans viewed Latinxs, and where did the films come from? In many ways, like the festival itself, the diversity of the films was the whole point. An article from the festival's earlier years said that the films ranged from "dramas to roguish comedies, political satires to social documentaries."[17] Some of the films were made in and were about Chicago. One titled *Silent Shame* was about the AIDS crisis in Chicago, told through the story of two lovers and based on "field research" in the city's AIDS clinics. Another, titled *Rudy Lozano*, was about a Mexican American who ran for alderman in 1982 and was murdered the very next year.[18] Another still was titled *Immigrant Nation! The Battle for the Dream*, about the Mexican-born immigrant Elvira Arellano, who found sanctuary in the Adalberto United Methodist Church in Humboldt Park, and immigrant rights activism more broadly.[19] Even these films made in and about Chicago for the most part represented local varieties of episodes that most Latinx communities in the United States experienced as well. They were not particularly midwestern, even if they were set in the Midwest.

But the vast majority of films arrived from every corner of the Americas to give festival audiences an expansive view of what it meant to be Latinx in Chicago and the United States more broadly. In the late 1980s, the films were about Panama, Mexico, Chile, Colombia, the US-Mexico borderlands, and other places. Early festivals highlighted the work of Spanish filmmakers, including Pedro Almodovar, Spain's "leading comic talent," and Luis Buñuel, the Spanish surrealist who worked with the artist Salvador Dalí. In 1987 they were about subjects as various as the musician Ruben Blades, the artist Frida Kahlo, the dictator Augusto Pinochet, Juan Seguín, a Tejano who fought at the Alamo, and the Mexican writer Octavio Paz, as well as the Colombian author Gabriel García Márquez.[20] In 1988 they included a documentary about a Haitian poet living in Brooklyn, a musical comedy about 1940s Rio de Janeiro, a biopic about Simón Bolívar, a drama about forty citizens of the Dominican Republic who stowed away in a boat headed for the United States, a "docudrama" about African slaves in nineteenth-century Latin America, and so many other topics.

That is, films were about Latin America's cultural and literary icons, contemporary politics, and historical episodes throughout Latin America that, seen together, gave viewers a sense of the transnational and hemispheric influences that shaped Latinx identity in the late twentieth century. *Frida, naturaleza viva* (Frida still life), a 1983 film by the Mexican director Paul Leduc that debuted in the United States at the 1987 festival, was the first biopic about "Latin America's most popular artist." Also at the 1987 festival, the Australian David Bradbury's documentary, *Chile, hasta cuando* (Chile, when will it end?), was about the horrors of the Pinochet dictatorship in 1985, when an 8.0 earthquake killed two hundred and injured more than two thousand Chileans, and when the politically motivated murder of three opposition leaders caused a national and international scandal. For the non-Latinx festivalgoers from Chicago who saw these films, the message would have been clear that the history, culture, and politics of the city's Latinx residents were shaped by places and ideas far beyond the city itself.

The films Vargas selected have displayed his main beliefs about Latinxs in the United States. Amid rising fears of undocumented Mexican immigrants, Cuba's *marielitos* making landfall in southern Florida, and drug smuggling across the US-Mexico border and the Caribbean Sea, the films at the festival showed Latinxs in a different light. Their cultural influences could be traced back to Spain. They were attuned to political developments throughout the hemisphere, lamenting human rights abuses in Chile and the Central American wars that led to the mass movement of refugees. They also appreciated art and literature produced by Latin American masters. They were historically informed about the imperial contests between the United States and Latin America that helped forge Latinx populations and senses of self. The mayor of Chicago, the city's megarich, and the festival's corporate donors would gain from these films an understanding of the deep histories and humanity of peoples of Latin American descent, especially those residing in the United States and Chicago in particular. With such an understanding, the hope was that they would not possibly believe some of the things they saw on television or heard on the radio, that all Latinxs are poor immigrants, drug dealers, or criminals of one sort or another.

Therefore, beyond the creation of a hemispheric and even transatlantic Latinx identity—one that included Latin Americans and Europeans—the Chicago Latino Film Festival helped to create a distinctly cosmopolitan Latinx identity. The Latinx attendees who came from Chicago, other US cities, and throughout Latin America and even Europe had means, either because they could afford to make the long trek to Chicago or because they were upwardly mobile Latinxs from Chicago who could afford passes to the festival.[21] Passes to the film cost a considerable sum, so at least some interested in participating have been excluded by the expense of attending.

The Cuban American author Achy Obejas, who in the early 1990s worked as a reporter for the *Chicago Tribune*, described the scene at the 1993 Chicago Latino Film Festival as principally about hobnobbing. She wrote, "Anybody who's anybody in the Hispanic community seemed to have turned out for Chicago Latino Cinema's annual film fest." The films and all of the events, like the opening gala, were completely sold out. "Chicago's young Hispanic professional elite was certainly present," she wrote in an almost curious tone, as if she were surprised at the networking and opportunism on display in the name of celebrating what it meant to be Latinx in Chicago and beyond. She quoted a Spanish filmmaker who said, "My god, it's a schmooze fest." He showed her his fistful of business cards to demonstrate the connections he had made—an extensive global network of Latinxs networked with heavyweight paper.[22] Even for Latin American and Latinx professionals who had the resources to travel from far and near to attend the Chicago Latino Film Festival, such opportunities for networking, community formation, and placemaking were few and far between. I did not look into how Chicago's "Hispanic professional elite" engaged with, supported, and built up the city's Latinx community when they were not at the festival—whether they saw the festival as an opportunity merely for their own professional advancement or believed that it benefited Chicago's broader Latinx community by performing middle-class respectability at the same time that the films drew attention to real challenges faced by Latinxs in Chicago and beyond.

No matter how expansive the Chicago Latino Film Festival's vision of *latinidad*, it has only represented a slice of what it means to be Latinx in the city, and with such a large and diverse Latinx population, it's unlikely that any single example of Latinx placemaking could hope to do anything more.

The films themselves have presented difficult subjects with a great deal of complexity. But as a gathering, the festival is ephemeral, located primarily in the well-to-do downtown business district, with a target audience that, in equal measure, is Latinx and non-Latinx. As Vargas has long insisted, one of the main goals of the festival was to change the ideas of non-Latinxs about Latinx people. He has wanted to show them as fully human, as members of complicated communities with internal contradictions. If the films he and others selected could show Latinx communities in all their complexity, non-Latinx viewers might come to see Latinxs as not all that different from them. And if the humanity and complexity of Latinxs were recognized, well, then that might lead to real change, visibility, and opportunities for Latinxs in Chicago, including Colombians, Ecuadorians, Peruvians, and other Latinxs who are even less represented but nevertheless present as a part of the city's Latinx community.

If judging the success or failure of the Chicago Latino Film Festival depends on whether it has changed the minds and then the behavior of non-Latinxs toward Latinxs, then the results have been mixed. Over the lifetime of the Chicago Latino Film Festival, Latinxs in Chicago have experienced the same discrimination to which Latinxs throughout the region and across the United States have been subjected. And if the conditions of Latinxs in the city have improved, it is as much the result of efforts of grassroots arts organizations, labor organizers, and immigrant rights activists as of the Chicago Latino Film Festival.

Similarly, if we are to judge the Chicago Latino Film Festival by how much or how little it has represented or served the Latinx community in Chicago—and this is indeed the litmus by which Latinx placemakers have often been judged—then this measure would also suggest that results have not been uniformly positive. To be sure, Vargas and the other organizers of the festival have made it possible for Chicago's Latinx communities to participate in festival events by organizing some screenings in Latinx neighborhoods and by busing thousands of Latinx youth to the festival to see some of the films. According to Vargas, trips to the festival by Latinx youth were consciousness-raising experiences; they taught Latinx youth about their histories, the places where they and their families had come from. The fact that 90 percent of the films were in Spanish and Portuguese was a "revelation" to them. Providing enlightening experiences for Latinx children in Chicago has always been part of the goal for Vargas, that the festival might serve as an "opportunity" for Latinx youth to learn about the diversity of Latinx cultures and the possibility of connecting with their own heritage.[23]

Nevertheless, very few of the movies that get screened have been made by Latinx filmmakers from Chicago or are about Chicago. The festival takes place at a theater that is hardly representative of Latinx space in Chicago. Its branding seems more in line with the city government's desire to project an image of Chicago as a global city than to reflect and uplift Chicago's Latinx community. And what Achy Obejas wrote about the film festival's galas more than twenty-five years ago rings true today. They are still fancy affairs where you would be likely to find Chicago's Latinx middle class schmoozing over cocktails and hors d'oeuvres. It should be noted, of course, that Chicago's Hispanic professional elite are no less members of Chicago's Latinx community, and gatherings attended by them are still examples of Latinx placemaking in the city, even if they are distinguished by their economic and socially upward mobility.

But because the Chicago Latino Film Festival is not an example of Latinx placemaking akin to physical spaces visited or otherwise occupied by Latinxs, it forces us to think about it as a Latinx place a little bit differently. Even though Latinxs attend the event and do occupy the space of the festival and related gatherings for the festival's duration, the festival primarily makes space for Latinxs in Chicago discursively by expanding our understanding of what *latinidad* means and by endeavoring to change minds about who Latinxs are. This effort maps out a different kind of Latinx place than more physical locations that are opened year-round and serve members of Chicago's Latinx community every day. Unfortunately, the representations of *latinidad* at the festival quickly disappear from sight and from mind.

The Chicago Latino Film Festival has combatted discrimination by displaying the diversity, complexity, and depth of Latinx and Latin American culture. In 1988 Vargas, according to the *Chicago Tribune*, said that many Americans "associate Latinos with the *barrio*, welfare and washing dishes." Instead, he and Lilia Delgado, the chair of Chicago Latino Cinema's newly formed board of directors, said they wanted to show people what "life is like" for both Latin Americans in their home countries and Latinxs in the United States. Ultimately, they wanted to "gain some recognition and respect" for Latinxs in Chicago, and they hoped that the films they showed would "help Latino children develop self-esteem and pride for their heritage."[24] In a 1990 interview with the paper, just as the festival was becoming better known not only in Chicago but also among filmmakers and aficionados throughout the United States and Latin America, Vargas said, "I'm very much interested in breaking stereotypes." For Vargas, film was the best medium for changing Americans' minds about Latinxs because it hit them emotionally. Films touched all of the viewer's senses. As Vargas put it almost twenty years later, in 2009, "A good film has the power to make you smell the food."[25]

Vargas and other festival organizers have said that they aspired to show non-Latinxs who Latinxs are, that they are good at more things than "doing laundry at a hotel, cutting the grass, babysitting, picking fruits and doing construction."[26] His guiding idea has been that by depicting the humanity and emotional depth of Latin Americans and Latinxs from throughout the hemisphere, the festival will combat stereotypes that have served to marginalize Latinxs, immigrants, and Latin Americans socially, politically, and economically. The Chicago Latino Film Festival has in fact established a cultural geography and framework for how to understand *latinidad* in Chicago, the United States, and the world. The Chicago Latino Film Festival has helped to create a space for Latinxs in Chicago through the repetition of its staging year in and year out, even in the midst of the coronavirus pandemic.

Mapping out the cultural geography of *latinidad* is a laudable goal, one that will always have a place alongside other instances of Latinx placemaking that aim to claim space for Latinxs in the Midwest. Within Chicago, the Chicago Latino Film Festival—and its parent organization, the International Latino Cultural Center—can therefore be compared with other institutions such as the National Museum of Mexican Art and the Puerto Rican Cultural Center. Even if the benefits of the Chicago Latino Film Festival are less visible or tangible for Latinxs than brick-and-mortar organizations that more directly serve Chicago's Latinx communities, it should be understood as a complement to other examples of placemaking that also seek to improve the lives of Chicago's Latinx residents; the film festival is like other media organizations that promote justice for Latinxs, even if it goes about its work in different ways.

The Chicago Latino Film Festival has created an almost impossibly broad and cosmopolitan Latinx identity, one that is local and hemispheric, particular and diverse, articulated in Portuguese and Spanish, and located in a midwestern city with established Latinx neighborhoods but also rooted in a downtown commercial center traversed but not necessarily inhabited by Chicago's Latinx populations. But instead of a Latinx identity coming apart at the seams, the Latinx identity created by the Chicago Latino Film Festival is one that is defined by these contradictions, managing to corral them all simultaneously under one very big umbrella—the festival itself. As such, the Chicago Latino Film Festival has done more than demonstrate the humanity of Latinxs in Chicago and the Americas, that they are not only janitors, dishwashers, and menial laborers. It has helped to create a hemispheric and cosmopolitan Latinx identity that operated alongside other definitions of what it meant to be Latinx in the Midwest, as well as a place for Latinxs in Chicago that may complement but will always only offer a limited view of what it means to be Latinx in the city. The vision of *latinidad* represented by the Chicago Latino Film Festival is therefore expansive and myopic at the same time.

Notes

1. Roger Almendarez, "Representational Scales: Latinx Media Production in Chicago, 1953–2012" (PhD diss., Northwestern University, 2018), chap. 3.

2. Elizabeth Barrios, "The Chicago Latino Film Festival: Shaping Latin American / Latino Cinema in the United States," *Transnational Cinemas*, July 2018, 1–15.

3. See the introduction to Cindy Hing-Yuk Wong, *Film Festivals: Culture, People, and Power on the Global Screen* (New Brunswick, NJ: Rutgers University Press, 2011).

4. Arlene Dávila, *Latino Spin: Public Image and the Whitewashing of Race* (New York: New York University Press, 2008), 71.

5. Teresa Córdova, "Harold Washington and the Rise of Latino Electoral Politics in Chicago, 1982–1987," in *Chicano Politics and Society in the Late Twentieth Century*, ed. David Montejano (Austin: University of Texas Press, 1998).

6. Chicago Latino Film Festival, New York Latino Film Festival, Miami International Film Festival (https://chicagolatinofilmfestival.org/about-us/; https://nylatino filmfestival.com/2021/about/; https://miamifilmfestival.com/festivals/).

7. Judy Hevrdejs, "Reel Winner, Seasoning Gives Latino Film Fest a Hot Lineup," *Chicago Tribune*, September 20, 1988, E3.

8. Judy Hevrdejs, "A Passion for Moving Pictures," *Chicago Tribune*, September 27, 1990, N_B1.

9. "Festival to Showcase Culture, People," *Chicago Daily Herald*, April 12, 2009, "Reflejos" section, 10.

10. Javacia Harris Bowser, "A Reel Legacy," *Hispanic Executive*, 2011.

11. Ibid.

12. Thomas Sugrue, *The Origins of the Urban Crisis: Race and Inequality in Postwar Detroit*, updated ed. (Princeton, NJ: Princeton University Press, 2014).

13. Sandoval-Strausz, *Barrio America*.

14. On the growth of Rogers Park's Latinx community, see Peña, *Performing Piety*.

15. Dean Golemis, "Latin American Diversity Captured in Films at Festival," *Chicago Tribune*, September 23, 1988, G6.

16. Judy Hevrdejs, "A Passion for Moving Pictures," *Chicago Tribune*, September 27, 1990, N_B1.

17. Golemis, "Latin American Diversity," G6.

18. "Festival to Showcase Culture, People," *Chicago Daily Herald*, April 12, 2009, "Reflejos" section, 10.

19. Elena Ferrarin, "Lights, Camera, Action! Local Filmmakers Share Their Inspiration, Struggles," *Chicago Daily Herald*, April 11, 2010, "Reflejos" section, 18.

20. Dave Kehr, "Latino Film Fest Basks in Financial Bright Lights," *Chicago Tribune*, June 18, 1987, D14; Dave Kehr, "Through Latin Eyes," *Chicago Tribune*, September 22, 1989, CNA5.

21. Judy Hevrdejs, "A Passion for Moving Pictures," *Chicago Tribune*, September 27, 1990, N_B1.

22. Achy Obejas, "It's Standing Room Only at Latino Cinema's Annual Fest," *Chicago Tribune*, September 26, 1993, E5.

23. Wendy Moncada, "Apoyo para el Festival de Cine Latino en Chicago," *Chicago Daily Herald*, February 17, 2013, "Reflejos" section, 32.

24. Golemis, "Latin American Diversity," G6.

25. "Festival to Showcase," 10.

26. Patrick McDonald, "Interview: Founder Pepe Vargas of Chicago Latino Film Festival on Closing Night, May 4, 2017," *HollywoodChicago.com*, May 4, 2017, http://www.hollywoodchicago.com/news/27491/interview-founder-pepe-vargas-of-chicago-latino-film-festival-on-closing-night-may-4-2017.

CHAPTER 14

Living Lakes

Performing Latinx and Black History

RAMÓN H. RIVERA-SERVERA

Moving Up North

This chapter concerns a contemporary performance piece about the histories of northward migration to the Midwest by African American and Latinx communities. It also explores the ways artists and scholars approach and tell the story of those who found possibilities and plenty of challenges as they sought to make place and advance a life in the region. Much like the historical narratives *The Living Lakes* as a performance explores, I draw on my own autoethnographic sense of motion, as I, too, arrived in the Midwest at a time of inhospitable atmospheric shifts in the Latinx geographies of this country. I open with my own narrative of travel into this geographic expanse and the placemaking Latinx studies enacts as a field of scholarly practice.

It is a scorching hot summer day in Phoenix, Arizona. It is May 2007, and my partner and I have just finished packing the last of our belongings into two compact vehicles. We are getting ready to caravan the eighteen-hundred-mile trek from the mountainous Sonoran Desert to the flat midwestern prairies and wetlands of the Chicago metro region. We are migrating for labor, a Mexican-born dance maker raised in the urban, coastal environs of the San Francisco Bay Area and a Puerto Rican–born and –raised dance and performance scholar, at times practitioner, who came into being within the urban/suburban routes of the San Juan metro region. Like many in our extended kin, this is not our first time on the move for the next gig, nor are our reasons for the move entirely about the greener pastures on the other side.

Arizona's heat this summer is atmospheric, but not just environmentally so. We are literally caught in the fire of hostile legislative efforts meant to make the significantly Indigenous and *mexicano* state increasingly more hostile to Latinx migration. It is three years before the infamous Support Our Law Enforcement and Safe Neighborhoods Act Arizona Senate Bill (AZ SB 1070) would attempt to unconstitutionally mobilize local police force and other state and county measures to aggressively pursue federal immigration law enforcement.[1] This will be one of the most aggressive legal assaults on undocumented immigrants to the United States and one of the most embarrassing moments in the state's recent history. However, the heat is already rising, as we are three years ahead of the Arizona Tax Payer and Citizen Protection Act (Proposition 200), a 2004 warm-up to SB 1070 requiring proof of citizenship to access state-managed social services. The Legal Arizona Workers Act, a legislative measure requiring heightened identity and work eligibility verification, is now being discussed at the Arizona legislature and will be approved by July 2007 and implemented in January 2008.

Yes, at a time when the housing market came crashing down and the legal obstacles to make a life in the Grand Canyon State went precipitously up for many, we packed our bags and left.[2] We were part of a mass exit that resulted in a 40 percent drop in the Mexican-born immigrant arrivals to the state after 2007.[3] Let me be clear, we were not undocumented migrants, as my partner's status was regularized in the 1980s during the amnesty approved by President Reagan, and my status as a colonial subject in Puerto Rico with citizenship granted, at minimum, safer access to cross-border mobility.[4] But these biographies easily disappeared into the everyday of practices of racism and xenophobia that characterized our environs, and we were indeed targeted within the collectivized "outsiderness" of our people. At the very university where we worked, during a technical rehearsal for one of his dance pieces about Mexican labor, my partner, demonstrating an elegantly abstracted rendition of cotton picking—one of Arizona's historic cash crops—as dance, was mockingly asked by the technical director in a theater full of students to "do the wetback pose."

We were not undocumented migrants, but we felt the heat just right. While Phoenix, much like the state of Arizona, is about 30 percent Latinx (with Mexicans representing the largest component part of the community at above 90 percent of the total Latinx population), its politics have been significantly dominated by Anglo-American social conservatism and libertarian attitudes toward economics and governance.[5] Anti-immigrant politics have taken center stage in Phoenix, as the capital city and intense legislative debates, as well as the public antics of agents such as Maricopa County sheriff Joe Arpaio, have fed the national airwaves with fresh fodder for xenophobic sentiments and actions nationally. As Latinx residents of this simmering anti-Mexican environ, we were indeed targets of quotidian hostility and felt the push out of its increasingly unhospitable political environment. So we set in motion into what felt like a mass exodus from the forty-eighth state.

Accounts of the slowdown of Mexican migration to the state among our circles of artists and activists tended to simply assume a southward directionality, even suggest a return border crossing. However, our anecdotal experience of that eighteen-hundred-mile drive also gave us a sense of a northern route. As we repeatedly encountered other Mexicanxs and Latinxs following the northbound route, the greetings while refilling gas, the complicit smiles while grabbing to-go tacos of varying quality along the changing landscapes, and the parking lot or hotel reception acknowledgments while overnighting at LaQuinta Inns created a sense of coordinated motion. The actual numbers do not exist to substantiate my claims about this move, about the significance of this journey. In fact, the Chicago metro region, like most metropolitan areas in 2007, would lose rather than gain a very significant percentage of Mexican population.[6] Nonetheless, our travel north to the Midwest felt like collective motion, an escape from the affective heat of Arizona. Our sense of space, our yearning for sure footing or safe emplacement overrode the demographic reality of our environs, rendering perceived and idealized space as our most bodily felt real. In this sense, our desirous dreaming for safe harbor was not unlike the accumulation of desires rendered in Tomás Rivera's short story "The Salamanders"[7] and so vividly recalled by Omar Valerio-Jiménez, Santiago Vaquera-Vázquez, and Claire F. Fox as a "future-oriented call for social justice."[8]

It was impossible, at least in our emotionally heightened journey, not to identify parallels with the Great Migration, which saw millions of African Americans escape the rural US South in search of better opportunities in the Northeast and Midwest from 1916 to 1970 and similar prior waves of Mexican migrants and other Latinx communities, including Puerto Ricans, who similarly ventured into the region since the early twentieth century in search of economic opportunity in the agricultural, industrial, and service industries of the Midwest, as so many chapters in this volume document. However, while we made our way to the midwestern mecca of Chicago with what felt at the time to be a mass of Brown exiles, African Americans were exiting our site of arrival, dissipating from the downtown core, pushed out by a political economy of racial expunction.[9] Decades of policy making to destroy large public housing complexes near the city center and biased practices in policing to further "manage" Black circulation in the metropolis, combined with increased lack of opportunity in education, employment, healthcare and basic survival needs such as food and leisure, gave a Chicago broad and cold shoulder to Black possibility. Even in the midst of the Barack Obama hope machine, which resulted in the election of the first African American president in the history of the United States, Black Chicago was under siege. For us, Phoenix was heating up in hatred toward Latinx folks (conveniently at a time when the armies of Brown labor were no longer necessary to sustain the new housing economy, halted by the bursting of the bubble).[10] Chicago was simply becoming chilly toward Black life (conveniently at a time when downtown real estate speculation struggled to maintain its boom despite the impending expansion of the housing crisis to the Midwest).

Disciplinary Arrivals, or How We Map Our Place in/through Movement

I open this chapter with a return to this 2007 journey—the danced performance of labor and the accompanying racist attack that set in motion our move to the Midwest—because it highlights both the spatial and affective qualities of my own orientations as a scholar, then recently arrived to the Midwest, and now more than a decade later assuming the analysis of its significance as marking a Latinx choreography and geography of placemaking in/to the region. That is, I can only understand my situated place as a Latinx scholar doing Latinx studies in the US Midwest if I turn to the moves and movements that have brought me here. These traveled trajectories, the qualitative nature of how I've moved along them, have shaped my sense of how I have come to understand this place as home. Similarly, the two artists whose collaborative work I focus on in this chapter engage with narratives of departure toward and arrival into the Midwest. These narratives and the performance works that result from them are shaped by a political economy of labor and anchored in an affective economy of race. More specifically, they explore the ways in which African Americans and Latinxs arriving into the region or born in the region as a result of earlier arrivals experienced the relationship between labor, leisure, and the environs of the midwestern expanse through choreography. I find in this collaborative work both aesthetic and affective insights that are useful to a broader theorization of placemaking in the Latinx Midwest.

In what follows, I turn to *The Living Lakes* project, a dance performance collaboration between Joel Valentín-Martínez and Anita González, in order to pursue the role of the aesthetic (movement and choreography in particular) as important analytics for understanding Latinx placemaking. Admittedly, I am also interested in pursuing such kinesthetic orientation beyond the interpretive exercise of a close reading in order to theorize placemaking more broadly. I apply the traveled itineraries and the qualitative nuance of the choreographic to more accurately mark the ongoingness of the very project of making a midwestern Latinx studies manifest as a historically deep and situated insistence in the durational presence of Latinx populations in the region. However, I am just as invested in how these kinesthetic logics shape our understanding of the moves and movements that continue to shape and reshape such social, cultural, and affective formations as *latinidad*, even in the institutionalized scholarly forms our academic efforts take, including publications such as this one that seek to emplace and sustain Latinx studies in and as of the Midwest.

The first of these two artists is Joel Valentín-Martínez, a dancer and choreographer of Mexican descent who was born in the valley of Lake Chapala in Jalisco, Mexico, and raised in the San Francisco Bay Area, who performed for fifteen years with New York–based Jamaican choreographer Garth Fagan's legendary Afro-modern dance troupe and has developed a second career as a choreographer based in Chicago. He develops research-based dance projects often focused on Latinx political and economic history, especially as they shape migration. His technique is grounded in Afro-Mexican aesthetic frameworks of *son jarocho*, a musical style typical of the coastal state of Veracruz, Mexico, and the Afromodern vocabulary of Fagan technique. Full disclosure, Valentín-Martínez is also my life partner, the dancer targeted as the wetback in my opening example, and my companion in that long drive into the Midwest. He served on the faculty at Northwestern University's Department of Theatre and is now on the faculty at the University of Texas at Austin.

The other artist is Anita González, an African American dancer (of Afro-Cuban and Bahamian heritage), choreographer, director, deviser, librettist, and all-around performance maker, as well as scholar. A multigenre artist known as an early performer in Jawole Willa Zolar's legendary New York–based Black feminist dance troupe Urban Bush Women, she is an expert in Afro-Mexican dance practices of *jarocho* and has published two monographs on the subject.[11] Counting with a long life and professional experience between New York and Florida, she was professor of theater at the University of Michigan before joining the faculty at Georgetown University in Washington, DC.

The collaboration undertaken by this duo of performance makers and academics, invested as they are in Latinx and Afrodiasporic aesthetics, especially between Mexico and the United States, and with their storied practice in the New York–based Black dance scene, focused on developing a project about labor and migration in the Midwest, and it prompted me to reflect on my and our own work as academics engaging the region. Central to my query is precisely an invitation to us to make sense in both literal and conceptual ways of our routes to and arrivals into the Midwest, of our desire to map and emplace this place as a Latinx place. Our documentation of practices of placemaking, as well as our constitution of that place through practices of academic framing, narration, and, ultimately, transference of those frameworks and narratives to our students through our pedagogy, makes the Midwest Latinx through travel. That is, I keep coming back to our own collective arrival or what it means to desire the realization of a Latinx Midwest from the vantage point of our traveled *latinidades*: Valentín-Martínez's and González's as artists venturing into this exploration, and my own as a scholar trying to make sense of the Midwest while also making the Midwest in my own narrative account of their work and the region as it emerges in my description and interpretation. A project about Latinx labor migration in the Midwest and its rendition in aesthetic performance directs me to think about our collective labor migrations to the midwestern academy and, as is the case for so many of us in this collaborative project focused on expressive practices and cultural institutions, our pursuit of the aesthetic as our principal academic labor commitment. I am interested in teasing here how the Midwest is both a situated and a traveled site, how it emerges as origin, background, even environment in relation to our movement toward and within it. As such, the choreographic as an aesthetic analytic for understanding and for putting things into motion becomes my primary optic. Dance, the literal scripting and rendition of choreography for spectatorial contemplation, is my object of study.

The Living Lakes: The Social Work of Aesthetics

The Living Lakes, as this Valentín-Martínez and González collaborative project is titled, is a dance performance piece and also a research query into the choreographies of labor migration and leisure of African American and Latinx experience in the Midwest. It proclaims that the lakes are more than static landscape, that they are alive or that they contain life within and around them. This creative research project was initiated in the academy as part of a project intent in pursuing the Midwest in and through performance and thus far has circulated its representation of the Latinx Midwest beyond the academy through an experimental performance platform in Chicago.

The first collaborative residency for *The Living Lakes* was hosted in Ann Arbor during the summer of 2015 under the auspices of the Perform Midwest umbrella, organized by Holly Hughes, a professor of art at the University of Michigan. Perform Midwest brought together three teams of artists and scholars from across the Midwest to explore different critical aspects of the Midwest through performance. Valentín-Martínez and González worked with dance scholar Cindy García on the histories of African American and Latinx labor migration to the Midwest.[12]

The collaborative research project between Valentín-Martínez and González continued for another three years with a rotating roster of artistic collaborators who participated in a second residency at Northwestern University and a Michigan workshop in 2016; a workshop production in Chicago's Links Hall, one of the region's longest-running experimental performance spaces, in 2017; and a second Chicago program at Links Hall in 2018.[13] For each iteration of the project, González and Valentín-Martínez assembled a team of musicians, dancers/performers, and image makers to tackle anew the same archive of histories, images, sounds, and movements that iconically represented labor migrancy in the region: post–Mexican Revolution northward migration at the top of the twentieth century and 1940s African American migration into the region.[14] Along with these two large historical movements, they have pursued the quotidian experiences, or lower-frequency movements, that accompany historical change, such as less historically marked migrations, encounters with the new landscape and climate, searches for food that recall or assist in making this new place home, pursuit of leisure as respite from the stresses of everyday survival, and the articulation of a sense of place, of community, from the traveled history and situated practices of becoming Latinx or Black in the Midwest. Anchoring all of these procedures of travel, arrival, and transformation of this new destination into a place of belonging is the aesthetic not just as a tool for recording and representing these experiences that accumulate as historical event but as the very social procedure through which history becomes palpable, experiential in and as performance. This social work of aesthetics is the placemaking strategy that *The Living Lakes* identifies and models for us as both analytic and methodology of Latinx placemaking.

In her essay on cultural poesis in everyday life, performance studies and dance scholar Judith Hamera reminds us that "the social work of aesthetics is especially central to performance, where the labors of creation and the dynamics of consumption are explicitly communal and corporeal, and where corporeality and sociality are remade as surely as a formal event may be produced."[15] This is precisely what I believe dance as an aesthetic practice both unravels within and choreographs the social achieves in González and Valentín-Martínez's collaboration. Shaping both the research process of the collective of artists involved in mapping the history of Latinx and African American migration to the region and the representational strategies for relating those histories to wider audiences, the aesthetic functioned as both a procedure of knowing, of becoming acquainted with place and its history, and an exercise in externalizing that collectively attained knowledge. The aesthetic served a double function of what anthropologist and performance scholar Dorinne Kondo has described as the capacity of the aesthetic to "make worlds through form and narrative."[16] As such, placemaking in *The Living Lakes* took place in at least two registers: the internal social world of aesthetic labor undertaken by the collective of artists to learn and conceptualize their environment through their choreographic procedures, and the formal public performance that circulated the work of that first effort outward before others. This effort was grounded in an understanding of both the geography before them and the aesthetic as process and platform not simply as predetermined objects but as dynamic catalysts for the social collectivity that emerges from their engagement and activation.

González and Valentín-Martínez's description of the project connects Hamera's embodied understanding of the aesthetic in the quotidian realm, which I extend to the exercise of art making, with Kondo's enthusiasm for the propositional potential of the worlds animated by the work (and the practices) of art. They explain it on their project website thusly: "*The Living Lakes* considers the Great Lakes as connectors and sites of conflict and dissonance among multi-ethnic communities. *Living Lakes* examines economies of labor, commerce and transport through projections coupled with theatrical sound and dance movement." Working through iconic images and narratives rendered in visual, literary, or historical archives that locate "historic moments of ethnic presence in the American Midwest," they query the ways "African American and Mexican American people find refuge, solace, work and pleasure in the frozen landscape of the Great Lakes region between 1910 and 1930." Bringing their conceptualization of the lakes as "connectors and sites" to the procedures of "theatrical sound and dance movement" positions quotidian and artistic dynamics for understanding geography as dynamically resulting from experiences of movement. Furthermore, understanding these choreographies to be shaped by "economies of labor, commerce and transport" articulates an intimacy between political economy and the aesthetic rendition of place in both quotidian and formal theatrical realms, the worldmaking power of the aesthetic both Hamera and Kondo are so invested in championing in their respective arguments about performance.[17]

I now turn to three critical moments in *The Living Lakes* when the aesthetic, in quotidian and presentational realms, productively mined dynamics of placemaking, both historical and contemporary, to produce a version of the Midwest as resulting from Latinx and African American migratory experience. In turning to the performance procedures activated by González and Valentín-Martínez—staging scenes of origin and arrival in relation to landscape, the encounter between the performer's body and the historical archive, and choreographed contiguity between the work and leisure rendered in the piece—I hope to illustrate how in *The Living Lakes*, González and Valentín-Martínez mine a history of placemaking while venturing themselves into a practice of placemaking in and through aesthetic and academic labor. Ultimately, it is this intersection between the deeply localized research into the history of place (and the placemaking of others) and the speculative process of creatively animating our work and experience in place in the present (artistic, academic, and otherwise) that I argue we share as academics of the Latinx Midwest, similarly venturing into encounters and conceptions of Latinx placemaking and advancing practices and concepts of our own.

Choreographing Arrivals: Landscape Contexts and Migratory Logics

The 2018 version of *The Living Lakes* opens at Lake Michigan's shoreline. The stage is bare and silent. It awakens with the shrill vibration emergent from rubbing slowly in vertical motion against the cymbal's edge and a chilling deep blue light shining from above. Still in the midst of partial darkness, we hear the sounds of bare feet stepping against hardwood floors and begin to make out the silhouettes of bodies, slowly becoming illuminated and visible as the lights warm and performers strut back and forth from each side of the stage, crossing each other center stage, in groups of yet-undetermined numbers and identities. As the lights make the two musicians upstage right visible, we begin to discern five performers who reach the front of the stage and assume a line formation facing the audience. Performers stand straight, arms relaxed, slightly tugged against the sides of the body, and they face forward past the audience, staring longingly into an imaginary horizon as a soft insistent note on the keyboard marks their spatial limit and invites them into a careful tilting of their head down toward an exploration of their feet and the terrain immediately before and beyond them. We are at the threshold between water and land.

Performers slowly progress onto a balance on the left leg, slightly raising their right foot, intimating an accompanying shoulder protraction, as if to signal a step forward. Instead of stepping forth, all four performers point their feet and gently lower them toward the imaginary edge in unison, quickly flexing their legs upward and backward closer to the hip at the moment of contact with the floor to sustain a balance on the felt leg. They arch forward, crossing arms with a slight shrug of the shoulders as if reacting to sudden contact with a freezing cold surface. We have arrived not only at the water's edge but also at the initiation of a new shared experience with place, both socially and environmentally. That is, the difference announced in the opening scene, where our partial view animated a plurality of bodies and trajectories that introduced the ensemble in motion with and past each other, is here equalized before a line that defines this collective of humans standing before us from a phenomenon larger than and different from whatever the elements that distinguished them from one another just seconds prior. Movement toward the lake's threshold has literally, in the choreographic progression of the piece, consolidated the ensemble in their difference as a unit of shared experience. This is a collective experience of movement toward the shoreline, of the social inaugurated by the coincidence of arrival and by their experience of contact with the environment.

The commonality of experience based on this choreographed arrival does not default into a homogenizing gesture. Instead, the piece goes on to pursue the frictions and pleasures of intersecting intimacies across shared territories. Dancers slowly lower their feet and return to a straightened back position as they begin to walk backward, retreating from the audience, relaxing arms to the sides, and breaking the line formation to initiate more individual explorations of space, still slow, still skeptically shocked by the coldness of that first contact. Light levels rise enough for the audience to note the diverse racial makeup of the cast—three visibly Afro-descended, one Asian-presenting, and a white-presenting performer. Along with a Black and a white presenting a duo of musicians, the cast challenges monolithic renditions of light brownness mythologized as the racial imaginary of *latinidad* and introduces a wider range of possible landings for the ethnic umbrella *latinidad* as the term often invites.

González and Valentín-Martínez's pursuit of the shared experiences of African American and Latinx migration into the shores of Lake Michigan deploys choreographic methodologies in hopes of unearthing a shared sensorium of arrival into the region and an equally embodied experience of the practices of placemaking that have allowed both communities to sustain lives and thrive despite what can frequently seem an unwelcome atmosphere, as documented in so much work in this volume. To that end, the sensorial attunement to the midwestern landscape, sensing bodily the geographic and natural phenomena of the region, became a key dramaturgical device for the working collective, as well as for the formal representational choices of the piece. Starting with their initial developmental residency in Ann Arbor in 2015, the team of collaborators incorporated both archival research (to which I will turn shortly) along with site visits along the shores of Lake Michigan, including an extensive research trip to Michigan's Upper Peninsula.

During their site visits, collaborators gathered visual material and walked and experienced bodily in situ the range of landscapes that comprise the region. These embodied investigations informed choreographic choices. This is especially noticeable in the sequence that follows. As performers begin to explore space more freely, they also become less individuated as humans by assuming, in movement, the shapes and motions of the landscape they have initially encountered at the lake's threshold, which coincides with the same line that divides the performance space from the audience. The directionality of northward Latinx and African American migration first orients, in the choreographic arrangement of the piece, toward the shore and its horizon at the opening of the piece. The audience, placed on the other side of the shoreline, in the direction of the imaginary horizon, witnesses the affective charge of that longing for an uncertain but desired futurity as dancers look past us in performed embodied expectation before the retraction prompted by the geographic limit and the environmental assault of the freezing lake. But matters are sure to turn.

"Cold winds blowing, blowing / Ice sheets gather-thicken," recites one of the performers standing next to the musicians as dancers continue to explore movement around them in arm extensions that lead to S-curve swiveling—from head to neck to hip to knee—of the entire body. The movement is meant to evoke winds, grasses and water moving to the forces of them, and ice formations—in water and land—moving and resisting movement from the forces of wind and water. Counterbalancing these curvaceous movement routines, initially individual and now in unison, the ensemble progresses along the performance area and slowly lowers the level of the action until all are on the floor, replicating the S-curve routines on a transversal plane. "Cold winds blowing blowing / Alas alas / Women sleep death sleep / Children sleep long sleep / Alas alas / Long wounds / Snow wounds / Wind blowing, blowing," continues to proclaim our performer, now to a sustained jazz beat on the cymbal, as she progresses to the front of the playing area and the rest of the performers slowly stand up and exit the stage.

This scene of nature mimicry, of kinesthetically performing qualities of environmental phenomena both to index our orientation to place and to narrate our embodied experience of it, serves both as an important articulation of the landscapes that constitute place and the logics of migration central to the choreographic strategy of the piece. That is, landscape stands in for a difference that is not just about nature but that signals the migratory movements that characterize the arrival of both African Americans and Latinx communities into the region. This is a critical positioning of the experience of *The Living Lakes* as a work that understands the predicament of Black and Brown experience in the region as resulting from colonial settlement histories. In fact, the opening sequence I have been describing, which takes no more than four minutes into the forty-five-minute piece, was also the result of significant dramaturgical adjustment over the four-year period of the project.

Initially meant to mark Indigenous presence in the region, earlier versions of the project similarly sought to inaugurate the performance with a scene that squarely announced landscape as intricately in relation to human presence. In the 2015 workshop, the piece opened as the above-cited poem was heard without musical accompaniment, as unembodied amplified sound on an empty stage. As the poem unfolds, describing the region's landscape and animal and human experience of it, Potawatomi performer and community historian Jefferson Ballew stands center stage, saluting the four cardinal points in full tribal ceremonial dress as he gradually removes pieces of his regalia and carefully places them on a mannequin torso stand center stage. We come to know landscape as the traditional image of Indigenous presence in ceremonial practice is transformed into the more familiar, quotidian image of a man in sweats and T-shirt, still donning a roach and other ritual objects. At the poem's conclusion, Ballew kneels before the audience in salute, and lights go out before a section of urban arrivals to an upbeat jazz rhythm ensues.

Native American studies and history professor Philip Deloria, then on faculty at the University of Michigan, participated as a member of the research team that informed the project during this early part of its development. At a postperformance talk-back he expressed some concern that this opening scene risked collapsing Native American presence simply into an "originary" natural presence, much like landscape, without accounting for a contemporary continuity. In this sense the ascription of proximity to the natural as a choreographic procedure ran the risk of problematically exacerbating long-held stereotypical repertoires that assumed Indigenous character to be collapsible with natural phenomena.[18] Deloria commented, "To what extent are Indian people going to be represented as being in nature or of nature? And as human beings living in nature in a certain kind of relationship that is one way of thinking about it. Indians who get conflated with nature and turn into sand and trees and things like that it becomes a different kind of thing."[19]

While the scene was meant to signal a Native presence that held both traditional and contemporary investments in place through the sequential shift in costuming, the embodied methodology to experience and stage nature as a significant aspect of midwestern experience was not intended to be exclusively applied to Native American representation. In fact, González and Valentín-Martínez were invested in exploring the ways in which embodied research through the somatic procedures of choreography allowed the creative team, and ultimately audiences witnessing the resulting work, to engage with the history of migration from a different, more intimate and critically conceived spatiotemporal framework.[20] Thinking about African American and Latinx experience as marked by much longer histories of movement (forced migrations from slavery to survival relocations) and by the much slower appearance of the effects of an environmental degradation and violence that have accumulated since those early experiences, they went about adopting a nonlinear approach to their rendition of time and a choreographic logic to their understanding of place.

Detaching this choreographic procedure from the iconicity of the Indigenous regalia and the ritual invocation of the directional salute opened up the possibilities of what theorist Donna J. Haraway has called for in the invitation to a curious practice, to think with other beings, human and nonhuman alike. These insistences on being with require a focus on temporal layering in order to remain situated, as Haraway explains: "Neither the critters nor the people could have existed or could endure without each other in ongoing, curious practices. Attached to ongoing pasts, they bring each other forward in thick presents and still possible futures; they stay with the trouble in speculative fabulation."[21] Becoming sand or trees or of nature, as Deloria worried in his postperformance commentary, was not an exercise in representational stereotyping but a choreographic attempt at being in or, better yet, being with and part of nature and caring for its, our, well-being.

In their introduction to a recently published volume on ecocriticism in Latin American and Latinx cultural production, Ilka Kressner, Ana María Mutis, and Elizabeth M. Pettinaroli invoke Rob Nixon's concept of slow violence in order to identify the "specific form of environmental destruction that unfolds gradually over long periods of time and is dispersed beyond national boundaries, ecosystems, and elements."[22] Thinking specifically about the ways African American and Latinx arrivals into the Midwest are shaped by extended histories of colonization and the dispersed map these histories have grafted onto a globalized migratory landscape, and understanding the ways in which these experiences have environmental implications slow to manifest in nature and on the body alike, González and Valentín-Martínez insisted on an articulation of this mutuality of body and environment. They did not focus exclusively on the negativity a concept like slow violence might intimate as an analytic but with an awareness that community formation in the region was undergirded by a significant number of traumatic histories and contemporary violence. Rendering this complexity required an aesthetic mode that allowed for those linkages between historical accounts and contemporary contexts to be properly held onstage.

Omi Osun Joni L. Jones's theorization of the jazz aesthetic is helpful in understanding the ways in which the piece renders this temporality consequential to the emplacement of the Midwest nonlinearly.[23] Describing a mode of performance practice grounded in the aesthetics of jazz, Yoruba spirituality, and a Black feminist and queer politics, Jones adopts African performance scholar Margaret Thompson Drewal's concept of "seriation," or the deep contextualization of historical knowledge in the now, to describe the ways that simultaneous temporalities with relevance to the present moment may coexist in a work of art.[24] Similarly, in bringing together variegated histories into a shared geography, *The Living Lakes* overlays multiple temporalities of migration (e.g., the transatlantic slave trade, cross-border migration, northbound labor intranational migration), labor histories (e.g., slavery, indentured agricultural labor, industrial boom, postindustrial economies), activism (e.g., abolitionism, unionization, civil rights activism), and leisure (e.g., sports, music, popular entertainments, outdoor recreation). Through their embodied research practice, González and Valentín-Martínez orient choreographic technique toward an investment in history and make that history consequential to the performed presence. Their choreographing of the archive, I argue, furthers this approach.

Choreographing the Archive:
Placemaking between Image and Body

The Living Lakes drew another significant amount of its source material from archival visual sources on the history of migration into the Midwest. These sources, much like the environmental sources discussed above, were processed somatically and incorporated into the presentational performance. The "ethnic presence" in the Midwest González and Valentín-Martínez researched over the course of the project was found in a wide range of visual sources and rendered in movement through a recurrence to situated, strategic stasis. While their work is a "dance piece," there is a preponderance toward sculptural still moments or tableaus. I believe that this is in part due to the performance's relationship to the photographic and painterly archive as one of the primary sources of material for the dance's dramaturgical exploration of labor and leisure along Lake Michigan's shores. It is also a continuation of their procedures of placemaking through kinesthetic exploration of sources and sites. Before or in front of the historical record of the archival image, they put body in purposeful, if not always exuberant, movement. But these tableaus are also moments of collective emplacement where Black and Latinx groupings become situated, fixed, and grounded but not captured, no longer so much attached to the stillness of the photograph or painting but intentionally setting foot on the ground in order to make it theirs.

Valentín-Martínez's research into African American and Latinx migration into the Midwest predates his work on *The Living Lakes*. While researching another work in 2013, he encountered an exhibition titled *They Seek a City: Chicago and the Art of Migration, 1910–1950* at the Art Institute of Chicago.[25] *Train Station*, a 1935 painting by Walter Ellison depicting a segregated southern rail station during the Great Migration, became a primary inspiration for his choreography of the opening abstract movement scene that opens the piece, as well as the urban migration scenes that follow. Valentín-Martínez became enthralled by the multidirectionality of movement combined with the concomitant clash of affective orientations to the experience of travel. Fear, hope, desire, despair all seemed to intermix in the chaos of a scene marked by the clear distinctions between race and its geographic orientation: whites orient to the left side of the painting where signs point to the South, Miami in particular, and African Americans concentrate on the right side of the painting, headed north, with a particularly crowded entrance into the Chicago gate.

Valentín-Martínez worked with dancers not to re-create an archival record but to activate a speculative account of what might be the narrative of the painting, informed by the extensive historical research undertaken as part of the project. In rehearsing narratives, Valentín-Martínez and dancers also rehearsed gestures, walking patterns, particular urgencies that might prompt speed or imagined ailments that might prompt a slower pace. Similar to their explorations of natural phenomena, the attempt in this process was to animate the archive with an empathetic relationship to those that the lives of performers, mostly of color and living in the Midwest, could assume to be in some manner connected to.

Putting forth or down of the body energetically to match sensorially the suggested physicality of the archival image, the distance of the materiality of the history it records, and the affective response that the rendering of this tension animates brings me back to the claims about placemaking that structure our collective query in our current project and that inaugurates my own frictive interrelation of the experience of region (Southwest/Midwest) or place (Phoenix/Chicago) to history as experiential. But this is not rigidly factual either, as, for example, my own felt sense of the urgent northward escape from Phoenix to the Midwest ultimately did not align with the actual directional trends of Latina/o demographic redistribution nationally and south of the border. Of course, I don't mean to challenge the weight of historical facts here but to insist on the realm of the speculative, embodied, and the affective in shaping the ways we ultimately experience history.

In further explaining their methodologies as performance makers, González and Valentín-Martínez observe that they "use tableaus, dance movement landscapes, projections and vocalized soundscapes to tell the story of multi-ethnic families making a place for themselves as they travel from South to North, from rural landscapes of Mexico and Mississippi, to icy farmlands and urban industrial cities like Detroit, Chicago or Kalamazoo."[26] These practices of placemaking, especially those between 1910 and 1950 intimated by the painterly photographic archive assembled, are also activated in the now as practices of placemaking for González and Valentín-Martínez, who intuit bodily routes of motion between the corporeality documented in the image (dress, stance, proxemic arrangement to others and things) and the sensorial and affectively dense experience of site visits, or fieldwork, undertaken as part of the project as explained above. This vacillation between the documentation of placemaking and the experience of placemaking results from that very exercise, particularly in instances where this process occurs through aesthetic technologies, principally dance and movement.

As our colleagues Omar Valerio-Jiménez, Santiago Vaquera-Vázquez, and Claire F. Fox argue in their introduction to the groundbreaking *The Latina/o Midwest Reader*, "Placemaking is not necessarily the domain of architects and city planners, but rather refers to the collective, everyday forms of communication and community formation practiced by Latina/o midwesterners, who construct what Maria Cotera describes in her chapter as 'narratives of belonging' through diverse self-representational strategies, including performance, storytelling, art and visual culture, bilingualism, and soundscapes, as well as through their physical presence in churches, workplaces, schools, nightclubs, community centers, and museums."[27] In rendering the Latinx Midwest as and through movement and in relation to other Midwests (African American, Native American), González and Valentín-Martínez remind us of the ways the body might stand in not just for the singularity of a subject but as an entity in full relation to our surroundings, human and nonhuman. In interweaving the history and experience of migration through choreographic experiments that move from body to landscape and back and account for the ways these relations accrue over long periods and unwieldy routes, *The Living Lakes* models a research practice, an aesthetic, and an ethic of placemaking attuned to what has come before us so that we may advance into a future relation to our environment, both natural and social, that is more carefully committed to sustainability and reparation.

Labor and Leisure: The Social Aesthetics of Pleasure in a Latinx Midwest

If *The Living Lakes* opens with a beautiful but ominous encounter with the biting touch of unknown nature and moves us to the violent traffic of urban migration, its remaining time is devoted to scenes of intimate sharing of both labor and leisure in the new expanse. Here, the focus on interethnic/racial relations is staged in spaces drawn as much from historical sources as from contemporary situations. Choreography changes from an orientation toward abstract movement of natural forces or ensemble rendition of collective experience to more intimate scales of social exchange. Partner dancing characterizes a significant portion of the choreography as the piece goes on to explore labor transitions from agricultural routines to industrial ones and leisure in the Latinx and African American celebratory platforms of the region, from *quinceañeras* to jazz clubs. In these scenes, rendered in shorter, episodic, and more explicitly realistic sequences, performers make place in the intimate exchange of the couple dance, as well as in the ritual collectivities of the circle dance. Relating to one another in shared weight, synched rhythms, negotiated touch, dancers model how performance choreographs protocols of *convivencia diaria*, to return to the intimate cohabitation theorized by Milagros Ricourt and Ruby Danta as we discussed in the introduction to this volume, that give rise to a sense of collective belonging to place out of accruing intimate exchanges.[28]

It is important that these scenes in *The Living Lakes* are intermixed. Much like the historical sequencing of the project jumps back and forth between then and now, the intimacies of work and play are not determined to be in opposition to one another. The ease with which we move from rapid-fire renditions of agricultural or industrial labor to a *quinceañera* festivity, a summer retreat, and a closing jazz celebration scene, all similarly moving from mimetic to abstract movement, renders the labor of placemaking as equally distributed between formal and informal platforms and opens up the space for considering the very act of artmaking, choreography included, as a crucial methodology of placemaking. This is the social work of the aesthetic Hamera points to, with the worldmaking potential for which Kondo so enthusiastically advocates.

Ultimately, the historical work *The Living Lakes* seeks to do is reparative work. It is a revisiting of history as a way of "staying with the trouble" of our experience, to parse Haraway, and figure out ways of sustaining into the future. A single scene of choreographed abstraction punctures the choreographic realism of this latter part of the performance. As an archival slide of a segregated public park sign in Chicago is projected onto the back wall of the performance space, performers enter in performed agony—sharp abdominal contractions, dramatic facial expression, tense shoulder and necks—and traverse across the space simply effecting a mood change prompted by the projected image. This scene is not the only scene of pain represented in the piece, but it stands alone at this moment near the conclusion of the piece. It reminds us, as Kondo states, that "reparative worldmaking necessarily navigates through violence, devastation, shattering, to work towards integration."[29]

From this painful reminder of what remains the Midwest's most segregated urban center, *The Living Lakes* brings us into a celebratory closing with a series of rapid-fire successions of festivities in Black and Brown. A Mexican American working-class *quinceañera* party, a middle-class African American pageant in Idelwild, Michigan, and a jazz club dance celebration finale bring us into celebratory motion to see the ways Latinx and African Americans have insisted in their presence and celebrated their endurance in these harsh environments. Choreographic procedures, dance cultures, movement analytics emerge in *The Living Lakes* as social and formal aesthetics with explanatory and experiential potential to carry our history forward through protocols of animation that seek to make place through the labor of our bodies, creative and otherwise.

I know I am dwelling in scalar trouble, between the arrivals and departures from one region to another, the feet-on-the-ground local experiences that texture my understanding of them, between the placemaking practices of others and my own, and between the urgency of an academic project to situate the Latinx Midwest while noticing the traveled paths, the residual marks of the traffic it sustains. And it is toward an understanding of this unwieldy choreography that I turn to the social aesthetics of dance to set in motion rather than set in place *The Living Lakes*.

Latinx Studies in Motion: Unmooring the Roots

It is the summer of 2017, and Hurricanes Irma and María have wreaked havoc through the archipelago of Puerto Rico. I have not received news from my family for more than ten days, and I have begun to despair over what the future holds. I prepare for the potential relocation of my family, especially my mother, by searching for a place of living that might accommodate us. I set out instinctually toward the lakeshore. An hour-long drive takes me to the Indiana Dunes National Lakeshore, now a national park. I park my car and walk in the direction of the shore. Barefoot, I feel the texture of the sand, feel the lightness of the saltless lake air, and walk into the cold pebble-floor beach until the water reaches my midthighs. This place is the familiar unfamiliar of my diasporic life. I have become in and of the Midwest after twelve years in the region, the longest I have lived anywhere outside of my place of birth. I have made place and made peace with what may or may not be replicated in this new location. I wonder how much I might be able to re-create for my mother should she need to be evacuated. I wonder if, like me, she will be able to adapt and adopt the lake as if it was our ocean. I stand still at the water's edge, contemplating a horizon of possibilities not entirely my own, and I get ready for another possible journey, this time, as always, not entirely only my own, shaping the places we come to be and live Latinx.

Notes

1. AZ SB 1070 was signed into law by then governor Janet Brewer on April 23, 2010. It was subsequently challenged in court, including preliminary injunctions of many of its provisions. In *Arizona v. the United States*, 567 U.S. 387, the Supreme Court upheld the provision of the law that allowed immigration status checks in routine local law enforcement, but it struck down provisions that went beyond federal authority on immigration controls.

2. On the housing market crash in Arizona, see Vikas Bajaj, "In Arizona, 'For Sale' Is a Sign of the Times," *New York Times*, November 7, 2006, New York ed., A1.

3. See Rogelio Sáenz's analysis based on the 2008 and 2013 American Community Surveys: "A Transformation in Mexican Migration to the United States," *Carsey Research, National Issue Brief #86*, Carsey School of Public Policy, University of New Hampshire, Summer 2015.

4. The Immigration Reform and Control Act of 1986, signed into law by President Ronald Raegan on November 6, 1986, raised the legal stakes against the hiring of undocumented immigrants (requiring employee status verification) while normalizing the status of undocumented immigrants who had arrived in the United States prior to January 1, 1982, and who live continuously in the country provided they had no criminal record, paid a leveled fine, and owed no taxes. The employee status verification simply pushed the undocumented labor market into the hands of subcontractor intermediaries who assumed the risks of verification. Undocumented migration continued to rise despite the provisions of the 1986 act.

5. According to 2019 estimates by the US Census Bureau, a third of the population of Arizona identifies as Hispanic or Latino, and about 5 percent belongs to a North American Indigenous nation, with Phoenix being the only urban center in the United States with a Native American population surpassing one hundred thousand. See "Arizona Quick Facts," Census Report, https://www.census.gov/quickfacts/fact/table/AZ/RHI325218#RHI325218.

6. See Tanvi Mirsa, "Why Immigrants Are Leaving Chicago," *CITYLAB*, March 31, 2017, https://www.citylab.com/equity/2017/03/behind-chicagos-population-decline/520611/.

7. Tomás Rivera, "Las salamandras / The Salamanders," in *Tomás Rivera: The Complete Works*, ed. Julián Olivares (Houston: Arte Público Press, 2008), 127–30, 159–61.

8. Valerio-Jiménez, Vaquera-Vázquez, and Fox, *The Latina/o Midwest Reader*, 16.

9. US Census reports from 2000 and 2010 demonstrate a 17 percent decline (close to 180,000 individuals) in Chicago's African American population.

10. See Cristina Gallardo-Sanidad, "Constructing Arizona: The Lives and Labor of Mexicans in the Valley of the Sun," in *Mexican Workers and the Making of Arizona*, ed. Luis F. B. Plascencia and Gloria H. Cuádraz (Tucson: University of Arizona Press, 2018), 270–300.

11. See Anita González, *Jarocho's Soul: Cultural Identity and AfroMexican Dance* (Lanham, MD: University Press of America, 2004); and González, *Afro-Mexico: Dancing between Myth and Reality* (Austin: University of Texas Press, 2010).

12. Cindy García is associate professor of dance at the University of Minnesota Twin Cities.

13. Links Hall is a Chicago experimental performance space and incubator founded in 1978 by three experimental choreographers. A member of the National Performance Network since 1998, it is both one of the city's primary platforms for experimental performance and one of the Midwest's longest-running independent performance venues. For more information, see www.linkshall.org.

14. Collaborators for *The Living Lakes* included the following artists: University of Michigan–Ann Arbor (summer 2015), performers: Jefferson Ballew, Janel Speelman, Marcus White, Shanice Rollins, Patty Solozano; University of Michigan–Ann Arbor (summer 2017): Jonathan Girling (composer), Will Simpson (video design), performers: Marty Gray, Lauryn Hobbs, Simon Longnight, Callie Munn, Alexandra Reynolds, and Isabel Stein; *Living Lakes* performance as part of Performing Home curated by Cynthia Bond at Links Hall, Chicago (October 2017): Andrew Baldwin (musician), Jonathan Girling (composer), Will Simpson (video artist), performers: Keila Hamed-Ramos, Ben Locke, Keewa Nurullah, Joel Valentín-Martínez; Performing Midwest Links Hall, Chicago (June 2018): Egan Franke, Andrew Baldwin (musicians), Jonathan Girling (composer), Will Simpson (video artist), performers: Keewah Narullah, Dwight Alaba, Kitty Morris, Jordan Alix Curnow, Duoduo Wang.

15. Judith Hamera, "Performance, Performativity, and Cultural Poesis in Practices of Everyday Life," in *The Sage Handbook of Performance Studies*, ed. Judith A. Hamera and D. Soyini Madison (London: Sage, 2006), 47.

16. Dorinne Kondo, *Worldmaking: Race, Performance, and the Work of Creativity* (Durham, NC: Duke University Press, 2018), 44.

17. http://thelivinglakes.com.

18. For an extended discussion of the ways non-Indian Americans have played out fantasies of Indianness that include conceptions of nature, see Philip J. Deloria, *Playing Indian* (New Haven, CT: Yale University Press, 1998).

19. Philip Deloria, postperformance discussion, University of Michigan–Ann Arbor, July 17, 2015.

20. Correspondence with the artists.

21. Donna J. Haraway, *Staying with the Trouble: Making Kin in the Chthulucene* (Durham, NC: Duke University Press, 2016), 133.

22. Ilka Kressner, Ana María Mutis, and Elizabeth M. Pettinaroli, eds., *Ecofictions, Ecorealities, and Slow Violence in Latin America and the Latinx World* (London: Routledge, 2019).

23. Omi Osun Joni L. Jones, *Theatrical Jazz: Performance, àṣẹ, and the Power of the Present Moment* (Columbus: Ohio University Press, 2015).

24. Margaret Thompson Drewal, *Yoruba Ritual: Performers, Play, Agency* (Bloomington: Indiana University Press, 1992).

25. Other important sources for the project included photographic collections of the Works Progress Administration documenting bracero Mexican laborers to the United States and the Jack Delano photographic collections of Puerto Ricans in the 1940s.

26. *The Living Lakes* website, http://thelivinglakes.com.

27. Valerio-Jiménez, Vaquera-Vázquez, and Fox, *The Latina/o Midwest*, 18.

28. Ricourt and Danta, *Hispanas de Queens*.

29. Kondo, *Worldmaking*, 33.

Bibliography

Literary, Performative, Cinematic, and Video Work

Abel, Jessica. *La Perdida*. New York: Pantheon Books, 2006.

Abrazos. Dir. Luis Argueta. New Day Films, 2014.

AbUSed: The Postville Raid. Dir. Luis Argueta and Vivan Rivas. Maya Media / New Day Films, 2011.

Arroyo, Fred. *The Region of Lost Names*. Tucson: University of Arizona Press, 2008.

———. *Sown in Earth: Essays of Memory and Belonging*. Tucson: University of Arizona Press, 2020.

———. *Western Avenue and Other Fictions*. Tucson: University of Arizona Press, 2012.

Arroyo, Rane. "Being: An Essay on Being a Midwestern Writer [poem]." In "Compass Rose: Introduction." *Midwestern Miscellany* 30 (Fall 2002): 7–14.

———. *The Portable Famine*. Kansas City, MO: BkMk Press, 2005.

Borzutzky, Daniel. *Lake Michigan*. Pittsburgh: University of Pittsburgh Press, 2018.

———. *The Performance of Becoming Human*. Brooklyn, NY: Brooklyn Arts Press, 2016.

Cárdenas, Brenda. *Boomerang: Poems*. Tempe, AZ: Bilingual Press / Editorial Bilingüe, 2009.

Carrillo, Albino. *In the City of Smoking Mirrors*. Tucson: University of Arizona Press, 2004.

Carrillo, H. G. *Loosing My Espanish*. New York: Anchor Books, 2005.

Castillo, Ana. *Loverboys: Stories*. New York: W. W. Norton, 1996.

———. *Massacre of the Dreamers: Essays on Xicanisma*. Albuquerque: University of New Mexico Press, 1994.

———. *The Mixquiahuala Letters*. Binghamton, NY: Bilingual Press / Editorial Bilingüe, 1989.

———. *My Father Was a Toltec and Selected Poems*. New York: W. W. Norton, 1995.

———. *Peel My Love Like an Onion: A Novel*. New York: Anchor / Random House, 1999.

———. *Sapogonia: An Anti-romance in 3/8 Meter*. New York: Doubleday, 1990.

———. *Watercolor Women, Opaque Men: A Novel in Verse.* Willimantic, CT: Curbstone Press, 2005.

Cintrón, Esperanza Malave. *Chocolate City Latina.* Jamaica Plain, MA: Swank Books, 2005.

———. *What Keeps Me Sane: Poems.* Detroit: Lotus Press, 2013.

Cintrón, Esperanza, Lillien Waller, and Lina Cintrón. *Visions of a Post-apocalyptic Sunrise: Detroit Poems.* Ithaca, NY: Stockport Flats, 2014.

Cintron, Ralph., ed. *ECOS: A Latino Journal of People's Culture and Literature* 2, no. 1 (1982).

Cisneros, Sandra. *Caramelo.* New York: Knopf / Random House, 2002.

———. *House of My Own.* New York: Vintage Books, 2016.

———. *The House on Mango Street.* Houston: Arte Público Press, 1985.

Cumpián, Carlos. *14 Abriles: Poems.* Chicago: March Abrazo Press, 2010.

———. *Armadillo Charm.* Chicago: Tía Chucha Press, 1996.

———. *Coyote Sun.* Chicago: March Abrazo Press, 1990.

dsmperforming. "*Tomas and the Library Lady* Experience." https://www.youtube.com/watch?time_continue=17&v=ME4RKb1TISA.

feastoffun. "Cooking with Drag Queens: How to Make Tostones." Nov 16, 2010. Video. http://youtu.be/TA05Vl3FoV0.

———. "Faustina—Mini Episode #1—How to Apply Makeup." FeastofFun.com, 11 November 2011. http://feastoffun.com/videos/2011/11/11/video-faustina-mini-episode-1-how-to-apply-makeup/.

———. "The Fire Eating Drag Princess." June 6, 2009. http://youtu.be/J2xe7JgkiGg.

———. "Forced Feminization." June 3, 2009. http://youtu.be/7hdJioRGsYM.

Fernós, Fausto. *El Chow De Faustina* (Linda Montano episode, 9 October 1994). *YouTube,* March 5, 2007. http://youtu.be/qeRKDGAQY-0.

———. "PHOTO: Time Traveling Bunny Cake Follows Gay Couple." Feast of Fun.com, December 1, 2010. https://feastoffun.com/topics/people/2010/12/01/photo-time-traveling-bunny-cake-follows-gay-couple/.

González, Anita and Joel Valentín-Martínez with ensemble. *The Living Lakes.*

Gressman, Erica, *Wall of Skin.*

———. *Monster Wedding.*

———. *Full Frontal Biopsy.*

———. *Circuit Witch.*

———. *Disco Butoh.*

———. *Limbs.*

Hernández, David, ed. *Nosotros: A Collection of Latino Poetry and Graphics from Chicago.*

Special issue, *Revista Chicano-Riqueña* 5, no. 1 (1977).

———. *Roof Top Piper.* Chicago: Tía Chucha Press, 1991.

Hernandez Linares, Leticia, Ruben Martinez, and Hector Tobar. *The Wandering Song: Central American Writing in the United States.* San Fernando, CA: Tía Chucha Press, 2017.

Hijuelos, Oscar. *Dark Dude*. New York: Atheneum Books for Young Readers, 2009.

Kurtz, Julia K., and Susan Dobinsky. *Mirroring Hispanic Culture: Murals in Chicago*. Chicago: Illinois Humanities Council, 1987.

La Fountain-Stokes, Lawrence. *Abolición del pato*. Carolina, Puerto Rico: Terranova Editores, 2013.

Levins Morales, Aurora, and Rosario Morales. *Cosecha and Other Stories*. Cambridge, MA: Palabrera Press, 2014.

———. *Getting Home Alive*. Ithaca, NY: Firebrand Books, 1986.

The Living Lakes website, http://thelivinglakes.com.

López, Lourdes Lugo. *Poemas que me desnudan y me definen*. Chicago: Editorial El Coquí Publishers, 1992.

Lucas, Maria Elena. *Forged under the Sun / Forjada bajo el sol*. Edited by Fran Leeper Buss. Ann Arbor: University of Michigan Press, 1993.

Machado, Carmen María. *In the Dream House: A Memoir*. Minneapolis: Graywolf Press, 2019.

MANTIS. *FULL*. Self-published, 2019.

Martinez, Rubén. *Crossing Over: A Mexican Family on the Migrant Trail*. New York: Picador USA, 2002.

Martínez-Serros, Hugo. *The Last Laugh and Other Stories*. Houston: Arte Público Press, 1988.

Mendoza, Louis G. "Conversations across 'Our America': Latinoization and the New Geographies of Latinas/os." In *The Latina/o Midwest Reader*, edited by Omar Valerio-Jiménez, Santiago Vaquera-Vásquez, and Claire F. Fox, 25–41. Urbana: University of Illinois Press, 2017.

———. *A Journey around Our America: A Memoir on Cycling, Immigration, and the Latinoization of the U.S.* Austin: University of Texas Press, 2012.

Menes, Orlando. *Fetish*. Lincoln: University of Nebraska Press, 2013.

Mercier, Paloma. *Ten Letters: Belmont*. Self-published, 2019.

Mireles, Oscar. *I Didn't Know There Were Latinos in Wisconsin: 30 Hispanic Writers*. Vol. 2. Madison, WI: Focus Communications, 1999.

Mora, Pat. *Tomás and the Library Lady*. Adapted for the stage by José Cruz Gonzáles, directed by Ismael Lara Jr. Northwestern University, March 2021. https://wirtz .northwestern.edu/tomas-and-the-library-lady/.

———. *Tomás and the Library Lady*. Illustrated by Raúl Colón. New York: Knopf, 1997. [Spanish-language edition: *Tomás y la señora de la biblioteca*. Translated by Amy Diane Prince. New York: Dragonfly, 1997.]

Morales, Iris, dir. *¡Palante, Siempre Palante! The Young Lords*. 1996, P.O.V. Documentary Series, PBS. [film]

"Ninth Annual Cleveland Performance Art Festival 1996 Invitational Artists." Performance Art Festival 1997. Can no longer be accessed. http://web.ulib.csuohio .edu/PAF97/paf_index.html.

Nothing Like the Holidays. Dir. Alfredo de Villa and Alison Swan. Hamburg: Hamburg Medien Haus, 2010.

Obejas, Achy. *Memory Mambo: A Novel*. Pittsburgh: Cleis Press, 1996.

———. *We Came All the Way from Cuba So You Could Dress Like That?* Pittsburgh: Cleis Press, 1994.

On the Downlow. Dir. Garcia Tadeo. 2004.

Osborne, Karen Lee, and William J. Spurlin. *Reclaiming the Heartland: Lesbian and Gay Voices from the Midwest*. Minneapolis: University of Minnesota Press, 1996.

Parson-Nesbitt, Julie, Luis J. Rodriguez, and Michael Warr, eds. *Power Lines: A Decade of Poetry from Chicago's Guild Complex*. Chicago: Tía Chucha Press, 1999.

Puerto Rican Diaspora: Lorain, Ohio. Produced by Erica Soto and Richard Unapanta. 2017. https://vimeo.com/220523605.

Ramirez, Alexa. *A CTA Love Letter*. Self-published, 2019.

Rebel Betty Arte. *El Barrio No Se Vende*. Self-published, 2017.

———. *The Gentrification of Chicago*. Self-published, 2018.

———. *Mujer en Revolución*. Self-published, 2018.

Rivera, Tomás. *Tomás Rivera: The Complete Works*. Edited by Julián Olivares. Houston: Arte Público Press, 1991.

Rodriguez, Leonardo. *They Have to Be Puerto Ricans*. Chicago: Adams Press, 1988.

Rodríguez, Luis J. *My Nature Is Hunger: New & Selected Poems, 1989–2004*. Willimantic, CT: Curbstone Press, 2005.

———. *Poems across the Pavement*. Chicago: Tía Chucha Press, 1989.

Sánchez, Erika L. *I Am Not Your Perfect Mexican Daughter*. New York: Alfred A. Knopf Books for Young Readers, 2017.

Saona, Margarita. *Comehoras*. Lima: Editora Mesa Redonda, 2008.

Souchet, Clementina. *Clementina: Historia sin fin*. Mexico City: Impresa Madero, 1986.

Torres, Daniel. *Morirás si da una primavera: Una novelita azul*. Coral Gables, FL: University of Miami, North-South Center, Iberian Studies Institute, 1993.

Unfreedom. Dir. José Toledo. 2014. https://www.youtube.com/watch?v=aEtxQ-erfD8.

Varela, Frank. *Serpent Underfoot*. Chicago: March/Abrazo Press, 1993.

Vázquez Paz, Johanny. *Streetwise Poems / Poemas callejeros*. Bay City, MI: Mayapple Press, 2007.

#ZINEmercado. *Compilation Zine*. Self-published, 2018.

Secondary Literature

Abarca, Meredith E. *Voices in the Kitchen: Views of Food and the World from Working-Class Mexican and Mexican American Women*. College Station: Texas A&M University Press, 2006.

Ahmed, Sara. *Strange Encounters: Embodied Others in Post-coloniality*. New York: Routledge, 2000.

Ahn, Ilsup. "Economy of 'Invisible Debt' and Ethics of 'Radical Hospitality': Toward a Paradigm Change of Hospitality from 'Gift' to 'Forgiveness.'" *Journal of Religious Ethics* 38, no. 2 (June 2010): 243–67.

Airriess, Christopher A., and Inés M. Miyares, eds. *Contemporary Ethnic Geographies in America*. Lanham, MD: Rowman & Littlefield, 2007.

Albarracín, Julia. *At the Core and in the Margins: Incorporation of Mexican Immigrants in Two Rural Midwestern Communities*. East Lansing: Michigan State University Press, 2016.

Alvarado, Karina O., Alicia Ivonne Estrada, and Ester E. Hernández, eds. *U.S. Central Americans: Reconstructing Memories, Struggles, and Communities of Resistance*. Tucson: University of Arizona Press, 2017.

American Dream. Dir. Barbara Kopple. 1990.

Aparicio, Frances R. *Negotiating Latinidad: Intralatina/o Lives in Chicago*. Urbana: University of Illinois Press, 2019.

———. "Not Fully Boricuas: Puerto Rican Intralatino/as in Chicago." *Centro Journal* 28, no. 2 (Fall 2016): 154–79.

———. "Reading the 'Latino' in Latino Studies: Toward Re-imagining Our Academic Location." *Discourse* 21, no. 3 (1999): 3–18.

Aparicio, Frances R., and Susana Chávez-Silverman. *Tropicalizations: Transcultural Representations of Latinidad*. Hanover, NH: University Press of New England, 1997.

Arredondo, Gabriela. *Mexican Chicago: Race, Identity, and Nation, 1916–1939*. Urbana: University of Illinois Press, 2003.

Arreola, Daniel D., ed. *Hispanic Spaces, Latino Places: Community and Cultural Diversity in Contemporary America*. Austin: University of Texas Press, 2004.

———. *Tejano South Texas: A Mexican American Cultural Province*. Austin: University of Texas Press, 2002.

Auslander, Philip. *Liveness: Performance in a Mediatized Culture*. 2nd ed. London: Routledge, 2008.

Avila, Eric. *Popular Culture in the Age of White Flight: Fear and Fantasy in Suburban Los Angeles*. Berkeley: University of California Press, 2006.

Avilés-Santiago, Manuel G. *Puerto Rican Soldiers and Second-Class Citizenship: Representations in Media*. New York: Palgrave Macmillan, 2014.

Bada, Xóchitl. *Mexican Hometown Associations in Chicagoacán: From Local to Transnational Civic Engagement*. New Brunswick, NJ: Rutgers University Press, 2014.

Badillo, David. "The Catholic Church and the Making of Mexican-American Parish Communities in the Midwest." In *Mexican Americans and the Catholic Church, 1900–1965*, edited by Jay P. Dolan and Gilberto M. Hinojosa, 223–308. Notre Dame, IN: University of Notre Dame Press, 1994.

Baier, Elizabeth. "25 Years Ago, Hormel Strike Changed Austin, Industry." *MPR News*, August 17, 2010. https://www.mprnews.org/story/2010/08/17/austin-hormel-strike.

Baim, Tracy, and Owen Keehnen. *Jim Flint: The Boy from Peoria*. Chicago: Prairie Ave. Productions, 2011.

Balassiano, Katia, and Marta Maria Maldonado. "Placemaking in Rural New Gateway Communities." *Community Development Journal* 50, no. 4 (October 2015): 644–60.

Bau, Ignatius. *The Ground Is Holy: Church Sanctuary and Central American Refugees*. Mahwah, NJ: Paulist Press, 1985.

Berry, Richard. "Podcasting: Considering the Evolution of the Medium and Its Association with the Word 'Radio.'" *Radio Journal: International Studies in Broadcast and Audio Media* 14, no. 1 (April 2016): 7–22.

Blackwell, Maylei. ¡Chicana Power! Contested Histories of Feminism in the Chicano Movement. Austin: University of Texas Press, 2011.

Boff, Leonardo, and Clodovis Boff. Introducing Liberation Theology. Maryknoll, NY: Orbis Books, 1987.

Bosse, Joanna. "Salsa Dance as Cosmopolitan Formation: Cooperation, Conflict, and Commerce in the Midwest US." Ethnomusicology Forum 22, no. 2 (2013): 210–31.

Bourriaud, Nicolas. Relational Aesthetics. Translated by Simon Pleasance and Fronza Woods. Dijon: Les Presses de Réel, 1998, 2002.

Brady, Mary Pat. Extinct Lands, Temporal Geographies: Chicana Literature and the Urgency of Space. Durham, NC: Duke University Press, 2002.

Bretherton, Luke. Hospitality as Holiness: Christian Witness amid Moral Diversity. Hampshire, UK: Ashgate, 2006.

Broughton, Chad. Boom, Bust, Exodus: The Rust Belt, the Maquilas, and a Tale of Two Cities. Oxford: Oxford University Press, 2015.

Buell, Lawrence. The Future of Environmental Criticism: Environmental Crisis and Literary Imagination. Malden, MA: Blackwell Publishing, 2005.

Buff, Rachel Ida. Against the Deportation Terror: Organizing for Immigrant Rights in the Twentieth Century. Philadelphia: Temple University Press, 2017.

Burgess, Jean, and Joshua Green. YouTube: Online Video and Participatory Culture. Cambridge, MA: Polity, 2009.

Butler, Judith. Gender Trouble: Feminism and the Subversion of Identity. New York: Routledge, 1991.

Cacho, Lisa Marie. Social Death: Racialized Rightlessness and the Criminalization of the Unprotected. New York: New York University Press, 2012.

Cadava, Geraldo L. Standing on Common Ground: The Making of the Sunbelt Borderland. Cambridge, MA: Harvard University Press, 2013.

Cadaval, Olivia. Creating a Latino Identity in the Nation's Capital: The Latino Festival. New York: Taylor & Francis, 1998.

Cadena, Marisol de la. Earth Beings: Ecologies of Practice across Andean Worlds. Durham, NC: Duke University Press, 2015.

Calafell, Bernadette Maria and Shane T. Moreman. "Envisioning an Academic Readership: Latina/o Performativities per the Form of Publication," Text and Performance Quarterly 29, no. 2 (2009): 123-30.

Caminero-Santangelo, Marta. "Documenting the Undocumented: Life Narratives of Unauthorized Immigrants." Biography 35, no. 3 (Summer 2012): 449–71.

Cantwell, Christopher, Heath W. Carter, and Janine Giordano Drake, eds. The Pew and the Picket Line: Christianity and the American Working Class. Urbana: University of Illinois Press, 2016.

Carrigan, William D., and Clive Webb. Forgotten Dead: Mob Violence against Mexicans in the United States, 1848–1928. Oxford: Oxford University Press, 2013.

Carrillo Rowe, Aimee. "Vendidas y Devueltas: Queer Times and Color Lines in Chicana/o Performance." Meridians 11, no. 2 (2011): 114–46.

Castanha, Tony. The Myth of Indigenous Caribbean Extinction: Continuity and Reclamation in Borikén (Puerto Rico). New York: Palgrave Macmillan, 2011.

Castellanos, M. Bianet. "Rewriting the Mexican Immigrant Narrative: Situating Indigeneity in Maya Women's Stories." *Latino Studies* 15, no. 2 (2017): 219–41.

Certeau, Michel de. *The Practice of Everyday Life*. Minneapolis: University of Minnesota Press, 1998.

Chabram-Dernersesian, Angie. "Chicana! Rican? No, Chicana-Riqueña! Refashioning the Transnational Connection." In *Multiculturalism: A Critical Reader*, edited by D. T. Goldberg. Oxford: Blackwell, 1994.

Chappell, David. *A Stone of Hope: Prophetic Religion and the Death of Jim Crow*. Chapel Hill: University of North Carolina Press, 2005.

Chase, Cheryl. "Hermaphrodites with Attitude: Mapping the Emergence of Intersex Political Activism." *GLQ: A Journal of Lesbian and Gay Studies* 7, no. 4 (1998): 189–211.

Chavoya, C. Ondine, and Rita Gonzalez, eds. *Asco: Elite of the Obscure: A Retrospective, 1972–1987*. Ostfildern, Germany: Hatje Cantz; Williamstown, MA: Williams College Museum of Art; Los Angeles: Los Angeles County Museum of Art, 2011.

Cheney-Lippold, John. *We Are Data: Algorithms and the Making of Our Digital Selves*. New York: New York University Press, 2017.

Cintron, Ralph. *Angels' Town: Chero Ways, Gang Life and Rhetorics of Everyday*. Boston: Beacon Press, 1997.

Clammer, John. "Performing Ethnicity: Performance, Gender, Body and Belief in the Construction and Signaling of Identity." *Ethnic and Racial Studies* 38, no. 13 (2015): 2159–66. doi:10.1080/01419870.2015.1045305.

Clark, Timothy. *The Cambridge Introduction to Literature and the Environment*. Cambridge: Cambridge University Press, 2011.

The Cockettes. Dir. David Weissman, Bill Weber, and Richard Koldewyn. GranDelusion, Strand Releasing Home Video, [2002].

Colín, Ernesto. *Indigenous Education through Dance and Ceremony: A Mexican Palimpsest*. New York: Palgrave Macmillan, 2014.

Conradson, David, and Deirdre Mckay. "Translocal Subjectivities: Mobility, Connection, Emotion." *Mobilities* 2, no. 2 (2007): 167–74. doi:10.1080/17450100701381524.

Consedine, M. Raphael. *One Pace Beyond: The Life of Nano Nagel*. Victoria, Australia: Presentation Congregation of Victoria, 1977.

Coutin, Susan Bibler. *The Culture of Protest: Religious Activism and the U.S. Sanctuary Movement*. Boulder, CO: Westview Press, 1993.

———. "From Refugees to Immigrants: The Legalization Strategies of Salvadoran Immigrants and Activists." *International Migration Review* 32, no. 4 (Winter 1998): 901–25.

Cowie, Jefferson. *Capital Moves: RCA's Seventy-Year Quest for Cheap Labor*. New York: New Press, 2001.

———. *Stayin' Alive: The 1970s and the Last Days of the Working Class*. New York: New Press, 2010.

Cruz-Malavé, Arnaldo. "Between Irony and Belief: The Queer Diasporic Underground Aesthetics of José Rodríguez-Soltero and Mario Montez." *GLQ* 21, no. 4 (October 2015): 585–615.

Cullen, Art. "Melting Pot Never Boils," *Storm Lake Times*, April 26, 2016, http://www
.stormlake.com/articles/melting-pot-never-boils.

———. "The View from Iowa: Where Immigrants Are at the Heart of America's
Culture War." *The Guardian,* September 17, 2018, https://www.theguardian.com/
society/2018/sep/17/the-view-from-iowa-where-immigrants-are-at-the-heart-of
-americas-culture-war?CMP=share_btn_fb.

Cunningham, Hilary. *God and Caesar at the Rio Grande: Sanctuary and the Politics
of Religion.* Minneapolis: University of Minnesota Press, 1995.

Cutler, John Alba. *The Ends of Assimilation: The Formation of Chicano Literature.*
Oxford: Oxford University Press, 2015.

Danky, James P., and Wayne A. Wiegand, eds. *Print Culture in a Diverse America.*
Urbana: University of Illinois Press, 1998.

Datta, Ayona, and Katherine Brickell. *Translocal Geographies: Spaces, Places, Connections.* London: Taylor and Francis, 2016.

Davalos, Karen Mary. *Chicana/o Remix: Art and Errata Since the Sixties.* New York:
NYU Press, 2017.

———. *Exhibiting Mestizaje: Mexican American Museums in the Diaspora.* Albuquerque: University of New Mexico Press, 2001.

———. "Innovation through Tradition: The Aesthetic of *Día de los Muertos*," in *Día de
los Muertos: A Cultural Legacy; Past, Present, and Future,* edited by Mary Thomas,
21-29. Curators, Linda Vallejo and Betty Ann Brown. Los Angeles: Self Help Graphics and Art, 2017.

———. "A Poetics of Love and Rescue in the Collection of Chicana/o Art," *Latino
Studies* 5 (2007): 76-103.

———. "Sin vergüenza: Chicana Feminist Theorizing," Chicana Studies special double
issue. *Feminist Studies* 34, no. 1 & 2 (2008): 151-71.

———. *Yolanda M. López.* Los Angeles: UCLA Chicano Studies Research Center
Press, 2008.

Davis, Mike. *Magical Urbanism: Latinos Reinvent the U.S. City.* London: Verso, 2007.

De Genova, Nicholas. *Working the Boundaries: Race, Space, and "Illegality" in Mexican
Chicago.* Durham, NC: Duke University Press, 2005.

De Genova, Nicholas, and Ana Yolanda Ramos-Zayas. *Latino Crossings: Mexicans,
Puerto Ricans, and the Politics of Race and Citizenship.* New York: Routledge, 2003.

DeGúzman, Mará. "LatinX Botanical Epistemologies." *Cultural Dynamics* 31, no. 1–2
(2019): 108–24.

Delgadillo, Theresa. "Exiles, Migrants, Settlers, and Natives: Literary Representations
of Chicano/as and Mexicans in the Midwest." Occasional Paper No. 64 (August
1999), 1–11. Michigan State University, Julian Samora Research Institute. https://
jsri.msu.edu/publications/occasional-papers.

———. "The Ideal Immigrant." *Aztlán: A Journal of Chicano Studies* 36, no. 1 (2011): 37–67.

———. *Latina Lives in Milwaukee.* Urbana: University of Illinois Press, 2015.

———. "Learning from Mexican and Native Women." *Mujeres Talk,* August 20, 2012.

http://library.osu.edu/blogs/mujerestalk/2012/08/20/learning-from-mexican-and
-native-women/.

———. "Living Without a Car." *Mujeres Talk*, May 10, 2012, https://mujerestalk.org/
2012/05/10/living-without-a-car/.

———. *Spiritual Mestizaje: Religion, Gender, Race, and Nation in Contemporary Chicana Narrative*. Durham: Duke University Press, 2011.

———. ". . . y no se lo tragó la tierra." In *Dictionary of Midwestern Literature, Volume Two: Dimensions of the Midwestern Literary Imagination*, edited by Philip A.
Greasley. Bloomington: Indiana University Press, 2016.

Deloria, Philip J. *Playing Indian*. New Haven, CT: Yale University Press, 1998.

Derrida, Jacques. *Of Hospitality*. Stanford, CA: Stanford University Press, 2000.

DiAngelo, Robin. *White Fragility: Why It's So Hard for White People to Talk about
Racism*. Boston: Beacon, 2018.

Diaz, Ella. "The Necessary Theater of the Royal Chicano Air Force." *Aztlán: A Journal
of Chicano Studies* 38, no. 2 (2013): 41-70.

Dietz, James. *Economic History of Puerto Rico: Institutional Change and Capitalist
Development*. Princeton, NJ: Princeton University Press, 1986.

Dolan, Jill. *Utopia in Performance: Finding Hope at the Theatre*. Ann Arbor: University
of Michigan Press, 2005.

Doty, Pamela. "Public-Access Cable TV: Who Cares?" *Journal of Communication* 25,
no. 3 (September 1975): 33–41.

Douglas, Mary, and Baron C. Isherwood. *The World of Goods: Towards an Anthropology of Consumption: with a New Introduction*. Rev. ed. London; New York:
Routledge, 1996.

Downey, Anthony. "Towards a Politics of (Relational) Aesthetics." *Third Text* 21, no.
3 (May 2007): 267–75.

Doyle, Jennifer. *Hold It Against Me: Difficulty and Emotion in Contemporary Art*.
Durham, NC: Duke University Press, 2013.

Duany, Jorge. *Blurred Borders: Transnational Migration between the Hispanic Caribbean and the United States*. Chapel Hill: University of North Carolina Press, 2011.

———. *The Puerto Rican Nation on the Move: Identities on the Island and in the United
States*. Chapel Hill: University of North Carolina Press, 2003.

———. *Puerto Rico: What Everyone Needs to Know®*. New York: Oxford University
Press, 2017.

Duncombe, Stephen. *Notes from Underground: Zines and the Politics of Alternative
Culture*. Portland, OR: Microcosm Publishing, 1997.

Dzi Croquettes. Dir. Tatiana Issa and Raphael Alvarez. TRIA Productions, Canal Brasil,
Imovision, 2009.

Ebaugh, Helen Rose, and Mary Curry. "Fictive Kin as Social Capital in New Immigrant
Communities." *Sociological Perspectives* 43, no. 2 (2000): 189–209.

Eisenbrandt, Matt. *Assassination of a Saint: The Plot to Murder Óscar Romero and the
Quest to Bring His Killers to Justice*. Berkeley: University of California Press, 2017.

Ellwanger, Joseph. *Strength for the Struggle: Insights from the Civil Rights Movement and Urban Ministry*. Milwaukee: Maven Mark Books, 2014.

Elmer, MacKenzie. "Dozens Rally in Mount Pleasant Day after ICE Arrested 32, Mourning Families Torn Apart and Demanding Answers." *Des Moines Register,* May 10, 2018. www.desmoinesregister.com.

Engelman, Ralph. *The Origins of Public Access Cable Television 1966–1972*. Columbia, SC: Association for Education in Journalism and Mass Communication, 1990.

Escobar, Edward, and James Lane, eds. *Forging a Community: The Latino Experience in Northwest Indiana*. Chicago: Cattails Press, 1987.

Escobedo, Elizabeth. *From Coveralls to Zoot Suits: The Lives of Mexican American Women on the World War II Home Front*. Chapel Hill: University of North Carolina Press, 2013.

Farr, Marcia. *Rancheros in Chicagoacán: Language and Identity in a Transnational Community*. Austin: University of Texas Press, 2006.

Feliciano-Santos, Sherina. "An Inconceivable Indigeneity? The Historical, Cultural, and Interactional Dimensions of Puerto Rican Taino Activism." PhD dissertation, University of Michigan, Ann Arbor, 2011.

———. "Negotiating Ethnoracial Configurations among Puerto Rican Taíno Activists." *Ethnic and Racial Studies* 42, no. 7 (2019): 1149–67.

Fernández, Delia. "Becoming Latino: Mexican and Puerto Rican Community Formation in Grand Rapids, Michigan, 1926–1964." *Michigan Historical Review* 39, no. 1 (2013).

———. "Rethinking the Urban and Rural Divide in Latino Labor, Recreation, and Activism in West Michigan, 1940s–1970s." *Labor History* 57, no. 4 (August 2016): 482–503.

Fernández, Lilia. *Brown in the Windy City: Mexicans and Puerto Ricans in Postwar Chicago*. Chicago: University of Chicago Press, 2012.

Fetta, Stephanie. *Shaming into Brown*. Columbus: Ohio State University Press, 2018.

Fife, John. "Civil Initiative." In *Trails of Hope and Terror: Testimonies on Immigration*, edited by Miguel A. de la Torre, 170–75. Maryknoll, NY: Orbis Books, 2009.

Findlay, Eileen. *We Are Left Without a Father Here: Masculinity, Domesticity, and Migration in Postwar Puerto Rico*. Durham, NC: Duke University Press, 2014.

Flores, Juan. *The Diaspora Strikes Back: Caribeño Tales of Learning and Turning*. New York: Routledge, 2009.

———. *Divided Borders: Essays on Puerto Rican Identity*. Houston: Arte Público Press, 1993.

Foley, Neil. *Quest for Equality: The Failed Promise of Black-Brown Solidarity*. Cambridge, MA: Harvard University Press, 2010.

———. *The White Scourge: Mexicans, Blacks, and Poor Whites in Texas Cotton Culture*. Berkeley: University of California Press, 1997.

Foley, Ryan J. "In Iowa City, Latinos Faced the Nation's Worst Bias in Home Loans." *Iowa City Press-Citizen,* February 15, 2018. www.press-citizen.com.

Fox, Claire F. "Commentary: The Transnational Turn and the Hemispheric Return." *American Literary History* 18, no. 3 (Autumn 2006): 638–47.

———. *The Fence and the River: Culture and Politics at the U.S.-Mexico Border.* Minneapolis: University of Minnesota Press, 1999.

———. *Making Art Panamerican: Cultural Policy and the Cold War.* Minneapolis: University of Minnesota Press, 2013.

Fox, Ragan. "Sober Drag Queens, Digital Forests, and Bloated 'Lesbians': Performing Gay Identities Online." *Qualitative Inquiry* 14, no. 7 (October 2008): 1245–63.

Franks, Mary Anne. "How to Feel Like a Woman, or Why Punishment Is a Drag." *UCLA Law Review* 61, no. 3 (2014): 566–605.

Fraser, Nancy. "Rethinking the Public Sphere: A Contribution to the Critique of Actually Existing." *Social Text,* no. 25–56 (1990): 56–80.

Freedman, Eric. "Public Access / Private Confession: Home Video as (Queer) Community Television." In *The Television Studies Reader,* edited by Robert C. Allen and Annette Hill, 343–53. London: Routledge, 2004.

Ganz, Cheryl, and Margaret Strobel. *Pots of Promise: Mexicans and Pottery at Hull-House, 1920–40.* Urbana: University of Illinois Press with Jane Addams Hull-House Museum, 2004.

Garcia, Alma M., ed. *Chicana Feminist Thought: The Basic Historical Writings.* New York: Routledge, 1997.

Garcia, Cindy. *Salsa Crossings: Dancing Latinidad in Los Angeles.* Durham, NC: Duke University Press, 2013.

García, Lorena, and Mérida Rúa. "Processing *Latinidad*: Mapping Latino Urban Landscapes through Chicago Ethnic Festivals." *Latino Studies* 5, no. 3 (2007): 317–39.

García, María Cristina. *Seeking Refuge: Central American Migration to Mexico, the United States, and Canada.* Berkeley: University of California Press, 2006.

García-Peña, Lorgia. *The Borders of Dominicanidad: Race, Nation, and Archives of Contradiction.* Durham, NC: Duke University Press, 2016.

Goeman, Mishuana. "Land as Life." In *Native Studies Keywords,* edited by Stephanie Nohelani Teves, Andrea Smith, and Michelle H. Raheja, 71-89. Tucson: University of Arizona Press, 2015.

Goetz, Edward G., Brittany Lewis, Anthony Damiano, and Molly Calhoun. *The Diversity of Gentrification: Multiple Forms of Gentrification in Minneapolis and St. Paul.* Minneapolis: University of Minnesota Press, 2019.

Goldberg, David. *Black Firefighters and the FDNY: The Struggle for Jobs, Justice, and Equity in New York City.* Chapel Hill: University of North Carolina Press, 2017.

Golden, Renny, and Michael McConnell. *Sanctuary: The New Underground Railroad.* Maryknoll, NY: Orbis Books, 1986.

Goldman, Dara E. *Out of Bounds: Islands and the Demarcation of Identity in the Hispanic Caribbean.* Lewisburg, PA: Bucknell University Press, 2008.

Goldman, Shifra M. "Siqueiros and Three Early Murals in Los Angeles." *Art Journal* 33, no. 4 (Summer 1974): 321–27.

Gómez, Laura E. *Manifest Destinies: The Making of the Mexican American Race.* New York: New York University Press, 2008.

González, Anita. *Afro-Mexico: Dancing between Myth and Reality*. Austin: University of Texas Press, 2010.

———. *Jarocho's Soul: Cultural Identity and AfroMexican Dance*. Lanham, MD: University Press of America, 2004.

González, José Gamaliel. *Bringing Aztlán to Mexican Chicago: My Life, My Work, My Art*. Urbana: University of Illinois Press, 2010.

González, Sergio M. "Interethnic Catholicism and Transnational Religious Connections: Milwaukee's Mexican Mission Chapel of Our Lady of Guadalupe, 1924–1929." *Journal of American Ethnic History* 36, no. 1 (Fall 2016): 5–30.

Gosse, Van. "'The North American Front': Central American Solidarity in the Reagan Era." In *Reshaping the US Left: Popular Struggles in the 1980s*, edited by Mike Davis and Michael Sprinker, 11–50. New York: Verso, 1988.

Grabell, Michael. "Sold for Parts: Case Farms Took Advantage of Immigrant Workers Then Used U.S. Immigration Law Against Them When They Got Hurt or Fought Back." *ProPublica*, May 1, 2017. https://www.propublica.org/article/case-farms-chicken-industry-immigrant-workers-and-american-labor-law.

Grady, Karen. "Lowrider Art and Latino Students in the Rural Midwest." In *Education in the New Latino Diaspora: Policy and the Politics of Identity*, edited by Stanton Wortham, Enrique G. Murillo, and Edmund T. Hamann. Westport, CT: Ablex Publisher, 2002.

Guha, Ramachandra, and J. Martinez-Alier. *Varieties of Environmentalism: Essays North and South*. London: Earthscan Publications, 1997.

Guidotti-Hernández, Nicole M. "Affective Communities and Millennial Desires: Latinx, or Why My Computer Won't Recognize Latina/o." *Cultural Dynamics* 29, no. 3 (2017): 141–59.

Gutiérrez, David. *Walls and Mirrors: Mexican Americans, Mexican Immigrants, and the Politics of Ethnicity*. Berkeley: University of California Press, 1995.

Gutiérrez, Gustavo. *A Theology of Liberation: History, Politics, and Salvation*. 15th anniversary ed. Maryknoll, NY: Orbis Books, 1988.

Gutiérrez, Ramón A., and Geneviéve Fabre, eds. *Feasts and Celebrations in North American Ethnic Communities*. Albuquerque: University of New Mexico Press, 1995.

Hames-García, Michael. "How to Tell a Mestizo from an Enchirito®: Colonialism and National Culture in the Borderlands." *Diacritics* 30, no. 4 (2000): 102-22.

Hames-García, Michael, and Ernesto Javier Martínez, eds. *Gay Latino Studies: A Critical Reader*. Durham, NC: Duke University Press, 2011.

Haraway, Donna J. *Staying with the Trouble: Making Kin in the Chthulucene*. Durham, NC: Duke University Press, 2016.

Harnish, David. "Tejano Music in the Urbanizing Midwest: The Musical Story of Conjunto Master Jesse Ponce." *Journal of the Society for American Music* 3, no. 2 (May 2009): 195–219.

Harvey, Paul. *Freedom's Coming: Religious Culture and the Shaping of the South from the Civil War through the Civil Rights Era*. Chapel Hill: University of North Carolina Press, 2007.

Haslip-Viera, Gabriel, et al., eds. *Taíno Revival: Critical Perspectives on Puerto Rican Identity and Cultural Politics*. Princeton, NJ: Markus Wiener Publishers, 2001.

Hayden, Dolores. *The Power of Place: Urban Landscapes as Public History*. Cambridge, MA: MIT Press, 1997.

Herrera, Brian Eugenio. *Latin Numbers: Playing Latino in Twentieth-Century U.S. Popular Performance*. Ann Arbor: University of Michigan Press, 2015.

Herrera, Olga. "'Street of Ouzo, Arak, and Tequila': Recalling the Marvelous Strangeness of Chicago's New West Side with Carlos Cortéz, Sandra Cisneros, and Daniel J. Martinez." *MELUS: Multi-ethnic Literature of the United States* 42, no. 1 (2017): 162–85.

Herrera, Olga, V. A. Sorell, and Gilberto Cardenas. *Toward the Preservation of a Heritage: Latin American and Latino Art in the Midwestern United States*. Notre Dame, IN: Institute for Latino Studies, 2008.

Hinderer Cruz, Max Jorge. "TROPICAMP: Some Notes on Hélio Oiticica's 1971 Text." *Afterall* 28 (Autumn/Winter 2011): n.p. https://www.afterall.org/journal/issue.28/tropicamp-pre-and-post-tropic-lia-at-once-some-contextual-notes-onh-lio-oiticica-s-1971-te.

Hinojosa, Felipe. *Latino Mennonites: Civil Rights, Faith, and Evangelical Culture*. Baltimore, MD: Johns Hopkins University Press, 2014.

Innis-Jimenez, Michael. *Steel Barrio: The Great Mexican Migration to South Chicago, 1915–1940*. New York: NYU Press, 2013.

Izzo, Amanda. *Liberal Christianity and Women's Global Activism: The YWCA of the USA and the Maryknoll Sisters*. New Brunswick, NJ: Rutgers University Press, 2018.

Jelks, Randal Maurice. *African Americans in the Furniture City: The Struggle for Civil Rights in Grand Rapids*. Urbana: University of Illinois Press, 2006.

Jirasek, Rita Arias, and Carlos Tortolero. *Mexican Chicago*. Chicago: Arcadia Publishing, 2001.

Johnson, E. Patrick, and Ramón H. Rivera-Servera, eds. *Blacktino Queer Performance*. Durham, NC: Duke University Press, 2016.

Jones, John Paul, III, et al. "Neil Smith's Scale." *Antipode* 49, no. S1 (2017): 138–52.

Jones, Omi Osun Joni L. *Theatrical Jazz: Performance, àṣẹ, and the Power of the Present Moment*. Columbus: Ohio University Press, 2015.Kanellos, Nicolás. "Recovering and Re-constructing Early Twentieth-Century Hispanic Immigrant Print Culture in the US." *American Literary History* 19, no. 2 (2007): 438–55.

Kanellos, Nicolás, and Helvetia Martell. *Hispanic Periodicals in the United States, Origins to 1960: A Brief History and Comprehensive Bibliography*. Houston: Arte Público Press, 2000.

Kanter, Deborah. "Making Mexican Parishes: Ethnic Succession in Chicago Churches, 1947–1977." *U.S. Catholic Historian* 30, no. 2 (2012): 35–58.

Katznelson, Ira. *When Affirmative Action Was White: An Untold History of Racial Inequality in Twentieth-Century America*. New York: W. W. Norton & Company, 2005.

Kemper, Robert V. "The Compadrazgo in Urban Mexico." *Anthropological Quarterly* 55, no. 1 (January 1982): 17–30.

Kennedy, Randall. *For Discrimination: Race, Affirmative Action, and the Law*. New York: Vintage Books, 2015.

Kiel, Doug. "Untaming the Mild Frontier: In Search of New Midwestern Histories." *Middle West Review* 1, no. 1 (Fall 2014): 9–38.

Kolko, Jed. "How Much Slower Would the U.S. Grow without Immigration? In Many Places, a Lot." *New York Times*, April 14, 2019. https://www.nytimes.com/2019/04/18/upshot/how-much-slower-would-the-us-grow-without-immigration-in-many-places-a-lot.html.

Kondo, Dorinne. *Worldmaking: Race, Performance, and the Work of Creativity*. Durham, NC: Duke University Press, 2018.

Korrol, Virginia Sánchez. *From Colonia to Community: The History of Puerto Ricans in New York City*. Berkeley: University of California Press, 1994.

Lacey, J. "Sonic Placemaking: Three Approaches and Ten Attributes for the Creation of Enduring Urban Sound Art Installations." *Organised Sound* 21, no. 2 (2016): 147–59.

La Fountain-Stokes, Lawrence. "The Queer Politics of Spanglish." *Critical Moment* 9 (2005).

———. *Queer Ricans: Cultures and Sexualities in the Diaspora*. Minneapolis: University of Minnesota Press, 2009.

———. "Translocas: Migration, Homosexuality, and Transvestism in Recent Puerto Rican Performance." *emisférica* 8, no. 1 (Summer 2011), http://archive.hemispheric institute.org/hemi/en/e-misferica-81/lafountain.

———. *Translocas: The Politics of Puerto Rican Drag and Trans Performance*. Ann Arbor: University of Michigan Press, 2021.

La Fountain-Stokes, Lawrence, Lourdes Torres, and Ramón H. Rivera-Servera. "Towards an Archive of Latina/o Queer Chicago: Art, Politics, and Social Performance." In *Out in Chicago: LGBT History at the Crossroads*, edited by Jill Austin and Jennifer Brier, 127–53. Chicago: Chicago History Museum, 2011.

Laó-Montes, Agustín, and Arlene Dávila, eds. *Mambo Montage: The Latinization of New York*. New York: Columbia University Press, 2001.

Lara, Jesus J. *Latino Placemaking and Planning: Cultural Resilience and Strategies for Reurbanization*. Tucson: University of Arizona Press, 2018.

The Latina Feminist Group, eds. *Telling to Live: Latina Feminist Testimonios*. Durham, NC: Duke University Press, 2001.

Latorre, Guisela. *Walls of Empowerment: Chicana/o Indigenist Murals of California*. Austin: University of Texas Press, 2008.

The Leadership Conference on Civil and Human Rights. "Trump Administration Civil and Human Rights Rollbacks." CivilRights.org. https://civilrights.org/trump -rollbacks/.

Lefebvre, Henri. *The Production of Space*. Translated by Donald Nicolson-Smith. Malden, MA: Blackwell Publishing, 1974.

Lepecki, André. *Exhausting Dance: Performance and the Politics of Movement*. New York: Routledge, 2006.

Le Talek, Jean-Yves. *Folles de France: Repenser l'homosexualité masculine*. Paris: La Découverte, 2008.

Levi, Jerome M. "Hidden Transcripts among the Rarámuri: Culture, Resistance, and Interethnic Relations in Northern Mexico." *American Ethnologist* 26, no. 1 (February 1999): 90–113.

Licona, Adela C. *Zines in Third Spaces: Radical Cooperation and Borderlands Rhetoric.* Albany: State University of New York Press, 2013.

Licona, Adela, and Marta Maria Maldonado. "The Social Production of Latin@ Visibilities and Invisibilities: Geographies of Power in Small Town America." *Antipode* 46, no. 2 (2014): 517–36.

Lidstrom, David P., and Adriana López Ramírez. "Pioneers and Followers: Migrant Selectivity and the Development of U.S. Migration Streams in Latin America." *Annals of the American Academy of Political and Social Science* 63, no. 1 (2010): 53–77.

Limón, José E. "*Al Norte* toward Home: Texas, the Midwest, and Mexican American Critical Regionalism." In *The Latina/o Midwest Reader*, edited by Omar Valerio-Jiménez et al., 40–56. Urbana: University of Illinois Press, 2017.

Loescher, Gil. "Humanitarianism and Politics in Central America." *Political Science Quarterly* 103, no. 2 (Summer 1988): 295–320.

López, Antonio. *Unbecoming Blackness: The Diaspora Cultures of Afro-Cuban America.* New York: New York University Press, 2012.

Lovink, Geert, and Sabine Niederer, eds. *Video Vortex Reader: Responses to YouTube.* INC Reader #4. Amsterdam: Institute of Network Cultures, 2008.

Lupton, Julia Reinhard. "Hospitality." In *Early Modern Theatricality*, edited by Henry S. Turner. Oxford Twenty-First Century Approaches to Literature. Oxford: Oxford University Press, 2013.

Lyman, Jessica Lopez. "Revitalizing Poetics: Latin@s Reshape South Minneapolis." *Chicana/Latina Studies* 15, no. 2 (2016): 33–61.

Lynch, Barbara Deutsch. "The Garden and the Sea: U.S. Latino Environmental Discourses and Mainstream Environmentalism." *Social Problems* 40, no. 1 (February 1993): 108–24.

Mager, Astrid. "Algorithmic Ideology: How Capitalist Society Shapes Search Engines." *Information, Communication and Society* 15, no. 5 (2012): 769–87.

Manning, Erin. *Politics of Touch: Sense, Movement, Sovereignty.* Minneapolis: University of Minnesota Press, 2007.

Marchi, Regina M. *Day of the Dead in the USA: The Migration and Transformation of a Cultural Phenomenon.* New Brunswick, NJ: Rutgers University Press, 2009.

Markusen, Ann, and Anne Gadwa. *Creative Placemaking.* Washington, DC: National Endowment for the Arts, 2010.

Martinez, Anne. *Catholic Borderlands: Mapping Catholicism onto American Empire, 1905–1935.* Lincoln: University of Nebraska Press, 2014.

Martínez, Norell. "Femzines, Artivism, and Altar Aesthetics: Third Wave Feminism Chicana Style." *Chiricú Journal: Latina/o Literatures, Arts, and Cultures* 2, no. 2 (2018): 45–67.

Martínez, Ruben O. *Latinos in the Midwest.* East Lansing: Michigan State University Press, 2011.

McCarthy, Maura, PBVM. Interview in *Surviving Globalization in Three Latin Ameri-*

can Communities, Part Two: Bolivia, edited by Denis Lynn Daly Heyck, 182–93. Peterborough, ON: Broadview, 2002.

McDonnell, Judith, and Cileine de Lourenco. "You're Brazilian, Right? What Kind of Brazilian Are You? The Racialization of Brazilian Immigrant Women." *Ethnic and Racial Studies* 32, no. 2 (2009): 239–56.

McMillian, John. *Smoking Typewriters: The Sixties Underground Press and the Rise of Alternative Media in America.* New York: Oxford University Press, 2011.

Medina, Lara and Gilbert R. Cadena. "Días de los Muertos: Public Ritual, Community Renewal, and Popular Religion in Los Angeles." In *Horizons of the Sacred*, edited by Timothy M. Matovina and Gary Riebe-Estrella, 69-94. Ithaca, NY: Cornell University Press, 2002.

Milian, Claudia. *Latining America: Black-Brown Passages and the Coloring of Latina/o Studies.* Athens: University of Georgia Press, 2013.

Millard, Ann V., and Jorge Chapa. *Apple Pie and Enchiladas: Latino Newcomers in the Rural Midwest.* Austin: University of Texas Press, 2004.

Milstead, Frances, Kevin Heffernan, and Steve Yeager. *My Son Divine.* Los Angeles: Alyson Books, 2001.

Montano, Linda M. *Letters from Linda M. Montano.* Edited by Jennie Klein. London: Routledge, 2005.

Mooney Smith, Lisa. *Knowledge Transfer in Higher Education: Collaboration in the Arts.* New York: Palgrave Macmillan, 2012.

Moraga, Cherríe, Gloria Anzaldúa, and Toni Cade Bambara, eds. *This Bridge Called My Back: Writing by Radical Women of Color.* New York: Kitchen Table Press, 1981.

Morales, Ed. "Latinos in Alternative Media: Latinos as an Alternative Media Paradigm." In *Contemporary Latina/o Media: Production, Circulation, Politics*, edited by Arlene Dávila and Yeidy M. Rivero, 322–36. New York: New York University Press, 2014.

Morgensen, Scott Lauria. "Ancient Roots through Settled Land: Imagining Indigeneity and Place among Radical Faeries." In *Spaces between Us: Queer Settler Colonialism and Indigenous Decolonization*, 127-60. Minneapolis: University of Minnesota Press, 2011.

Mumm, Jesse Stewart. "When the White People Come: Gentrification and Race in Puerto Rican Chicago." PhD dissertation, Northwestern University, 2014.

Muñoz, José Esteban. *Cruising Utopia: The Then and There of Queer Futurity.* New York: NYU Press, 2009.

———. *Disidentifications: Queers of Color and the Performance of Politics.* Minneapolis: University of Minnesota Press, 1999.

———. "Feeling Brown, Feeling Down: Latina Affect, the Performativity of Race, and the Depressive Position." *Signs* 31, no. 3 (2006): 675–88.

———. *The Sense of Brown.* Edited and with an introduction by Joshua Chambers-Letson and Tavia Nyong'o. Durham, NC: Duke University Press, 2020.

Murray, Jennifer Lynn. "The Chicago Religious Task Force on Central America: Moral Defiance in the Face of U.S. Policy, 1980-1992." MA thesis, University of Wisconsin–Eau Claire, 2012.

Nakamura, Lisa. *Digitizing Race: Visual Cultures of the Internet*. Minneapolis: University of Minnesota Press, 2007.

Negrón-Muntaner, Frances. *Boricua Pop: Puerto Ricans and the Latinization of American Culture*. New York: New York University Press, 2004.

———. "The Gang's Not All Here: The State of Latinos in Contemporary US Media." In *Politics, Contemporary Latina/o Media: Production, Circulation*, edited by Arlene Dávila and Yeidy M. Rivero, 103–24. New York: New York University Press, 2014.

———, ed. *None of the Above: Puerto Ricans in the Global Era*. New York: Palgrave Macmillan, 2007.

Newton, Esther. *Mother Camp: Female Impersonators in America*. 1972; Chicago: University of Chicago Press, 1979.

Noble, Safiya Umoja. *Algorithms of Oppression: How Search Engines Reinforce Racism*. New York: New York University Press, 2018.

Nunn, Jerry. "'Feast' Duo Still Having Fun after 13 Years." *Windy City Times*, December 27, 2017, 18. ProQuest.

Obejas, Achy. "'Feast of Fools'—a Celebration of Diversity. Colorful Fausto Fernós—an Appropriate Host for Radical Faeries." *Chicago Tribune*, March 31, 2000, 28.

Oiticica, Hélio. "Mario Montez, Tropicamp." *Afterall* 28 (2011): 16–21. https://www.afterall.org/journal/issue.28/mario-montez-tropicamp.

Oiticica, Hélio, and Mario Montez. "Héliotape with Mario Montez (1971)." *Criticism* 56, no. 2 (2014): 379–404.

Orozco, Myrna, and Reverend Noel Anderson. "Sanctuary in the Age of Trump: The Rise of the Movement a Year into the Trump Administration." Church World Service, January 2018. https://www.sanctuarynotdeportation.org/sanctuary-report-2018.html.

Orsi, Robert. *Thank You, St. Jude: Women's Devotion to the Patron Saint of Hopeless Causes*. New Haven, CT: Yale University Press, 1998.

Ortiz Cuadra, Cruz Miguel. *Eating Puerto Rico: A History of Food, Culture, and Identity*. Translated by Russ Davidson. Chapel Hill: University of North Carolina Press, 2013.

Osborn, Bradley. "The *Feast of Fools*: The Fiercest Gay Podcast in the Universe." BradleyOsborn.com, December 2006.

Padilla, Felix M. *Latino Ethnic Consciousness: The Case of Mexican Americans and Puerto Ricans in Chicago*. Notre Dame, IN: University of Notre Dame Press, 1985.

———. *Puerto Rican Chicago*. Notre Dame: University of Notre Dame Press, 1987.

Pallares, Amalia. *Family Activism: Immigrant Struggles and the Politics of Noncitizenship*. New Brunswick, NJ: Rutgers University Press, 2015.

Pallares, Amalia, and Nilda Flores-González, eds. *¡Marcha! Latino Chicago and the Immigrant Rights Movement*. Urbana: University of Illinois Press, 2010.

Peña, Elaine. "Beyond Mexico: Guadalupan Sacred Space Production and Mobilization in a Chicago Suburb." *American Quarterly* 60, no. 3 (September 2008): 721–47.

———. *Performing Piety: Making Space Sacred with the Virgin of Guadalupe*. Berkeley: University of California Press, 2011.

Pérez, Gina M. *The Near Northwest Side Story: Migration, Displacement, and Puerto Rican Families*. Berkeley: University of California Press, 2004.

Pérez, Gina M., Frank A. Guridy, and Adrian Burgos Jr., eds. *Beyond El Barrio: Everyday Life in Latina/o America*. New York: New York University Press, 2010.

Pérez, Laura E. *Chicana Art: The Politics of Spiritual and Aesthetic Altarities*. Durham, NC: Duke University Press, 2007.

Pew Research Center. "The Shifting Religious Identity of Latinos in the United States." May 7, 2014. https://www.pewresearch.org/wp-content/uploads/sites/7/2014/05/Latinos-Religion-07-22-full-report.pdf.

Pirie, Sophie H. "The Origins of a Political Trial: The Sanctuary Movement and Political Justice." *Yale Journal of Law & the Humanities* 2, no. 2 (1990): 381–416.

Potowski, Kim, and Janine Matts. "MexiRicans: Interethnic Language and Identity." *Journal of Language, Identity and Education* 7, no. 2 (2008): 137–60.

Povinelli, Elizabeth A. *Economies of Abandonment: Social Belonging and Endurance in Late Liberalism*. Durham, NC: Duke University Press, 2011.

Power, Margaret, and Julie A. Charlip. "Introduction: On Solidarity." *Latin American Perspectives* 36, no. 6 (November 2009): 3–9.

Poyo, Gerald E. "'Integration without Assimilation': Cuban Catholics in Miami, 1960–1980." *U.S. Catholic Historian* 20, no. 4 (Fall 2002): 91–109.

Quijano, Aníbal, and Immanuel Wallerstein. "Americanity as a Concept, or the Americas in the Modern World-System." *International Social Science Journal* 44, no. 4 (1992): 549–57.

Ramírez, Leonard G. *Chicanas of 18th Street: Narratives of a Movement from Latino Chicago*. Urbana: University of Illinois Press, 2011.

Ramírez, Sara A., and Norma E. Cantú. "Publishing Work That Matters: Third Woman Press and Its Impact on Chicana and Latina Publishing." *Diálogo* 20, no. 2 (2017): 77–85.

Ramirez-Valles, Jesus. *Compañeros: Latino Activists in the Face of AIDS*. Urbana: University of Illinois Press, 2011.

Ramos-Zayas, Ana Y. "Between 'Cultural Excess' and Racial 'Invisibility': Brazilians and the Commercialization of Culture in Newark." *Becoming Brazuca: Brazilian Immigration to the United States* (2008): 271–86.

———. *National Performances: The Politics of Class, Race, and Space in Puerto Rican Chicago*. Chicago: University of Chicago Press, 2003.

Rast, Raymond W. "Cultivating a Shared Sense of Place: Ethnic Mexicans and the Environment in Twentieth-Century Kansas City." *Diálogo* 21, no. 1 (2018): 35–49.

Reay, Riccki. "*I Am the Queen*: Latest Trailer Sashays In." *Movie TV Tech Geeks*, October 13, 2015. https://movietvtechgeeks.com/i-am-the-queen-latest-trailer-sashays-in/.

Reinfelder, Monika, ed. *Amazon to Zami: Towards a Global Lesbian Feminism*. London: Cassell, 1996.

Rentas Torres, Sandra. "Cuando el hogar es la escuela." *El Nuevo Día*, April 13, 1983, 42–43.

Ricourt, Milagros, and Ruby Danta. *Hispanas de Queens: Latino Panethnicity in a New York City Neighborhood*. Ithaca, NY: Cornell University Press, 2003.

Rios, Michael, and Joshua Watkins. "Beyond 'Place': Translocal Placemaking of the

Hmong Diaspora." *Journal of Planning Education and Research* 35, no. 2 (2015): 209–19.

Rivera-Servera, Ramón H. *Performing Queer Latinidad: Dance, Sexuality, Politics.* Ann Arbor: University of Michigan Press, 2012.

Robinson, Todd. *A City within a City: The Black Freedom Struggle in Grand Rapids.* Philadelphia: Temple University Press, 2012.

Rodríguez, Juana María. *Queer Latinidad: Identity Practices, Discursive Places.* New York: NYU Press, 2003.

Rodriguez, Marc Simon. *The Tejano Diaspora: Mexican Americanism and Ethnic Politics in Texas and Wisconsin.* Chapel Hill: University of North Carolina Press, 2011.

Rodríguez, Richard T. "X Marks the Spot." *Cultural Dynamics* 29, no. 3 (2017): 202–13.

Rosaldo, Renato. "Cultural Citizenship and Educational Democracy." *Cultural Anthropology* 9, no. 3 (1994): 402–11.

Rosello, Mireille. *Postcolonial Hospitality: The Immigrant as Guest.* Stanford, CA: Stanford University Press, 2001.

Rúa, Mérida. "Colao Subjectivities: PortoMex and MexiRican Perspectives on Language and Identity." *Centro Journal* 13, no. 2 (2001).

———. *A Grounded Identidad: Making New Lives in Chicago's Puerto Rican Neighborhoods.* Oxford: Oxford University Press, 2012.

———, ed. *Latino Urban Ethnography and the Work of Elena Padilla.* Urbana: University of Illinois Press, 2010.

Rudolph, Jennifer Domino. *Embodying Latino Masculinities: Producing Masculatinidad.* New York: Palgrave Macmillan, 2012.

Ruiz, Sandra. *Ricanness: Enduring Time in Anticolonial Performance.* New York: NYU Press, 2019.

Ruiz, Vicki. *From out of the Shadows: Mexican Women in Twentieth-Century America.* New York: Oxford University Press, 2008.

Rupp, Leila J., and Verta Taylor. *Drag Queens at the 801 Cabaret.* Chicago: University of Chicago Press, 2003.

Saldívar, José David. *Trans-Americanity: Subaltern Modernities, Global Coloniality, and the Cultures of Greater Mexico.* Durham, NC: Duke University Press, 2011.

Saldívar, Ramón. *Chicano Narrative: The Dialectics of Difference.* Madison: University of Wisconsin Press, 1990.

Salvatierra, Alexia. "Sacred Refuge." *Sojourners* 36, no. 9 (September/October 2007): 12–20.

Samora, Julian, and Richard A. Lamanna. *Mexican Americans in a Midwest Metropolis: A Study of East Chicago.* Los Angeles: University of California Mexican-American Study Project, 1967.

Sandoval, Chela. *Methodology of the Oppressed.* Minneapolis: University of Minnesota Press, 2000.

Sánchez, George J. *Becoming Mexican American: Ethnicity, Culture, and Identity in Chicano Los Angeles, 1900–1945.* New York: Oxford University Press, 1993.

Sandoval, Gerardo Francisco. "Transnational Placemaking in Small-Town America."

In *Diálogos: Placemaking in Latino Communities*, edited by Michael Rios, Leonardo Vazquez, and Lucrezia Miranda, 50–66. New York: Routledge, 2012.

Sandoval, Gerardo Francisco, and Marta Maria Maldonado. "Latino Urbanism Revisited: Placemaking in New Gateways and the Urban-Rural Interface." *Journal of Urbanism: International Research on Placemaking and Urban Sustainability* 5, no. 2–3 (2012): 193–218. doi:10.1080/17549175.2012.693123.

Sandoval-Sánchez, Alberto. *José Can You See? Latinos on and off Broadway*. Madison: University of Wisconsin Press, 1999.

Sandoval-Strausz, Andrew K. *Barrio America: How Latino Immigrants Saved the American City*. New York: Basic Books, 2019.

———. "*Viewpoint*: Latino Vernaculars and the Emerging National Landscape." *Buildings & Landscapes* 20, no. 1 (Spring 2013): 1–18.

Schechner, Richard. *Performance Theory*. New York: Routledge, 1988.

Schjeldahl, Peter. "The Song of a Nation: Walt Whitman at Two Hundred." *New Yorker Magazine*, Art World section, June 24, 2019, 74–75.

Schneekloth, Lynda H., and Robert G. Shibley. *Placemaking: The Art and Practice of Building Communities*. New York: John Wiley & Sons, 1995.

Schwartz, Stuart. *Slaves, Peasants, and Rebels: Reconsidering Brazilian Slavery*. Urbana: University of Illinois Press, 1992.

Shapiro, Gregg. "Feast of Fools Takes Gay Podcasting to New Heights." AfterElton.com, August 22, 2006. http://www.afterellen.com/archive/elton/people/2006/8/fausto.html.

Sharpe, Christina. *In the Wake: On Blackness and Being*. Durham, NC: Duke University Press, 2016.

Shear, Michael D., and Julie Hirschfeld Davis. "Trump Moves to End DACA and Calls on Congress to Act." *New York Times*, September 5, 2017. https://www.nytimes.com/2017/09/05/us/politics/trump-daca-dreamers-immigration.html.

Smith, Christian. *The Emergence of Liberation Theology: Radical Religion and Social Movement Theory*. Chicago: University of Chicago Press, 1991.

Smith, Ryan. "Students Meet to Discuss Trump Chants Made during Game." KCCI Des Moines, February 25, 2016. www.kcci.com.

Smith Richards, Jennifer. "Hispanics Lead Population Growth in Ohio." *Columbus Dispatch*, June 26, 2014. http://www.dispatch.com/content/stories/local/2014/06/26/hispanics-lead-state-population-increases.html.

Soja, Edward. *Postmodern Geographies: The Reassertion of Space in Critical Social Theory*. London: Verso, 2011.

Solomon, Serena. "A Bold Artist, a Quiet Texas Town and the Heritage of the Borderland." *New York Times*, February 16, 2018. https://www.nytimes.com/2018/02/16/arts/design/michael-tracy-san-ygnacio-texas.html.

Soto, Erica, and Richard Unapanta. "Puerto Rican Diaspora: Lorain, Ohio." *Vimeo*. June 6, 2017. https://vimeo.com/220523605.

Sotomayor, Antonio. *The Sovereign Colony: Olympic Sport, National Identity, and International Politics in Puerto Rico*. Lincoln: University of Nebraska Press, 2016.

Stark, David. "Parish Registers as a Window to the Past: Reconstructing the Demographic Behavior of the Enslaved Population in Eighteenth-Century Arecibo, Puerto Rico." *Colonial Latin American Historical Review,* no. 15 (Winter 2006): 1–30.

Stern, Alexandra Minna. *Eugenic Nation: Faults and Frontiers of Better Breeding in Modern America.* Berkeley: University of California Press, 2005.

Stevens, Nolan, Megan Uhrig, and Paola McDowell. "Ohio Hispanic Voters: Eligibility, Participation, and Preferences." PDF. Ohio Commission on Hispanic/Latino Affairs, April 15, 2013.

Suárez, Juan A. "Jack Smith, Hélio Oiticica, Tropicalism." *Criticism* 56, no. 2 (2014): 295–328.

Sugrue, Thomas. *The Origins of the Urban Crisis: Race and Inequality in Postwar Detroit.* Updated ed. Princeton, NJ: Princeton University Press, 2014.

Sze, Julie, ed. *Sustainability: Approaches to Environmental Justice and Social Power.* New York: New York University Press Scholarship Online, 2018. DOI: 10.18574/nyu/9781479894567.001.0001.

Ta, Linh. "Racist Chant Targets Iowa High School Basketball Players." *Des Moines Register,* January 25, 2018. https://www.desmoinesregister.com/.

Taylor, Diana. *The Archive and the Repertoire: Performing Cultural Memory in the Americas.* Durham, NC: Duke University Press, 2003.

———, ed. *Negotiating Performance: Gender, Sexuality, and Theatricality in Latin/o America.* Durham, NC: Duke University Press, 1994.

Todd, Molly. "'We Were Part of the Revolutionary Movement There': Wisconsin Peace Progressives and Solidarity with El Salvador in the Reagan Era." *Journal of Civil and Human Rights* 3, no. 1 (Spring/Summer 2017): 1–56.

Toro, Ana Teresa. "La mancha que nos une." *El Nuevo Día,* December 25, 2012. http://www.elnuevodia.com/lamanchaquenosune-1414028.html.

Torres, Lourdes. "Building a Translengua in Latina Lesbian Organizing." *Journal of Lesbian Studies* 20, no. 2 (2016): 272–88.

Tosta, Antonio Luciano de Andrade. "The Hispanic and Luso-Brazilian World: Latino, Eu? The Paradoxical Interplay of Identity in Brazuca Literature." *Hispania* 87, no. 3 (2004): 576–85.

Treviño, Roberto R. *The Church in the Barrio: Mexican American Ethno-Catholicism in Houston.* Chapel Hill: University of North Carolina Press, 2006.

Tuan, Yi-Fu. "Place: An Experiential Perspective." *Geographical Review* 65, no. 2 (1975): 151–65.

———. *Topophilia: A Study of Environmental Perception, Attitudes, and Values.* Englewood Cliffs, NJ: Prentice-Hall, 1974.

United States Conference of Catholic Bishops and Conferencia del Episcopado Mexicano. *Strangers No Longer: Together on the Journey of Hope.* Washington, DC: United States Conference of Catholic Bishops, 2003.

Urayoán, Noel. *In Visible Movement: Nuyorican Poetry from the Sixties to Slam.* Iowa City: University of Iowa Press, 2014.

Urrieta, Luis, Jr. "Identity, Violence, and Authenticity: Challenging Static Conceptions of Identity." *Latino Studies* 15, no. 2 (2017): 254–61.

Valdés, Dennis Nodín. *Al Norte: Agricultural Workers in the Great Lakes Region, 1917–1970.* 1st ed. Mexican American Monographs, no. 13. Austin: University of Texas Press, 1991.

———. *Barrios Norteños: St. Paul and Midwestern Mexican Communities in the Twentieth Century.* Austin: University of Texas Press, 2000.

Valdés, Dionicio. *Mexicans in Minnesota.* Minneapolis: Minnesota Historical Society Press, 2005.

Valdivia, Angharad N., and Matt Garcia, eds. *Mapping Latina/o Studies: An Interdisciplinary Reader.* New York: Peter Lang, 2012.

Valerio-Jiménez, Omar. "Racializing Mexican Immigrants in the Heartland: Iowa's Early Mexican Communities, 1880–1930." *Annals of Iowa* 75, no. 1 (Winter 2016): 1–46.

Valerio-Jiménez, Omar, Santiago Vaquera-Vásquez, and Claire F. Fox, eds. *The Latina/o Midwest Reader.* Urbana: University of Illinois Press, 2017.

Vargas, Deborah R. "Ruminations on *Lo Sucio* as a Latino Queer Analytic." *American Quarterly* 66, no. 3 (September 2014): 715–26.

Vargas, Deborah R., Nancy Raquel Mirabal, and Lawrence Fountain-Stokes, eds. *Keywords for Latina/o Studies.* New York: New York University Press, 2017.

Vargas, Zaragosa. *Labor Rights Are Civil Rights: Mexican American Workers in Twentieth-Century America.* Princeton, NJ: Princeton University Press, 2007.

———. *Proletarians of the North: A History of Mexican Industrial Workers in Detroit and the Midwest, 1917–1933.* Berkeley: University of California Press, 1999.

Vega, Sujey. *Latino Heartland: Of Borders and Belonging in the Midwest.* New York: New York University Press, 2015.

Velazquez, Mirelsie. "Solidarity and Empowerment in Chicago's Puerto Rican Print Culture." *Latino Studies* 12, no. 1 (2014): 88–110.

Villa, Raúl Homero. *Barrio Logos: Space and Place in Urban Chicano Literature and Culture.* Austin: University of Texas Press, 2000.

Wald, Sarah D., David J. Vázquez, Priscilla Solis Ybarra, and Sarah Jaquette Ray, eds. *Latinx Environmentalisms: Place, Justice, and the Decolonial.* Philadelphia: Temple University Press, 2019.

Warner, Michael. "Publics and Counterpublics." *Public Culture* 14, no. 1 (2002): 49–90.

Waszak, Mary Ellen. *A Guide to Chicago's Zine Scene & Alternative Press.* Chicago: iWrite Publications Inc., 2006.

Western Reserve Historical Society. *The Mexican Community in Lorain Ohio.* Rev. ed. Lorain, OH: Western Reserve Historical Society, 1999.

Wilkinson, Kenton T. *Spanish-Language Television in the United States: Fifty Years of Development.* New York: Routledge, 2016.

Winston, Bryan. *Mapping the Mexican Midwest.* https://mappingthemexicanmidwest.bryanwinston.org/.

Ybarra, Priscilla Solis. *Writing the Goodlife: Mexican American Literature and the Environment.* Tucson: University of Arizona Press, 2016.

Yukich, Grace. *One Family under God: Immigration Politics and Progressive Religion in America.* Oxford: Oxford University Press, 2013.

Zentos, Nicholas J., and Wendy Marley. "Hispanic Community." *Encyclopedia of Cleveland History*. Case Western Reserve University. May 11, 2018. https://case.edu/ech/articles/h/hispanic-community.

Zimmerman, Marc. *Defending Their Own in the Cold: The Cultural Turns of U.S. Puerto Ricans*. Urbana: University of Illinois Press, 2011.

Zubieta, Sebastián. "Interview with Linda Ronstadt." *Review: Literature and Arts of the Americas* 42, no. 1 (2009): 102–6.

Contributors

EMILIANO AGUILAR JR. is a PhD candidate in history at Northwestern University. His research focuses on how ethnic Mexicans and Puerto Ricans navigate and utilize machine politics to further their inclusion within East Chicago, Indiana. He is interested in themes such as politics, labor, corruption, and organizing.

GERALDO L. CADAVA is a professor of history and Latina and Latino studies at Northwestern University. He is the author of *The Hispanic Republican: The Shaping of an American Political Identity, from Nixon to Trump* (Ecco, 2019) and *Standing on Common Ground: The Making of a Sunbelt Borderland* (Harvard, 2013).

KAREN MARY DAVALOS, professor of Chicano and Latino studies at the University of Minnesota, Twin Cities, is a leading scholar of Chicana/o/x art, with four books on the subject: *Exhibiting Mestizaje* (UNM Press, 2001); *The Mexican Museum of San Francisco Papers, 1971–2006* (UCLA Chicano Studies Research Center Press, 2010), the Silver Prize winner of the International Latino Book Award for Best Reference Book in English; and a prize-winning monograph, *Yolanda M. López* (distributed by UMN Press, 2008). Her latest book, *Chicana/o Remix: Art and Errata since the Sixties* (NYU Press, 2017) exposes and challenges untenable methods in art history. With Constance Cortez, she is building "Rhizomes of Mexican American Art since 1848," an online digital tool linking art collections and related documents from libraries, archives, and museums. She serves on the board of directors of Self Help Graphics & Art.

THERESA DELGADILLO is a professor of English and Chican@ and Latin@ studies at the University of Wisconsin–Madison. She is the author of numerous journal articles and chapters, as well as two books, *Latina Lives in Milwaukee* (Illinois, 2015) and *Spiritual Mestizaje: Religion, Gender, Race, and Nation in Contemporary Chicana Narrative* (Duke, 2011). She is also the founder of the online academic venue *Mujeres Talk* and a cofounder of its successor site, *Latinx Talk*.

DELIA FERNÁNDEZ-JONES is an assistant professor of history at Michigan State University. Her research centers on Latino placemaking in the Midwest. She is particularly interested in how Latinos transform the places they live in to suit their political, economic, and social needs. Her forthcoming book is in press with the University of Illinois Press.

LAURA FERNÁNDEZ is a visiting assistant professor of Hispanic studies at Bates College. Her research centers on Latinx popular culture, and she is at present engaged in examining the representation of Latinxs and Latinidad in various television series set in the Midwest.

CLAIRE F. FOX is M. F. Carpenter Professor of English at the University of Iowa. She is the author of *Making Art Panamerican: Cultural Policy and the Cold War* (Minnesota, 2013) and *The Fence and the River: Culture and Politics at the U.S.-Mexico Border* (Minnesota, 1999). With Omar Valerio-Jiménez and Santiago Vaquera-Vásquez, she edited *The Latina/o Midwest Reader* (Illinois, Latinos in Chicago and the Midwest series, 2017). Her current research focuses on art and performance at heritage sites in the Americas.

SERGIO M. GONZÁLEZ is an assistant professor of Latinx studies at Marquette University. A historian of twentieth-century US immigration, labor, and religion, his scholarship focuses on the development of Latinx communities in the American Midwest. He is the author of *Mexicans in Wisconsin* (Wisconsin Historical Society Press).

Born in Waterloo, Iowa, Sr. CARMEN HERNANDEZ is a member of the Sisters of the Presentation of the Blessed Virgin Mary (also known as the Presentation Sisters), located in Dubuque, Iowa. In 2013, she became the founding executive director of La Luz Hispana community center in Hampton, Iowa, a position that she held for five years, until returning to Dubuque in 2018 to assume her current role as congregational leader of the Sisters of the Presentation.

LAWRENCE LA FOUNTAIN-STOKES is professor of American culture, Romance languages and literatures, and women's and gender studies at the University of Michigan, Ann Arbor. He is author of *Queer Ricans: Cultures and*

Sexualities in the Diaspora (2009). His book *Translocas: The Politics of Puerto Rican Drag and Trans Performance* (University of Michigan Press, 2021) is part of the Triangulations: Lesbian/Gay/Queer Theater/Drama/Performance series. Larry performs in drag as Lola von Miramar since 2010 and has appeared in several episodes of the YouTube series *Cooking with Drag Queens*.

MARIE LERMA received her PhD in women's, gender, and sexuality studies at the Ohio State University in 2020. She is a storyteller, writer, instructor, and interdisciplinary researcher who is interested in social justice, art, feminism, environmentalism, Latinx communities, and more.

RAMÓN H. RIVERA-SERVERA is dean of the College of Fine Arts and professor of theatre and dance at the University of Texas at Austin. He is author and editor of numerous books on Latinx and Black feminist and queer performance, including *Performing Queer Latinidad: Dance, Sexuality, Politics* (Michigan, 2012); *Blacktino Queer Performance* (Duke, 2016); *Queer Nightlife* (Michigan, 2021); and *Performance in the Borderlands* (Palgrave, 2010).

ARIANA RUÍZ is an assistant professor of Chicanx Latinx literature and culture at the University of California San Diego. Before joining UCSD, she was an assistant professor at the University of Iowa. Her research and teaching areas include Latinx literary and cultural studies, cultural citizenship, feminist and gender studies, and cultural geography. She is particularly interested in how travel and mobility are explored in Latina/x cultural expression.

SANDRA RUIZ is an associate professor of Latina/Latino studies and English at the University of Illinois at Urbana-Champaign. She is the author of *Ricanness: Enduring Time in Anticolonial Performance* (NYU Press, 2019) and a co-series editor of Minoritarian Aesthetics (NYU Press). She is the coauthor with Hypatia Vourloumis of *Formless Formation: Vignettes for the End of the World* (Autonomedia Press, 2021). Ruiz has recently received a Humanities Research Institute Fellowship to work on her book project *Minoritarian Pedagogy: Psychoanalytic Affections in the Space of Aesthetics*.

LEILA VIEIRA is a PhD candidate in Latin American literatures and cultures at the Department of Spanish and Portuguese at the Ohio State University. Her research interests are on Latinx literature and other cultural products, specifically those by and about Brazilian migrants to the United States.

J. GIBRAN VILLALOBOS is an administrator, curator, and art historian. He is assistant curator at the Museum of Contemporary Art Chicago. He has held posts as partnerships and community engagement manager for the Chicago Architecture Biennial, cultural liaison for the Chicago Park District, and curator in residence for the Chicago Cultural Center. In 2016 he attended the Advocacy Leadership Institute and was invited to the White House Office of Public Engagement, the National Endowment for the Arts, and the Congressional Hispanic Caucus to speak to issues affecting Latinos in Chicago. In 2017 he launched an inaugural summit of Latinx artists and administrators across the United States; for this project he was awarded the Act Up Award by the Chicago Community Trust. His work has been presented at the Fabrica de Arte Cubano during the 2017 Havana Biennial. In 2019 he was an inaugural recipient of the Field Foundation's Leaders for a New Chicago Award, as well as the Americans for the Arts 2019 Leaders of Color Fellowship. In 2020 he was accepted to the Civic Leadership Academy at the University of Chicago Harris School of Public Policy, where he worked with government and nonprofit sector participants to think about effective policy for Chicago's cultural industries. He serves on the auxiliary board for the National Museum of Mexican Art and is chair of the Chicago Artists Coalition board of directors. He is a faculty lecturer at the School of the Art Institute of Chicago in the Department of Arts Administration & Policy. Gibran holds a BA in art history and a BS in public relations from Northern Arizona University and an MA in arts administration and policy and MA in modern art history and theory from the School of the Art Institute of Chicago.

Index

activism: disability, 238; immigrant justice, 183–84, 185; labor rights, 12; Latinx, 2; social justice, 12, zines and, 110. *See also* Concerned Latins Organization (CLO); sanctuary movement

aesthetics: DIY aesthetics, 137–38; jazz aesthetics, 280; placemaking and, 271, 275; social work of, 274–75

Afanador, Armando, 255, 256

affirmative action: defined, 205; deindustrialization and, 205–6; in East Chicago, 204, 207–20; Equal Employment Opportunity Act of 1972, 217; gender and, 207; opposition to, 213–14, 217; as "quota" system, 217

African Americans: in East Chicago, 204–8, 211; interactions with Latinxs at summer ethnic festivals, 236–38; migration to Midwest, 268, 270, 273, 279–81; Puerto Rican and African American children, 24

Afro-Latinxs: Afro-Puerto Ricans, 93; anti-Blackness and, 5, 93; festival dance performances, 237; summer ethnic festivals and, 236–38

agency: in Festival de las Calaveras, 165; hospitality and, 48; Latina/o print culture and, 114–15; placemaking and, 88, 102; in Tomás Rivera, 45–46; tropicalization and, 64

Aguilar, Emiliano, Jr., 14

Aguilar, Maria, 97, 98

Aguirre, Albert, 92

Ahmed, Sarah, 117, 118

Ahn, Ilsup, 50

Alarcón, Francisco, X., 161

Alarcón, Norma, 112–13

Alinsky Institute, 209, 211

Allsup, Carl, 206

Almendarez, Roger, 253

Alvarez, Monica, 140, 146n1

Americanness, 10

Anderson, Benedict, 116

Anderson, Carolina Báez, 102

Anderson, Nels, 120

anti-Blackness, 24; Black Latinxs and, 5, 93

Anzaldúa, Ahmed, 167–68, 179n38

Anzaldúa, Gloria, 115, 179n38; on code switching, 123

Aparicio, Frances R., 7, 63, 64

archives: Catholic Church records, 89, 95; historical erasure and, 89, 103; reading against the grain, 89

Arellano, Elvira, 197, 260

Arizola, Angelita, 99–102

Arizona: anti-immigrant politics in, 5, 268–71; Latinxs in, 260, 286n5; migration to, 270; racism in, 269

Arizona SB 1070 (Support Our Law Enforcement and Safe Neighborhoods Act), 5, 268–69, 285n1

Arpaio, Joe, 269

Arriola, Oscar, 111, 118–26, 130n59

art: avant-garde, 135–46; difficult, 136–38, 143; heteronormativity and, 141; perfor-

American, 34; *milpas* and, 34; of mixed Mexican and Puerto Rican communities, 97–98; place and, 1–2; social and political, 239; of support for immigrant Latinx communities, 150, 152–53
Sze, Julie, 1

Tainos: narratives of extermination, 72; reclamation of, 72–73; summer ethnic festivals and, 237–38
Taylor, Diana, 59n10, 69
third space, 128n34; code switching and, 123, 125; summer ethnic festivals as, 226; zines as, 115–16
Third Woman (journal), 112–13, 128n34
Third Woman Press, 112–13
Tlalnepantla Arts, 164, 178n24
Tobar, Leah, 99
Tomás and the Library Lady (Mora), 53–55; hospitality in, 58
Toro, Ana Teresa, 77
Torres, Jema, 140, 146n1
trans: use of term, 83n37
transculturation, 13
transloca performance, 62–63, 65, 78. *See also* Fernós, Fausto
Treviño, Roberto, 197
Troche, Rose, 66, 82n21
tropicalization, queer, 64–65
tropicamp, 63, 69–71
Tropicana, Carmelita (Alina Troyano), 65, 79n4
Trump, Donald: anti-immigrant policies of, 56; anti-Latinx rhetoric of, 239–40; bigotry of, 4; defunding of sanctuary cities, 59n18; xenophobic policies of, 240; xenophobic rhetoric of, 197–98
Tuan, Yi-Fu, 180n58

urban renewal, 123, 209; displacement and, 257
Urrieta, Luis, 163

Valentín-Martínez, Joel, 15, 271–76; methodology of, 282–83; migration research of, 281–82; placemaking practices of, 282–83. See also *Living Lakes, The*
Valerio-Jiménez, Omar, 270, 283
Vaquera-Vásquez, Santiago, 270, 283
Vargas, Daniel, 94, 95
Vargas, Deborah R., 77
Vargas, Guadalupe, 94, 95
Vargas, Pepe, 254, 255–56, 258–59, 263–65

Vasquez, Consuelo, 94
Vasquez, Daniel, 94, 96
Vasquez, Juan, 99–100
Vasquez, Rosa, 99–100
Vega, Julio, 99
Vega, Sujey, 7, 225, 227
Velázquez, Mirelsie, 112–13
Ventura, Carlos, 215
Vieira, Leila, 14, 56
Villalobos, J. Gibran, 14; founding of LARD, 156–57; testimony of, 154–58
violence: of becoming, 136, 146n4; in *The Last Laugh*, 32; against queers of color, 142; state-sanctioned, 5, 139, 182–83; of urban migration, 283
visibility: in Chicago, 110
Vogel, Ken, 201n41

Washington, Harold, 202n45
Waters, John, 75–76
Weakland, Rembert, 190
Western Avenue and Other Stories (Arroyo), 25, 35–38; form of, 35
white flight, 205
whiteness, 87; *blanqueamiento*, 100; Dutch CRC and, 90; Mexican Americans and, 100; MexiRicans and, 100; of Midwest, 10; punk and, 115; riot grrrl and, 115; zines and, 115, 118; of zine studies, 13–14
Wilkinson, Kenton T., 68
Wisconsin: Latinxs in, 190, 201n30, 201n39; sanctuary movement in, 190–94, 202n45
Wong, Cindy, 254
Woodward, Thomas, 182

Ybarra, Priscilla Solis, 1–2; on environmentalism in Mexican American literature, 39n10; on environmental justice, 40n17; on goodlife writing, 25, 27, 42n57, 43n65
Ybarra-Fausto, Tomás, 113
Youngstown, Ohio, 90; ethnic summer festival in, 225, 227, 229–30, 237–38, 240–44, 251n85

Zavala, Alvaro, 117–18
Zenteotl Project, 164
Zimmerman, Marc, 74
#ZINEmercado, 111, 118–26, 124 fig. 5.1, 130n60; community building and, 119, 122, 125–26, 130n56; *Compilation Zine*, 125, 126; inclusivity of, 122–23; mission of, 122; placemaking practices of, 125; promotion of, 123, 124 fig. 5.1, 125,

130n55; Zine Hobo, 119–20, 121, 124 fig.
5.1, 131n68
zines: belonging and, 115; as counterpublics, 115; cut and paste style, 114; defined,
111; festivals, 117–18, 121, 129nn48–49;
gentrification and, 38; periodization of,
111–12; self-publication methods, 112;
whiteness and, 115, 118. *See also* #ZINE-
mercado; zines, Latinx

zines, Latinx, 110–26; activism through, 110;
in Chicago, 116–17; placemaking and,
110–11, 125; as third space, 115–16
zine studies: whiteness of, 13–14
Zobl, Elke, 112
"Zoo Island" (Rivera story), 44–55; agency
in, 45–46; hospitality in, 46–47, 53, 58;
migrant labor in, 44; placemaking in,
44–45, 48

Latinos in Chicago and the Midwest

The University of Illinois Press
is a founding member of the
Association of University Presses.

University of Illinois Press
1325 South Oak Street
Champaign, IL 61820-6903
www.press.uillinois.edu